Ian Nicholas Wood
Europe in Late Antiquity

Oldenbourg
Grundriss der Geschichte

———

Edited by Hans Beck, Karl-Joachim Hölkeskamp,
Achim Landwehr, Steffen Patzold, and
Benedikt Stuchtey

Volume 43

Ian Nicholas Wood

Europe in Late Antiquity

—

DE GRUYTER
OLDENBOURG

ISBN 978-3-11-035264-1
e-ISBN (PDF) 978-3-11-035265-8
e-ISBN (EPUB) 978-3-11-039758-1
ISSN 2190-2976

Library of Congress Control Number: 2024948397

Bibliographic information published by the Deutsche Nationalbibliothek
The Deutsche Nationalbibliothek lists this publication in the Deutsche Nationalbibliografie;
detailed bibliographic data are available on the Internet at http://dnb.dnb.de.

© 2025 Walter de Gruyter GmbH, Berlin/Boston, Genthiner Straße 13, 10785 Berlin
Typesetting: bsix information exchange GmbH, Braunschweig
Printing and binding: CPI books GmbH, Leck

www.degruyter.com
Questions about General Product Safety Regulation:
productsafety@degruyterbrill.com

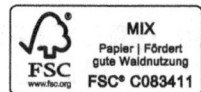

MIX
Papier | Fördert
gute Waldnutzung
FSC
www.fsc.org FSC® C083411

Editors' Foreword

Since 1978, the series *Oldenbourg Grundriss der Geschichte* (Oldenbourg Outline of History) has served both students and teachers as an important means of orientation, delivering what its title promises: an outline, a plan providing insights from a bird's-eye view which would be difficult to gain from other perspectives.

The series has held fast to its main purpose since its inception. In a proven three-part structure, each volume first provides an introduction to the given historic subject. The second part is devoted to a thorough survey of the research, providing newcomers with the given area an overview of current and past debates. Equally, trained historians and newcomers are increasingly challenged to keep up to date on the major ramifications of a research topic, in view of the characteristic complexity, international scope, and temporal depth of such discussions. At this point the series is a crucial aid – and this is the key feature which significantly distinguishes it from other publications of its kind. Each volume is rounded up by a third part which offers an extensive bibliography.

In the course of its own history, the *Oldenbourg Grundriss der Geschichte* series has responded to the changes in research, debate, and study of history. It has gradually expanded to include new subject areas. The series overall is no longer exclusively devoted to a survey starting in Greek and Roman antiquity, scrutinizing the European Middle Ages at length, then arriving in the present, broadly understood as the modern era. While this chronological tour of German and European history remains fundamental for an orientation in relation to historic events, its scope is increasingly being broadened by volumes on special themes and non-European subjects. Thus the series documents the substantive changes that are continuously taking place in the study of history.

The *Oldenbourg Grundriss der Geschichte* series presents these topics to students who want to explore not only the substance, but also the research history of a complex field. At the same time, they are intended to support teachers in their endeavours to communicate such topics in lectures and seminars. Nevertheless, the primary objective remains accurately to portray past times, the more recent as well as the more remote, not simply by representing them as

https://doi.org/10.1515/9783110352658-201

events and structures, but by showing that the scholarly treatment of them is a part of their history.

Hans Beck
Karl-Joachim Hölkeskamp
Achim Landwehr
Steffen Patzold
Benedikt Stuchtey

Foreword

This survey of Late Antiquity is the result of more than half a century of study of the period, initially in Oxford under the guidance of Henry Mayr-Harting, Peter Brown, Sabine McCormack, John Matthews, and Michael Wallace-Hadrill. My contemporaries, among an array of fine early-medievalists, included Chris Wickham and Roger Collins. From Oxford, I moved to London, where I learnt a great deal from Jinty Nelson and Wendy Davies before taking up a job in Leeds. I subsequently had the great good fortune of being a co-ordinator of the European Science Foundation's project on the Transformation of the Roman World, which brought me into contact with many of the European scholars working on the centuries from the fourth to the eighth.

The book itself is the result of a commission from Steffen Patzold, to whom I am extremely grateful, not just for the commission, but also for the opportunity to hold a fellowship in Tübingen, in the Kolleg-Forschergruppe "Migration und Mobilität in Spätantike und Frühmittelalter", which gave me access to one of the best German research libraries. I am equally (perhaps even more) indebted to the four "Hilfskräfte", Gabriel Anhegger, Derek Benson, Nicolai Böckler, and Luis Probst. They transformed my footnotes into the citation system of the OGG volumes – which all the scholars I know who have contributed to the series will understand is a remarkably difficult task.

It would be impossible to list everyone to whom I am indebted for what they have taught me about Late Antiquity and the early Middle Ages, but I cannot leave out any mention of Herwig Wolfram, who introduced me to the world of Austrian scholarship (not least to Walter Pohl, Helmut Reimitz, Max Diesenberger and Richard Corradini), and by extension to the broader world of German and Central European research. I offer the book to Herwig as a poor payment for an enormous intellectual debt.

https://doi.org/10.1515/9783110352658-202

Inhaltsverzeichnis

I Historical Survey

1 Introduction

The idea that Late Antiquity should be considered as a period in its own right has only come to be generally accepted since the publication in 1971 of Peter Brown's *World of Late Antiquity* [2: Brown 1971], although the concepts of *Spätantike* in Germany and *Antiquité tardive* in France already existed in the mid twentieth century [1.2: Liebeschuetz 2004; 3: Cancik/Schneider (eds.), vol. 15, cols. 1013–4]. In the last half century there has been what Andrea Giardina has described as an 'esplosione di tardoantico' [1.2: Giardina 1999]. As with all historical periods, one can debate where the beginning and end points should be. Should one begin with the death of the last member of the Severan dynasty in 235, with Diocletian, whose rule ended the so-called Third Century Crisis, or with Constantine, who promoted Christianity as the official religion of the Empire? And should one end with Justinian or with Heraclius and the rise of Islam? Or, from the point of view of the post-Roman West, should one end with Justinian's conquest of Africa and Italy, or with the arrival of Columbanus on the continent in c. 590, and the revival of Christian contacts with the British Isles?

Recent emphasis on the history of climate change and Plague adds new parameters. One way of defining the period is to begin it at a relatively early date from the end of the Roman Climatic Optimum and with the Plague of Cyprian (249), named after the bishop of Carthage who refers to its impact, and as ending with the catastrophic aftermath the Plague of Justinian (542), which stretched into the early seventh century and beyond. This ending period has even been identified as the Late Roman Little Ice Age (536–c. 570 or c. 660) [3: Harper 2011; Little 2007]. According to this catastrophist reading, Late Antiquity may be said to begin with the Third-Century Crisis which led to fundamental changes in the structure of the Empire, and ended immediately before the break-up of the Eastern Mediterranean World at the hands of the forces of Islam.

The impact of these environmental factors has, however, been questioned [9: Haldon/Elton/Huebner/Izdebski/Mordechai/Newfield 2018; Mordechai/Eisenberg 2019 and 2020], although it is clear that the historian should bear in mind changes in climate and environment. Yet,

Late Antiquity

Environment

https://doi.org/10.1515/9783110352658-001

even if the significance of plague is a matter of some debate, the period between the late third century and the end of the sixth is effectively the period that has been defined as Late Antiquity.

Mediterranean world

Rather than looking for chronological precision, it is easiest to define Late Antiquity by describing the historical situation at its beginning and its end, noting the contrasts between the two. At the start of the period, one can talk about a Mediterranean-dominated world which was part of a single political entity – regardless of how well that entity was functioning in political or economic terms. At its heart was the Mediterranean itself, which helped unify what was a very diverse world, as it had throughout the Classical period. The Roman Empire certainly faced difficulties in terms of internal civil wars as well as external threats in the late third and at the beginning of the fourth century, but it was still capable of raising the funds to pay the army and the governmental machine. It was also a pagan empire which allowed the practice of numerous different religions but was united in its promotion of a single imperial cult, which effectively served as a means of showing loyalty to the State.

The divided Mediterranean

At the end of Late Antiquity, the Mediterranean no longer maintained its central position. It had ceased to be the unifying feature that it had been. Nor was there a Mediterranean-wide empire. Rather, there was an eastern Mediterranean world that was still united under Byzantine rule, at least until the rise of Islam from the 630s onwards. Attached to this bloc were territories in Italy, North Africa and on the coast of Spain that were under the control of Constantinople. Elsewhere in the western parts of continental Europe and in Britain territory was divided between several successor states. These states did not rely on a sizeable administration, nor did they maintain a standing army, paid for by taxation. Rather, they made use of a system of military obligations, which meant that theoretically they could call on a very substantial pool of warriors if need be – although in practice they rarely did so. Equally important, the Byzantine Empire of the eastern Mediterranean and the successor states of the West were all Christian. The Church, although in many respects it was made up of small units ('micro-Christendoms', as they have been described) [3: BROWN 2013, pp. 355–79], was a significant presence not just in religious, but also in social, economic and political terms. Despite its divisions, the Church was a single institution, and it was well funded in terms of wealth and, unlike earlier pagan institutions, in terms of land [9:

Wood 2013]. By the seventh century there had been a shift from a pagan Mediterranean World to a Christian European World, which would form the basis of western Christendom for the next millennium [8: Wood 2018; 5.5: Wood 2022].

In other words, a central feature of Late Antiquity is that it was a period of transition. All historical periods are, of course, periods of transition, but some see greater change, and change at a greater pace, than others. This is certainly the case for the late-antique period. It is effectively the chronological core of what in Marxist terms has been termed the passage from Antiquity to Feudalism, or, more neatly (and with the changes from Feudalism to Capitalism in the period of the Renaissance and Reformation in mind), 'the Other Transition' [3: Anderson 1974; 11: Wickham 1984].

As a period of transition, Late Antiquity has been treated differently by classicists and medievalists, by historians of different disciplines (religious, secular), and by archaeologists. Classicists tend to regard Late Antiquity as the end of the Ancient World, while medievalists approach it as the beginning of the Middle Ages. Not that there is unanimity of approach among all the classicists or all the medievalists. A particular area of disagreement is the question of the significance of the barbarian migrations, and the destruction that they caused [11.2: Goffart 2006]. There is also division between Roman and early medieval archaeologists, with each group concentrating on different types of site and tending to see either decline or settlement. Historians of religion used to treat the period primarily as the Patristic Age, stressing the significance of its theologians (among them Ambrose, Jerome and Augustine) – and also as a period of ecumenical councils (five out of seven of which fall into the years from 325 to 553). More recently it has also been studied from a socio-religious viewpoint, with emphasis being placed on belief and cult, and in particular on the cult of the saints [7: Brown 1981, 2015; Wiśniewski 2019].

Classical and medieval readings

All these approaches have some validity. The problem, therefore, in studying the Late Antique period as a whole is to give due weight to each of these different approaches. There is a political history of the fall of the West Roman Empire and its replacement by the successor states. There is a socio-economic history of the collapse of an imperial aristocracy, of the settlement of barbarian incomers, of urban decline, and changes in the management of land – elements in the 'other transition' of Marxist historiography. For the final half century or more of Late Antiquity the question of the impact of plague, the occurrence of which is unambiguous, has also to be considered. There is a history of the weaking of classical culture, and there is a religious history of the establishment of the Church. None of these aspects of the period's history is free-standing, and they all need to be borne in mind.

To state that the development of Late Antiquity marked a change from a pagan, imperial world dominated by the military to a world of Christian kingdoms ruled by non-Roman rulers is no more than to describe the beginning and the end of a period of profound change. It does not explain that change. Simple recourse to environmental determinism [3: HARPER 2011] is questionable, and certainly inadequate. Before attention was ever paid to the end of the Roman Climatic Optimum, the Cyprianic Plague and the Late Roman Little Ice Age, historians had set down well over two hundred causes of the Fall of the Roman Empire, some more obviously significant than others [1.2: DEMANDT 1984, [2]2015]. In what follows, a few of the dominant explanations have been singled out. Most obviously, there are the internal weaknesses of the Empire, including the inherent problems in its political, social and economic structure. But there is also the question of the impact of the barbarians. At the same time, while not following Gibbon's view that the Church played a central role in the Fall of Rome, it is vital that one gives due weight to the history of religion: Late Antiquity is characterised as much by its extraordinary religious vitality as by its political and economic decline. These issues underlie the narrative structure of what follows. But as one of the great twentieth-century interpreters of the Late Roman Empire, John Bagnell Bury, argued, hazard, or contingency, is a major issue in historical development. Who was ruling or in command at a particular moment could have major influence on the immediate outcome of events.

2 Diocletian (284–305) and Constantine (306–337)

2.1 The Third-Century Crisis and the Tetrarchy

In political terms, Late Antiquity is usually seen to begin with the reign of Diocletian, whose seizure of power in 284 following the death of the emperor Carus marked the end of a long period of political instability which had begun with the murder of Severus Alexander in 235. This ended a period in which imperial rule had been largely hereditary (although new emperors unquestionably required military support and senatorial approval). Thereafter, the army was effectively the sole arbiter in choosing an emperor. In the fifty years following the death of Severus at least 26 men claimed the imperial title: on average, therefore, in that half century an emperor held the throne for two years [3: ANDO 2012]. Diocletian, by contrast, retained his position until his abdication in 305, when he retired to his palace in Split, where he lived until 316. Holding the reins of power as he did for more than two decades, he was able to institute a number of reforms that ensured the survival of the Empire into the fifth century, and in the East well beyond that [2: JONES 1964].

Recent study of climate change and of environmental history has, however, suggested that the socio-economic factors underlying the crisis that lasted from the death of Severus Alexander to the accession of Diocletian continued to haunt the Empire through the fourth century [4.1: JOHNE/HARTMANN/GERHARD 2008; 3: HARPER 2011]. It is, therefore, worth looking back to the Third-Century crisis, which may be said to have begun not with the end of the Severan dynasty in 235, but rather with the reign of Philip the Arab, who took the imperial title in 244, following the death of Gordian III in the course of a campaign against the Persians. Philip managed to withdraw the Roman army from Mesopotamia, albeit at the cost of paying the Persians a considerable amount of tribute. He then turned his attention to the Danube frontier. By 248 his reign seemed successful enough for him to celebrate the millennium of the foundation of Rome, with a major display of public games, the *ludi saeculares*. But the following year disaster struck. The army on the Danube revolted and backed Decius as emperor. Perhaps more significant for the long term was the so-called Plague of Cyprian, which broke out in 249 [3: HARPER 2011]. It may have lasted until 270, and it was therefore present through the first half of the Third-Century Crisis, and its effects clearly lasted yet longer. The exact nature of the plague is unclear, and the pathogen involved was probably not the same as that in the Justinianic Plague of the sixth century, but it seems to have been damaging enough. Sensing the weakness of the Roman Empire in its immediate aftermath, Goths crossed the Danube in 250/1, and they subsequently raided Asia Minor, as did the Persians under Shapur, who also attacked Syria in 252, while Franks and *Alamanni* crossed the Rhine in 256.

Rebellion in Gaul and Syria

Although the narrative of the Third-Century Crisis reads like a succession of imperial usurpations, coupled with threats from across the borders of the Empire, which led to the temporary establishment of independent regions in Gaul and Britain (the 'Gallic Empire') and Syria, the impact of a changing climate and of the plague, may have been more fundamental, if, as seems likely, it resulted in a manpower crisis, which would have led to a decline in economic production, and thus in tax yields, and also to problems in military recruitment and in the emperor's ability to pay the army. This in turn initially led to massive devaluation of the coinage. The devaluation was to lead to further discontent among the troops, which was a major cause of the succession of usurpations during the quarter of a century from 259 to 284.

Persecution

One other major response to the crisis was persecution, above all of Christians. Since the disasters meted on the Empire were thought to have been inflicted by the gods, public displays of sacrifice were required, and those who refused to comply were punished. Hence the Third-Century Crisis and its immediate aftermath saw the Decian Persecution in 250, that of Aurelian in 274, and the Great Persecution of 303–11. In terms of strengthening reverence for the Empire's gods this seems to have had a negative effect, and indeed Christianity was transformed in the course of the persecutions from being the religion of a relatively insignificant minority of the population to being the chosen religion of an emperor, Constantine, after 312.

Military reform

In time, however, the Empire did succeed in reversing the problems affecting the military. This was the result, in part, of a change in the emperors themselves, who after 268 were almost exclusively men of military background, rather than members of the senatorial aristocracy. Indeed, senators were banned from high military office. Between 268 and 610 most emperors came from the Danubian provinces, a frontier region of the Empire which had long been a major recruiting area for the army. The first of the Danubian emperors, Claudius II (Gothicus) (268–70), began to reward his troops with donatives in gold, rather than paying them in debased silver – a decision that has been seen as marking the beginning of Late Antiquity [3: HARPER 2011]. Certainly, the gold *solidus* came to be central to the late antique economy [4.2: BANAJI 2001].

Although Claudius and his immediate successors all had short reigns, they effectively dealt with the immediate dangers presented by Persian and barbarian invaders. They also brought those areas of the Empire that had broken away from Rome, Syria and Gaul, back into the fold. Odenathus of Palmyra had managed to defend the Syrian frontier against the Persians, and as a result had created an independent Palmyrine Empire, but after his death the emperor Aurelian defeated his widow Zenobia, and in 272 he reconquered Syria [4.1: HARTMANN 2001]. In the West another breakaway region, known as the Gallic Empire, had been formed by generals unsatisfied by the actions of the central government to deal with the threat posed to Gaul and Britain by the barbarians [4.1: DRINKWATER 1987]. Following his overthrow of Zenobia, in 274 Aurelian defeated the Gallic emperor Tetricus I at the Battle of Châlons and reintegrated Gaul and Britain into the Empire. But if the threat from outside forces had largely been overcome before Diocletian's accession, the need to strengthen the frontiers against outside threats remained, as did the underlying problem of military rivalry within the Roman Empire.

Diocletian understood that part of the problem facing the Roman Empire was its sheer size [4.1: BARNES 1982; 3: CHASTAGNOL 1982; 4.1: KOLB 1987; REES 2004; ROBERTO 2014]. As a result, he divided it, initially by appointing Maximian as western Caesar in 285, promoting him to the office of Augustus in 286, and then in 293 by creating two additional Caesars, Constantius in the West and Galerius in the East. There were, thus, two emperors in each half of the Empire, a senior and a junior. The intention was that in time the two *Augusti* should retire: the Caesars should take their places, and two new junior appointments should be made. The new system was known as the Tetrarchy. This was to be a meritocracy: family ties were not to influence the choice of emperor, although once appointed, an individual emperor might marry the daughter of a colleague. At the same time the status of the emperor was elevated through the elaboration of court ritual and the enhancement of imperial title, which raised the emperor to near-divine status. A new uniform imperial style was developed, as is apparent from the coinage (where the four emperors are represented in a similar manner) and from the so-called Porphyry Tetrarchs – a group statue (or pair of statues) that was presumably carved for Diocletian's capital in Nicomedia,

Diocletian and the Tetrarchy

but was taken from there to Constantinople, and now survives in Venice [4.1: L'ORANGE 1965].

Reform of the provinces

In addition to dividing the imperial office, Diocletian also took care to divide the provinces of the Empire, thus weakening the power of individual governors. The number of provinces was increased from roughly fifty to nearly one hundred. They were organised into twelve dioceses, which were themselves grouped into four prefectures [2: JONES 1964]. At the same time greater distinction was made between civilian and military office holding, thus further weakening the power of individual generals and governors. But while this reorganisation had the benefit of reducing the likelihood of rebellion against the emperor, and while it may also have made government more efficient, it unquestionably enlarged the bureaucracy, and thus added to the costs of the imperial administration. The number of fourth-century administrators has been estimated at 35,000 [4.2: KELLY 2004], but this figure almost certainly underestimates the number of minor officials and drudges, as well as those active at the local level of the *civitas*.

Economic reform

Having sought to address the danger of renewed civil war within the Empire, Diocletian turned to the question of the economy, initially (and not altogether successfully) introducing a reform of the coinage, which, following on from the innovations of Claudius Gothicus, was based on a gold standard. After Diocletian's reform in 301 the major unit of account was no longer the silver *denarius* of the early Empire, but the gold *solidus*. A further reform, however, was needed under Constantine, who both reduced the weight of the *solidus* and had many more minted, making it much more important for the functioning of the economy. Also in 301, Diocletian issued an Edict of Maximum Prices [4.1: BRANDT 2004], primarily because inflation was causing havoc with the payment of the army and with the value of remuneration received by the troops. This, however, proved unworkable. In addition, Diocletian embarked on reform of the tax system, which involved the raising of taxes per head (*capitatio*) and on land (*iugatio*) – though the land was assessed by its economic viability rather than its acreage. The assessment was made by imperial officials, but the taxes, which were levied in gold, were collected by the decurions, effectively city counsellors, who had to make good the shortfall if they failed to raise the full amount. Not surprisingly there is evidence in the

Theodosian Code that men tried to avoid holding the office of decurion.

The most famous of Diocletian's actions was his instigation of the Great Persecution, which was subsequently recorded by a Christian member of Diocletian's court, Lactantius, as well as by the historian and bishop of Caesarea, Eusebius, and also by the authors of numerous martyr acts (most of which date from a good deal later in time). The Great Persecution is, indeed, the aspect of Diocletian's reign that is best covered in our sources – almost all of which come from the pens of Christians and are therefore extremely hostile to the emperor [4.1: Lane Fox 1986]. It would seem that Diocletian began removing Christians from the army shortly after his accession, but from 303 onwards, under the increasing influence of the eastern Caesar Galerius, he moved to full-scale persecution, although the policy was not pursued with equal zeal throughout the Empire. The western Caesar Constantius was remembered as not being a persecutor, but since he was the father of Constantine the image of him as tolerant may in part result from later Christian bias in favour of the Constantinian dynasty. Underlying the persecution was a concern to promote the imperial cult and associated reverence for the four ruling emperors, each of whom was associated with a deity. Diocletian's religious policy was, therefore, closely associated with the unity and preservation of the Empire.

The Great Persecution

It is important to understand that, despite the importance of the imperial cult for the maintenance of political unity, Roman paganism was not a single institutionalised religion. Although there was an acknowledged Olympian pantheon whose deities were revered in temples presided over by priests, there were numerous gods and goddesses outside that pantheon which an individual might worship [4.1: Beard/North/Price 1998]. The temples were enriched by offerings of treasure, but unlike the Christian churches of the Middle Ages, and in contrast with the situation in Egypt and Asia Minor in the Hellenistic Age, in the later Roman period they were not endowed with major landed possessions. Moreover, unlike the Christian priesthood, which was a vocation lasting until death, the pagan office of priest was largely honorific, with leading civic individuals taking office usually for a limited period of time.

Paganism

For the most part the Roman State was not concerned about the religious beliefs of an individual. It was, however, concerned to propitiate the gods, whose favour to the Empire might be withdrawn, and, equally significant, it was concerned with loyalty to the person and genius of the emperor, and it was participation in the imperial cult that was demanded of the citizens. Unlike the adherents of most other sects (with the exception of the Jews whose reservations were recognised by the Empire) the Christians felt unable to offer sacrifice (that is to burn incense) to the emperor's genius, and as a result could be regarded as disloyal to the State.

The end of
Diocletian's reign

Initiating the Persecution was the last of Diocletian's major acts. In 305, having already ruled over the Empire for twenty years, he retired from office, forcing his colleague Maximian to do the same. Galerius was elevated to the position of Augustus in the East, with Constantius as his colleague in the West. In accordance with Diocletian's plans the new Caesars, Maximinus and Severus, were not related to their seniors.

At the moment of his resignation, Diocletian would seem to have had a relatively successful reign: the frontiers were safe, and the Empire was united under its tetrarchs. There had been at least one major challenge. In c. 288 Carausius, a naval commander in the Channel, revolted against Maximian, having been accused of colluding with the pirates he was supposed to suppress. Initially, the revolt had some success in Britain and northern Gaul, and Maximian came to a peace agreement. In 293, however, the Caesar Constantius made preparations against Carausius, who was murdered by his fellow rebel, Allectus. The reconquest of Britain followed in 296. What might have turned into a revival of the Gallic Empire had been brought to an end [10: CASEY 1995; 4.1: WILLIAMS 2004]. But while Diocletian and his colleagues would seem in 305 to have restored the Roman Empire, problems remained, and indeed new problems had been created. The administrative reforms brought with them huge costs. And at the same time the structure of the Tetrarchy itself, with its four rulers appointed without regard for any dynastic ambitions, was open to challenge.

2.2 The Emergence of Constantine

Competition for power

The structure of the Tetrarchy was the first part of Diocletian's legacy to crumble. Within a year of the emperor's retirement, it was under threat. Constantius died unexpectedly in York. Galerius, the Eastern Augustus, raised the western Caesar, Severus, in his place

[4.2: LENSKI 2006]. But the army at York elevated Constantius' son, the young Constantine, to his father's office, thus overturning the non-dynastic pattern that Diocletian had attempted to establish. Maxentius, the son of the retired Maximian, then added to the chaos by challenging and overthrowing Severus, and this in turn led Maximian to come out of retirement, with the result that there was one official Augustus (Galerius), three self-proclaimed *Augusti* (Constantine, Maxentius and Maximian), and one official Caesar, the eastern Maximinus [4.2: LEPPIN/ZIEMSSEN 2007]. After negotiations involving the retired Diocletian in 308, a new solution was proposed for the West, with Licinius as Augustus and Constantine as Caesar. This, however, did not end the political conflicts, which continued for a further fifteen years. In 310 Constantine forced the aged Maximian to commit suicide; Galerius died of natural causes the following year, which led Licinius to divide the Eastern Empire with Maximinus. Shortly afterwards, Constantine defeated Maxentius at the Battle of the Milvian Bridge outside Rome in 312. This was the supposed moment of his conversion to Christianity. In the East, Licinius defeated Maximinus in 313. There were then two *Augusti* from 313 to 324, when Constantine defeated Licinius. The Tetrarchy was firmly at an end. Diocletian's attempt to solve the problem of military rivalry at the highest levels of the Empire had failed. It was a problem that would never be solved.

Having defeated Licinius, Constantine turned to providing his solution to the problem of ruling the Empire [4.2: ODAHL 2004; POTTER 2012: VAN DAM 2007]. He decided to create a new capital in Byzantium on the Bosporus. In that, he was to some extent following in the footsteps of Diocletian. For centuries emperors had tended not to reside in Rome. Although it was the Empire's ideological centre, most emperors were concerned far more with the state of the frontiers, and their places of residence reflected their concerns. Diocletian had decided to use Nicomedia, which lay on the southern side of the Bosporus, almost opposite Byzantium, as his main base. From there he could respond quickly to problems on his northern and eastern frontiers. In choosing Byzantium, Constantine acknowledged the wisdom of his predecessor in opting for a base on the Bosporus, but at the same time he chose a site that was not associated with the previous regime. And in one particular way his rule marked a breach with what had come before, for while Diocletian

The rule of Constantine

and Galerius had tried to make pagan cult a touchstone of adhesion to the Empire, Constantine instead embraced Christianity.

The state of Christianity

It is not easy to assess the state of Christianity by the year 310. Most scholars would accept that around 10 per cent of the Empire's population was already Christian by that time. Until recently it was assumed that these Christians were to be found largely in cities, but statistically this has shown to be unlikely [4a: ROBINSON 2017, criticising the figures of MACMULLEN 1984, and STARK 1996]. The possibility that there were significant numbers of Christians in the countryside (much of which was, of course, closely tied to the cities), challenges the argument that Christianity in 300 was largely a religion of the middle class, and of the Hellenised Jews [4a: STARK 1996]. At the same time, it would be wrong to deny that Christianity had made some inroads into middle and upper-class society, even in Rome itself [7: SESSA 2007]. Despite this, Constantine's ultimate choice of a new religion is surprising.

Constantine's conversion

The exact process of Constantine's conversion is unclear, not least because our main narratives are stridently Christian and provide simple and impossibly clear-cut versions of events [4.1: BARNES 1981]. It is possible that Constantine did indeed embrace Christianity at the time of his conflict with Maxentius in 312. Certainly, he was already inclined to monotheism, although he seems to have understood this largely in terms of the cult of the Unconquered Sun. Galerius had called an end to the persecution of Christians before his own death in 311. In 313 in what is known as the Edict of Milan Constantine and Licinius jointly proclaimed the legality of the Christian religion. A year later, Constantine involved himself directly in the affairs of the Christian Church by calling the Council of Arles, which, among other issues, dealt with the Donatists, an African ecclesiastical movement that had taken an extremely harsh line against those who had given in to pressure in the course of the Great Persecution.

The Council of Nicaea and the Homoeans

Constantine would show even greater commitment to the Christian Church in 325, when he called the Council of Nicaea, above all to deal with a further problem of doctrine – the question of the nature of the Trinity, and most especially of the relationship between the three aspects God the Father, God the Son and God the Holy Spirit [4.2: AYRES 2004]. Were the three persons in the Trinity equal or not? The precise nature of the Trinity had been thrown into question by disagreements between the priest Arius, who saw a hierarchy (with God the Father as the senior figure, Jesus Christ as second to Him, and the Holy Spirit as being below both of them), and his opponents, who saw equality between the three persons in the Godhead [4.2: WILLIAMS 1987]. Nicaea ruled against Arius, and in so doing stated that all the persons of the Trinity were of the same substance. This, however, introduced a controversial term (*homoousios* – 'of one substance'), and the debate rumbled on for much of the Late Antique period, with the Goths following the version of Arianism – which strictly speaking should be termed 'homoean' (which is to say that it did not claim that the three persons in the Godhead were of one substance, but that they were similar) – which was only condemned in Visigothic Spain at the Third Council of Toledo in 589. This heresy still had significant adherents in Lombard Italy as late as the 670s. But although Nicaea did not permanently solve the Arian problem, it was regarded as the first of the Ecumenical Councils, and it was looked back to as the fount of orthodox doctrine – although what is usually referred to as the Nicene Creed is a later modification of its statement of belief issued at Constantinople in 381.

When considering Constantine's interventions in Church doctrine, it is important to understand that during the centuries between the crucifixion of Christ and the conversion of the emperor the development of Christianity had been regional and had depended on the influence of individual religious leaders whose interpretation of the new religion varied. Periods of persecution had not helped the creation of any doctrinal uniformity. But, in any case, the bases on which such uniformity might have been established were not in place. There was, as yet, no established canon of the Bible: that would only be defined in the late fourth century [7: McDONALD 2011]. Not surprisingly, there was no universally accepted interpretation of Christian doctrine. Different cities and different schools of thought had emerged. One effect of Constantine's conversion, and of his bringing the leaders of different communities together in council, was to make apparent the variety of doctrines and to make necessary the formulation of an agreed interpretation of the newly recognised religion. Despite the conflict within the Church, the most powerful of the bishops gradually established their authority, effectively shifting Constantine himself from being a master at forming consensus to pursuing an increasingly coercive line [4.2: DRAKE 2000]. Even so the establishment of a generally ac-

Christian division

cepted orthodoxy was only achieved over many years, and as a result of much bitterness and much rewriting of history.

Constantine and the Church

A text written from a non-Christian viewpoint, the *Epitome de Caesaribus* by Aurelius Victor presents Constantine as extraordinary for the first ten years of his reign, a bandit for the next ten years, and for the final decade as a little boy 'because of his unrestrained generosity' (*decem annis praestantissimus, duodecim sequentibus latro, decem novissimis pupillus ob profusiones immodicas nominatus*) [4.1: BIRD 1984, 1994]. It is tempting to assume that this estimate of his generosity includes his gifts to the Church. While Constantine was concerned with doctrinal divisions within Christianity, he was also remembered as having supported the Church financially, not least in Rome. The evidence for this is to be found in the *Liber Pontificalis*, the collection of papal biographies put together initially in the sixth century. Although there are reasons for thinking that the collection was initially created in the early part of that century, some of the lists of donations that are to be found at the end of individual biographies cannot date to earlier than the reconquest of Italy by Justinian [129: MCKITTERICK 2020; 14.1: MONTINARO 2015]. It is, therefore, fairly clear that we cannot trust the lists of Constantinian endowments, especially those of St Peter's, St Paul's and the Lateran baptistery. The *Liber Pontificalis* also claims, entirely fraudulently, that Pope Silvester was responsible for the emperor's conversion.

Helena in the Holy Land

We can be more certain about a lengthy visit to the Holy Land, made between 326 and 328 by the emperor's mother, Helena, in the course of which she endowed several churches, and at the same time effectively established a model for pilgrimage to the holy sites. Sources from the second half of the fourth century claim that in the course of her visit she was responsible for the discovery of the relic of the True Cross [7: HUNT 1984]. Whether or not the story is a total fiction, the relic was on display in Jerusalem by 380 [4.2: DRIJVERS 1992].

Constantine's baptism

Yet, despite the clear attachment of Constantine and his mother to Christianity, the emperor's position remained enigmatic. He continued to allow the building of temples in his name. And it was only on his deathbed that he was baptised. This delayed baptism in itself, however, was not a matter of great significance – infant baptism was not yet normal practice within the Christian churches, and, since the ritual was understood to wash away sins previously committed, there was much to be said for leaving it to a moment when one was unlikely to sin any further.

And a good deal may have been weighing on Constantine's conscience. In 326 he had ordered the execution of his son Crispus, and shortly afterwards he had his wife Fausta (the daughter of Maximian and sister of Maxentius) drowned, the exact reasons for which are unclear. But for some later historians, including the Church Father Jerome, worse still was the fact that when the emperor finally did accept baptism on his deathbed in 337, it was at the hands of Eusebius of Nicomedia, who was regarded by many as an Arian, even though he had been present at Nicaea, and the position he upheld was not that of Arius but the 'homoean' modification of it. The conversion of the first Christian Emperor was not as perfect as many later writers would have liked [4.3: Humphries 1997]. And in any case the Christianisation of the Empire was still in its early stages at the time of his death.

2.3 Military Reform

In 337 Christianity was not yet a dominant force in the Roman Empire, despite the monuments financed by the imperial family in Rome, Constantinople and the Holy Land. A far greater recipient of public largesse, and indeed the main beneficiary of imperial taxes, was the army. John Lydus writing in the sixth century talks of an army of 389,704 soldiers and a navy of 45,562 sailors in the days of Diocletian, while another sixth-century author, Zosimus, provides figures which imply that 581,000 soldiers were involved in the civil wars of 312. Although these numbers have been questioned, they are not out of line with the information provided by the late-fourth- and early-fifth-century lists included in the *Notitia Dignitatum*, which are thought to suggest an army of between 400,000 and 600,000. If these figures are remotely accurate, there were well over ten times more soldiers in the army than there were regular officials employed in the bureaucracy. What proportion of the total population this amounted to, however, is unclear: assessments of the population of the Later Roman Empire range from 20 million to 200 million, although a figure towards the lower end is most likely, and 55 million seems a reasonable guess [4.2: Campbell 2005; Elton

The army

2006; 6: Le Bohec/Wolff 2004; 4.1: Southern/Dixon 1996; 4.2: Tomlin 1988; 6: Tomlin 2000].

Military reforms
In terms of numbers, the army of Diocletian and Constantine probably did not differ radically from those of the Principate. Nevertheless, the structure of the army was reformed. Reform began in the days of Diocletian as part of his division of military and civilian administration. The number of legions was effectively doubled, although the size of each legion seems to have been much reduced. In line with the division of offices and the increase in the number of legions, 20 *duces* (generals) were appointed. Following a prohibition put in place by Gallienus (253–68), none of them were of senatorial extraction.

Constantine appears to have continued Diocletian's reforms, although there is some debate as to which emperor effected which changes. Certainly, Constantine disbanded the Praetorian Guard, which had previously been based in Rome, following the defeat of Maxentius. At the same time, he divided the army into frontier troops, *limitanei*, on the one hand, and non-frontier troops, *comitatenses* and *palatini* (palace guards), on the other [6: Isaac 1988]. The *comitatenses* (and indeed the *palatini*) were a force that could be deployed wherever needed, whether against foreign invaders or against internal challengers to imperial power.

The majority of the *comitatenses* were initially drawn from frontier troops, an act which the pagan historian Zosimus, writing around 500, regarded as weakening the defences of the Empire. If this were the case, however, it was not immediately apparent, and when considering the criticisms levelled against Constantine by Zosimus, one has always to remember that the historian was a pagan who was intent on blaming the first Christian emperor for as many of the Empire's problems as he could.

The *Notitia Dignitatum* suggests that there were 195,500 members of the *limitanei*, 104,000 *comitatenses*, and 3,500 *palatini* in the Eastern half of the Empire. The information in the western section of the *Notitia* is, unfortunately, less complete, but if the proportions in the West were similar to those in the East, there were substantially larger numbers of *limitanei* than *of comitatenses* [4.1: Treadgold 1995, pp. 44–59]. It would seem that even after Constantine's reforms, the majority of the troops were still to be found on the frontiers. In other words, the Roman Empire was essentially a military state, but this was only really apparent in the frontier provinces.

2.4 Towns and Villas

Away from the frontiers, and from the centres of mining, where there was also a military presence to protect imperial resources, the late Roman World was dominated by its towns and villas. The most important towns were regional centres, *civitas* capitals (the term *civitas* referred both to a city and to its dependent territory), and as such they were the seats of local government. In time they would also develop into diocesan centres and thus provide a structure for ecclesiastical organisation, which was modelled on the administrative structures of the provinces [9: Brogiolo/Gauthier/Christie 2000; Brogiolo/Ward Perkins 1999; Grigg 2013; Lavan 2001; Rich 1992].

The *civitas* capitals

The Third-Century Crisis had seen some decline in urban life. The Plague of Cyprian in 249 probably had an effect on large parts of the Empire, which may already have been suffering from a general decline in climatic conditions, although the evidence is far from conclusive; and in some areas, there seem to have been improvements in the environmental conditions [3: Harper 2011]. There is, however, plenty of evidence, particularly in Gaul, for the fortification of city centres, reflecting a fear of barbarians and the general uncertainty of the time. But, in some instances (as at Le Mans), the building of impressive new walls was a statement of civic pride. The fourth century saw some urban revival, although there is little to match the great building programmes that had been paid for by the aristocracy in the early Empire. And, as yet, there was no major expansion of church building (despite the foundations endowed by the imperial family).

In general, there appears to have been a distinction between the two halves of the Empire. In the West, cities tended first and foremost to be centres of regional government rather than economic centres; whereas in the East, there is more evidence for commerce and manufacture. Although there certainly was trade in the West, its economy seems to have been dominated far more by the landed estates of the aristocracy, whereas the Eastern economy was very much more urban.

The upper tier of the aristocracy was massively rich, with families holding estates across the whole Empire. It has been estimated that senators of the highest level, perhaps the top 1 % of the population, had an annual income of 384,000 *solidi*, those below them of 72,000 *solidi*, or the income of 80,000 family farms per year [3: Wick-

Senatorial property

HAM 2005, 155–68]. Such a concentration of wealth in the hands of so small a group would be highly unusual in historical terms – and the figures are certainly misleading [9: LEPPIN 2021]. Clearly the late-Roman aristocracy was extremely wealthy, but we need to treat the written sources with a certain amount of caution. The surviving evidence of the prosperity of the richest members of the senatorial aristocracy is most apparent in the archaeological discoveries of their villas. Their wealth came in part from the exploitation of their landed resources. In some areas they made heavy use of slaves, although the extent of the so-called *latifundia* has been called into question. Without doubt, however, this was a slave-owning society, and it was not only the rich who had them [3: HARPER 2011]. The aristocracy seems also to have profited from their fiscal responsibilities, and it was these that gave them access to the gold *solidi*, which is a distinctive aspect of the late Roman economy [4.2: BANAJI 2001].

Civic duties of the
upper classes

By tradition, the aristocracy understood that it had an obligation towards the state. The ideal aristocratic life was one of leisure (*otium*), but it was accepted that a member of the senatorial aristocracy should at various periods of his life be active in the affairs of the region, the state and even the Empire, and this involved the abandonment of leisure and thus participation in its mirror image, *negotium*. Some individuals, especially members of the greatest families, undertook to hold in turn one of the great offices of State, governorships, and above all the consulship – that is, to follow the *cursus honorum*.

At a lower level of the social scale, the minor aristocracy, urban middle classes, and the landed gentry, were also expected to be active, as decurions, in civic life, as members of their local urban councils (*curiae*) [6: BAUMANN 2014]. Initially, to be a *curialis* had been a mark of honour, and in the age of prosperity that characterised the early Empire, members of the order had been pleased to contribute to the amenities of their towns. But to them, also, passed the burden of ensuring that taxes were raised. If they failed, the shortfall was their responsibility. As a result, their position became increasingly unattractive, especially given the continuing pressure on manpower and agricultural production that hung over the Later Empire even in the centuries when there was no extreme outbreak of disease, between the Plague of Cyprian and that of Justinian. Increasingly, men of curial standing tried to find ways of avoiding the honour, or its obligations. One possible route after 312 was to enter the ranks of the Christian clergy. Since decurions had, as part of their civic duties, on occasion to participate in pagan ceremonies, Constantine prohibited clergy from being members of the decurionate. One unintended consequence of this legislation was to prompt men to enter the Church in order to avoid taking on the obligations of a decurion, which led to further legislation banning such a move.

Given the increasing burdens that fell on Roman taxpayers and on the class responsible for the collection of taxes as well as the enhancement of civic amenities, it is no surprise that there was a slow degradation of life in the towns and cities of the Later Empire. Few new public buildings and works can be ascribed to this period. The one exception to this is the building of churches, which in some ways belongs to the long-established tradition of Roman, and even Hellenistic, public munificence. However, despite the evidence for a handful of ecclesiastical buildings, extensive construction of churches appears to have been a development of the mid to late fourth century, and it was increasingly common through the fifth and sixth centuries.

Urban decline

The breakdown of the old social order, however, did not occur overnight. Although the curial class was under pressure, it did not vanish. Indeed, in most cities the *curia* continued to be active to the end of the Late Antique period. But from the fourth century onwards churchmen became increasingly involved in what had been the tasks of the *curiales* and the decurions. In time, bishops and senior clergy emerged as central figures in the life and organisation of their cities, although this was a slow and uneven development. In local terms, episcopal authority varied from city to city, depending in part on the influence of an individual bishop.

3 The House of Constantine and the Development of the Church

3.1 Constantius II (337–361)

On the death of Constantine in 337 his three sons, Constantine II, Constantius II, and Constans succeeded [4.3: BAKER-BRIAN/TOUGHER 2020]. Other, more distant members of the family were ruthlessly eliminated, probably at the instigation of Constantius. Their father

The sons of Constantine

had steadily promoted a notion of dynastic rule from very early in his career, and effectively the Empire would be ruled by two dynasties (that of Constantine and that of Valentinian and Theodosius) from Constantine's defeat of the last of his rivals in 324 down to 455, albeit with a continuing input from the military. Constantius took over much of the Eastern Empire, leaving the West to his brothers, who were soon at odds with each other. Constantine was killed in 340, and Constans seized the territory he had controlled. He conducted a campaign against the Franks in 341–2, and he visited Britain in 343, perhaps to deal with threats from the Picts and Scots. By the end of the decade, however, he had lost the support of the **Magnentius** western army, which raised Magnentius to the imperial throne in 350 in his place. Constans himself was murdered. The challenge of ambitious generals and the support they could raise from their troops, which Diocletian had hoped to end, had resurfaced. Constantius, who up until this moment had been largely concerned to ward off attacks launched by the Persian shah Shapur II, marched west and defeated the usurper in 351, forcing him into Gaul. He defeated Magnentius again in 353, and the usurper subsequently committed suicide. In between his two campaigns against Magnentius, Constantius turned his attention to the defence of the Danube frontier; and following the final defeat of the usurper, he campaigned successfully against the *Alamanni*, a confederation of barbarian peoples who had emerged in the angle between the Rhine and the Danube which had previously been dominated by the *Marcomanni* [4.2: ELTON 1996; 12.6: DRINKWATER 2007].

Gallus and Julian   In 351, Constantius raised his cousin Gallus to the rank of Caesar, in order to help in the governance of the Empire. In 354, however, unhappy with the activities of Gallus in the East, he ordered his execution. Immediately afterwards. he was faced with a rebellion led by Silvanus, who had previously been a supporter of Magnentius. Like a number of the leading military figures of the period, Silvanus was a general of Frankish extraction – several barbarians pursued a distinguished military career in the decades before the migration of Goths into the Empire in 376, though Silvanus was unusual in also making a bid for the imperial title [2: STROHEKER 1965, pp. 9–29]. Following the quick suppression of the attempted usurpation of Silvanus in 355, Constantius decided to raise his last remaining cousin, Julian, to the rank of Caesar, setting him the task of defending the Rhine frontier. Then, after a campaign against the *Alamanni*, the senior emperor travelled to Rome.

Our knowledge of Constantius' visit to the imperial city, his only one, in 357 is dominated by the description provided by Ammianus Marcellinus, which concentrates on the emperor's relations with the senatorial aristocracy. But it is clear that much more was at stake. In 354, the emperor had deposed a number of bishops who were opposed to his homoean theological position, which his religious critics deliberately portrayed as Arianism [4.3: HUMPHRIES 1997; STEVENSON 2014]. Among them was the bishop of Rome, Liberius. In his place, Constantius appointed Felix, whose theological views were more in keeping with the emperor's. Support for Liberius, however, remained strong in the city, where there was opposition to the emperor's appointee. It seems significant that archaeological evidence for the building of St Peter's suggests that construction took place in precisely 357, the year that Constantius visited Rome [4.2: WESTALL 2015]. It is also likely that the emperor sponsored work at St Paul's, and perhaps at the Lateran Baptistery. In other words, Constantius, in 357, may have been responsible for much of what the *Liber Pontificalis* attributed to Constantine. One may guess that this was part of an attempt to enhance the pious credentials of the emperor and to shore up support for Felix. Renewed troubles on the Danube, however, drew Constantius from the city and left Felix exposed to his enemies. The dispute between Felix and Liberius was later regarded by the papacy as an embarrassment that needed to be hidden away, and the *Liber Pontificalis* even claimed that Felix was executed by Constantius. As for the emperor's endowment of the holy sites of the city, papal tradition chose to ignore it, preferring to see Constantine as the great benefactor. This, one might note, is part of a wider rewriting of the religious histories of Constantine and Constantius that is to be found in the ecclesiastical sources [4.3: HUMPHRIES 1997].

In 360, Constantius turned his attention back to the East, having failed to avert renewed threats from Shapur in 357–8. He left Julian to deal with the continuing danger posed by the *Alamanni*. Following some military successes, however, the western Caesar revolted against his cousin, claiming the title of Augustus. In 361, before he could return West to deal with the revolt, Constantius died in Mopsucrene, having been baptised by bishop Euzoius at Antioch, leaving Julian as sole Augustus.

Constantius II in Rome, 357

The death of Constantius

3.2 The Theological Crisis

Athanasius and the homoeans

In the long run, the religious crisis that confronted Constantius was to be as significant as the military threats from the Persians, the Franks and the *Alamanni*, as well as from the usurpers Magnentius, Silvanus, and finally Julian. Central to this was the continuing conflict over Arianism that had not been solved at Nicaea [4.2: HANSON 1988; 4.3: KLEIN 1977; BARNES 1993; BARCELÓ 2004]. Here, the leading figure was Athanasius, who had been present as a deacon at the Council but who was subsequently appointed bishop of Alexandria in 328, a post that he held until his death in 373 [7: WIPSZYCKA 2015]. He very quickly came into conflict with a number of leading bishops who had taken a moderate position over Arianism – most notably Eusebius of Nicomedia. Eusebius and his fellows did not defend the Arian doctrine condemned at Nicaea, but nor were they happy with the term 'homoousios' ('of one substance'), which the council had adopted, embracing instead the theological position that goes under the name of 'homoean', stressing the similarity of the persons in the Trinity while avoiding a statement that they were of the same substance. Although Eusebius and his colleagues were not adherents of the precise doctrine put forward by Arius, Athanasius and his supporters, managed to brand their opponents as Arians. Initially, however, it was Eusebius who held the upper hand.

Athanasius' exiles

Constantine himself had exiled Athanasius to Trier in Gaul in 335, for the extremity of his anti-Arian stance and for supposedly having threatened to cut off the supply of corn from Alexandria to Constantinople. In Trier, however, the exiled Athanasius was well received by the local bishop. Athanasius returned to Alexandria after Constantine's death, only to be exiled once again, by Constantius, in 338, this time to Rome, where again he received support from western bishops, including Julius I, the bishop of Rome. He was supported by the Council of Sardica in 343, but he was unable to return to Alexandria until 346. Constantius ordered his exile once again in 356, when he fled to Upper Egypt. Then, in 359, at Councils held simultaneously on the emperor's orders at Rimini in Italy and at Seleucia in Isauria, there was an attempt to secure the acceptance of a new 'homoean' creed which had been formulated at Sirmium (which dropped the offending term 'homoousios'). The attempt, however, failed. Two years later, Constantius died, and his successor, Julian, allowed the return of Athanasius and other exiles to their sees. A year later, in 362, the bishop was exiled once again and returned to Upper Egypt. Following Julian's death, the new emperor Jovian restored Athanasius to Alexandria in 363, but his successor, the Arian Valens, renewed the sentence of exile two years later. This time, however, the exiled bishop remained in the vicinity of Alexandria until he was allowed to return in 366. Thereafter, he remained in his diocese, continuing to promote the theological position set out at Nicaea until his death in 373.

Although the phrase 'Athanasius contra mundum' ('Athanasius against the world') would seem to imply that he alone stood against the rest of the world, the bishop of Alexandria was one of a significant group of bishops who opposed the homoean position promoted by Constantius [4.3: Flower 2016]. In addition to Liberius of Rome, among the other leading pro-Nicene figures who suffered exile there was Hilary of Poitiers [4.3: Stevenson 2014]. Athanasius played a central role in the theological disputes of the mid fourth century at least in part because, as bishop of Alexandria, he led a city of particular importance: both religious (it was a Patriarchate and associated with St Mark), and economic (because of the Egyptian grain supply) [7: Wipszycka 2015]. In addition, his periods of exile had repercussions, putting him in contact with like-minded clergy from across the Roman World, western as well as eastern. And this also meant that he disseminated news and ideas of one of the most distinctive features of Egyptian Christianity: asceticism, both eremitic and monastic.

Fellow exiles

3.3 Asceticism

In his two periods of exile in Upper Egypt, Athanasius spent time in one of the heartlands of an ascetic movement, which he recorded in his *Life of Antony*. This provided an account of the great desert saint who had been born in c. 251. At the age of eighteen, on the death of his parents, Antony had opted for the ascetic life. Initially he lived with other ascetics in the Nitrian desert, west of Alexandria. Subsequently, however, he moved further south to Arsinoë in the Fayum, where he lived alone in an abandoned fort. During the Great Persecution he is said to have returned to Alexandria, to give support to the persecuted, but he then travelled south again, this time to the desert east of the Nile. He made one further visit to Alexandria, in

Antony of Egypt

338, to intervene in the Arian controversy. He died in 356 [7: WIPSZY-CKA 2018, 2021].

*Athanasius' Life
of Antony*

At almost exactly the time of Antony's death, Athanasius was driven into exile for the third time. For a persecuted defender of Nicene doctrine, the career of the hermit presented an ideal subject. The holy man had ministered to fellow Christians during the Great Persecution, and he had travelled to Alexandria specifically to engage in anti-Arian polemic. Moreover, Athanasius had met him – he claimed that he had done so often, but this may have been an exaggeration. He certainly knew disciples of Antony, including bishop Serapion of Thmuis. The *Life of Antony* was, therefore, a text that had particular significance for Athanasius at the moment when it was written.

It was, however, to have influence way beyond the context of its composition. Probably originally written in Greek, it was translated into several other languages, including Coptic and Latin. In both the Greek East and the Latin West, it provided a model for writing about holy men. Already in the fourth century, it was well known in Gaul and Italy, inspiring Martin, bishop of Tours and founder of the monasteries of Ligugé and Marmoutier, as well as the great theologians Jerome and Augustine.

Pachomius

Antony was not, in fact, the earliest Christian ascetic, nor was his style of asceticism the only one on offer in Egypt, or in the equally ascetic environment of Palestine. According to Jerome, the first hermit was Paul of Thebes (the ancient city on the site of modern Luxor). A generation younger than Antony was Pachomius [7: ROUSSEAU 1985, 1999]. He was born to a pagan family in Thebes in 292. He encountered Christianity in the course of a brief enforced career in the army, and thereafter converted. He adopted the ascetic lifestyle as the disciple of the hermit Palaemon before moving closer to Antony. He then had a vision that prompted him to set up communities for ascetics, in the style of Macarios, who had developed the notion of the *lavra* (a monastic community, as opposed to a hermitage), for those who could not live up to Antony's solitary eremitism. His first monastery of Tabennisi, founded at some point before 323, attracted large numbers, and further foundations followed. He was visited by Athanasius in 333, and also by the Cappadocian bishop and theologian Basil of Caesarea, who adopted many of his ideas.

Antony, Pachomius, and Athanasius put Egyptian monasticism firmly on the map. By the later fourth century, they had numerous imitators whose sayings were gathered by visitors, such as Palladius of Galatea, the author of the *Lausiac History*, written in 419–20, and John Cassian, a cleric from the region to the west of the Black Sea who founded a monastery at Marseille in Gaul in c. 415 where he wrote two of the classics of ascetic life, the *Institutiones* and the *Collationes*. These played an important role, alongside the *Life of Antony*, in transmitting the ideals of the Egyptian monks to the West [7: GOODRICH 2007]. In addition to would-be ascetics intent on gaining advice from visiting the monks of Egypt, pilgrims who were beginning to imitate Helena in her journey to the Holy Land also stopped off to witness the piety of the region. Alexandria and the hermitages of the Nitrian desert were incorporated into a standard pilgrimage route to Jerusalem.

The transmission of monastic ideals

Exactly how numerous the holy men were is some matter of debate. Edward Gibbon in *The Decline and Fall of the Roman Empire* repeated with horror the figures given by fourth- and fifth-century authors who talk of 50,000 attending the Easter celebrations led by Pachomius, and 10,000 monks and 20,000 nuns to be found in the oasis city of Oxyrhynchus. These figures are frankly improbable, and they have not been supported by archaeological findings. But, unquestionably, the ascetics were numerous. It is certainly possible that there were 600 communities in the region of Alexandria, and that the largest of them held 200 or 300 monks or nuns [7: WIPSZYCKA 2018]. Without any doubt, when they acted en masse (as they occasionally did), the monks of the region of Alexandria could exert considerable influence on ecclesiastical politics [7: WIPSZYCKA 2015].

Numbers of ascetics

3.4 Julian (361–3)

Athanasius' doctrinal conflicts, and the emergence and spread of the ascetic movement, were the shape of things to come – pointing firmly towards a world dominated by Christianity, its doctrinal debates, and the ascetic movement. Paganism, however, was still a force to be reckoned with. Indeed, as late as 384, the senator Symmachus, writing in his third *Relatio*, could claim that pagans were in the majority in the senate, while the Christianisation of the countryside certainly lasted into the fifth, and in some regions the sixth and seventh centuries.

Julian's upbringing   The final flowering of State Paganism, however, came with the rule of Julian, the successor of Constantius, and the third of Athanasius' persecuting emperors [4.4: NESSELRATH 2013; TEITLER 2017]. Julian, like his half-brother Gallus, was one of the few male members of the Constantinian family to survive the purge carried out by Constantius in 337. He was, however, brought up away from the imperial limelight. Although officially he was cared for by Eusebius of Nicomedia, the bishop who had baptised Constantine, he was educated in a traditional Greek manner first by the eunuch Mardonius and then by the philosopher Maximus of Ephesus. As a result, he developed a reverence for Neo-Platonic philosophy, while behaving to the outside world as a Christian [4.4: ATHANASSIADI 1981, 1988; BOWERSOCK 1978].

Julian as western Caesar   His unexpected appointment as Caesar in 355 necessitated the development of different, military qualities. Faced with incursions into Gaul by the *Alamanni* between 356 and 359, he conducted a series of remarkably successful campaigns in the Rhineland. In addition, according to the late fourth-century historian Ammianus Marcellinus, he also demonstrated a considerable amount of administrative skill. His success, however, led to conflict with Constantius, who had been preoccupied with the Persian threat. Before civil war actually erupted, however, the older emperor died, leaving Julian as sole Augustus in 361.

Julian as sole emperor   Julian now turned against those who had been supporters of Constantius, presenting his actions as a move towards the restoration of an older style of rule. This also extended to his public abjuration of Christianity. Increasingly anti-Christian policies followed. His first actions were to lift restrictions on those Christian groups that had themselves been persecuted, but subsequently he set about preventing Christians from such actions as teaching. At the same time, he tried to refashion pagan cult along Christian lines, creating the equivalent of a Church-structure by appointing regional high priests who in their turn were to appoint appropriate individuals to a revived priesthood. Meanwhile, he himself ridiculed Christian belief in his own philosophical and satirical writings.

Whether this would seriously have challenged Christianity, however, was never tested. In 363, Julian turned his attention to the Persian frontier, which Constantius had left two years previously and which had proved to be the graveyard of a number of emperors, including Gordian III and Valerian in the third century. Initially the campaign went well, and the Roman forces even moved within reach of the Persian capital Ctesiphon. His generals advised against undertaking a long siege, and Julian agreed to withdraw, petulantly burning the boats he had been using on the Persian river system. The retreat proved disastrous, not least because the Persians had employed a scorched earth policy, depriving the Roman troops of food. Even worse, the emperor was wounded in mysterious circumstances (later Christian sources claimed the miraculous intervention of saint Mercurius). He died shortly after, leaving his second in command, Jovian, with the problem of extricating the army from Persian soil.

3.5 Valentinian I (364–375)

Back in the territory of the Empire, having made a humiliating peace with the Persians, Jovian reversed Julian's religious policy, and he also allowed the return of Athanasius to Alexandria. But his reign lasted no more than a year. He was replaced by Valentinian [4.5: RAIMONDI 2001], who promptly appointed his brother Valens as co-emperor. The senior Augustus then turned his attention to renewed problems in Gaul. Julian's departure had left the Rhine frontier open to attacks from the *Alamanni*. In addition to these threats, in 367 Britain was threatened by what Ammianus Marcellinus called the Great Conspiracy, when Picts, *Attacotti* and Scots (that is Irish) attacked the insular Roman province at the same moment as Franks and Saxons launched raids across the Channel from the lands to the east of the Rhine mouth [8: MATTHEWS 1989]. Whether or not the various barbarian groups had planned a united onslaught, they presented a major problem that was not dealt with until Valentinian sent Theodosius the Elder to Britain in 368. The energies of the emperor himself were directed towards the Alaman threat [4.2: ELTON 1996; 12.6: DRINKWATER 2007]. This was further complicated by the arrival in the Rhineland of a substantial number of Burgundians. The figure of 80,000 Burgundians that is given in the sources is suspiciously large: it probably means little more than a large number – the same number occurs several times in late-antique sources, with regard to the size of armies and numbers of the dead as well

Problems in the Rhineland and in Britain

The Burgundians

as those receiving the corn dole in Constantinople. Whatever the scale of the Burgundian forces, Valentinian made use of their arrival, directing the newcomers against the *Alamanni*.

Although Rome had long been troubled by the barbarians established on the far side of their frontier, the Burgundians were the first in a line of migrating peoples to appear on the borders of the Empire. Exactly where they had originated is unclear, but prior to their move to the Rhineland, they seem to have been settled in Bohemia. In all probability, their move was not dictated by the same forces that would prompt the migration of Goths in 376. Certainly, in the 360s they were not the direct victims of Hunnic aggression, unlike the Goths a decade later. Their move westwards is unlikely to have been an early response to the build-up of Hunnic pressure in the steppes to the east of the Black Sea. Initially they did not cross into imperial territory, but they were a hint of problems to come.

Problems in North Africa and on the Danube

Nor were these the only military challenges faced by Valentinian. In North Africa, Firmus, the son of the Berber prince Nubel, proclaimed himself emperor in 372. Valentinian sent the Spanish general Theodosius to deal with the uprising, which he successfully suppressed in 375. Theodosius, however, was then executed in mysterious circumstances. Meanwhile, the *Quadi* and the Sarmatians attacked the Danube frontier in response to the aggressive policies of the Romans. Valentinian moved up to Pannonia in 374, where he spent the winter. But he died the following year, apparently as a result of an apoplectic fit, following a meeting with envoys from the *Quadi* who objected to the building of Roman fortresses on their territory. For Ammianus Marcellinus, Valentinian was a notably irascible and cruel emperor who even kept two bears to whom he threw convicts, including senators convicted of dabbling in magic. His death, in a fit of rage, is of a piece with Ammianus' account of his character. He was, however, one of the last emperors to successfully defend the frontiers of the Western Empire. And the Codex Theodosianus reveals him to have been an active legislator [4.5: Schmidt-Hofner 2008].

3.6 Valens (364–378)

The eastern frontier

Despite the revolt of Firmus, Valentinian's reign had been largely concerned with threats to the Northern frontier. During this period, his brother Valens was concerned primarily with the continuing threat from the Persians on the eastern frontier [4.5: Lenski 2002]. Although Jovian had bought peace with Shapur in order to extricate the remnants of Julian's army, the Persian threat remained. But this was not the only military problem that Valens had to face: at the very start of his reign, in 365–6, he had to deal with the rebellion of Procopius, a cousin of Julian. After some difficulty, Procopius was defeated and executed. Valens then decided to attack the *Tervingi*, a group of Goths living to the north of the lower Danube, led by Athanaric, who had provided support for the usurper. As a result, the emperor crossed the Danube and marched into Gothic territory in 367 and again in 369, when Athanaric came to terms.

The treaty with the Goths allowed Valens to turn his attention back to the Eastern frontier, and particularly to the kingdom of Armenia, the control of which Jovian had ceded to Persians in 363. This concession, however, had left the Roman provinces of eastern Asia Minor dangerously open to Persian intervention. Valens intervened in Armenian affairs once again, and a truce was negotiated in 371, but the situation remained tense, not least because there were rebellions in the Roman territory of Isauria. Valens was thus fully occupied with Eastern affairs when his brother Valentinian died, and his nephew Gratian succeeded to the western throne in 375.

At the same time, he involved himself in religious issues. Unlike Valentinian, who was a committed Catholic, Valens was a supporter of the homoean position. As such he was responsible for the final exile of Athanasius in 365, although he allowed the return of the patriarch to Alexandria the following year. Athanasius was not the only Nicene bishop to suffer at his hands: among other exiles were the Cappadocian Father Gregory of Nyssa and Eusebius of Samosata. When Athanasius died in 373, Valens ensured that his successor as patriarch was an Arian, Lucius, while other Nicene clergy of Alexandria were sent to work in the mines [4.2: Hanson 1988]. He also supported the appointment of an Arian, in preference to a Nicene candidate, as bishop of Constantinople in 369. His hostility towards the Nicene party, however, was inconsistent, depending on political circumstances. In the period immediately before his final and fatal encounter with the Goths in 378, he appears to have allowed the return of several leaders, including Peter of Alexandria. Even so, he was remembered as the last of the persecuting emper-

Valens and Arianism

ors. His failure against the Goths, however, was even more disastrous for his reputation, and for the Empire itself.

4 The failure of the House of Valentinian

4.1 The Goths before 376

Although the Rhine and Danube frontiers had been a constant cause for concern for the Empire for the first three quarters of the fourth century, the threats had largely been kept under control [4.5: WOL-FRAM 2009; 11.1: KULIKOWSKI 2007]. There has even been the suggestion that individual emperors exaggerated the problem posed by the *Alamanni* in particular, to impress the general population [12.6: DRINKWATER 2007]. The most substantial foreign threat had come not from the Germanic barbarians, but from the Persians [11.1: LEE 1993]. This changed in 376 with the arrival of substantial numbers of Gothic migrants on the banks of the Danube, fleeing from the threat of the Huns.

The Goths north of the Danube   The Goths had long been settled in the lands that stretched north of the Lower Danube, up to the modern territory of Poland and as far east as the coast of the Black Sea and the Crimea [4.5: WOLFRAM 2009; 11.1: KULIKOWSKI 2007; 12.3: HEATHER 1991]. They appear in written sources, which show that they were present in the regions of the Wielbark and Chernyakov cultures that have been identified by archaeologists. There were several Gothic groups, of whom the most notable were the *Greutungi* and the *Tervingi*.

Goths had raided the Empire from as early as 238. Thereafter they took advantage of the state of the Empire in the aftermath of the Plague of Cyprian to cross the Danube, and subsequently to launch seaborne raids on Asia Minor. In 255 they fought against and killed the emperor Decius. As a result of the raids on Asia Minor, Romans, including Roman Christians, were taken prisoner. The last of their maritime attacks took place in 275, but frontier conflict escalated after the arrival of the *Tervingi* on the Lower Danube in 291. In 332, however, Constantine, having defeated the Goths, negotiated a treaty with them [4.5: WOLFRAM 2009; 11.1: KULIKOWSKI 2007; 12.3: HEATHER 1991]. Subsequently, there was an increase of recruitment of Goths into the Roman army, which was effectively an escalation of a tradition of employing barbarians as federates [on the federates: 4.1: LANIADO 2015].

In the aftermath of the treaty, at some point between 332 and 337, Ulfila, a Goth who was descended from Cappadocian captives, spent time in the Empire, where he was consecrated as bishop for the Christians 'in the Getic land' by the homoean Eusebius of Nicomedia [2: THOMPSON 1966; 11.1: HEATHER/MATTHEWS 1991; 11: GHELLER 2017]. Ulfila returned to Gothic territory, where he was active as a missionary. In 347/8, however, there was a persecution of Christians among the *Tervingi*, probably as a reaction to renewed military hostilities with Rome. Ulfila and his flock moved to the Roman province of Moesia with the agreement of Constantius II. It was probably there that he translated the Bible into Gothic. He attended at least one Church council (the homoean Council of Constantinople in 360). It is possible that he had some influence on the *Tervingi* even after his departure from their territory. He was said to have had contact with Fritigern, one of the Tervingian leaders of the 370s. The dominant Tervingian before 376, however, was Fritigern's opponent Athanaric, who attacked the Empire in 369, but subsequently concluded a treaty with Valens. In 372, he launched a new, and apparently wider ranging, persecution of the Christians among the Goths, which saw the martyrdom of Saba, whose death provides us with the best account of life in the Gothic world prior to the entry of the *Tervingi* into the Empire [2: THOMPSON 1966; 11: Gheller 2017]. Ulfila himself lived on until 383, and thus witnessed the cataclysmic events of 376–8. His position as a homoean would have significance for the development of Gothic Christianity.

Ulfila and the origins of Gothic Christianity

4.2 The Hunnic Threat

Despite the wars of Constantine, Constantius, and of Valens, following the defeat of Procopius, an uneasy relationship had developed along the Lower Danube between the *Tervingi* and the Romans since 291. This was suddenly broken in c. 376 by the arrival of the Huns north of the Black Sea. These were a group of Asiatic nomads who had unexpectedly moved westwards. Such nomads had always been a force in Central Asia, and they had regularly caused problems to the Chinese Empire to the East and the Persian Empire to the South. It would appear that they looked further west in the later

The arrival of the Huns

fourth century as a result of climatic crisis in the central steppe lands. Whereas there were major environmental catastrophes within the Empire in the third and sixth centuries, the only catastrophe to have a significant impact on the Roman World in the fourth century took place way outside the Mediterranean zone. The 350s and 60s was a period of extreme drought in Central Asia, and it is probable that this drove the nomads from their normal areas of activity, bringing them into conflict with the semi-nomadic peoples to the north of the Caucasus and then with the sedentary peoples to the west of the Volga and Dnieper [11.3: MAENCHEN-HELFEN 1973; SINOR 1990; SCHMAUDER 2009; KIM 2016; DI COSMO/MAAS 2018].

The defeat of the Greutungi Their first known victims were the Alans of the Northern Caucasus [12.5: ALEMANY 2000]. The Huns then attacked the *Greutungi*, at the time probably the most powerful of the Goths, who were based between the Crimea and the Polish marshes. However numerous they were, and that is an issue that cannot be answered, the Huns were effectively an irresistible force because of their speed and because of their archery: they were horsemen, and they used a particularly powerful weapon, the reflex bow, which being short was ideally suited to fighting on horseback, and which had a range of 150 metres.

Ermaneric, the ruler of the *Greutungi*, attempted to oppose the Hunnic threat, but was defeated and committed suicide. In some legendary accounts, there were significant internal divisions within the *Greutungi* which rendered them weak in the face of the Hunnic onslaught. The majority of the *Greutungi* soon submitted to the Huns, although some moved south to join the *Tervingi* under Athanaric, who is said to have vowed to remain in his native land. However, he was unable to defend it. Although for a while he did stay north of the Danube, a substantial number of Goths – mainly *Tervingi*, but with some *Greutungi* who had escaped the Huns – led by Alaviv and Athanaric's old rival Fritigern petitioned to enter the Empire.

4.3 The Gothic Crossing of the Danube (376)

At the moment of the arrival of the Goths on the banks of the Danube the two emperors, Valens and his nephew Gratian, were fully occupied with other frontier problems. Although he was only

8 years old at the time, Gratian had already been elevated to the position of Augustus by his father Valentinian in 367 – in an act that initiated a sequence of appointments of child emperors, which in time would lead to a growing emphasis on the non-military aspects of imperial rule, ritual and involvement in religion [4.5: McEvoy 2013]. On his father's death in 375 Gratian took charge of the Gallic provinces, leaving the rest of the Western Empire theoretically in the hands of his young brother Valentinian II. In 376, he was campaigning against the *Alamanni*, despite still being no more than seventeen years old.

At the same time, Valens was faced with a much more serious threat from the Persians [4.5: Lenski 2002]. He was, therefore, in no position to block the entry of the Gothic migrants into the Balkan provinces at the moment of their arrival on the banks of the Danube. Instead, he agreed to what was supposed to have been a controlled settlement, in which the Goths were meant to give up their arms on entry into the Empire. To allow a sizeable number of barbarians into the Empire under strict terms was not a novel act: previous emperors, including Constantius II, had settled large groups of immigrant barbarians within the Empire. They were regarded as *dediticii*, supplicants, who, like federates, might be expected to swell the ranks of the Roman fighters [4.5: Heather 1991; 3: Halsall 2007; 11.1: Mathisen 2020]. The incoming Goths may also have been expected to accept Christianity in the context of their settlement [11.1: Heather 1986; 11: Gheller 2017]. And in this the Romans may have been partially successful. Certainly, there are few references to pagan Goths after 376. The homoean version of Christianity that they came to accept was that championed not only by Ulfila, and probably Fritigern, but also by Valens, and this would have repercussions later. The acceptance of the homoean Creed meant that the Goths came to be doctrinally opposed to the Romans for whom Nicene Christianity became the orthodox position, following the legislation of Theodosius I.

The entry into the Empire, however, was badly managed. The officials charged with supervising the arrival and settlement of the Goths were later described as corrupt, taking bribes, and seizing the opportunity to enslave children. They therefore failed to ensure that the Goths gave up their weapons. In all probability, the accusations have some truth in them; but it is also important to note that the officials, who were not from the highest level of the imperial

Terms of settlement

Administrative failure

army or bureaucracy, were faced with a very considerable logistical operation. The Romans were not just dealing with the *Tervingi* of Alaviv and Fritigern, but also with *Greutungi* under Alatheus, Safrax and Farnobius, as well as *Taifali*. Not all of these had been given permission to enter the Empire. And they may not all have crossed the Danube at the same place.

Fritigern's revolt and the battle of Adrianople

Moreover, once the incomers had entered the Empire, they had to be provided for. The provision of food and living space presented a further logistical nightmare. Here relations soon broke down. The Roman commander Lupicinus tried to win over Alaviv and Fritigern, but when their followers demanded access to food supplies, he ordered the killing of the Gothic leaders and their retinues. Fritigern escaped, gathered the Gothic forces, and defeated and killed Lupicinus. Following his victory, he was joined not only by Goths (although not by the Moesian Goths with whom Ulfila was associated), but also by Thracian miners and Roman slaves. At this point it was clear that Valens could no longer afford to concentrate his energies on the Persian frontier, but that he had to take personal charge of the Balkan crisis [4.5: LENSKI 2002]. He also asked his nephew Gratian for support. Not realising the scale of the crisis, the western emperor sent some troops, but he did not himself hurry to the Balkans. The result was a devastating defeat of the East Roman army at Adrianople in 378, when, according to Ammianus Marcellinus, two thirds of the imperial forces were destroyed largely at the hands of the Gothic cavalry. For Ammianus the Roman defeat was the worst since Cannae at the hands of Hannibal. The emperor himself died, supposedly burnt to death in a hut in which he had taken refuge: for later Catholic historians, this was a fitting end for an Arian, or more accurately homoean, heretic.

The scale of the Gothic forces

There is no question that the battle was a devastating blow for the Romans and that it took years for the eastern army to repair its losses. It also left the Balkans effectively undefended – and arguably the Empire's Balkan provinces never fully recovered. At the same time, it is important not to overestimate the scale of the threat posed by the *Tervingi* and their allies. Historians sometimes talk of hundreds of thousands of barbarians entering the Empire, and it is true that the only figure we have is that given by Eunapius, who talks of 200,000 Goths reaching the Danube – but this is surely an exaggeration, and in any case refers to the barbarians gathered on the northern bank of the river and not to those who were able to cross into Roman territory. In fact, no specific figures are provided by our sources for the Gothic incomers in 376 – unlike the Burgundians in the 360s, or the Vandals and their allies when they crossed to Africa in 429, both of which groups are stated to have been 80,000 strong, a figure that, in the case of the Vandals, is said to include women, children and the elderly, as well as fighting men. Historians have, therefore, resorted to estimating the size of the Gothic army at Adrianople from the account of the battle provided by Ammianus and from what is known of the imperial forces at the time. A generally accepted figure for the Gothic army is of 15,000/20,000 men – which would suggest that the overall size of the immigrant group, including women and children, was similar to that of the Vandals in 429. Although, in the Burgundian case, the figure would seem to be symbolic, a similar figure of around 80,000 is a plausible estimate for the number of Goths who crossed the Danube.

It is important, however, to set this figure into context. The Roman army of the fourth century is usually reckoned to have been made up of 400,000 to 600,000 men, while the *Notitia Dignitatum* suggests that there were 104,000 *comitatenses*, leaving aside the 195,500 *limitanei* and 3,500 *palatini*, in the late-fourth-century army of the East. Perhaps ten per cent of these eastern forces fought at Adrianople. The Gothic soldiers, in other words, were not a vast horde that could swamp the Roman military. Moreover, 80,000 men, women and children would have been dwarfed by the population of the Empire, which might have been anything between 20 and 200 million. 80,000 is the number of recipients of free corn in fourth-century Constantinople. These figures have been compared with the numbers of migrants to enter Europe in the first decade of the twenty-first century [8: Wood 2018].

Yet, while the figures of the incoming barbarians are relatively low, the migrants certainly presented the Empire with a considerable problem. In particular, given the delicate ecological balance that existed within the Empire, the need to feed a sudden influx of people, and to do so within territory now open to the ravages of war, even relatively small numbers would have had a significant impact.

Equally important for the immediate future, the loss of so many Roman troops in a single day was a disaster. Although the fourth century did not see any environmental disaster on the scale wrought between 249 and 270 by the Plague of Cyprian, or by the

The aftermath of the Gothic victory

Justinianic Plague in the decades after 542, the Roman Empire did not have the manpower surplus to instantly make good the loss of perhaps 20,000 troops, while the devastation of the Balkans, caused by the wanderings of the Goths over the next twenty years, was a serious loss in terms of imperial revenue. The impact of the Gothic arrival and of the battle of Adrianople was considerable, despite the relatively low numbers of barbarians involved.

4.4 Restoration under Theodosius I (379–395)

Theodosius I and the Balkan problem

In the immediate aftermath of the Roman defeat, Gratian elevated Theodosius to the position of eastern Augustus [5.1: ERNESTI 1998; LANÇON 2014; LEPPIN 2003; WILLIAMS/FRIELL 1994]. Unlike most of the emperors between 268 and 610, Theodosius did not come from a Balkan family, but he was certainly of military stock. He was the son of the general also called Theodosius who had put down the Great Conspiracy directed against Britain in 367/8 and the rebellion of Firmus in North Africa, but who had subsequently been executed on the orders of Valentinian. At the same moment, the younger Theodosius was involved in an unfortunate campaign against the Sarmatians, for which Valentinian dismissed him from his post. Despite this, Gratian called Theodosius out of retirement and set him to deal with the Gothic problem, which had spread from Thrace into Dacia and Macedonia, territories that were subject to the western emperor.

Although Theodosius did not have uninterrupted success against the Goths, his generals inflicted a major defeat on them as early as 379. He did, however, have to call upon Gratian for aid in 380/1. But by the autumn of 382, the Goths had come to terms. Not only that, Athanaric, who had remained outside the Empire in 376, submitted to Theodosius in Constantinople in 381, shortly before he died. Unfortunately, the exact terms agreed with the Goths in 382 are unknown, although it would seem that they were allowed to settle in the Danube basin, and many subsequently served in the Roman army. It appeared that the Gothic problem had been solved – and indeed that it had helped to ease the Empire's problem of military recruitment. That it erupted again in the last years of the fourth century was the result of military conflict between ambitious generals at the highest levels of the Empire. The continuing divisions within the Roman military were more damaging for the future than the arrival of the Goths.

Although Gratian had some success against the *Alamanni* in the Upper Rhine, Britain saw a renewed threat from the Picts and Scots in 381. This was quickly dealt with by the *comes Britanniae*, Magnus Maximus, but his victory led his troops to acclaim him as emperor, and he crossed to Gaul [6: Wijnendaele 2020]. Gratian's troops deserted him and he fled to Lyon, where he was assassinated in 383. Maximus probably hoped that his elevation would gain the approval of Theodosius, since he had previously campaigned alongside Theodosius' father.

Magnus Maximus

There remained another Augustus in the West, Gratian's younger brother Valentinian II, who had been proclaimed emperor at the age of four in 375 on the death of his father. Despite his youth, the bishop of Milan, Ambrose, and the Frankish general Bauto moved to support the young emperor. A compromise was reached in 384, probably at the instigation of Theodosius. Maximus was left in control of Gaul, Britain, Spain and Africa, while Valentinian and Theodosius ruled jointly in Italy. This situation lasted for three years, but in 387 Maximus moved against Valentinian, who fled to Theodosius for protection. The older emperor then turned on Maximus, defeating him at the Battle of the River Save and executing him in 388. Theodosius remained in the West until 391, when he left Valentinian in Gaul in the charge of Arbogast, a situation which the young emperor found oppressive and which culminated in Valentinian's murder or suicide in 392. Arbogast then raised Eugenius to the position of emperor [6: Szidat 1979]. This action prompted Theodosius' return, and the defeat of the usurper at the Battle of the River Frigidus in 394, where the loss of men on both sides was considerable. Eugenius was captured and executed and Arbogast committed suicide. Although Theodosius emerged triumphant, the combined troop losses from the battles of the Save and Frigidus, less than twenty years after Adrianople, inevitably weakened Roman military capability further.

Eugenius

Theodosius was now in sole control of the Empire even though he had granted the imperial title to both his sons [4.5: McEvoy 2013]. He had already conferred the title of Augustus on his elder son, Arcadius, in 383, probably to ensure his succession in the East. Ten years after the elevation of Arcadius, in 393, Theodosius raised his younger son Honorius to the position of Augustus. But neither son

The elevation of Arcadius and Honorius

was old enough to rule: Arcadius had been born in 377/8, and Honorius in 384. Thus, the pattern of 'child rule' initiated by Valentinian I with the elevation of Gratian was continued. Even so, with the re-unification of the Empire, the suppression of the threats posed by the Goths within the Balkans, and the *Alamanni*, Picts and Scots outside the frontiers, it may have seemed that the crises of the later fourth century were over. The appearance was illusory. Theodosius died suddenly in 395, leaving two boys, one aged 18 and the other 10, as emperors of East and West. Arrangements were made to ensure an effective regency, but they were instantly disputed, with Stilicho, who in military terms had been Theodosius' right-hand man, claiming to be responsible for both emperors, only to find his claim blocked in Constantinople by the eunuch Rufinus.

The consequences of the civil wars

Moreover, although it may have seemed that Theodosius had solved the Empire's immediate problems, the civil wars between Theodosius and first Maximus and then Eugenius had taken their toll. Maximus had moved large numbers of troops out of Britain, leaving the island province open to attacks by Picts, Scots and Saxons, as would become apparent in subsequent years. At the same time, the bloodshed on both sides, first at the Battle of the River Save (between Theodosius and Magnus Maximus) and subsequently at the River Frigidus (between Theodosius and Eugenius), had been considerable. The Empire could ill afford such casualties, especially in the aftermath of the battle of Adrianople. Maximus and Eugenius had, moreover, directed attention away from the Gothic settlement in the Balkans. Militarily, the Theodosian restoration was only temporary. Far more permanent were the changes that had taken place in the position of the Church and of churchmen since the death of Valentinian.

5 The Consolidation of the Church

5.1 The Council of Constantinople 381

Theododius and the Church

Theodosius is remembered as much for his commitment to Catholicism as for his restoration of the Empire following the deaths of Valens, Gratian and Valentinian [5.1: Maraval 2009]. Even before he had concluded a truce with the Goths, he had summoned the Council of Constantinople, which met in 381. The council had been called in part to deal with the appointment of a new bishop to the see of Constantinople, following Theodosius' removal of the homoean Demophilus. This resulted in an attempt, backed by Peter, the successor of Athanasius in Alexandria, to appoint Maximus the Cynic, who was, however, opposed by the local population. They wished to see the appointment of Gregory of Nazianzus. As a result, Theodosius turned to Damasus, the bishop of Rome, for advice, and at his suggestion he summoned a council of bishops.

Gregory was appointed patriarch, and he presided over the first part of the Council. One of the so-called Cappadocian Fathers, along with the brothers Basil of Caesarea and Gregory of Nyssa, he was a staunch defender of the Nicene position, which had been championed by Athanasius, up until his death in 373 [7: McGuckin 2001]. Perhaps as a result of sickness, however, Gregory soon offered his resignation from the episcopate and from the presidency of the council. A civil servant, Nectarius, was appointed in his place.

Despite the retirement of Gregory, the major pronouncements of Constantinople concerned the condemnation of Arianism and other related heresies. As such, it marked the end of the homoean dominance of the imperial Church in the East, which had been the situation from the time of Constantius II to that of Valens, except during the reign of Julian. Although Athanasius had not lived to see the triumph of Nicaea, from 381 onwards the Nicene position constituted orthodoxy. It is almost certain that what is now called the Nicene Creed was drawn up at the Council: this was the opinion stated by the bishops of Chalcedon in 451, although some modern scholars have expressed doubts as to whether they were correct [4.2: Kelly 1960; 7: Ritter 1965]. Whether or not the Creed was set down in 381, the Nicene position of the Council is clear.

The Nicene Creed

Also important was the third canon of the Council, which stated that the Bishop of Constantinople should 'have the prerogative of honour after the Bishop of Rome, because Constantinople is New Rome'. Because of its suggestion of parity between the two sees this was not a claim that was welcome in Rome, where it would store up problems for the future. Nor was Constantinople's new status welcome in the established patriarchates of Alexandria, Antioch and Jerusalem, all of which had New Testament justification for their authority. This was not the case for Constantinople, which makes no appearance in the Bible and whose importance was determined entirely by the status of the city as an imperial capital. Its

Constantinople as new Rome

dignity was, however, affirmed in the canons of the Council of 381, which would come to be regarded as the Second Ecumenical Council of the Church, following that of Nicaea.

5.2 Ambrose (374–397), Gratian (367–383), Magnus Maximus (383–388), and Theodosius I (379–395)

The Council of Constantinople marked the triumph of Nicene doctrine over that of the Homoeans. There were other aspects to the victory of the Catholic party. In the West, the dominant figure in the Catholic triumph was the bishop of Milan, Ambrose [4.5: McLynn 1994; Dassmann 2004; 7: Moorhead 2014]. He had been governor of the north Italian province of Liguria and Emilia at the time of the death of the homoean bishop, Auxentius, in 374. When a riot nearly broke out during the election of a successor, Ambrose intervened in his official capacity, only to find himself elected to the bishopric, even though he had held no church office and was not even baptised. He refused the appointment, but he was effectively forced to accept when the emperor Gratian intervened, praising the choice.

Ambrose was to prove an extremely active bishop who had a major effect on both the Church and the Roman State – more so, indeed, than did the bishops of Rome of his day. That he was so influential was the result not only of his own energy, but also of the fact that for much of his episcopate the West Roman imperial court was resident in Milan [4.5: McLynn 1994; Löx 2013]. As a result, he had plenty of opportunity to intervene in matters of religious and political importance. And having already held a provincial governorship, as well as being a man of considerable rhetorical talent, he exploited his episcopal position more effectively than any of his contemporaries.

A good example of his ability to influence the imperial court is his intervention in the Altar of Victory controversy in 384 [14.1: Klein 1972; 5.1: Cameron 2011]. The Altar of Victory had been set up in the Senate House in Rome in 29 BC by Augustus, to celebrate the defeat of Mark Antony and Cleopatra at the Battle of Actium. It was removed for religious reasons by the emperor Constantius II in 357, only to be restored by Julian. It was removed again by Gratian in 382 but following the emperor's death in 384 the senator Quintus Aurelius Symmachus appealed to Valentinian II to restore it. Symmachus' argument survives as his Third *Relatio*, which provides an important insight into the continuing significance of paganism among the senatorial aristocracy. Symmachus claimed that the pagans were still a majority in the senate. His defence of tradition, however, was firmly opposed by Ambrose – despite the fact that the two men happened to be related. The result was that Valentinian did not reinstate the altar, although it was briefly restored to the Senate House during the rule of the usurping emperor Eugenius, between 392 and 394.

The Altar of Victory controversy shows Ambrose influencing imperial policy. Other events actually show him successfully opposing emperors and members of the imperial family, even though he was usually a stalwart supporter of the houses of Valentinian and Theodosius, intervening in 384 to protect Valentinian II from the demands of Magnus Maximus, and delivering major orations to mark the funerals of Valentinian and Theodosius I.

The first of the bishop's conflicts with the imperial court arose over doctrine [4.5: McLYNN 1994; LÖX 2013]. From early in his episcopate Ambrose had established himself as a leader of the anti-homoeans. In 381, he was responsible for the Council of Aquileia, whose decrees theologically echoed those of the Council of Constantinople held the same year. The homoeans, however, still had support in the West, most notably from Justina, widow of Valentinian I and mother of Valentinian II. The first major confrontation between her and Ambrose occurred in 385, when she demanded that he hand over a *basilica* to the homoean cleric Auxentius (the younger), which the bishop refused to do. She made the demand again a year later, when Ambrose in response pointedly commented on the orthodoxy of the usurping emperor Magnus Maximus, who had sanctioned the execution of the charismatic ascetic Priscillian and who posed a major threat to the government of Valentinian. The bishop also manipulated opinion against Justina through his discovery and translation of the supposed bodies of the martyrs Gervasius and Protasius. In so doing he established something of a vogue for the unearthing and reburial of martyrs by Catholic bishops. As early as the 390s, Theodore of Octodurum (Sitten) unearthed the bodies of Maurice and the Theban legion at Agaune, on the banks of the Rhône, above its entry into the Lac Leman [14.4: NÄF 2011]. Ambrose's orchestration of the public mood also involved the use of hymns.

Justina

The relics of Gervasius and Protasius

In his conflict with Justina, Ambrose was opposing an imperial lady whom he regarded as heretical. By contrast, he recognised Theodosius as impeccably orthodox. Nevertheless, on two separate occasions, he came into open conflict with the Catholic emperor [4.5: McLʏɴɴ 1994]. The first occasion followed an episode in 388, when the bishop of the eastern city of Callinicum incited a group of monks to burn a synagogue. Theodosius ordered the punishment of the monks and the rebuilding of the synagogue. Ambrose was outraged and wrote to the emperor. When this had no effect, he publicly refused to give Theodosius communion until he had rescinded the punishment.

The synagogue at Callinicum

The second occasion was yet more dramatic. In 390, following the murder of the Gothic general Butheric in Thessalonika, Theodosius issued an order that culminated in the massacre of numerous citizens. Ambrose again reacted by writing to the emperor, telling him that he would not allow him to take communion unless he performed penance. Once more the emperor gave way.

The massacre at Thessalonika

Ambrose directly challenged the emperor and the imperial family with greater success than any bishop before him. Athanasius had been as implacable in standing up for his beliefs, but he was forced into exile on several occasions. Ambrose was able to face down both Justina and Theodosius. In part this was because, as bishop of the city that for the moment was the standard place of imperial residence in the West, he was well placed politically. But his successes were unusual. A generation later, the conflict between the empress Eudoxia, the wife of Arcadius, and the patriarch of Constantinople, John Chrysostom, led to the bishop's death in exile [5.2: Lɪᴇʙᴇsᴄʜᴜᴇᴛᴢ 1990]. In the sixth century, bishops of Rome found themselves forced to obey the emperor Justinian, despite the fact that by that time the only imperial ruler was based in Constantinople. Ambrose's career, however, is a demonstration of the growing influence of the Church, and not just over matters of doctrine.

5.3 Damasus (366–384)

Ambrose was easily the most influential bishop in the Western Empire in the last quarter of the fourth century, far more so than any incumbent of the see of Rome. Nevertheless, this was also a period in which the status of the bishopric of Rome was considerably enhanced, although it was not yet described as the papacy, nor indeed was the word *papa* used for the bishop. The key figure in the developments of the fourth century was Damasus, pope from 366 to 384.

Damasus and Ursinus were both elected bishop of Rome in a disputed election, following the death of Liberius in 366. According to the canons, bishops (including the bishop of Rome) were to be elected by the clergy and people of their city. Ursinus seems to have had the backing of the majority of the Roman clergy, while Damasus had that of the aristocracy. Documents preserved in the sixth-century collection of letters known as the *Collectio Avellana* claim that Damasus' supporters had previously backed Felix, whom Constantius had appointed as a replacement for Liberius in 355. The conflict was only concluded by the rulings of a synod in 368.

The disputed papal election of 366

Despite, and perhaps because of the controversial nature of his election, Damasus was more active than most of his Roman predecessors [7: REUTTER 2009]. In 382 he presided over a council in Rome which, among other acts, established a canonical list of Old and New Testament books. His concern for the Biblical text also led him to encourage Jerome, who served as his secretary between 382 and 385, to revise the Latin text of the Bible, which produced the Vulgate [7: McDONALD 2011].

The text of the Vulgate

Not quite as far reaching, but of considerable importance for the development of Rome as a Christian city, was Damasus' promotion of the cult of Roman martyrs. Just as the conflict between Felix and Liberius seems to have provided a background for Constantius' building at St Peter's, St Paul's and perhaps at the Lateran baptistery, so too that between Ursinus and Damasus apparently lay behind the development of the shrines of those who had died in the persecutions. Damasus restored the church of San Lorenzo fuori le Mura, and he developed the catacombs as centres of cult, as is shown by numerous epigrams, some of which he wrote himself [4.5: LÖX 2013: 7: TROUT 2015]. These were inscribed and set up at various tombs. Damasus thus deliberately associated himself with the Roman martyrs. This did not, however, lead to a vogue for pilgrimage to the catacombs, or to shrines of the Roman martyrs, which seems to be a development of the Carolingian era [7: DENZEY LEWIS 2020].

The extent to which successive conflicts within the Church of the city of Rome affected the position and representation of the bishop is striking. One can point not only to developments at the time of conflict between Liberius and Felix, and Ursinus and Damasus, but also in the subsequent century and a half, to the effects the disputed elections of Eulalius and Boniface (418–9), and of Symmachus and Laurentius (498–502). Some of the earliest biographies contained in the *Liber Pontificalis* were written in the context of the Laurentian schism [14.3: COHEN 2015].

The concern with Rome as a city of apostles and martyrs needs also to be considered against the ruling of the Council of Constantinople of 381, which had recognised the eastern imperial city as New Rome and effectively raised it to the same status as Rome itself. Hitherto, although there had been no official hierarchy among the major metropolitan dioceses, there had been a recognition that those cities which were most closely associated with the events of the New Testament (Jerusalem, Alexandria, Antioch and Rome) held higher patriarchal status, with Rome being particularly significant, both because it was the imperial capital and because it housed the bodies of two apostles, Peter and Paul. The elevation of Constantinople not only to the level of a Patriarchate, but also to the title of New Rome, offered a challenge to the ecclesiastical hierarchy.

The promotion of the cult of the martyrs by Damasus would seem to be a reaction both to the pope's disputed election and also to the new status of Constantinople. Only Rome could claim the bodies of two apostles: no apostle had lived or died in Constantinople. And Rome could also claim to be surrounded by the shrines of hundreds of martyrs. Effectively the promotion of the cult of the Roman martyrs marked an important step in the establishment of the primacy of the bishopric of Rome, although the evolution of papal primacy was slow, and was not fully achieved for centuries. The authority of the pope outside Rome was only established piecemeal, for instance through intervention in other regions of the Roman World, as in the elevation of the status of the bishopric of Arles by Pope Zosimus in 417, which took place against the background of conflict within the south Gallic Church, and of the attempt of the court of Honorius to reassert order in Gaul. Even more important, papal opinion was sought in the course of the Nestorian and Monophysite debates of the eastern Church, although no pope was present at the councils of Ephesus and Chalcedon.

5.4 Two Fathers of the Latin Church: Jerome (d. 420) and Augustine (354–430)

Just as the second half of the fourth century saw a major development in the status of Rome as a dominant ecclesiastical centre, so too it witnessed one of the intellectual highpoints of the Christian Church. The period from the fourth to the end of the sixth century saw the production of a considerable number of works of theology, above all Biblical commentaries, but also works which established the main doctrinal positions of the Church.

We have already noted the importance of Ambrose, and of Jerome's work on the text of the Bible. Jerome's stay in Rome was relatively short, although it was of considerable significance, and not just because of his support for Damasus and the beginnings of the production of the Vulgate text of the Latin Bible [7: KELLY 1975; REBENICH 1992, English translation: 2002; CAIN/LÖSSL 2009; MCDONALD 2011]. He also acted as the spiritual confessor of a number of senatorial ladies, advising them to adopt an ascetic lifestyle. This is well illustrated by several of his surviving letters, addressed to Marcella and to Paula and her daughters Blaesilla and Eustochium, which are regarded as classics of spiritual advice. Jerome was not the only such spiritual adviser at the time: among his contemporaries was the Briton Pelagius, whose theological views on the need for good works, as opposed to divine grace, would become a major bone of contention in the early years of the fifth century and would lead to his condemnation at the Synod of Diospolis (in Palestine) in 416.

Jerome

Jerome, however, fell afoul of the authorities in Rome before Pelagius did. When Damasus died in 384, he lost his major patron and protector. His relations with the widow Paula were thought to be suspicious, and he was effectively forced to leave the city. He travelled east, and after a visit to Egypt, which inspired him to take up the monastic life personally, moved on to Palestine, where he established himself in a cave in Bethlehem. There he once again became the spiritual adviser of numerous friends, and in particular of some of the senatorial ladies he had advised in Rome, including Paula and Eustochium. It was in Bethlehem that he completed his work on the Vulgate, which he based where possible on the original Hebrew, and not just on the Greek text. It was also there that he wrote most of his commentaries on individual books of the Bible, and it was from there that he launched his attack on Pelagius.

Augustine

Pelagius' other great adversary, Augustine, was slightly younger than Jerome [7: Brown 1967; Fuhrer 2004; O'Donnell 2005; Rosen 2015; Lane Fox 2015, 2017]. A provincial from North Africa, as a young man he had seemed to be destined for a public career as a rhetorician. He moved from Carthage to Rome, and then in 383 on to Milan, where he taught rhetoric. Although his mother, Monica, was a devout Catholic, he himself had joined the Manichaean sect whose dualist beliefs in Good and Evil had emerged out of third-century Persia. In Milan, however, he abandoned Manichaeism to embrace Neoplatonic philosophy. He then fell under the influence of Ambrose, and in 386 became a staunch Christian. As a result, he abandoned his post as *rhetor*, and in 388 moved back to North Africa. Having entered the priesthood in 391, he was elected bishop of Hippo Regius in 395. He charted the story of his move towards being a Christian in his *Confessions* of 397–8 – a work of autobiography that, however, needs to be read in full awareness of the fact that the narrative tells its story in a highly tendentious fashion [ed. 15.7/Augustine: O'Donnell 1992; Hammond 2014–6; 7: Lane Fox 2015, 2017].

As bishop, Augustine carried out his pastoral duties, which included the regular preaching of sermons, copies of which were widely circulated almost immediately. He engaged in intellectual combat with Manichaeism as well as the local African heresy of Donatism, and in the second decade of the fifth century with Pelagianism. These theological battles underpinned many of his theological works, which effectively mapped out much of what would come to be understood as orthodox Catholic doctrine – although some of his ideas were certainly misunderstood by his contemporaries and by subsequent generations [7: Markus 1970]. His most substantial work, however, the *City of God*, was inspired not by intra-Christian doctrinal debate, but by the sack of Rome by the Visigoths in 410, which had prompted pagans to claim that conversion to Christianity had led to the abandonment of the Eternal City by its gods. In contrasting the secular world and its history, philosophy, and culture with the City of God, Augustine formulated a Christian worldview that effectively denied worldly and secular values [7: O'Daly 1999; Wetzel 2012].

The City of God was completed in 426; three years later, a substantial body of barbarians, led by the Vandal king Gaiseric, crossed the Straights of Gibraltar to Africa. They moved eastwards and reached Hippo Regius in 430, laying siege to the city at precisely the time that Augustine was dying. He did not live to see its capture.

5.5 The Church Historians

Augustine's reading of history was very much at odds with the Christian historiography that had emerged in the course of the fourth century. At its heart were a number of works written during and immediately after the reign of Constantine by Eusebius of Caesarea. The most influential of these were the *Ecclesiastical History* and the *Chronicle*, which provided an annalistic history of the World down to c. 325. The *Life of Constantine*, which is of great value to modern historians, was little known in Late Antiquity or the early Middle Ages [4.2: CAMERON/HALL 1999]. The *Ecclesiastical History*, which covered the period from the days of the apostles down to 324 and thus dealt with the expansion and persecution of the Church down to the days of Constantine, was translated into Latin by Jerome's sometime friend Rufinus, and the work in both Greek and Latin provided the model for all later ecclesiastical histories [15.7/Rufinus of Aquileia: HUMPHRIES 2008]. It also influenced more general historical works that covered ecclesiastical matters (as, for instance, the late sixth-century *Ten Books of Histories* by Gregory of Tours). The *Chronicle*, which has not survived in its entirety, was divided into an epitome of universal history and the so-called Canons of the Chronicle. These arranged the histories of individual empires and peoples into parallel columns in which entries were inserted alongside the appropriate date, which allowed events to be viewed synchronically. The dates were all given according to a variety of different systems, including the regnal dates of kings and emperors and Olympiads (a four-year chronological cycle determined by the Olympic games) as well as the years from the birth of Abraham (which could be calculated from a close reading of the Old Testament); it did not, however, use the system of *anno domini* dates which was employed by Dionysius Exiguus in his Easter Table of 525 and only entered general currency from the eighth century onwards. The second part of Eusebius' *Chronicle* has survived in its entirety in a Latin translation made by Jerome (although it does not, in fact, survive in the original Greek). Both of Eusebius' major

Eusebius and ecclesiastical history

The chronicle of Eusebius

historical works presented a vision of the steady triumph of Christianity and of the Christian Empire [5.2: BURGESS/KULIKOWSKI 2013].

This Christian triumphalism was challenged by the events of the late fourth and fifth centuries. Nevertheless, in its Latin form the *Chronicle* of Eusebius became the model for subsequent late-antique and early-medieval chronicles in the Latin West [5.2: BURGESS/KULIKOWSKI 2013]. Jerome himself continued Eusebius' *Chronicle* from 325 to 379 and subsequent writers added to Jerome's continuation. Thus, Prosper of Aquitaine started to add annalistic entries in 433 and continued until 455, while in *Gallaecia* Hydatius continued Jerome's *Chronicle* down to 469 [5.4: BURGESS 1993]. An anonymous chronicler, writing in Gaul probably towards the end of the fifth century, also compiled a continuation to Jerome, concluding his narrative at some point around 452 (the dating systems followed for the fifth-century entries are unfortunately in conflict) [5.4: BURGESS 2001; KÖTTER/SCARDINO 2017]. The following centuries saw yet more continuators, including Cassiodorus, Marcellinus Comes [12.9: CROKE 1995], and Victor of Tunnuna and John of Biclaro in the sixth century as well as Isidore in the seventh [12.3: CARDELLE DE HARTMANN 2001]. Although these chroniclers could no longer present the optimistic reading of history that Eusebius had set out and in which the Christian Empire marked a historical apogee, they still presented what was essentially a history of Salvation, in which events of the Old and above all those of the New Testament provided a central strand.

Although the Chronicle genre dominated the historiography of the Western Empire in the fifth century, not every historian adopted its form. Like Eusebius and Jerome, Orosius in his *Seven Books of Histories against the Pagans*, written in c. 416/7, composed a universal history, and not just an account of Rome or its Empire. But the format he chose to do so was a more rhetorical one [5.1: ARNAUD-LINDET 1990–1; VAN NUFFELEN 2012]. Writing at the request of Augustine, Orosius set about denying the pagan claim that the conversion of the Empire to Christianity had led to decline and to the sack of Rome. The final book, with its account of the closing years of the fourth century and the beginning of the fifth, only sustains the argument with difficulty. Even so, Orosius' work would become one of the chief sources and models for subsequent western historians writing in the early Middle Ages.

Marcellinus Comes' apart, the Chronicle tradition was largely a western affair. In the Greek East it was Eusebius' *Ecclesiastical History* that provided the chief model for historical writing. And here, because the East suffered much less than the West in the early fifth century, it was easier to adopt Eusebius' positive reading of events. Thus, both Socrates and Sozomen could write *Ecclesiastical Histories* in which the Christian Empire was still a significant force [4.2: HANSEN/PERICHON/MARAVAL, 2004–7; GRILLET/SABBAH/FESTUGIÈRE/ANGLEVIEL DE LA BEAUMELLE 1983–2008; 3: PELIKAN 1987]. What these two historiographical traditions also demonstrate, however, is the extent to which history, and the understanding of the past, had been christianised. Of course, as we will see, there were still writers who did not conform to this tradition: in the fourth century, there was Ammianus Marcellinus (who took Tacitus as his model), and in the sixth the pagan Zosimus, as well as Procopius (who looked back to Thucydides) and his continuator Agathias. But the dominant modes of historical discourse were Christian ones.

5.6 The Poets: Prudentius, Paulinus of Pella and Dracontius (348-post 405)

Alongside theology and history, the fourth century also witnessed the creation of a strong tradition of Christian poetry. Already in the days of Constantine the Spaniard Juvencus wrote a verse account of the events of the Gospels. The tradition of writing Biblical epic continued down to the end of the fifth century, with Cyprian's *Heptateuch* and the versifications of Genesis and Exodus by Avitus of Vienne, and into the sixth century with Arator's retelling of the Acts of the Apostles [7: ROBERTS 1985; 13: NODES 1993; GREEN 2006]. Less tied to pre-existing texts, at the end of the fourth century another Spaniard, Prudentius, wrote a number of works, including an allegorical poem on the war between Virtue and Vice, the *Psychomachia*, as well as a large collection of verses, the *Peristephanon*, recounting tales of the Christian martyrs [7: PALMER, 1989; ROBERTS 1993; FRISCH 2020]. In addition, he contributed to the debate over the Altar of Victory in his *Contra Symmachum*.

The crises of the fifth century also elicited works from a number of poets, including the *Commonitorium* of Orientius of Auch and the *Eucharisticos* of Paulinus of Pella, which describes the disasters

Orientius and Paulinus of Pella

that hit the poet in the course of the barbarian invasions of Gaul [15.7/Paulinus of Pella: Moussy 1974; 7: Lucarini 2006]. Prosper of Aquitaine is thought by several scholars to have been the author of the *De Providentia Dei* [7: Marcovich 1989]. Although the poem of Paulinus presents a remarkable picture of the experience of an aristocrat living through the early fifth century, the main significance of most of these works for the historian is the evidence they provide of the Christianisation of literary culture, which is also apparent in the Christian poems of Dracontius, the *Satisfactio ad Gun-*

Dracontius — *thamundum* and the *De laudibus Dei* [7: Moussy/Camus 2002]. Although Dracontius also wrote works that belonged much more firmly in the classical tradition, including his version of the Orestes myth, the late fourth and early fifth centuries essentially mark a cultural revolution. Christianity had made an impact on all walks of life.

6 Secular Culture

6.1 Rhetoric and Panegyric

Of course, the establishment of new genres of Christian writing did not mean the instant collapse of long-established classical traditions. Augustine himself had been trained as a *rhetor*, and this is apparent from his sermons. Indeed, much of the sermon literature of the fourth, fifth and sixth centuries shows a degree of rhetorical skill, and it would seem to have been appreciated in those terms [7: Vessey 2013]. Rhetoric continued to be important throughout the fifth century, and indeed into the sixth [8: Kaster 1988].

Martianus Capella and — The classic description of the seven liberal arts – grammar, the liberal arts — logic, rhetoric, arithmetic, geometry, astronomy, music – is to be found in the *De nuptiis philologiae et Mercurii* ('On the marriage of Philology and Mercury') of Martianus Capella, writing in Africa, probably in the late fifth century [8: Shanzer 1986], although Konrad Vössing, among others, prefers an earlier date [7: Vössing 2008]. The division of these subjects into the *trivium* (grammar, logic and rhetoric) and the *quadrivium* (arithmetic, geometry, astronomy and music) only appears in the sixth century (a coinage perhaps of Boethius or Cassiodorus). Martianus Capella's work continued to be cited throughout the early Middle Ages, although the evidence for the teaching of the liberal arts fades after the late fifth century, which is when we last hear of the existence of grammarians and of schools of rhetoric in the West. Although the fourth and fifth centuries were a golden age of rhetoric, one can talk of a decline, even a collapse, in the teaching of grammar and rhetoric in the sixth century, despite the fact that books of grammar were still being copied and indeed took on considerable importance in Ireland and Anglo-Saxon England, where Latin had to be learnt as a foreign language [13: Law 1997]. On the continent, the decline in rhetoric and grammar went hand in hand with linguistic change, which saw Latin move ever further from its classical form towards proto-Romance, and thus towards the early forms of Italian, Spanish, Portuguese and French [13: Wright 1982; Banniard 1992]. The decline in the use of classical grammar, however, did not lead to a complete break in literary culture.

Above all, the fourth and fifth centuries were an age in which panegyric had a role to play at the heart of imperial politics. Emperors, generals, and leading members of the senatorial aristocracy used panegyric to set out and justify policy or to offer coded criticism [5.2: Cameron 1970; 13: MacCormack 1976; 4.1: Nixon/Rodgers 1994; 8: Müller-Rettig 2008–12; 8: Rees 2012; 3: Omissi 2018]. Panegyrics were delivered at the great occasions of the political year, notably when a man began his consulship. Although consular office itself did not convey any great power, holding the consulship was regarded as a mark of extreme honour, and emperors frequently took the office or appointed especially favoured individuals. Apart from anything else, consuls gave their names to the year in which they held office. — Panegyric

Panegyrics had long been delivered on the occasion of taking up the consulship. Pliny, for instance, had delivered a speech of thanks (*Gratiarum Actio*) to Trajan in AD 100, for being appointed *consul suffectus*. In the late third and fourth centuries Pliny's speech was regarded as the ideal model for a panegyric. Its importance was made abundantly clear in the late fourth century when it was placed at the head of a collection of panegyrics, known as the *Panegyrici Latini*, which was put together by a Gallic *rhetor*, Pacatus, in or shortly after 389, when he delivered his own panegyric in praise of Theodosius I [4.1: Nixon/Rodgers 1994]. With the single exception of Pliny's panegyric, the collection made by Pacatus covers the century from 289 onwards. There are panegyrics addressed to Diocletian's colleague, Maximian, to his Caesar, Constantius Chlorus, to — The *Panegyrici Latini*

Constantine (and other members of his family), and to the emperor Julian. In their praise of the actions of individual emperors (for instance of the actions of Maximian and Constantius in northern Gaul and Britain during the 290s), these texts provide us with precious evidence.

Symmachus and Ambrose

In addition to this collection of panegyrics and other works of the same genre, we also have a number of other public speeches, delivered to influence or justify imperial policy in the fourth century. *Relationes* delivered by the senator Symmachus in the 380s survive and provide crucial information on the Altar of Victory controversy [8: BARROW 1976]. Symmachus' opponent, Ambrose, himself a great rhetorician as well as a bishop and theologian, composed substantial speeches to mark the deaths of Gratian and of Theodosius [4.5: LIEBESCHUETZ 2005]. From this political world we also have the works of Ausonius, teacher of rhetoric at the schools of Bordeaux, who was subsequently appointed tutor to the young Gratian by the emperor Valentinian I. From Ausonius, in addition to a substantial number of poems, there is a *Gratiarum Actio*, offered to Gratian for appointing him to the consulship [4.5: GIBSON 2019; SIVAN 1993].

Ausonius

Greek panegyrics

Alongside these Latin works of the fourth century there are the texts of Greek speeches, notably by the emperor Julian himself, that provide major information for understanding the emperor's policies and his reign [3: OMISSI 2018]. A particularly significant number of speeches have survived from the pen of the rhetor Libanius, active in Antioch, one of the major centres of the Eastern Empire. These include a funerary oration on Julian as well as numerous works that shed light on life in Antioch itself. In addition, there are panegyrical works by Themistius (whose speeches provide crucial information on politics in the Eastern Empire during the reigns of Julian, Valentinian and Valens, and of Theodosius) [4.3: HEATHER/ MONCUR 2001; VANDERSPOEL 1995]. From the next generation there are rhetorical works of Synesius (a rhetor who ended up as bishop of Ptolemais in Libya), whose *De Regno* sheds light on the political ideology of the court of Theodosius' son Arcadius. It is also central to his *Egyptian Tale* which provides vital information on the revolt of the *magister militum* Gainas [5.2: CAMERON/LONG 1993; 6: HAGL 1997].

Merobaudes

Panegyric continued to be of importance into the fifth and even the sixth centuries. From the mid fifth-century West fragments of panegyrics by Merobaudes survive [5.3: CLOVER 1971], and from the sixth there is a lengthy speech on the Ostrogothic ruler Theodoric, written by Ennodius of Pavia [13: Rohr 1995], as well as works by Cassiodorus [13: MacCormack 1976]. These are all in prose, although many of the panegyric texts that survive from the very late fourth and fifth centuries are in verse, which seems to have become the dominant mode for such public statements for a brief period.

Ennodius and Cassiodorus

The shift from prose to verse, and indeed to a highly allusive style, full of mythological references (comparable to those of the *Egyptian Tale* of Synesius), would seem to be associated above all with the panegyrics of Claudian, written primarily to justify the policies of the *magister militum* (and power behind the imperial throne) Stilicho in the opening decade of the fifth century [5.2: Cameron 1970].

Claudian

From the middle decades of the same century there survive several verse panegyrics written by Sidonius Apollinaris, directed towards a sequence of emperors, Avitus, Majorian and Anthemius. Here Sidonius is sometimes found to be acting as spokesman for the emperor, and sometimes (as in the case of the panegyric on Majorian) excusing the actions of those who had previously opposed the emperor.

Sidonius

Panegyrics in verse, as in prose, were still being composed after the death of Sidonius. In the East, Corippus wrote his *In Laudem Iustini* for Justin II in 565 [6: Cameron 1976a], while the Italian poet Venantius Fortunatus wrote a number of very much shorter panegyrical works on Merovingian rulers [12.7: Reydellet 1981], following his move to Francia in the late sixth century. He would eventually be elected to the bishopric of Poitiers. The genre thus continued to be important well beyond the deposition of the last western emperor in 476.

Sixth-century verse panegyrics

6.2 Letters

The panegyrics and the speeches of the fourth and fifth centuries are very public texts, although the public to which they were addressed was only a very small and very elite proportion of the population (unlike much of the sermon literature, which was delivered in church, but also circulated in manuscript form, sometimes widely, to judge from the surviving manuscripts and from textual citations in other works). The audience of the panegyrics thus overlaps with that of many of the friendship letters that survive from fourth, fifth and sixth centuries and are preserved in letter collections, which constitute another of the distinctive bodies of evidence from the period [7: NEIL/ALLEN 2015; SOGNO/STORIN/WATTS 2017; 8: MÜLLER 2018].

The letters that survive from Late Antiquity can be divided into private and public, although there is a significant overlap in that private letters illustrate networks that were also employed for political and ecclesiastical purposes. Public letters might be administrative, legal or theological. Letters addressed by officials to the emperor, or indeed by *curiales* lobbying for their cities, were at the heart of the Roman administrative system. A significant percentage of imperial law contained in the Theodosian and Justinianic collections began as responses to appeals sent to the emperor [4.2: MILLAR 1977]. The *Variae* of Cassiodorus provide us with a collection of letters intended to illustrate the continuing *civilitas* of government in post-Roman Ostrogothic Italy in the early years of the sixth century [6: BJORNLIE 2013].

The *Variae* of Cassiodorus

Letters are also at the heart of ecclesiastical communication. Bishops lobbied the emperor, but in addition they wrote to one another and to their congregations. Just as there is an overlap between letters and secular legislation, so too there is an overlap between episcopal letters, theology and canon law [13: MATHISEN 1999; 8: WOOD 2018]. Letters are therefore one of our chief sources for the activities of bishops [15.7/Gelasius I: NEIL/ALLEN 2014].

Papal letters

There are important collections of letters from Pope Leo I (440–61) and Gelasius (492–6), and papal letters, like those of Ambrose, Augustine, and other Church Fathers, have survived in collections of canon law and theology. Thus, the *Collectio Dionysiana*, compiled by Dionysius Exiguus in the early sixth century, contains a substantial number of excerpts from papal letters. Another collection that also includes papal letters from the fifth and sixth centuries, as well as imperial documents, the *Collectio Avellana* is thought to have been put together by a private individual at some point between 556 and 561 [12.9: BLAIR-DIXON 2007; LIZZI TESTA/MARCONI 2019].

In addition to what they tell us about the functioning of Church and State, letters and letter collections are also a key to our understanding of late-antique aristocratic society. Initially, of course, private letters had a very small circulation, but in the fourth and fifth centuries a number of authors gathered their letters into collections, which were circulated among a wider, although still limited, circle. One should, however, note, that not all the collections of letters that have come down to us were put together by their authors or by near contemporaries: several of them are compilations of the Carolingian period [8: WOOD 2018]. These letters and letter collections provide a remarkable insight into the workings of elite society: its maintenance of communication and its exploitation of friendship to promote and protect oneself, one's friends, and one's family. Indeed friendship, *amicitia*, is a central theme of these letters, and a major feature of the structure of aristocratic society. *Amicitia* Aristocrats relied on friends and acquaintances to help them in their political and legal lobbying and in preparing for the great games that high officials were expected to mount when they assumed office [8: MATTHEWS 1974]. The surviving letters of *amicitia* are our clearest evidence for the networks that were exploited by the senatorial elite.

Some of the authors of letters and letter collections we have already met in discussing rhetorical culture. Just as Pliny provided the chief model for the writers of panegyrics, so too were his letters the touchstone for the epistolary culture of the fourth and fifth centuries. Symmachus, Ambrose's opponent in the clash over the Altar of Victory, composed a substantial body of letters, which were gathered together into nine books (as were Pliny's) by his son [8: MATTHEWS 1974]. This was a model that was also ultimately copied by Symmachus Sidonius Apollinaris, although the number of books that he produced built up over time, and the final figure of nine seems not to have been envisaged when the first books of letters were put together. As we will see, Sidonius himself was the model for a subse- Sidonius Apollinaris quent generation of letter writers active in the early post-Roman period.

The letter collections of Symmachus and of Sidonius and his followers are a very particular group. The authors themselves came from the very highest level of society, and their writings provide us with the majority of our evidence for that elite. One other figure who by birth belonged to the same elite group, Paulinus of Nola, has also left us a number of letters [8: FABRE 1949; TROUT 1999; CONY- BEARE 2000]. Paulinus was initially a friend and correspondent of Au- Paulinus of Nola and sonius, but he came to associate himself increasingly with ascetics, Sulpicius Severus becoming bishop of Nola. He was a correspondent of Augustine (another writer who has left a substantial correspondence) as well as of Sulpicius Severus, the hagiographer of St Martin, and he was also author of a small cluster of letters. Although he broke with the secular world of Ausonius, Paulinus continued to work through the same patterns of friendship that were central to the secular aristocracy, but in so doing he gave them a strikingly Christian aura. Whereas for Symmachus, and indeed for Sidonius, friendship is most often described by the term *amicitia*, Paulinus tended to employ the term *caritas*, thus playing a significant role in the transformation of Roman into Christian friendship.

6.3 The Secular Historians

We have already noted that despite the importance of Christian historiography, there was no major break in secular history-writing in the fourth and fifth centuries [8: Rohrbacher 2002]. Indeed, just as Late Antiquity was a golden age of panegyric, so too it was a notable period of history-writing. Of particular importance to anyone wanting to understand the second and third quarters of the fourth century is the history written by Ammianus Marcellinus, a career soldier from the East, who ultimately made his way to Rome, where his audience was essentially members of the senatorial class [8:

Ammianus Marcellinus   Matthews 1989; 4.3: Barnes 1998; Drijvers/Hunt 1999; Kelly 2008]. Unfortunately, we lack the opening books of his histories, but he seems to have set out to continue the Annals of Tacitus: his work began with the reign of Nerva, although the surviving narrative only begins in 353 and continues up to 378, ending shortly after the battle of Adrianople. The surviving books of his History contain an extremely valuable account of the reigns of Constantius II, Julian, Valentinian and Valens. Having been a soldier, he provides detailed, sometimes eye-witness, information on military campaigns, especially on the eastern frontier and in Gaul.

Historia Augusta   In terms of the importance of his narrative Ammianus stands head and shoulders above other historians of the period, but other histories are nevertheless of considerable interest. The strangest, and most difficult to evaluate, is the *Historia Augusta*, a work purporting to have been written by six authors at the end of the third and beginning of the fourth century. This is made up of the biographies of thirty emperors, covering the period from 117 to 284. In form it follows the *Twelve Caesars* of Suetonius, in contrast to Ammianus' choice of Tacitus as model. Were the *Historia Augusta* to have been a reliable record of the second and third centuries it would have been an invaluable source. Unfortunately, it seems to be a rather fanciful account of that period, written not by six authors, but by one, active perhaps in the later decades of the century, although some have argued for composition in the time of Constantine [4.1: Syme 1968; Lippold 1998]. The writings of Ammianus may provide a *terminus post quem*. It has been argued that the *Life* of Aurelian contained in the *Historia Augusta* alludes to the consul of 400 of the same name, and that other Lives in the compilation also allude to events surrounding the fall of Gainas in that year [4.1: Pottier 2006]. Although it is often used as a quarry for facts (inevitably, given the poverty of our narrative evidence for the second and third centuries), it has more recently been studied as shedding light on the interests of a Roman audience in the decades in which Ammianus was active. That sections of the Roman aristocracy were intensely interested in history during this period is apparent from a letter by Symmachus which refers to the preparation of a new edition of Livy.

The 370s and 380s seem to have been a period of exceptional historiographical activity, and not just in the composition of major narratives in the style of Tacitus and Suetonius. In exactly these decades Eutropius wrote a Breviary of Roman history, running from the foundation of Rome in 753 BC down to 363 AD. For the early part of his story, he provides what is largely an abridgement of Livy. Thereafter his major source is unknown, but it seems to have been a now-lost history of the Caesars [4.1: Bird 1993]. This same source would seem to have been used by Aurelius Victor, whose *De Caesaribus* provides an epitome of Roman history from Augustus to 360, arranged, as the title suggests, into accounts of the reigns of emperors [4.1: Bird 1984, 1994; Stover/Woudhoysen 2023].

Eutropius and Aurelius Victor

After this great burst of history-writing there is something of a caesura. Historical writing in the fifth century is dominated by the Byzantine Church historians, Sozomen, Socrates and Theodoret, and by the western chroniclers following in the footsteps of Eusebius and Jerome, together with Orosius, who rewrote classical history to prove that the conversion of the Empire was not the disaster that the pagans were claiming, in the aftermath of the Gothic sack of Rome. Earlier traditions would only be revived in the sixth cen-

The Church historians

tury, when Procopius, and after him Agathias, looked back to the model of Thucydides.

7 The Sack of Rome and the First Barbarian Settlements

7.1 Stilicho (d. 408)

The division of east and west

In the aftermath of the disaster of Adrianople and of the revolt of Magnus Maximus, Theodosius had done much to re-establish the Empire, continuing its transformation into a Christian state. This achievement, however, was called into question following his death in 395. The emperor left two sons: Arcadius, who was already 18 years old, and Honorius, who was ten. Arcadius had been declared co-Augustus in the East as early as 383; Honorius was given the same status in the West in 393. Although Arcadius was almost of an age to rule when Theodosius died, Stilicho, who had become his military right-hand man, attempted to establish himself as regent for both sons of the dead emperor. The eastern Praetorian Prefect, Rufinus, however, seized control in Constantinople, leaving Stilicho in command of the West. This division between East and West and the frequent lack of cooperation between the two halves of the Empire would prove disastrous – although not fatal to the Roman State – over the course of the following two decades [3: O'FLYNN 1983; BÖRM 2018].

Rufinus and Eutropius

At the time of Theodosius' death, Stilicho was in Greece, at the head of an army of eastern and western troops. Rufinus persuaded Arcadius to recall the eastern forces and to order Stilicho to take his own troops back to the West [5.2: JANSSEN 2004]. The result was to allow the Visigoths, who had been trapped in Greece, freedom to move through the Balkans [4.5: HEATHER 1991]. Although Rufinus himself was killed by the Gothic *magister militum* Gainas before the end of the year, relations between Stilicho and the court of Constantinople did not improve during the four years from 395 to 399, when it was controlled by the eunuch Eutropius. Stilicho's relations with both Rufinus and Eutropius are detailed in poems of Claudian, who effectively acted as a mouthpiece for the western leader [5.2: CAMERON 1970]. Eutropius' successor, Anthemius, was a rather more emollient figure than either of his two predecessors, but Rufinus and Eutropius had crucially weakened the Stilicho's ability to deal with the barbarian threat in the closing years of the fourth century and the beginning of the fifth.

In 397, Stilicho failed to defeat the Visigoths, who by now were led by Alaric. He may well have been worried about the reliability of some of his troops, which included significant numbers of Goths, recruited into the Roman army since 376. He was also faced with problems in both North Africa and in Britain. In 402, however, he was successful in checking an invasion of Italy by Alaric, and he defeated the Gothic leader again the following year, forcing him to return to the Balkan province of Illyricum – territory that was divided between the Eastern and Western Empires and which Stilicho was keen to control. The threat posed by Alaric in 402, however, seems to have led the court to move from Milan to the harbour city of Ravenna, where it was also well protected by marshes. In the following decades it remained the preferred place of residence for the emperor and his family.

The Gothic problem

Then in 405 Radagaisus, with an army of Goths, Alans, Sueves and Vandals invaded Italy [4.5: Wolfram 2009; 3: Heather 2005]. They may have been reacting to renewed Hunnic activity to the north of the Danube. Orosius claims that there were 200,000 men in the army of Radagaisus. The figure is highly unlikely, but it does show that this was a significant force. After several months gathering a large enough army, and also enlisting the help of Huns under the leadership of Uldin, Stilicho successfully defeated the invasion, capturing Radagaisus at Fiesole outside Florence [6: Wijnendaele 2016]. This success, however, was short-lived. In order to deal with the threat posed by the invasion, Stilicho had to draw troops from the Rhineland, leaving that frontier exposed.

Radagaisus

7.2 The Year 406

According to Prosper of Aquitaine, a force of Vandals, Alans, and Sueves crossed the Rhine on 31st December 406. Some have questioned whether this date is a year too late, but in all probability it is correct. This means that the Rhine crossing occurred after one other disastrous event from Stilicho's point of view. In 406, Britain revolted against the court in Ravenna, elevating three usurpers in

Constantine III

turn, Marcus, Gratian, and then Constantine (III), who may have been reacting against Stilicho's removal of troops from the Rhine frontier. Although the first two of these usurpers were of little significance, Constantine posed a major threat not only to Stilicho, but also to the regime of Honorius. Having established himself in Britain, Constantine crossed to Gaul [10: DRINKWATER 1998: 4.1: KULIKOWSKI 2000].

The fall of Stilicho
Stilicho clearly took the threat of Constantine seriously, sending the Gothic general Sarus to oppose him. He was, however, unable to check Constantine's advance, in part because Alaric took advantage of events to move into Italy from the Balkans. At the same time, factions within the Roman army and at the court of Honorius turned openly against Stilicho, accusing him, amongst other things, of intending to place his son Eucherius on the imperial throne. The accusations were surely false, but in his reliance on Gothic troops Stilicho had alienated many at court. He was arrested in Ravenna and executed in 408 [5.2: WIJNENDAELE 2018].

406
It was against the background of Constantine's rebellion that the Vandals (who had originated to the south of Denmark), Alans (probably driven from north of the Caucasus by the Huns), and Sueves (apparently a segment of the *Alamanni*), having crossed the Rhine, moved into Gaul. It is important to note the absence of any evidence for a significant military response on the part of either Stilicho or Constantine. The internal divisions among the Romans (both those between Constantinople and Ravenna – which often served as the capital for Honorius, although the imperial family also spent time in Rome, which is where most of its members were buried – and those between Ravenna and Constantine III) had reduced the Roman ability to act. It was the civil war between Constantine and Honorius that allowed the Vandals, Alans and Sueves to plunder Gaul and settle in Spain.

Barbarian numbers
Prosper does not say how many barbarians there were in the groups that crossed the Rhine in 406, but they were numerous enough to overcome what Roman opposition there was. When the surviving Vandals and Alans crossed into North Africa after two decades in 429, they were fewer than 80,000. By that time the Sueves had settled in Gallaecia in north-west Spain. The Vandals and Alans themselves had certainly lost considerable numbers of men over the previous twenty years, but at the same time they had gained others, including Roman renegades and slaves. When dis-

cussing the Vandal crossing to Spain, Procopius states that previously the Vandals and Alans had numbered 50,000. This is unlikely to be an underestimate, although it does not include the Sueves. Taking the claims of Procopius as a point of comparison, we can guess that the barbarians who crossed the Rhine in 406 were in the tens, and not the hundreds, of thousands. For the three years from 406 to 409 they plundered their way across towards the Pyrenees and to Spain [11.2: WOOD 2019].

Their route is hard to piece together [12.4: BERNDT/STEINACHER 2008]. Much of the factually specific evidence is to be found in letters of Jerome, where he repeated news that had reached him in far-off Bethlehem. He mentions the destruction of various cities (Mainz, Worms, Speyer, Strasbourg, Arras and Thérouanne). In addition, some of the Christian poets writing in Gaul in the second and third decades of the fifth century make general reference to the destruction caused, but they do not provide a clear account of the passage of the barbarians in these years. Thus, we lack a clear narrative. Nevertheless, it is clear that some cities suffered badly in the course of the movement of the Vandals, Alans and Sueves, while other areas, including the north-west and the south-east of Gaul, were left untouched.

Jerome and accounts of destruction

Meanwhile, disagreement between Constantine III and his general Gerontius had turned into open warfare, allowing the peoples who crossed the Rhine in 406 to enter Spain three years later [10: ARCE 1988, 5.2: ARCE 2005; 10: DRINKWATER 1998; 11.1: KULIKOWSKI 2000]. In 411, they split up, dividing the Iberian peninsula between them. The division they made is interesting, because it suggests that initially the dominant group was that of the Alans, for it was they who settled in the most extensive and richest areas. Thus, they moved into Lusitania and Carthaginiensis, the Siling Vandals into Baetica, while the Hasding Vandals and Sueves settled in the north-western province of Gallaecia. On all this we are dependent on the *Chronicle* of Hydatius, resident in Gallaecia, in the city of Tuy, where he was writing in the middle of the fifth century.

Barbarians in Spain

7.3 The Year 410

In the immediate aftermath of their arrival in Spain, however, the Vandals, Alans and Sueves were a secondary problem for Honorius

The sieges of Rome

and his counsellors. Following the execution of Stilicho in 408, Alaric marched on Rome, besieging the city until the senate agreed to hand over considerable amounts of treasure and to liberate any Gothic slaves. What Alaric wanted above all was recognition from the emperor, including an official military position, which Honorius refused to confer, prompting a second siege of Rome. At the same time, the Gothic leader elevated the Roman senator Priscus Attalus to imperial office, and as a result gained the desired title of *magister militum*. Shortly after, however, Alaric began negotiations with Honorius and deposed Attalus. When the negotiations failed, he launched his third siege of Rome, and this time the city fell, although Alaric was careful to control the amount of destruction and in particular protected the city's churches [5.2: Arce 2018].

The sack of Rome   The capture of Rome prompted a series of different reactions [5.2: Meier/Patzold 2010; Lipps/Machado/von Rummel 2013]. Clearly, as Pelagius noted, it was a violent affair, despite Alaric's moderation. Above all, however, it was a shock, and one that prompted the remaining pagans to claim that it had been allowed by the gods because of the conversion of the Empire to Christianity. It was this reaction that caused Augustine to embark on writing *The City of God*, and encouraged Orosius to write the *Seven Books against the Pagans*. For Augustine, the sack of the city was a matter of transient significance when set against the divine plan of salvation and damnation [5.2: De Bruyn 1993], while for Orosius it was nothing like as bad as previous disasters had been [5.1: Van Nuffelen 2012]. Many Christians, however, did not see the events as they did, and Jerome, amongst others, lamented the sack of the old capital of the Empire.

The Sibylline Books   At the same time, one should note that pagans had long expected that disaster would strike Rome at around this time. A well-known legend related that when Romulus and Remus were digging the foundations of the city, Remus saw six vultures, but Romulus twelve. According to the Sibylline Books, this could be interpreted as meaning that Rome would last twelve centuries. Since the city was thought to have been founded in 753 BC (or thereabouts – there is inconsistency over the exact date), this meant that it would fail in the middle years of the fifth century. Such was the alarm over this prediction that Stilicho is said to have had the Sibylline Books burned in the last years of his exercise of power [3: Wood 2018].

The death of Alaric   Although Alaric succeeded in taking Rome, it brought him little advantage. He withdrew his army and marched south, intending, it would seem, to cross over to the fertile province of Africa [5.2: Arce 2018]. He died somewhere in Calabria, leaving his brother Athaulf to take command of Visigoths. In 411, the new Gothic leader led his people out of Italy into Gaul, where the usurpation of Constantine III had finally been checked by the *magister militum* Constantius.

It is striking that even at this stage the court in Ravenna seems to have regarded Roman usurpers as posing a greater threat than the barbarians. We can see this most clearly in a set of fragmentary annals, compiled apparently at the imperial court in Ravenna, but preserved only in two sheets of parchment of the Carolingian period, which seem to have been concerned to copy the original very carefully, in both the style of writing and in the illustrations. Unfortunately, we only have the entries for the years 411–12, 421–23, 427–29, 434–37, 440–3 and 452–4 [5.2: Bischoff/Koehler 1939]. Even so, it is striking that there is no direct mention of any barbarian group (although there is a reference to the destruction of Aquileia in 452, but not to the fact that the city was destroyed by Attila and the Huns). By contrast, usurpers and their downfall are noted, and are illustrated with the drawing of severed heads displayed on poles. So too, attention is paid to natural disasters, notably to earthquakes in 429 and 443. The implication is that barbarians were not the most important problem in the eyes of the imperial court. Other authors did not share the same perspective.

> The Ravenna Annals and the threat of usurpation

Above all, Hydatius, observing events from the north-west of Spain, and the anonymous author of the Chronicle of 452, who was apparently writing in Gaul (most likely the Rhône valley) towards the end of the fifth century, had a very different view of them. Nevertheless, the attitude of the Ravenna Annalist probably sheds some light on why the imperial court failed to coordinate a response to the arrival and settlement of the barbarians. For Honorius and his advisers, the barbarians were less of a threat than ambitious generals. Arguably they were right. In so far as barbarian groups did break up the unity of the Western Empire, they did so only because the infighting between imperial generals allowed them to do so.

> Hydatius

It is also important to remember that the destruction and the disruption of communication caused by the civil wars and by the presence of barbarians had significant side effects. The Empire depended on taxes to pay its troops. Civil war and the passage and settlement of barbarians denied an emperor and his agents access to territory to collect taxes. Valentinian III openly stated in one of his novels (that is edicts) (III) that he did not have the resources to pay the army and that he was unable to increase the land tax [11: Wick-ham 1984]. In another law, he asked members of the senatorial aristocracy to pay for recruits. Moreover, disruption also posed a problem for the recruitment of soldiers needed to replace those killed in war (as often as not in Roman civil wars). Not only was the Roman leadership divided, but as time wore on the resources available to the Empire contracted. Ultimately, by the second half of the fifth century, the imperial court was in no position to control the majority of the land of the Western Empire.

7.4 The Years 418/419

Having led the Visigoths into Gaul, Athaulf joined in the civil wars of the Romans, initially supporting, and then turning against Jovinus and his brother Sebastian, who had continued the uprising of Constantine III against the Ravenna court. Athaulf also married Galla Placidia, the sister of Honorius, who had fallen into Gothic hands in 410. He set up his own court in the Gallic city of Narbonne, and there he was heard to say that he had thought of overthrowing the Roman Empire but that he had subsequently changed his mind and decided instead to use his Gothic army to support Rome. Despite this, Constantius forced him and the Goths into Spain, where Athaulf was murdered by a Goth, Sigeric, who had a grudge against him. It is important to note that, like the Romans, the barbarians were themselves deeply divided. Sigeric was then killed, and Wallia took over leadership of the Goths. Among his first actions was the return of Athaulf's widow, Galla Placidia, to the Romans. Constantius immediately took her as his wife, and the two had a son, the later Valentinian III [3: O'Flynn 1983; Börm 2018].

It is sometimes claimed that Constantius starved the Goths into submission in Spain. This interpretation involves taking a number of fragments of information and joining them together. It is, however, an interpretation that is not particularly well founded, because some of the fragments used in this reconstruction may not relate to this moment in time. Moreover, it makes the events of the following years extremely difficult to understand, since the subsequent history of the Goths would seem to imply that they were in a position of some strength when negotiating with the Empire.

According to Prosper of Aquitaine, the Goths were granted Aquitaine in 419; the same event is assigned to the year 418 by Hydatius, while the Chronicle of 452 seems to place it in 414. Curiously historians have tended to accept Hydatius' date, even though, based in Gallaecia, under Suevic control at the time of writing, his access to information seems to have been intermittent. He was, moreover, writing almost half a century after the event. Prosper, by contrast, was talking about the region from which he had originated, and his chronicle is more nearly contemporary. We should probably accept Prosper's date, which means that the settlement of the Goths followed the establishment of the Council of the Gauls in 418, which was to meet annually in the city of Arles. In all probability, however, arrangements for the settlement were drawn out, beginning before and ending after the establishment of the Council [11.1: WOOD 1998; 12.3: SCHWARCZ 2001; MATHISEN 2018]. Hydatius may provide us with the date for Constantius' initial recall of the Visigoths from their war against the Vandals and Prosper with that of the conclusion of their settlement in Gaul.

The establishment of the Goths in Aquitaine does not look to be the result of total submission to Constantius. Rather, it would seem that the barbarians were getting more or less what they wanted: a place to settle, in a rich part of the Empire, close to where they had originally settled under Athaulf's leadership. The Romans surely expected something in return. A number of suggestions have been made to explain the settlement, none of them provable, but several worth bearing in mind [12.3: BURNS 1992; SCHARF 1992]. The court of Ravenna may have been keen to establish a military presence in Aquitaine with a view to checking further revolts against the government of Honorius. It is possible that there had been support for Constantine III and Jovinus in Aquitaine: the geography of the settlement may suggest that it was intended as a punishment for the local aristocracy. There is also the question of the emergence of *Bacaudae* in the territory to the north of the river Loire. We will return to this group of disaffected Romans.

Exactly how the Goths were settled is a matter of debate. The traditional view was that they were given land under a system of billeting known as *hospitalitas*, whereby a barbarian was given two-thirds of an allotment and one-third of its bondmen (according, at least, to one reading of the Burgundian laws). Walter Goffart challenged this assumption in an important book that suggested

The Visigothic settlement in Aquitaine

The accommodation of the Visigoths

that the Visigoths, and subsequent barbarian settlers, were given tax revenues rather than physical property [11.2: GOFFART 1980, 2006]. However, they must have been provided with places to live, as well as supplies of food or, more likely, the means of feeding themselves. The Latin sources use the phrase *ad habitandum* on a number of occasions [11.1: WOOD 1998; 11.4: PORENA/RIVIÈRE 2013]. At the same time, it is possible, indeed probable, that the barbarians were initially not allocated property in perpetuity. Here, it is useful to note a distinction in Roman law between *dominium* and *possessio* – that is, between ownership and occupation. It is possible that barbarians were not granted ownership, but given rights of occupation, and that this was counted against the tax obligations of the Roman owners.

However one understands the settlement of the Visigoths, it is clear that over time they thought they had a right to the territory they occupied. In other words, within a short period of time there was a *de facto* territorial settlement, even if it was not *de jure*. In the event, when they lost the land on which they had settled in the early sixth century, it was not because Romans asserted *dominium*, but rather because they were driven out by other barbarian groups, notably the Franks.

7.5 The Literary Response: Rutilius Namatianus and Paulinus of Pella

A great deal has been made of the reaction of the Romans to the devastation wrought by the barbarians on Gaul, Rome, and Spain in the course of the first decades of the fifth century. We have already noted the importance of the letters of Jerome for events in Gaul and Rome. For immediate reactions to the sack of Rome we also have a letter of Pelagius, as well as sermons of Augustine, and then we have the more deeply considered response of the latter in the *De Civitate Dei*, as well as the *Historia adversus Paganos* of Orosius, both responding to pagan interpretations of the fall of the city. In addition, Hydatius' *Chronicle* is of considerable value for the entry of the Vandals, Alans and Sueves into Spain, and for their impact on the peninsula.

There is, thus, a significant body of contemporary written material that casts light on Christian responses to the events of the years from 406 onwards. For a surviving pagan response (as opposed to those mediated through the polemics of Christians) we have to wait until the *Historia Nova* of Zosimus, written early in the sixth century in Constantinople – leaving aside the distinctly allusive poem *De Reditu Suo* of Rutilius Namatianus. The literary responses to the Germanic invasions were considered at length by Pierre Courcelle in his *Histoire littéraire des grandes invasions germaniques*, originally published in 1948, and subsequently revised, notably in a third edition in 1964 [5.2]. Courcelle's survey paints a picture of widespread disaster, followed by a brief period of optimism around the year 417, which was checked by the barbarian expansion in Gaul and Spain and only partially recreated with the successes of the Franks in the late fifth and early sixth centuries. In reading Courcelle's survey of the material, it is important to remember the date of its original publication, four years after the end of the Second World War. Like much of the work that came out of France in the 1940s and 50s, it reflects the experience of the German invasion and occupation.

Nevertheless, there certainly were writers, above all in Gaul, but also in Spain, who did register the disasters of the period. Thus Orientius, who has been identified as bishop of Auch, left a lengthy poem, the *Commonitorium*, which alludes to the destruction wrought by barbarians [14.1: FIELDING 2014]. Similarly, the *Carmen de Providentia Dei*, which is often thought to have been written in c. 416 by Prosper of Aquitaine (although some scholars have denied the attribution, on the grounds of opinions in the text that have been identified as Pelagian and anti-Augustinian, which is not in keeping with Prosper's theological position), presents a picture of a land that has suffered at the hands of the Goths [7: MARCOVICH 1989]. Prosper had already described the impact of the invasions, and the need for spiritual reform, in his *Ad uxorem*, as had the author of the *Epigramma* often attributed to Paulinus of Béziers [13: FO 1999; SMOLAK 1999].

The *Commonitorium* and the *Carmen de Providentia Dei* leave no doubt about the trauma experienced by those who witnessed the passage of the barbarians, and at very much closer quarters than did Jerome, writing in Bethlehem. It is, nevertheless, important not to be carried away by the picture that they present. Both poems are primarily theological exercises, and the descriptions of devastation

Orientius of Auch and Prosper of Aquitaine

are generalised statements concerned with the workings of divine providence.

Paulinus of Pella

An equally religious poem, but one that is very much more specific, is the *Eucharisticos* of Paulinus of Pella [15.7/Paulinus of Pella: Moussy 1974; 7: Lucarini 2006]. Paulinus was the grandson of the poet, rhetor, and consul, Ausonius. He had inherited a good deal of property and gained yet more through marriage. The first challenge to his fortune came with the arrival of the barbarians in Gaul. Initially he weathered this, becoming *comes privatae largitionis* to the usurper Priscus Attalus, at the time of the usurper's second elevation as emperor by Athaulf. But when Attalus was deposed and Athaulf withdrew from Bordeaux, Paulinus found himself at the mercy of barbarians, and he moved to the small town of Bazas, only to be caught up in a siege. Finally, he moved to Marseille, where he was lucky enough to benefit from the benevolence of a Visigoth who enabled him to live in his old house. Decades later he set down a poetic account of his experiences, presented as his Thanksgiving.

Because it provides us with a specific narrative, the *Eucharisticos* is a more telling account of events in Gaul in the first two decades of the fifth century than are the *Commonitorium* and the *Carmen de Providentia Dei*. Here we are faced with a clear picture of the disasters that could happen to a member of an extremely prosperous family. It is worth noting, however, that although Paulinus lost almost all of his inheritance, he suffered a good deal more than did members of other aristocratic families, including that of the future emperor Avitus and of his son-in-law Sidonius Apollinaris, who we find still in possession of their estates in the late fifth and sixth centuries. The old Gallo-Roman senatorial class did not come to an end in the fifth century. Paulinus suffered not simply from the arrival of the barbarians, but also from misjudgement. As a backer of Priscus Attalus, he was a member of a faction that lost out in the politics of the second and third decades of the fifth century.

Rutilius Namatianus

We have one other equally specific account of events of the period after 410 in the fragmentary poem *De Reditu Suo* of Rutilius Namatianus [5.2: Doblhofer 1972–7]. Like Paulinus, Rutilius was a member of the senatorial aristocracy, but he was also closely associated with the imperial court. His father had been governor of Tuscia, vicar of Britannia, and prefect of the city of Rome, which is also an office that Rutilius himself held, after having already been *magister officiorum*. He had, therefore, witnessed many of the major political events that had taken place in Italy since the death of Theodosius. Then in 416 he decided to return to his homeland in Gaul.

His poem, of which only the first book and fragments of the second survive, recounts his journey homewards. As he travelled up the Italian coast, he not only noted the state of the countryside following the damage caused by the Goths, and the subsequent move of Athaulf from Italy to Gaul, but he also visited senatorial friends, no doubt for political as well as social reasons. He was surely engaged in lobbying. We do not know precisely why he was travelling to Gaul, but he was doing so just as Constantius was dealing with the Visigoths, and it would seem likely that his journey had some political cause: perhaps preparation for the 418 establishment in Arles of the Council of the Gauls; perhaps even for the settlement of the Visigoths in Toulouse in 419. Certainly, although Rutilius describes a world that had recently suffered a great deal, he was optimistic for the future. He talks of a Renaissance, an *ordo renascendi* [4.5: Matthews 1975]. It is important to remember that there were those who thought that the worst was over in the decades immediately after 410, and that the Empire could be put back on its feet.

Because only the first and fragments of the second book of the *De Reditu Suo* survive we do not know anything about the author's actions on his return to Gaul, but we may have some indication of his concerns in the text of an anonymous play, the *Querolus*, which is addressed to an aristocrat named Rutilius, perhaps to be identified as Rutilius Namatianus himself [8: Jacquemard-Le Saos 1994; Lassandro/Romano 1991]. The play, which is the only example of such a work to survive from Late Antiquity, is a comedy about an incompetent landowner, but it includes interesting comments on the presence of communities north of the Loire who were living a free life. These men have been identified as members of what other sources, referring to Gaul, Spain, and the Alpine region, call the *Bacaudae*. Exactly who these were, is a matter of debate: Marxist historians have seen them as free peasants, others have seen them as landowners oppressed by the demands of the state [10: Thompson 1952; Van Dam 1985]. Certainly, they were not all agricultural labourers, since one of their leaders, Eudoxius, was a doctor, which implies a certain amount of learning, although he might still have been a slave. Whatever their social class, the *Bacaudae* presented

Querolus

Bacaudae

the government with a challenge, and it may have been one that concerned Rutilius, and it certainly concerned the court of Ravenna. In both the *Life of Germanus of Auxerre*, written by Constantius of Lyon in the later fifth century, and in the nearly contemporary Chronicle of 452, we see the Empire using Alan forces against them in the 420s and the 430s. There was indeed a sense that the Empire could be restored following the settlement of the Visigoths, and that the barbarians themselves could be used to effect that restoration.

Constantius of Lyon and the Chronicle of 452

8 The Political Failures of the Fifth Century

8.1 Success and Failure in Spain

In the immediate aftermath of the Visigothic settlement, the restoration of the Empire was a distinct possibility. Certainly, large areas of the West had dropped out of the control of the court of Ravenna, as much because of the uprising of Constantine III as because of the barbarians. Thus, Britain was not subject to imperial rule for much of the second and third decades of the fifth century, although shortly after 406 the Britons seem to have rejected Constantine's rule and to have asked Ravenna for help against the threats of the Picts of Scotland and the Scots of Ireland, as well as continental Saxons. In 410, Ravenna was unable provide help, and Britain was briefly left to its own devices. But by 429 at the latest, the island was once again subject to the emperor. So too Gaul north of the Loire was often outside imperial control in the years after 406, but central authority was also re-imposed at various moments in the 420s and 430s [12.10: Wood 1987; 5.2: Haarer 2014].

Britain

Attempts had already been made to regain control of Spain after the transfer of the Visigoths to Toulouse in 418/9. Either immediately before or after the move to Gaul, the Visigothic leader Wallia (who died in 419) campaigned successfully on behalf of the Empire against the Siling Vandals in Baetica, and against the Alans in Lusitania and Carthaginiensis. The Siling and Alan survivors of this campaign, however, joined forces with the Hasding Vandals, leaving one powerful Vandal group and the *Suevi* as the only major barbarian forces in Spain. In 420, the Roman general Asterius prevented the Vandals from destroying the *Suevi* in Gallaecia, but two years later another general, Castinus, suffered a heavy defeat at the hands

The Vandals in Spain

of the Vandals in part because of a failure to cooperate with count Boniface, who instead moved his forces to Africa. As a result, the Vandals were able to expand through much of the Spanish peninsula, taking Seville and Cartagena, and even reaching the Balearic Islands around 425 [12.3: THOMPSON 1982, 2005; 10: THOMPSON 1988].

The middle and later years of the 420s marked another setback for the Western court, and once again the problem was related as much to conflicts between Romans as to the dangers posed by the barbarians themselves. Constantius, the general who had overseen the settlement of the Visigoths and who had married Galla Placidia, subsequently taking the imperial title as Constantius III, died in 421 [3: O'FLYNN 1983; 5.2: LÜTKENHAUS 1998; 11.2: BÖRM 2018; 5.2: DUNN 2020]. Honorius died two years later, and since he had no direct heir, his death provoked a succession crisis. The emperor's sister Galla Placidia had fled east with her four-year old son Valentinian, and the head of the imperial writing office, the *primicerius notariorum*, Ioannes, seized the throne. He held it, however, for a mere two years before the Eastern emperor Theodosius II supported the return of Valentinian and Galla Placidia in 425 [5.2: SIVAN 2011].

The death of Constantius III

The accession of Valentinian III

This political crisis was further complicated by the rivalries of the western generals [3: O'FLYNN 1983; 5.3: STICKLER 2002; 5.2: WIJNENDAELE 2015]. In Italy, the leading figures were the patrician Felix, a supporter of Galla Placidia, and Flavius Aetius, who had supported the usurping emperor Ioannes. He had even brought Hunnic troops to the aid of the usurper, but he had subsequently come to terms with the empress. In Africa there was Boniface, who had been a consistent supporter of Galla Placidia. The establishment of Valentinian III as emperor in 425 did not end the crisis. Aetius turned first on Felix, and then on Boniface, who had been recalled to Italy. The result was open war between Boniface and Aetius, which concluded in 432 with the death of the former, despite actually defeating his rival. It was, therefore, not until the 430s that the Romans could concentrate on the barbarian problem.

The rise of Aetius

8.2 The Vandal Crossing to Africa

The conflict between Boniface and Aetius provided the background for the most serious development in the barbarian migrations: the crossing of the Vandals to North Africa, probably in 429 (although some sources place the event two years earlier) [12.4: BERNDT 2007, 2010; BERNDT/STEINACHER 2008]. Aetius even claimed that Boniface had invited the Vandals into Africa, but this is highly unlikely. Indeed, he had to defend the city of Hippo in 430 against the barbarians. If any Roman openly encouraged the Vandal crossing, it is more likely to have been Aetius, in which case his claim that Boniface had issued an invitation was probably propaganda that he spread after his opponent's death, in order to avoid being held responsible for what had become a major problem.

Vandal numbers   We have two accounts of the Vandal crossing, one from Victor of Vita, writing in North Africa at the end of the fifth century, and the other from Procopius, writing in Constantinople in the mid sixth century. Both accounts state that Gaiseric crossed the Straits of Gibraltar with a force of 80,000 people, but they also add important detail to modify that figure. For Victor the 80,000 included men and women of every age group and children. The fighting force was thus a great deal lower. According to Procopius, Gaiseric divided his people into 80 groups, each led by a *chiliarch*, that is, technically, a leader of 1,000. But within those groups there was a very mixed population (not just of Vandals, but also of other barbarians and even of runaway slaves). He also implies that no group actually contained as many 1,000, claiming that previously the Vandals had numbered a mere 50,000, but admitting that they had been joined by others.

The figure for the Vandal crossing is important because it is one of our few specific pieces of information for the size of the migrant groups, and it shows that we are not dealing with an overwhelming body of immigrants [11.2: WOOD 2019]. The Romans were unable to cope with them because they themselves were divided. The Vandals entered Africa at exactly the time that Boniface and Aetius were competing for recognition as the leading military figure in the Western Empire [5.2: WIJNENDAELE 2015]. Initially, Boniface was able to defend the city of Hippo against them, and indeed he received some support from the Byzantine court, which provided troops under Aspar, the Alano-Gothic son of the eastern *magister militum*, Ardaburius, who had brought Galla Placidia and Valentinian back to Italy. Aspar was able to negotiate a treaty with Gaiseric. But when Boniface left Africa for Italy, he left the African provinces open to the barbarians. In 435, the imperial government made a treaty with Gaiseric, conceding the northern part of Roman

The concessions of 435 and 442

Numidia. Four years later, Gaiseric broke the truce and besieged Carthage, prompting yet another treaty in 442 that gave the Vandals the provinces of Africa Proconsularis and Byzacena as well as parts of Numidia and Tripolitania.

This had two major implications. First, it removed from direct Roman control a major source of wheat, and one on which the city of Rome had depended on since the end of the Third Punic War in 146 BC. This, and subsequent Vandal gains in Africa and Sardinia, gave them what Christian Courtois described as the Empire of Corn (*l'empire du blé*) [2: Courtois 1955]. Second, it transferred into Vandal hands one of the greatest ports of the Mediterranean, Carthage. In 75 BC, Pompey had cleared the Mediterranean of pirates, and as a result the sea developed into the centre of the Empire, facilitating commerce as well as political and social movement. Although Henri Pirenne argued that the unity of the Mediterranean was not really broken until the expansion of Islam in the middle of the seventh century [2: Pirenne 1937], there can be no question that the Vandals had turned the coastal districts surrounding what had been the maritime centre of the Empire into a frontier zone. Communication across the length of the Mediterranean did not come to an end, but it was a good deal more dangerous than it had been in the fourth century and earlier.

Carthage

8.3 Success and Failure in Britain

The author of the *Chronicle of 452* seems to have thought that there were two particular periods when the barbarians caused substantial, even fatal, damage to the Western Empire. In one sequence of entries he grouped together a Saxon devastation of Britain, the arrival of the Vandals and Alans in Gaul, the entry of the Sueves into Spain, and the Gothic sack of Rome. Later, he listed, in this order, the Alan settlement in Valence, Saxon success in Britain, Alan settlement in Gallia Ulterior, Burgundian settlement in Sapaudia, and the Vandal capture of Carthage. The chronology of these annal entries is highly suspect, but the interpretation is interesting because it is one of the clearest statements of the opinion that the victories and settlements of the barbarians were at the heart of the fall of the Roman Empire in the West [11.1: Wood 1984].

The Chronicle of 452

410   The first devastation of Britain mentioned in the Chronicle would seem to have taken place around 410. It may have been this that prompted Britons to reaffirm their links with the court of Ravenna, which, however, was unable to offer any help. Britain remained outside imperial jurisdiction for at least the following decade. Indeed, it would appear that some Pelagians faced with persecution on the continent made their way to the island for safety in 418.

The Empire, however, had not yet abandoned the island. The province of Britannia is extensively described in the *Notitia Dignitatum*, an official list of offices that was initially compiled in the fourth century but which was still being revised in the early fifth century [10: Hassall 1976; 4.1: Kulikowski 2000]. Equally important, members of the Christian community on the island appealed for help against Pelagianism, which led to the sending of bishop Ger-

Germanus of Auxerre   manus of Auxerre to deal with the problem in 429. It would seem that he had some secular backing both on this occasion and also during a probable second visit to the island, which has been dated to various moments between 435 and 448, while others have even denied it altogether [11.1: Wood 1984; 7: Barrett 2009; 12.10: Higham 2014]. Whatever the correct date, it would seem clear that imperial authority was reintroduced into Britain during the 420s and 430s.

The appeal to Aetius   Exactly when that authority came to an end is unclear. There are few sources, and these are contradictory, at least in terms of their chronology. But at some point in the early 440s the council in Britain appealed to Aetius for help against renewed incursions from the Picts and Scots. As in c. 410, the imperial court was in no position to send troops, and so the Britons had to organise their own defence, which they did by employing Saxon federates. In doing so they were acting as Roman emperors had often acted, but they failed to remunerate the Saxons as they had agreed, which prompted the federates to rebel. This may be the Saxon take-over referred to in the Chronicle of 452. But even so, this was not yet the end of Roman Britain. Writing in the early sixth century, Gildas, who provides one of our main accounts of events, claimed that after a period of disaster, the Britons fought back, a point that may be supported by the *Life of Germanus of Auxerre* by Constantius, who states that Britain was peaceful at the time of writing, in other words c. 470. This British revival was led by a man called Ambrosius Aurelianus, who we might well understand to be a usurper in the same mould as Constantine III, or indeed Magnus Maximus before him. However we understand this, the majority of the old province of Britannia was not yet in the hands of barbarians before the end of the fifth century.

Ambrosius Aurelianus

8.4 Emperors and *magistri militum*

Despite the account provided by the *Chronicle of 452*, our evidence does not suggest that the barbarians overwhelmed the Roman Empire. Certainly, when we reach the late sixth century, most of what had been the Roman West was in barbarian hands, but the barbarians themselves had not intended to conquer Rome. Rather, the political structure of the later Empire had provided a context in which the successor states emerged in the course of the second half of the fifth century, and central to that political context was the failure of the imperial court, of its agents, above all its generals, and of the imperial aristocracy.

One major problem was the weakness of the emperors themselves in the half century following the death of Theodosius. Neither Arcadius nor Honorius were strong leaders. When Arcadius died in 408, he was succeeded by his son Theodosius, who had been born in 401. When Honorius died in 423, he left no son, and as we have seen, his heir Valentinian III, the son of his sister Galla Placidia, had to be installed on the western throne with Byzantine help in 425. Valentinian was only six at the time of his installation. His mother acted as regent until 437, and she continued to be influential until her death in 450. In other words, because there was an understanding that the emperor should be a direct descendant of Theodosius I, for a significant proportion of the period between 395 and 455 the titular head of one or the other half of the Empire was a child or an adolescent [4.5: McEvoy 2013]. Moreover, although all these child-emperors reached the age of maturity, none of them took on military duties when they did so.

Child emperors

Certainly, this did not mean that these emperors or their courts had no significance, but their lasting importance lay in the sphere of religion, law, and the ceremonial. Thus, the court of Arcadius in the East was deeply influenced by the emperor's wife, the pious Eudoxia, who was powerful enough even to remove John Chrysostom from his position as bishop of Constantinople [5.2: Liebeschuetz 1990;

McEvoy 2020]. The first regent for the young Theodosius II was Anthemius, but between 414 and 416 influence was chiefly exercised by the emperor's elder sister Pulcheria. After assuming sole rule, Theodosius immersed himself increasingly in religious issues (perhaps not surprisingly, as this would prove to be one of the crucial periods in the definition of Christian doctrine) [6: HOLUM 1982; MILLAR 2006; ELTON 2009; KELLY 2013]. Equally pious was his wife, Eudocia, who went on an extended pilgrimage to Jerusalem in 438 and subsequently retired there in 443 [6: HOLUM 1982]. Apart from this involvement in the Church, Theodosius was also responsible for the compilation of the great legal compendium, the *Codex Theodosianus*, which was issued in 438 [6: HARRIES/WOOD 1993; MATTHEWS 2000; MILLAR 2006; ELTON 2009; KELLY 2013; SALWAY 2013]. In other words, this was not a court without significance or influence, but it was not a military court. Much the same can be said of the court of Valentinian III, which initially was also dominated by a woman of notable piety, Galla Placidia, and which joined with Constantinople in issuing the *Theodosian Code*.

The Theodosian Code

Magistri militum   The effect of this sequence of non-military emperors was to transfer military authority to generals who did not hold imperial office. In the Byzantine East an Alano-Gothic dynasty, which included Ardaburius, his son Aspar, and grandsons Ardaburius and Patricius, dominated the scene from the 420s down to the 470s, and they proved to be remarkably competent and extremely loyal to a sequence of emperors. In the West, the generals, by contrast, were often in competition against one another, as we have seen in the case of Boniface and Aetius. Of course, soldier emperors had also been challenged throughout imperial history, but in the period following the death of Theodosius, the rivalry of generals, and opposition to them from within the court circle, was a significant factor in the failure to deal with the barbarian problem in the West [3: O'FLYNN 1983; MACGEORGE 2002; BÖRM 2018].

There were moments when one man gained control of the military and had some success in limiting the impact of the barbarian presence. But Stilicho found himself thwarted by Rufinus and Eutropius; Constantius III died too soon after taking control of the government. Aetius exercised military power for longer than either, although his early support for the usurper Ioannes may have rendered him suspect to Galla Placidia, and he eventually lost the trust of Valentinian III [5.3: STICKLER 2002].

Much of Aetius' military activity was concerned with re-establishing control of Gaul. Between making peace with Galla Placidia in 425 and engineering the fall of Felix in 430, he fought against the Visigoths who had taken advantage of the disputed imperial succession to expand their territory in Gaul, and he also fought against the Franks. After the death of Boniface, he turned against the Burgundians, defeating them in 436, and although they came to terms, he apparently encouraged the Huns to attack them the following year. At some subsequent point he settled surviving Burgundians in Sapaudia, in the region of Geneva and Neufchatel. Traditionally this event has been dated to 443, but unfortunately our sole information on this is to be found in the *Chronicle of 452*, the chronology of which is confused and unreliable. It is also unclear what proportion of the Burgundians who had survived the Hunnic onslaught were settled in Sapaudia. To judge by the archaeological evidence, there would not seem to have been significant numbers of them.

Aetius

In 437, the general Litorius had some success against the *Bacaudae*, the disaffected movement in northern Gaul which some have seen as a peasant uprising. Others have seen a wider group, including local aristocrats who had been alienated by the regime in Ravenna. When Litorius was killed in battle against the Visigoths in 439, Aetius returned to Gaul, where he managed to restore peace. In the 440s he also intervened in Spain, against both the Suevi, and against further groups of *Bacaudae*, although here he had a good deal less success.

Litorius

In attempting to restore imperial control of Gaul and Spain, Aetius employed barbarians against barbarians. He used Alans against the *Bacaudae*, and Huns against both the Burgundians and the Visigoths. He was particularly well placed to make use of Hunnic troops, having spent time as a hostage first with the Visigoth Alaric and then with the Hun Uldin. It was to the Huns he turned in 425 when he looked to find support for Ioannes. So too, he used the Huns against the Burgundians. Following Aetius' murder at the hands of Valentinian in 454 it was two Huns, Optila and Thraustila, who avenged him by killing the emperor a year later. It is not, therefore, surprising that although he led the imperial forces at the Battle of the Catalaunian Plains, he does not appear to have been the dominant figure in gathering together the confederation that faced the Hunnic king Attila when he attacked Gaul in 451. Nor was Aetius notably active the following year when Attila invaded Italy.

Aetius and the Huns

His earlier links with the Huns, and his confrontations with the Visigoths and the Burgundians, may have compromised his position as the leader of the Roman party against Attila.

8.5 Attila (d. 453)

The Huns The role of the Huns in the collapse of the Roman West is a complex one [3: HEATHER 2005; 11.3: SCHMAUDER 2009; KIM 2016]. That they were the cause of the migration of the *Tervingi* and of their establishment within the Roman Empire in 376 is clear. After 378, the Roman sources lose interest in them. In this period they were certainly exercising control of a vast area of land to the north of the Danube, subjugating most of the peoples in that region to their authority [4.5: HEATHER 1991; 11.3: SCHMAUDER 2009]. In all probability, the Goths under Radagaisus, who entered the Empire in 405, and the Vandals, Alans and Sueves who crossed the Rhine in 406 were escaping from their control. As we have noted, Stilicho defeated Radagaisus with the help of the Hunnic leader Uldin, who was also responsible for the execution of the rebellious eastern *magister militum*, Gainas, a Goth who had sought safety to the north of the Danube in c. 400. It was also to Uldin's court that Aetius was sent as hostage. It appears that Uldin died while the Roman was in captivity, for we also hear of Aetius as being in the custody of Charaton in 412/13.

Around the year 430, our sources for the Huns become more plentiful [11.3: THOMPSON 1996; MAENCHEN-HELFEN 1973]. At that date it would seem that they were subject to two rulers, the brothers Octar and Ruga or Rugila. The Church historian Socrates tells us that Octar was killed during a campaign against the Burgundians. Ruga was in power at the time of Aetius' conflict with Boniface, and it may have been to him that the Roman appealed when he went to get help for Ioannes in c. 425. Despite being on good terms with Aetius, Ruga apparently invaded the Eastern Empire in the 420s, which resulted in the Byzantines having to pay the Huns 350 pounds of gold annually.

The emergence of Attila Ruga had two other brothers, Oebarsius and Mundzuc, who was the father of Bleda and Attila. These last two first appear shortly after Ruga's death, at which point they negotiated a particularly harsh treaty with the East Romans at Margus in 435. As a result, the Eastern Empire's annual payment to the Huns was doubled, the Romans were forced to return fugitives who had fled from the Huns, and trading arrangements were made. For the following five years the Huns directed their military campaigns against the Persians, but in 441 they attacked the Balkans, claiming that the bishop of Margus had desecrated royal graves north of the Danube. They launched a major campaign in 443, which involved the destruction of several cities: Constantinople was only saved by the great city walls that been completed in 413. This led to yet more substantial payments. Shortly afterwards, Bleda was killed, leaving Attila as the sole king of the Huns [11.3: ANKE/EXTERNBRINK 2007; 4.3: KELLY 2008; MAAS 2014; ROSEN 2016].

In 447 Attila launched a further attack on the Eastern Empire, prompting Theodosius to negotiate another humiliating treaty, the Peace of Anatolius, in which the emperor may even have granted the Hunnic ruler the title of *magister militum*. In 449 there was a Byzantine attempt at assassinating Attila in the course of an embassy to the Hunnic court – the plan, however, was revealed and the envoys only just managed to avert a diplomatic disaster. Among those involved in the embassy was Priscus of Panium, who left an invaluable account of what he saw. A year later, Theodosius himself died. His successor, Marcian, instantly changed Byzantine policy towards the Huns, moving from appeasement to aggression.

Priscus of Panium

At the same moment, however, 450 Attila turned his attention to the West, supposedly intending to attack the Visigoths, although the Romans understood his intentions to be an attack on the Western Empire. The Hunnic army, which included warriors from numerous other peoples under their control, crossed into Gaul, capturing the city of Metz and also attacking other cities, supposedly causing a good deal of destruction, although here the evidence is hagiographical.

Attila in Gaul

The invasion was halted at the Catalaunian Plains by a confederacy largely made up of barbarian groups. Although Aetius was the general in overall command, according to Jordanes, writing in the mid sixth century, the Roman element in the army was remarkably small. This is fully in keeping with Valentinian's claim that he was having difficulty paying his troops. The barbarians, and especially the Visigoths, provided the majority of the forces. Perhaps because of the *magister militum*'s own connections with the Huns, and also his use of Huns against Visigoths and Burgundians, it is not surprising that the confederation seems to have been put to-

The Catalaunian Plains

gether by other members of the Roman senatorial aristocracy, above all Avitus, who had close connections with the Visigothic court.

Jordanes   Our fullest account of the battle is that provided by Jordanes in the *Getica*, composed in Constantinople in the mid sixth century, certainly with an eye to contemporary politics [6: WHATELY 2012]. The picture he gives is remarkably favourable to the Huns, and here it is worth remembering that his grandfather, as the secretary of the Alan Candac, had worked within the Hunnic Empire. However, not surprisingly the Visigoths are the heroes of Jordanes' account, even though their king, Theodoric, was killed in the course of the battle. Aetius, by contrast, is presented as cunning rather than heroic. We are told that he allowed the Huns to escape from the field of battle, aware that they might subsequently prove useful against the Goths. This may be a smear story. Despite his early contacts with the Huns, in the 440s Aetius had come to realise the danger they presented. Moreover, although the Western Empire was undoubtedly weaker than its Eastern counterpart, the court of Valentinian had actually been more consistently hostile towards Attila than that of Theodosius.

Attila in Italy   If Aetius did deliberately allow the Huns to withdraw from the battlefield in 451, he made a bad misjudgement. A year later, Attila invaded Italy, destroying the city of Aquileia as he entered the peninsula. Why he decided to attack Italy is unclear, although Valentinian III's sister, Honoria, had appealed to Attila for help following a violent disagreement with her brother. The Huns marched on Rome, but then mysteriously withdrew. Various explanations for the retreat have been offered. Not long after the event the papacy was claiming that Pope Leo had turned back the invaders with divine help. Less miraculous suggestions have been that Attila's army was struck by disease and that the new Byzantine emperor, Marcian, had threatened to attack the heartlands of the Huns. Or simply that Attila was withdrawing before the onset of winter [11.3: LINN 2019].

The death of Attila   Two years later Attila himself was dead, supposedly following a drunken wedding party. His death led to a disputed succession between his sons and to the uprising of several of the peoples who had been subject to his rule. The empire he had created collapsed very quickly. It had been held together, as can be seen in Priscus' account of Attila's court, by fear and lavish rewards, paid for by the vast sums of gold handed over by the Byzantines [11.3: BLOCKLEY 1983]. It was probably the peoples subject to the Huns who provided the bulk of the manpower.

However many Huns there were in the steppes, it is unlikely that vast hordes of them ever settled in Central Europe. This we can conclude from a consideration of the territory that they took as their heartlands, the Hungarian Plain. Although this looks nowadays to be a landscape that could house huge numbers of horsemen, before the canalisation of the river system by the Habsburgs in the nineteenth century much of it was marsh and prone to flooding. At all costs, the Hunnic threat evaporated very quickly, but in forcing other barbarian peoples to migrate across the Danube and the Rhine, and in the destruction wrought on cities of the Balkans, the Huns had played a significant role in the destabilisation of the Roman Empire. Moreover, with the death of Attila, peoples who had been subject to him, especially the *Greutungi*, took advantage of their new freedom to cross the Danube into the Balkans.

The Hungarian Plain

8.6 The Last Western Emperors

The defeat of Attila ought to have allowed the restoration of the Roman West. After all, a sequence of competent military emperors had reversed the third-century crisis that had threatened to destroy the Empire. But the terms of the restoration would have been different: the loss of direct control over territory and therefore of taxation meant that the revival of a Roman army would have been problematic. However, the Visigoths and Burgundians had willingly fought on behalf of Rome at the Catalaunian Plains, and although the Visigoths effectively had their own court in Toulouse, they did not have an independent kingdom [3: DELAPLACE 2015]. Nor, indeed, did the Burgundians, whose leaders acted as Roman officials down to the 470s: thereafter, they continued to see themselves as part of the Empire down to the 520s [12.3: WOOD 2021]. The Vandals in Africa presented a much greater problem, but they were not consistently hostile to Rome, and indeed a daughter of Valentinian III, Eudocia, was betrothed to Gaiseric's son Huneric [12.4: MERRILLS/MILES 2010]. Moreover, although the marriage only took place following the murder of Valentinian, after the princess had been seized in the course of the Vandal sack of Rome in 455, Huneric and his descendants prided themselves on their association with imperial blood. Equally important, although the Vandals survived several attempts by Eastern and Western emperors to overthrow their kingdom, they did so largely because of Roman incompetence and division. By the 530s, at least, the Vandals were incapable of standing up to a well-organised imperial campaign.

Valentinian III   Certainly, the Roman West after the 430s was far less able to field a major army than was Byzantium a century later: Valentinian III admitted in Novel III, vi that he could not raise the taxes to pay his troops, and he subsequently asked the aristocracy to provide money for individual soldiers [11: Wickham 1984]. But it was weakness and division within the Roman leadership, and more broadly among the senatorial class, that had allowed the development of a situation in which the emperor could no longer call on the resources needed to impose control. It was this that sabotaged any possibility of rebuilding the Western Empire.

After Attila's invasion of Italy, Aetius' influence was radically diminished. In 454, Valentinian III personally supervised his assassination. A year later, Huns, who had been members of Aetius' bodyguard, took revenge and killed the emperor himself. There is some evidence that the murders of both Aetius and Honorius were understood in apocalyptic terms. Throughout the fifth century there was an idea in circulation that Rome's fall was imminent [5.5: Wood 2022]. The interpretation of the twelve vultures of Romulus as indicating that the city would last twelve centuries pointed to both 454 and 455 as possible years in which Rome's power might come to an end. This might explain why the death of Aetius is one of two dates for the end of the Empire given by the Byzantine chronicler Mar-

The Sibylline oracle   cellinus Comes: it fulfilled the prediction of the Sibylline oracle. Sidonius in his panegyric on the emperor Avitus, delivered in 456, made explicit reference to the fact that the prophecy had not been fulfilled, suggesting that there were those who had argued otherwise. Moreover, the eschatalogical mood of the period continued, at least in the East, certainly as late as the reign of Anastasius.

The successors
of Valentinian   In the course of 21 years following the murder of Valentinian there were eight emperors in the West, none of them lasting for more than five years. There was the Italian senator Petronius Maximus who seized power on the death of Valentinian but only lasted for a few months. He was followed by the Gallic senator Avitus who was backed by the Visigoths but opposed by the Roman generals

Ricimer and Marjorian [3: O'FLYNN 1983; 5.4: MACGEORGE 2002; OPPEDIS-
ANO 2013]. The latter took the throne from 457 to 461, when he was
overthrown by his erstwhile ally, Ricimer, who appointed the south
Italian senator Libius Severus in his place. When Libius Severus   Ricimer
died, apparently of natural causes, in 465, there was a brief interregnum before the Eastern emperor Marcian sent Anthemius to
take the western throne [5.4: OPPEDISANO 2020]. Ricimer initially accepted Anthemius' appointment and even married his daughter,
but in 472 he turned against him, having him killed. He then appointed Olybrius, a western senator who had spent time in Constantinople, but within months both Ricimer and Olybrius had died
of natural causes. In his place Gundobad, the Burgundian nephew
and political heir of Ricimer, appointed Glycerius. At this moment
the Eastern emperor, Leo I, intervened, sending Julius Nepos to take
the throne. Glycerius was driven out, but survived to become a
bishop in Dalmatia, while Gundobad retired to Gaul where he
joined the Burgundians settled in the Rhône valley, but without giving up his title of *magister militum*. Nepos, who himself came from
Dalmatia, lasted less than a year before he too was removed by another of Ricimer's old allies, Orestes, who appointed as emperor his
young son Romulus Augustulus. A year later, in 476, the barbarian   The deposition of
general Odoacer killed Orestes and forced his son into retirement.   Romulus Augustulus
He sent the imperial insignia to Constantinople, thus implying that
there was henceforth to be one emperor, while he himself took
charge of the government of Italy and those territories to the north
of the Alps that were still under Roman control, as well as western
Dalmatia.

   Several interest groups obviously contributed to this rapid   Emperors and
turnover of emperors, at least two of whom, Majorian and An-   *magistri militum*
themius, were highly competent leaders who might well have been
successful in different circumstances. There was the senatorial aristocracy, which itself was regionally divided [9: MATHISEN 1993; 3: SALZ-
MAN 2021]. Petronius Maximus, Libius Severus, Olybrius and Glycerius were Italians: Avitus was a Gallo-Roman with Visigothic backing. Anthemius was an easterner, backed by Constantinople, as was
the Italian Olybrius and also Julius Nepos, who came from the western Balkans. There were the leading military figures: Majorian, as
well as Ricimer, arguably the most powerful individual in the West
between 456 and 472, Gundobad, Orestes and Odoacer [3: O'FLYNN
1983; MACGEORGE 2002; BÖRM 2018]. Majorian and Orestes were both

Romans, although Orestes, like Aetius before him, spent time at the Hunnic court. Ricimer, Gundobad and Odoacer were all barbarians in the service of the Empire. Ricimer was the son of the Suevic king Rechila and the grandson of the Visigothic king Wallia, but spent his whole career in the Roman army. Gundobad, who succeeded Ricimer as *magister militum praesentalis*, was the son of the Burgundian Gundioc, *magister militum per Gallias*, and the nephew of another *magister militum*, Chilperic. Odoacer's ethnic origins are unclear, as different sources make different claims, but like Gundobad, he came to political prominence in the service of Ricimer. Nor were these the only barbarians involved at the highest level of imperial politics. Avitus was backed by the Visigoth Theodoric II, while Olybrius had the backing of Gaiseric. As the husband of Valentinian III's daughter Placidia, Olybrius was the brother-in-law of Gaiseric's son Huneric who was married to Eudocia. The barbarians in this group were no more intent on destroying the Empire than were their Roman colleagues, but equally they were well placed to reject the authority of emperors who were not of their own choosing. Competition over control of imperial office was a major factor in permanently breaking the unity of the West.

8.7 The End of the Western Empire

The deposition of the young Romulus Augustulus is often seen as marking the end of the Western Empire, even though Romulus himself lived on for some while. Moreover, the deposed Julius Nepos was only killed in 480, and Glycerius outlived him. Odoacer saw himself as the agent of the emperor, who was now based solely in Constantinople. The first clear statement that the deposition of Romulus Augustulus marked the end of the Empire is to be found in the *Chronicle* of the Byzantine Marcellinus Comes, which would seem to have been initially compiled in 518 and then revised in c. 534 [5.5: CROKE 1983, 8: CROKE 2001]. Marcellinus provides two dates for the end of the Western Empire: 476 and the murder of Aetius in 454, which could be understood, as we have seen, to be the fulfilment of the Sibylline oracle. That the Western Empire ended with the murder of Aetius was clearly an opinion that Sidonius did not share, nor did the emperors who ruled in the years 455 to 476 or indeed those who appointed them. But it is important to note that, through the fifth and sixth centuries, there were differing views about whether the Empire fell, and if it did, when. And just as there were those who thought that the Empire continued after 455, there were plenty who considered that it continued after 476.

Elaborate theories have been advanced arguing that the development of the notion that the Western Empire came to an end with the deposition of Romulus Augustulus originated among nostalgic senatorial circles in the city of Rome itself [5.5: WES 1967]. It would seem more likely, however, that the opinion of Marcellinus and others in the Byzantine East, that the West Roman Empire ended in 476, reflects the pragmatic view of the early sixth-century Constantinopolitan court, for whom the absence of a western counterpart was simple political reality [5.5: CROKE 1983, 8: CROKE 2001].

8.8 Life in the Failing West

Of course, the problems that faced the Empire were not only political. Rather, there were deeply ingrained social and economic weaknesses that meant that there was widespread alienation within the Roman world. It is apparent in the emergence of the *Bacaudae* in The *Bacaudae*
Gaul and in Spain in the later fourth and early fifth centuries, whether or not they consisted mainly of peasantry or of minor landowners. The *Bacaudae* are attested in a number of narrative sources. They probably included the poor Romans who Orosius said rushed to join the barbarians, and they are surely the subject of comments in the one dramatic work to have survived, the *Querolus* [10: THOMPSON 1952; VAN DAM 1985; SÁNCHEZ LEÓN 1996]. They are described most fully by Salvian of Marseille. He states that they were men who had been oppressed by Roman *iudices* who had exacted too much from them and who had reduced them to the level of animals so that they lived like barbarians.

Salvian wrote his *magnum opus*, the *De Gubernatione Dei*, in Salvian
the 440s [3: BROWN 2012; 7: ELM 2017]. He refers to the failure of Litorius against the Visigoths at Toulouse in 439 and to the capture of Carthage by the Vandals in the same year, but he seems not to have known of the invasion of Gaul by the Huns in 451. The *De Gubernatione Dei* is a moral diatribe, listing the sins and evils of the Romans and comparing them unfavourably with the barbarians. For Salvian, the Empire was ruined by the injustice, corruption and greed

of the rich. For him, all the Romans suffered from the same vices, but it was the rich and powerful who were in a position to oppress the rest of the population, above all through the fiscal system. They (in fact not the senatorial aristocracy, but the curial class) extorted taxes and tribute from the ordinary people and thus rendered them destitute. As a result, men fled to the barbarians or joined the *Bacaudae*. Salvian says nothing about the fact that it was the State that made the tax demands, but he points rather to those who actually collected the taxes.

The Empire, and indeed the governing classes as a whole, was probably caught up in a spiral of decline. The end of the climatic optimum that had provided an economic base for the early Empire seems to have caused a general decline in agricultural productivity [3: HARPER 2011], although some regions (for instance northern Syria) were clearly thriving economically. It is likely that there was a population decline, although this would have been most marked in years of plague, above all from 542 onwards. To add to that, there was the destruction caused by the arrival of the barbarians, and equally by the civil wars between the Roman generals themselves. A reduced population and a weakened economy had to bear the brunt of fiscal demands made by the State, and those demands grew more onerous as the emperor had to ask for more and more. In a remarkable law of 444, Valentinian asked members of the highest aristocracy each to pay for three new recruits, and others are asked to pay for one or even for a third of a recruit.

Salvian is surely over-censorious on the tax collecting classes. The *curiales* were squeezed between the demands made by the government and the fact that they had to make good any shortfall. But the gulf between the truly rich (the senatorial aristocracy) and the vast majority of the population was undoubtedly extreme. Socially and economically the Empire was in a state of crisis, regardless of the arrival of the barbarians. In the fifth century a good proportion of the ordinary population were disaffected, at least according to Salvian. At the same time, to judge by the letters of Sidonius Apollinaris, many members of the senatorial aristocracy were interested only in maintaining their own lifestyle. It is not just Salvian, in the *De Gubernatione Dei* and in his even more radical *Letter of Timothy*, but also a number of Pelagian tracts that lambast the rich.

At the level of imperial politics, there was a small clique competing for power. That the Western Empire collapsed without much fuss is scarcely surprising. For the majority of the population, the political change from imperial to barbarian rule would have been negligible, especially as the barbarians tried to preserve the provincial life of the Western Empire as best they could. In so far as there was dynamic change, it was not in the secular but in the ecclesiastical world.

9 The Development of Christian Society

9.1 Theological Conflict in the Fifth-century West

While Rome was faced with the barbarian settlements, the Hunnic invasions, and the political infighting that led to the fall of the West, the Mediterranean World was also wracked by a series of theological debates which were themselves damaging to its unity but are a remarkable indication of the religious and spiritual vitality of the period. Most of these debates were played out in the Byzantine East, although the conciliar decrees of the Ecumenical councils that dealt with them circulated throughout the Christian World. But some debates were essentially western.

The problem of Arianism, which had supposedly been solved at   Arianism
Nicaea in 326 and then at Constantinople in 381 [4.2: AYRES 2004], re-emerged because the Visigoths had adopted the homoean version of Christianity in which the Trinity was not made up of equal persons, but rather formed a hierarchy in which God the Father was superior to Christ, and both together were superior to the Holy Spirit. It was a factor in Gainas' rebellion against Arcadius in 399. In the West, the Arianism of the Visigoths first became an issue during Alaric's Italian campaigns [11: GHELLER 2017]. Probably because of its adoption by the Visigoths, homoean Christianity also passed to the Vandals and the Ostrogoths. For a while it was imposed by the Visigoths on the Sueves; and it was adopted by one Burgundian ruler (Gundobad, who probably took his religious position from his uncle and mentor, the *magister militum* of Gothic extraction, Ricimer) [11: HEIL 2011; 14.1: WOOD 2018]. It was also adopted by the Lombards in the sixth century [12.11: FANNING 1981]. Burgundian Arianism was very short lived. Vandal and Ostrogothic Arianism was destroyed in the course of Justinian's conquest of Africa and Italy in the sixth century. After less than a hundred years as heretics, the Sueves re-

turned to orthodoxy in the later sixth century under the guidance of Martin of Braga. The Visigoths abandoned Arianism decisively under their king Reccared at the Third Council of Toledo in 589. The Lombards wavered between Arianism and Catholicism until well into the seventh century. Unfortunately, we have very little Arian theology from this period, although there are numerous denunciations of the heresy from the pens of Catholic bishops. These, however, largely repeat views that had already been aired in the fourth century. What is most striking is the relative insignificance of barbarian heresy [11: BERNDT/STEINACHER 2014]. It was a matter of importance at various moments – notably during the Vandal persecutions, in the last years of the Ostrogoth Theodoric, and in the days of the Visigothic king Leovigild; and Gregory of Tours claimed that it was a significant issue for Clovis [12.7: WOOD 1985]. For the most part, however, it caused little or no friction.

Pelagianism New areas of debate were opened up by the British ascetic Pelagius, who had moved to Rome in the 380s, and, like Jerome, had established himself as a religious mentor to members of the aristocracy. Shortly after 400, having read Augustine's *Confessions*, he wrote a critique of the bishop of Hippo's view of the workings of divine grace, stressing instead the importance of human free will [7: REES 1998; BONNER 2018; SQUIRES 2019]. Along with Rufinus and Celestius, he also challenged Augustine's notion of original sin as well as the efficacy of infant baptism. Beginning in 411, the bishop of Hippo wrote a number of works attacking Rufinus, Celestius and Pelagius, who by now was in Palestine, where he was also denounced by Jerome and Orosius. In 416, Pelagius was condemned by councils held in Milevis and Carthage, but in 417 Pope Zosimus refused to endorse the condemnation. The emperor Honorius, however, intervened and condemned both Pelagius and Celestius, and the pope then followed suit. The result was that Pelagius was driven out of Palestine and moved to Egypt. The pope's condemnation, however, was challenged by the southern Italian bishop, Julian of Eclanum, who also attacked Augustine. Julian moved to Egypt, and then to Cilicia, where he was protected by Theodore of Mopsuestia. In the late 420s, by now the leading Pelagian spokesman, he travelled to Constantinople, where he sought support from the patriarch Nestorius. Following the arrival of the papal condemnation, however, he was exiled from the imperial city. He and Celestius were further condemned by the Council of Ephesus in 431.

The Pelagian controversy was played out across the whole Mediterranean and involved a number of leading eastern clerics, most notably Theodore of Mopsuestia and Nestorius of Constantinople. It was, however, conducted in Latin, and was dominated by western theologians. Moreover, although the Augustinian party seemed to have won the argument by the time of the bishop of Hippo's death in 430, the legacy of the debate was long-lasting. Indeed, there was a broad body of opinion that Augustine had gone too far in his attack on Julian and that he had himself fallen into the heresy of Predestinarianism [10: Weaver 1996]. In the mid and late fifth century a number of leading theologians, most notably Faustus of Riez, attacked the doctrine of predestination, with the result that the dominant doctrinal position in Gaul was what has been described, misleadingly, as Semi-Pelagian. The Augustinian position would only be fully reasserted in Gaul at the Council of Orange in 529, presided over by bishop Caesarius of Arles.

Anti-augustinianism

9.2 The Councils of Ephesus and Chalcedon

Pelagianism and the debates that it engendered were major issues for the West, but for Christendom as a whole the more important theological quarrels were eastern and concerned the nature of the Christ: how could he be both truly God and man, as required by the Christian doctrine that had emerged in the course of the Arian conflict? One answer to this conundrum was formulated by the Antiochene priest Nestorius who made a distinction between Christ the *Logos*, the word of God, who was co-eternal with the Father, and Christ the son of the Virgin Mary, who he refused to call *Theotokos*, mother of God, describing her only as *Christotokos*, mother of Christ. For Nestorius, in other words, Christ had two natures which could not be entirely united. This was anathema in Alexandria, and especially to the patriarch Cyril (412–44).

Nestorius

The distinction between the two positions came to the fore following the appointment of Nestorius to the see of Constantinople in 428, where the ideas which he had developed without opposition in Antioch were subjected to public scrutiny, as a result of which Cyril appealed to Pope Celestine I, inviting him to condemn Nestorius as a heretic. The pope called upon Nestorius to recant. In response, the bishop of Constantinople persuaded the emperor Theodosius to

The council of
Ephesus 431
summon a council, which met at Ephesus. The meeting was somewhat chaotic. Not all the bishops arrived on time. Initially it looked
as if Nestorius would emerge triumphant, not least because it was
thought that he was supported by a sizeable body of imperial
troops. But, in part because the pope had already ruled against
Nestorius' teaching, the council concluded in condemning his doctrine of two natures [7: PRICE/GRAUMANN 2020].

This, however, was not the end of the issue. Certainly Nestorius,
his ideas, and his supporters were condemned within the Empire.
But the ideas of Nestorius continued to circulate, initially in Byzantine Mesopotamia (notably in Edessa) and subsequently beyond the
borders of the Roman World. They survived in Persia and also in
Christian communities in central Asia. It is in the material that was
preserved by these communities that we find Nestorius' own writings, as opposed to the ideas attributed to him by his opponents.

Equally important, the aftermath of Ephesus saw the development of a hard-line statement of Christ's single nature. This was
propounded primarily by the Constantinopolitan *archimandrite* Eutyches, who had been one of the leading opponents of Nestorius be-
Eutyches
fore and during the Council of Ephesus. For Eutyches, Christ had
only one nature, that of the Incarnate Word. As a result, he was condemned by a council held in Constantinople by the patriarch Fla-
The council of
Constantinople 448
vian in 448. The condemnation of Eutyches was supported by the
pope, who set out his doctrinal position in the so-called *Tome of Leo*
which he sent to Flavian. The decisions made in Constantinople,
however, prompted Dioscorus of Alexandria, with the approval of
The robber council of
Ephesus 449
Theodosius II, to summon a second council in Ephesus a year later,
which reinstated Eutyches and deposed Flavian, despite an intervention by Pope Leo, who condemned Ephesus II as a robber council (*latrocinium*).

The council of
Chalcedon 451
When Theodosius died in 450, his successor Marcian called a
further council, which was held at Chalcedon in 451, with Leo's approval [7: PRICE/GADDIS 2005; PRICE/WHITBY 2009]. This reaffirmed the
doctrine set out by Cyril at Ephesus I, stating that Christ had two
natures that were united in a single hypostasis (substance). This
was the position set in the *Tome* that Leo had already addressed to
The Tome of Leo
Flavian. The pope himself, however, did not attend the council, nor
indeed was there much western representation: only two bishops
and two priests. Given the threat posed by Attila, 451 was not an op-
portune moment for an ecumenical council from the Western point

of view. Tellingly, Prosper of Aquitaine does not mention Chalcedon under the correct year, which he reserves for Attila's campaign in Gaul, or 452, which is devoted to the Hunnic invasion of Italy, but instead states that Marcian issued the summons for the council in 450, and that the bishops met in 453, when they accepted the doctrine laid down by Pope Leo. For westerners, the council was less important than the threat posed by Attila, but even so it was regarded in the West as a doctrinal triumph for Leo. Subsequently, any challenge to the orthodoxy of the council was regarded with horror in the West, despite the fact that Leo never signed the acts of the council because they reaffirmed the ecclesiastical position of Constantinople as New Rome. But when in 543 Justinian condemned as Nestorian the writings of Theodore of Mopsuestia, Ibas and Theodoret, who had signed the acts of the council, he precipitated the Tri-Capitoline Schism. For westerners, to condemn any signatory of Chalcedon posthumously was tantamount to rejecting the canons of a council that had accepted the *Tome of Leo* [14.2: PRICE 2009; 7: PRICE/WHITBY 2009; CHAZELLE/CUBITT 2007].

The Tri-Capitoline schism

The bishops at Chalcedon condemned Eutyches and Diocorus. However, there remained a considerable body of support in the East, and especially in Egypt and parts of Syria, for the doctrine they championed. Monophysitism, as it came to be known, remained a force in the eastern Mediterranean down to the Arab conquest. On occasion it had adherents at the Byzantine court. The emperor Anastasius was a Monophysite, which prompted a number of western theologians to write works against Eutyches, as indeed they wrote against Nestorius. So too, the empress Theodora was a supporter of Monophysitism. Usually, however, the relations between the Monophysites and the imperial court in Constantinople were hostile. The resulting alienation of the Monophysite populations of the Middle East played into the hands of the Arabs in the 630s and 640s [7: FREND 1972].

Monophysitism

9.3 The Spread of Monasticism in the West

Despite the importance of the debates over Divine Grace and Free Will, and despite the perceived significance of the intervention of Pope Leo in the Christological debates of the mid fifth century, doctrinal matters were arguably less important for the development of the western Church (or Churches), and certainly for western society as a whole, than the less intellectual issues of the spread of monasticism and the growth of episcopal authority. In both cases, the fifth century only marked early stages in a process that would culminate after 600.

Antony and Athanasius

The early history of monasticism is largely centred on Egypt and Palestine [7: WIPSZYCKA 2018, 2021; 14.5: HIRSCHFELD 1992; PATRICH 1995]. But news of asceticism in the Nile Valley and in the Holy Land was brought back to the West by pilgrims and by exiles already in the mid fourth century [7: HUNT 1984; ROUSSEAU 1978; 14.5: DIJKSTRA/VAN DIJK 2006]. Most important, Athanasius, the patriarch of Alexandria, spent two periods of exile in the West, in Trier from 336 to 337, and in Rome, Italy and Gaul between 338 and 345. As the champion of St Antony, and subsequently his biographer, Athanasius was a key figure in the dissemination of ascetic ideas. Among the leading supporters of Athanasius in the West was the bishop of Poitiers, Hilary, the episcopal patron of Martin of Tours.

Martin of Tours and Hilary of Poitiers

Martin had been a career soldier, but he abandoned the army during the reign of Julian in Gaul, probably in 355, and joined the circle of Hilary who, however, was exiled from his see between 356 and 360 [7: STANCLIFFE 1983]. During this time Martin travelled to Pannonia, and then to Milan, where he came into conflict with the Arian bishop, Auxentius. When Hilary returned from exile, Martin rejoined him, establishing a monastic community at Ligugé, outside Poitiers. Although he was elected bishop of Tours in 371, he continued to follow a monastic lifestyle, founding another monastery at Marmoutier just outside his episcopal city. As bishop, Martin was active in the evangelisation of his still partially pagan diocese. He also intervened on behalf of the Spanish ascetic Priscillian, but was unable to prevent his execution on the orders of Magnus Maximus in 385. His episcopal style was controversial, being roundly condemned by some of his colleagues and praised by others. A hagiographical account of his life was written by the aristocrat Sulpicius Severus, supposedly before the saint's death in 397. Sulpicius subsequently enlarged the hagiographical dossier on Martin, adding two dialogues and three letters [7: FONTAINE 1967–9].

The *Life* of Martin

Although Sulpicius' *Vita Martini* is not primarily the *Life* of a monastic founder, the saint was remembered as one of the founders of western monasticism, and numerous early monasteries were regarded as following the model of Ligugé and Marmoutier.

The most substantial discussion of monasticism in Gaul, which would seem to have been the most important centre of monastic life in the late-Roman and early Medieval West, has presented Martin's foundations as one of the two most important centres of monastic influence [7: PRINZ 1965].

The second major centre was the island of Lérins, where Honoratus founded a monastery with the support of the local bishop of Fréjus, around the year 410 [7: CODOU/LAUWERS 2009; NÜRNBERG 1988]. The exact year is unknown, but it is often assumed that Honoratus moved to Lérins in the wake of the crossing of the Rhine by the Vandals, Alans and Sueves in 406. The origins of the island community would, then, fit neatly with the call for spiritual reform in the wake of the barbarian invasions, expressed in a number of Christian poems, notably the *Commonitorium* of Orientius of Auch, the *Ad uxorem* and *Carmen de Providentia Dei* of Prosper, and the *Epigramma* of Paulinus of Beziers. The first firm date for the community, however, is the departure of Honoratus from his island monastery when he was elected bishop of Arles in 427. By that time he had attracted a number of influential figures to the island, including Hilary, who would succeed him as bishop of Arles from 430–49, and Eucherius, who would become bishop of Lyon (c. 433–49) and set himself up with his wife and sons not on the island of Lérins itself, but on the neighbouring island of Ste-Marguerite. A significant number of aristocratic men who adopted the ascetic life at Lérins went on to become bishops of Gallic cities, and thus spread the ascetic traditions of the island monastery [7: MATHISEN 1989]. Eucherius, for instance, extolled his monastic experience in his *De laude eremi*, and also seems to have founded or supported communities in his diocese of Lyon.

At roughly the time that Honoratus established his community at Lérins, an ascetic from the region of the Lower Danube, who had spent time in Palestine and Egypt, John Cassian, moved to Marseille, where he set up the community of St Victor [7: GOODRICH 2007; ROUSSEAU 1978; LEYSER 2000]. As important as his foundation were the ascetic texts that he wrote: the *Institutes* and the *Conferences*, where he used his experiences in Egypt to set out models of coenobitic and eremitical monasticism. Among the dedicatees of his works were Honoratus and Eucherius.

These early Gallic monasteries produced nothing comparable to the *Rule of Benedict*, which was composed in mid-sixth-century

Lérins

Eucherius of Lyon

John Cassian

Monastic rules

Italy, although it is possible that one or more of a group of short texts known as the *Regulae Patrum* ('Rules of the Fathers'), emanated from Lérins, while others were written in the same milieu [7: DE VOGÜÉ 1982; 15.7/Regulae: PUZICHA 2010]. One of the first substantial monastic rules was written by another bishop who had spent time in Lérins, Caesarius of Arles. He wrote a rule for the nunnery that he established for his sister in c. 512 [14.5: DE VOGÜÉ/ COURREAU 1988]. It is probably significant that the text was written for a community of women by the founder-bishop who could not himself be the abbot. He subsequently adapted the text for monks. For the most part, however, it would seem that monastic communities followed the life-style dictated by their founders or their abbots, and that a hagiographical account of the founder could be used as the model for the organisation of the monastery: at least one saint's *Life*, the *Vita Patrum Iurensium*, which provides an account of the Jura Fathers, Romanus, Lupicinus and Eugendus, is explicitly described as a *vita vel regula*: 'life and/or rule' [10: MARTINE 1968; 14.5: WOOD 1981].

There had been earlier rules. Already in the fourth century Basil of Caesarea had written a letter of guidance for his sister, which came to be regarded as a Rule. In addition, there is a short text known as the *Regula Augustini* which may not have been written by Augustine himself. Moreover, some of the bishop of Hippo's letters, sermons and short tracts also deal with aspects of the ascetic life [14.5: LAWLESS 1990]. Above all they set out a monastic-style pattern of life for the cathedral clergy of Hippo, which would later become central to the creation of rules for canons. But it was the sixth century that saw the development of a genre of the monastic rule, beginning with those of Caesarius, which provided a model for later writers, including Aurelian of Arles. In addition there is the mysterious *Rule of the Master* which seems to have provided the chief model for Benedict (although the order of composition has been debated, with some seeing the *Rule of Benedict* as being the earlier of the two texts) [14.5: DE VOGÜÉ 1964–5, 1992; DUNN 1990, 1992]. The *Rule of the Master* may already have provided material for a rule ascribed to the early sixth-century Neapolitan abbot Eugippius, which, like the *Rule of Caesarius*, also makes use of Augustine's Rule [14.5: KRAUSGRUBER 1996].

In other words, there was no dominant monastic *Rule* in the early Middle Ages before the Carolingian period. Indeed, the monas-

Caesarius of Arles

The Jura Fathers

The Rule of Augustine

The Rule of the Master and Benedict

teries of the fifth, sixth, seventh and eighth centuries were unlike the regular institutions of later medieval centuries [14.5: Dunn 2000]. There was nothing like a Benedictine or Cistercian order before the eleventh and twelfth centuries. Initially, there were communities founded by aristocrats on their own estates, or occasionally founded by bishops or landowners for ascetics whom they admired. Some may have attracted significant numbers from a relatively early date: thousands of monks are said to have attended Martin's funeral. Clearly those communities that attracted large numbers must have acquired additional property, simply in order to provide the necessary provisions. But we can only trace the acquisition of monastic property once we reach a period for which we have charter evidence, which means the seventh century, by which time the monasteries were leading social and economic as well as spiritual centres.

9.4 Bishops and Priests

The fourth and fifth centuries saw the beginnings of the emergence of monasticism as a major force in the Roman World. The same is true for the episcopate. Historians have talked about *Bischofs-herrschaft*, 'episcopal lordship', and this description is well supported by the presentation of individual bishops in hagiography and on episcopal epitaphs [14.2: Heinzelmann 1976; Diefenbach 2013]. Such authority, however, was only established slowly and inconsistently.

    Bischofsherrschaft

    Constantine had stated that bishops in council alone had authority over religious matters, although not all later emperors or kings agreed. Constantine, perhaps in 318, also allowed parties in a legal dispute to transfer their case from a secular judge to a bishop. However, legislation preserved in the Theodosian and Justinianic Codes modified this. A law of 398 (*Corpus Iuris Civilis* I, 4, 7) insisted that both parties had to agree to the transfer, while a law of the following year (*Codex Theodosianus* 16, 11, 1) restricted a bishop's judicial authority to religious cases. The *Codex Justinianus* labels this ecclesiastical jurisdiction *episcopalis audientia* [7: Humfress 2011; Sirks 2013]. The popularity of these episcopal courts, however, is unclear. We have little evidence to show them in operation, except in the letters of Augustine and of Synesius of Cyrene. The individual courts

    Episcopalis audientia

probably depended greatly on the regard with which individual bishops were held. On the other hand, bishops could and did intervene more widely in lawsuits, as pastors and as patrons, that is as agreed arbitrators. Many bishops, most notably those who came from the curial or senatorial classes, effectively came to operate as patrons of their cities.

Episcopalis audientia did not automatically endow bishops with widespread authority. Rather, that authority had to be built up steadily [14.2: Rapp 2005; Sessa 2012; Allen/Neil 2013]. In some dioceses that was easier than in others. Ambrose benefited greatly from being bishop of an imperial capital [4.5: McLynn 1994; Löx 2013]. The bishops of Alexandria profited from the proximity of large numbers of monks who were liable to intervene in major protests [7: Wipszycka 2015]. The bishop of Rome gradually established leadership not only in his city but more widely in the Roman world, not least by playing on the centrality of Peter to the Christian faith. But in most places, bishops had a much harder job making their presence felt. Of course they presided over the religious cult of their episcopal cities, but according to Gregory of Tours, priests hostile to Sidonius Apollinaris, when he was bishop of Clermont, removed the mass book from which he conducted church services: he survived the experience, but as a great *rhetor* and as the author of Masses, he was well placed to ad lib.

Senatorial and non-senatorial bishops

Like Sidonius, many of the bishops we hear about, especially in fifth- and sixth-century Gaul, were aristocrats, though few were as aristocratic as the bishop of Clermont. It has been argued that with the drying up of opportunities for holding high secular office, senatorial families looked instead to maintain their status by seeking episcopal office. This may well be true in a number of instances, and especially in certain important cities, like Lyon, Vienne, Clermont, and even Tours (although there the city's importance derived almost entirely from the shrine of St Martin). It is not, however, the case that the majority of bishops whose origins can be identified came from the senatorial classes [14.2: Patzold 2014]. And the probability is that most of those about whom we know nothing (in other words the vast majority) did not come from leading aristocratic families.

Bishops, however, came to be at the head of important patronage networks which provided the backbone for their obligations as pastors. As such they were expected to look after the poor and sick, the widows and orphans [9: Brown 2002; Neri 1998; 7: Lizzi Testa 1989; Toneatto 2012]. They effectively controlled the poor relief of their cities. From the mid fifth century onwards there are papal instructions stating the income of a church was to be divided evenly between the bishop, his clergy, the maintenance of the Church fabric, and the poor (the so-called *quadripartum*). This was not, however, a universal division of Church income – in Spain, for instance, we find references to a threefold division: the *tertia*. These allocations of income gave the bishop of a rich see an immense amount of influence. On the other hand, it is probable that most sees were not well endowed before the late fifth or sixth centuries [12.8: Wood 2021]. With the exception of the problematic lists of donations to the Church of Rome recorded in the *Liber Pontificalis*, the majority of our evidence dates to the sixth and seventh centuries, which is the period from which the earliest authentic charters and wills date. Although Constantine seems to have endowed a small number of favoured churches with land, the portfolio of property controlled by most bishops in the fourth century was small. Many churches received gifts of treasure, but gifts of land, which provided a steadier income, seem initially to have been less common. In theory, bishops were supposed to leave the property that they had acquired after their election to their churches when they died, although we know from the comments of Gregory the Great that many did not do so. Nevertheless, over time churches did acquire vast amounts of property and wealth. By the late seventh century perhaps a third of the property of western Europe was in the hands of ecclesiastical institutions (that is to say bishoprics and monasteries), but that was certainly not the case two hundred years earlier [2: Wood 2013, 3: Wood 2018].

> The origins of episcopal wealth

The build-up of episcopal power was piecemeal. But the political and social uncertainty of the fifth century undoubtedly played into the hands of the more astute bishops [7: Allen/Neil 2013]. The arrival of barbarians brought destruction, enslavement and destitution. Some bishops reacted immediately to ransom captives and to alleviate poverty. We see this in a number of saint's Lives, for instance those of Augustine, Epiphanius of Pavia, and Caesarius of Arles [14.2: Klingshirn 1983, 1994; 9: Salzman 2017]. In so doing they not only carried out their pastoral duties, but they also created a large network of indebted families.

> Bishops and crisis management

As a result, by the beginning of the sixth century one can talk rightly about the exercise of *Bischofsherrschaft* in some cities, including Arles, Lyon and Vienne. This could lead to the complete overshadowing of the secular administration. As a result, there are places where the office of count (*comes*) declined in significance radically. But in other cities the *comes* was still a figure of importance in the seventh century [11: CLAUDE 1964; MURRAY 1986; 6: BARNWELL 1992]. The situation depended entirely on the cumulative impact of the actions of individuals and their exploitation of circumstances. The fourth, fifth and sixth centuries saw an erratic build-up of authority and of property on the part of the Church, or rather individual churches. It did not reach its zenith until the seventh and eighth centuries. But one can talk of a process of 'ecclesiasticisation', which would become one of the most notable developments of Late Antiquity.

The priesthood
The ecclesiastical hierarchy below the level of the bishop is remarkably difficult to trace in the late Roman and pre-Carolingian period [7: WIŚNIEWSKI 2019; 14.2: GODDING 2001]. We know of a whole array of church offices, running through archpriests, priests, archdeacons, deacons, subdeacons, and, in the greatest churches, readers, singers, and doorkeepers. Some of these must have been part-time occupations, but the priesthood was increasingly time-consuming (especially in the more populous centres); even so, some individual priests had to supplement their livelihood as scribes or teachers. For some dioceses, for instance Rome, Ravenna, and Auxerre, we have a good idea of the number of priests, deacons and clergy in lower orders. But for others evidence is lacking entirely. The duties of priests come to be clearly defined in the ninth century, but the canons of Church councils and references in the hagiography help to build up a picture of ecclesiastical practice already in the sixth century.

Parishes
The evidence for the subdivisions of a diocese – which we would define as parishes – is also patchy. Although the term *parrochia* does exist in our documentation for the sixth century, the establishment of a formal parish system was achieved over a very long period of time, and it was not fully in existence before the end of the First Millennium. Churches that we would regard as having the functions of parish churches were founded by individual landowners or bishops, and they reflect the interests of the founder and concerns with his or her estates, rather than any logical plan to

make provision for religious cult throughout a diocese. It is rare that we have anything that might be construed as a list of parishes; more usually passing references are our only evidence for the existence of a 'parish' church and a resident cleric. Even so, there are a handful of dioceses where the evidence is relatively good. Thus, we know that the diocese of Le Mans had at least 90 'parish' churches by c. 600 [5.5: Wood 2022].

9.5 The Cult of Saints

Because of the development of hagiographical writing, works both describing individual saints and covering the saints of a region or of a certain category, we are much better informed about the presence of shrines containing the relics of martyrs and confessors in some regions than in others. The effort to remember the Christian victims of the Roman persecutions had created a literature concerned with martyrs – some of which, especially the texts dealing with the martyrs of Rome, is extremely difficult to date, although most of the Roman *passiones* were written in the two and a half centuries after 425 [4.1: Lapidge 2018]. It is clear, however, that the cult of relics developed relatively quickly from the fourth century onwards [7: Wiśniewski 2019]. Equally important, there was a literature concerned with the ascetic holy men of Egypt and Palestine [14.5: Dijkstra/Van Dijk 2006]. This was influential throughout the Roman Empire, and in the West it led to the development of a hagiographical tradition from the late fourth century, when Sulpicius Severus wrote the *Life of Martin*, which was soon followed by hagiographical works concerned with ascetics associated with the island monastery of Lérins.

Martyr acts

The most extensive accounts of the cult of the saints come at the end of the sixth century, with the hagiographical works of Gregory of Tours followed by the *Dialogues* of Gregory the Great. Although the former compiled a collection of twenty Lives dedicated to individuals, it is in his books on the *Glory of the Martyrs* and the *Glory of the Confessors*, as well as those on the miracles of Martin and Julian, that we find the largest compendium of information on shrines and those who sought help at them. These works are largely a record of individual miracles, and in the case of the later books of the *De Virtutibus sancti Martini* they are a record of events that oc-

Gregory of Tours and Gregory the Great

curred at the saint's shrine during Gregory's episcopate [10: Van Dam 1985; 14.4: de Nie 2015].

Most of the pilgrims described by the bishop of Tours had not travelled far, and many of them are from the lower orders of society [10: Van Dam 1985]. It has become clear in recent years, however, that we should not see the cult of the saints as a type of popular religion, to be contrasted with the elite religion of the theologians. Bishops were often deeply involved in the promotion of the cults that existed in their dioceses (among the most distinguished being Ambrose of Milan) [4.5: Löx 2013], and theologians (not least, Gregory the Great) wrote about the miraculous [14.4: Dal Santo 2012].

In the West, our best written evidence for the cult of the saints comes from Gaul. The city of Rome has the archaeological evidence of the catacombs, but much of this was reconstructed in the sixteenth and nineteenth centuries [7: Nicolai/Bisconti/Mazzoleni 2000; Denzey Lewis 2020]. Elsewhere, there have been important excavations that shed light on individual cults. In Spain the shrine of Eulalia in Mérida has been well excavated [7: Bowes 2005; Jiménez/Sastre de Diego/Tejerizo García 2018]. In North Africa there is some evidence for shrines, above all for Donatist shrines, in written documentation, but even more important is the excavated evidence of inscriptions and of cult sites [7: Gui/Duval/Caillet 1992].

The cult of the saints thus provides an indication of the depth of the penetration of Christianity into society as whole. It adds a level of human detail to the figures of bishops, priests, dioceses, and churches, which we can establish. And it also provides further illustration of the development of the spiritual economy of the post-Roman World.

10 A Roman Commonwealth in the West

10.1 Odoacer (d. 493)

The deposition of Romulus Augustulus is usually taken to mark the end of the West Roman Empire. In its place there were a number of successor states, some of which, most obviously that of the Vandals in Africa, were already in existence before 476. As a statement of fact this is clearly correct, but it should not lead us to assume that contemporaries saw a major distinction between the situation in the West before and after the removal of the last Western emperor. In 476 it was by no means clear that Romulus would never be replaced, and indeed some contemporaries thought that Julius Nepos, who had been forced into retirement in Dalmatia in 475, continued to hold the imperial title until his assassination in 480. Moreover, most of the successor states still regarded the remaining emperor as a political superior, even though he was based in Constantinople. In other words, we enter a period that we can perhaps describe as that of a Byzantine Commonwealth, by analogy with the modern transformation of the British Empire into the British Commonwealth. Individual regions claimed a degree of independence, but at the same time they acknowledged that the emperor in Constantinople was still titular head of what had been the Roman world [8: Wood 2018].

This is most obviously the case in Italy. According to the Byzantine historian Malchus, Romulus Augustulus instructed the senate to write to the emperor Zeno, stating that there was no need for two emperors. The West Roman imperial regalia were sent to Constantinople [12.2: Jones 1962]. At the same time the senators asked the eastern emperor to raise Odoacer to the patriciate. Zeno continued to back Nepos, who was alive in Dalmatia, as emperor, but he did address Odoacer as *patricius*. Odoacer himself employed the title *rex* to define his position, but at the same time he issued coins in the name of Nepos, down to the moment of the ex-emperor's death in 480. Thereafter he continued to attempt to maintain good relations with the eastern court, despite falling out with the Eastern emperor Zeno when he invaded Illyricum in 486/7 [12.2: Cesa 1994; MacGeorge 2002; 3: Börm 2018]. A year later he attempted to make amends by sending the emperor a share of the booty taken from the *Rugi*, who were based in the region of Krems on the north bank of the Danube, whom he defeated in 487/8 [4.2: McCormick 1977].

Odoacer and Zeno

Despite his victory over the *Rugi*, he withdrew forces from the province of Noricum. This is most vividly described for us in the *Life of Severinus* written by Eugippius, which reports first a breakdown in paying the frontier troops and then the official evacuation of the region. As a result, the religious community attached to the cult of Severinus crossed the Alps and made its way down to the *Lucullanum* outside Naples, possibly to the very estate where the deposed emperor Romulus Augustulus was living.

The evacuation of Noricum

Odoacer's rule in Italy seems to have been well regarded, not least because he was very concerned to support the senate [9: CHASTAGNOL 1966; LA ROCCA/OPPEDISANO 2016]. But Zeno was determined to remove him from power, and he directed Theodoric the Ostrogoth against him in 489. Thereafter Odoacer ceased to issue coins in the name of the emperor, and he raised his son Thela to the position of Caesar. Theodoric, however, proved too much for him, and, having confined him to the city of Ravenna from 490–3, forced him to surrender and then had him killed.

10.2 The Gibichungs

Although Odoacer was responsible for the overthrow of the last Western Emperor, Italy in his day was still understood to be part of the Empire. The same was true of other regions of the West. When Gundobad left Italy for Gaul in 474, following the Byzantine rejection of Glycerius, who he had installed as emperor, he retained his title of *magister militum*, by which we should probably understand that he regarded himself as *magister militum praesentalis*. This was the office that he seems to have inherited from his patron, Ricimer. In Gaul his father Gundioc and his uncle Chilperic had held the titles of *magister militum per Gallias* and *patricius* [4.8: WOOD 2016, 2021]. Indeed, his uncle may still have been in office at the moment of Gundobad's return. The leading males of the Gibichung family were, thus, Roman career soldiers. Gundioc and Chilperic had initially come to prominence in c. 455 when they took over the city of Lyon with the agreement of the senators of the region. Although Majorian objected and drove them out, they returned after his overthrow, probably with the approval of Ricimer, who was married to Gundioc's sister. Thereafter they governed the valleys of the central and upper Rhône and Saône, as well as territory stretching into the Auvergne. They exercised power as Roman officials, even if their authority was unusual in that their offices were military rather than civilian.

Gundioc and Chilperic

Gundobad

Exactly when Gundobad took over from his uncle is unclear. Chilperic was certainly in post in 474, and Gundobad in 490. Historians have hypothesised that Gundobad removed Chilperic from power, but we have no means of knowing if this was the case. If he was in conflict with anyone in Gaul in 474, it would have been the

Visigoth Euric, who at the time was unquestionably intervening in the territory under Burgundian control. In 490, Gundobad took advantage of the war between Odoacer and Theodoric to plunder Liguria, but the damage was subsequently redressed. We next hear of Gundobad in 500, when his brother Godegisel joined the Frankish king Clovis and drove him out of Lyon and Vienne, forcing him to seek terms from the Visigothic stronghold of Avignon, where he had taken refuge. Thereafter, while Clovis was alive, Gundobad was effectively subordinate to the Merovingian king and as such joined in his campaigns against the Visigoths in 507 and in the years that followed [12.3: Wood 2010, 2012]. When Clovis died in 511, however, Gundobad was effectively the most powerful ruler in Gaul.

Godegisel and Clovis

Throughout this period, he occasionally used the title *rex*, but not *rex Burgundionum* [12.8: Wood 2014, 2016; 3: Eisenberg 2019]. In general, the earliest rulers of the successor states did not use titles that included the name of their people. Gundobad's claim to authority, however, was probably as *magister militum* and as *patricius*, even after 476. Certainly, towards the end of his life, he opened negotiations with the emperor Anastasius to transfer his Roman titles to his son Sigismund [12.8: Wood 2014], which is what eventually seems to have happened. In other words, down to the abdication of Sigismund in c. 522 the Gibichung family ruled as agents of the Empire, initially of Western emperors, and subsequently of their eastern successors.

The titles of rulers

When they legislated, they did so in conformity with imperial practice, although they were expanding their military authority more generally into the civilian sphere [12.8: Wood 2016]. Sidonius tells us that his friend Syagrius was regarded as a Solon of the Burgundians, which suggests that he was helping one of the *magistri militum* (probably Gundioc or Chilperic) with legislation. And Sidonius' own epitaph reveals that he gave laws to the barbarians. Given the involvement of Syagrius and Sidonius these laws are unlikely to have been Germanic in any way. Some of them may be included in the *Forma et Interpretatio Legum* (usually known as the *Lex Romana Burgundionum*), which appears to have been put together around 500. This is a compilation of extracts from Roman Law. Perhaps at approximately the same time another compilation was also issued, the so-called *Lex Burgundionum*, although its proper title is the *Liber Constitutionum*, which drew on the *Forma et Interpretatio*. This only survives in a revised recension from 517

Gibichung legislation

(in fact there seem to have been several revisions over the years). Although there are one or two clauses in the *Liber Constitutionum* which clearly refer to traditional practices among the non-Roman followers of Gundobad and Sigismund (the use of Germanic vocabulary makes this clear), the legislation is best seen as that of rulers who regarded themselves as *magistri militum* of the Roman Empire, continuing Roman practices as best they could [14.1: Wood 2018].

Christian doctrine   Apparently unlike his father and his uncle, Gundobad was an Arian, perhaps as a result of his close association with Ricimer [12.3: Wood 2010, 2012]. Although Avitus of Vienne and other Catholic bishops were keen to convert him, his heresy did not impinge in any way on his rule. His government was certainly tolerant in religious terms, and his son Sigismund converted to Catholicism well **Sigismund** before Gundobad's death, possibly as early as c. 500. Sigismund's reign, short though it was, was more problematic than that of his father. He almost immediately came into conflict with the Catholic episcopate, and he abdicated in c. 522, having killed his son at the prompting of his second wife [11.1: Wood 1998]. He retired to the monastery of Agaune, which he had founded in 515 [14.5: Brocard/ Vannotti/Wagner 2011]. The young Merovingian king Chlodomer took advantage of the situation and, spurred on by his mother, Clovis' widow Chrotechildis, who was herself a member of the Gibichung family, invaded Burgundian territory: Sigismund was taken out of monastic retirement and killed. However, his brother, Godomar, led a rear-guard action against Chlodomer, killing the Merovingian king at the Battle of Vézeronce. The Gibichung province survived for a further ten years before it was finally conquered by the Franks. Of Godomar's rule we know next to nothing. In all probability, unlike his brother or his father, he held no Roman office.

10.3 Ostrogoths

Theoric the Amal   Like Odoacer and the Gibichungs, the Ostrogothic king Theodoric was effectively a Roman ruler, albeit one whose authority depended on his barbarian following [12.9: Wiemer 2018]. Theoderic the Amal belonged to the tribe of the *Greutungi*, which had been subject to the Huns prior to the death of Attila in 453 [4.5: Wolfram 2009; Heather 1991]. Six years later, in the aftermath of the overthrow of Hunnic power, Theodoric himself was sent as a hostage to Constantinople and remained there for ten years. On returning to his people, he was elevated to the kingship alongside his father, Theudimir. Shortly afterwards he crossed the Danube to attack a group of Sarmatians in Singidunum. Once in the Balkans, he found himself in competition with another leader of *Greutungi*, also called Theodoric, nicknamed *Strabo*, 'the Squinter'. The two Theodorics were in competition, each of them trying to secure approval from the Eastern emperor from 470 to 481, when Theodoric the Squinter died in an accident. As a result, Theodoric the Amal was left in a very strong position as leader of all the Balkan Goths and was a potential threat to the emperor, who had previously benefitted from playing the two Theodorics off against each other. Initially, however, the emperor Zeno responded by appointing Theodoric to the post of *magister militum praesentalis* in 483, as well as *patricius* and even consul in 484. Odoacer's ill-judged entry into Illyricum in 486/7, however, gave the emperor Zeno an excuse to send Theodoric and his Greutungian forces westwards. Odoacer survived until he was killed by Theodoric in 493.

Having defeated Odoacer, Theodoric attempted to negotiate an official position for himself with the new emperor Anastasius [12.2: Jones 1962; 12.1: Arnold 2014]. When none was forthcoming, his military following hailed him as king, although he himself did not use the title *rex Gotorum* – just as Gundobad did not use the title *rex Burgundionum*. In 498, however, Anastasius returned the West Roman regalia that Odoacer had sent to Constantinople in 476. He also allowed Theodoric to name the western consul for each year. In imperial eyes, the Ostrogothic ruler was now the senior figure in the West, despite Gundobad's longstanding position as *magister militum*, an office that he had held since 472. Theodoric had only been granted the equivalent eastern position in 483.

Although Theodoric did not hold the imperial title, he was, as Odoacer had been, heir to the imperial government, which was something that distinguished him from his barbarian peers in the West who had essentially taken over provincial government [12.1: Arnold 2014; Arnold/Bjornlie/Sessa 2018]. Based in Ravenna, he occupied a city that had intermittently been a capital for West Roman emperors before 476. His government was entirely Roman in style, as we can see from the *Variae* of Cassiodorus. This collection of letters was probably put together by Cassiodorus when he was effectively in exile in Constantinople in c. 550. It was carefully edited,

Theodoric Strabo

Theodoric in Italy

The government of Italy

and some texts were clearly rewritten for political reasons [6: Bjorn-LIE 2013]. In other words, it is not a simple record of Ostrogothic government. Even so, the fact that it provides some of our clearest information on late- and post-Roman offices is an indication of the extent to which Theodoric's rule was a continuation of later Roman rule in Italy. Perhaps significantly Gregory of Tours, in the late sixth century, remembered Theodoric as king of Italy and not king of the Goths.

Ostrogothic marriages

Theodoric attempted to exert influence beyond Italy. This is most apparent in his diplomacy. One sister, Amalafrida, was married to the Vandal king Thrasamund. One daughter, Theodegotha, married the Visigoth Alaric II, another, Ostrogotho Areagni, the Burgundian Sigismund [12.8: Shanzer 1996]. Theodoric himself married Audofleda, a sister of Clovis. Following Clovis' victory over a group of *Alamanni* in 506, the Ostrogothic ruler welcomed the survivors into his kingdom. He tried to prevent war between Clovis and Alaric. When his intervention failed and Alaric was killed in 507, he sent troops against Gundobad, who had supported the Franks, seizing territory on the fringes of the Alps. In the name of Alaric's son Amalaric, he also took over control of the territory in southern Gaul and Spain that remained in Visigothic hands.

Intervention in Gaul

The Ostrogothic army

The one major divergence between Roman and Ostrogothic rule concerned the army [12.1: Halsall 2016]. Romans could and did fight for Theodoric – one of his most important generals, Liberius, Praetorian Prefect in Italy from c. 493–500 and then in Gaul from 510 onwards, had already fought for Odoacer. He distinguished himself in organising the settlement of Theodoric's followers. In the aftermath of the death of the Visigothic king Alaric II at Vouillé, he was sent to Gaul to take charge of the areas remaining under Gothic control [6: O'Donnell 1981]. Even so, the army that he commanded was conceived of as Gothic, although the troops themselves were urged to display the Roman virtues of *civilitas*.

Theodoric and
the Church

For most of his reign Theodoric succeeded in presenting himself as a fine ruler in Italy, despite his Arianism. He was careful not to intervene in the affairs of the Catholic Church, even when there was a disputed papal election. His Arianism did, however, emerge as problematic in his last years [12.9: Moorhead 1983, 1992]. In 518 Anastasius died, and Justin I took over the Eastern Empire. Anastasius had been a supporter of Monophysitism and was therefore regarded as unorthodox by both the Catholics and the Arians in Italy.

Justin and his nephew Justinian, who succeeded him in 527, were both aggressively orthodox and embarked upon of policy of rededicating Arian churches to Catholic cult. As a result, Theodoric sent the pope, John, to Constantinople to protest. On his return in 523 he was accused of treason and imprisoned; he died in custody in 526.

At the same time two leading senators, Symmachus and Boethius, were executed as traitors. Albinus, a friend of Boethius, had been accused by another senator, Cyprian, of wishing to see a restoration of imperial rule. Boethius and his father-in-law Symmachus then intervened on behalf of Albinus, with the result that they too were condemned. The deaths of Boethius, Symmachus and John were regarded as the one major blot on Theodoric's reign. In the event, however, much more important was the king's failure to ensure that he had a male heir. He had no son. He may have hoped that a grandson by one of his daughters could succeed him. There is some indication that he saw Sigistrix, the son of Ostrogotho Areagni and the Burgundian Sigismund, as a potential heir, but the boy was murdered by his father in 522. In 519, one other daughter of Theodoric, Amalasuntha, had married the Gothic noble Eutharic and had given birth to a son, Athalaric, and a daughter, Matasuntha. Eutharic himself died in 523, with the result that when Theodoric died his position was taken by his infant grandson, while Amalasuntha acted as guardian. Amalasuntha tried to maintain good relations with Byzantium, but there were groups among the Goths who did not favour the romanising policies that she and her father wished to pursue [12.9: VITIELLO 2017].

The deaths of Boethius and Symmachus

The search for an heir

10.4 Visigoths and Sueves

The Ostrogoths only entered the Empire following the death of Attila and the uprisings against his successors. The Visigoths, by contrast, were the first of the barbarian peoples to cross into Roman territory in the course of the *Völkerwanderungszeit*. Subsequently, their relations with Constantinople and Rome varied. Maltreatment after their arrival led them to fight against Valens and then against Theodosius. They were then caught up in the conflicts between Constantinople and Rome, which led to their move into Italy and to Alaric's sack of Rome in 410 [4.5: WOLFRAM 2009; 12.3: HEATHER 1991]. Despite the violence, however, they were not intent on destroying the

Empire. Alaric was keen to obtain imperial recognition, and although his successor Athaulf did, supposedly, consider fighting against the Romans, he decided instead to use his military power in support of Rome. It is possible that some Visigoths were less inclined to cooperate with the Empire, but Wallia came to terms with Constantius with the result that he and his people were settled in Aquitaine, as Roman federates, in 419. Thereafter, there were moments when Visigothic and Roman forces came into conflict, but for the most part the Visigoths supported the Empire, most notably at the Battle of the Catalaunian Plains. They also intervened in imperial politics, backing the elevation of Avitus as emperor in 455 [3: DELAPLACE 2015].

Euric   Following the deposition of Avitus in 456, their relations with West Roman emperors were determined by the confusion of imperial politics rather than any inbuilt hostility towards the Empire, at least up until the death of Theodoric II in 466. Euric, Theodoric's brother, killer, and successor, was more inclined to exploit the political chaos for his ends. Like his predecessors, he fought against the Sueves in Spain, but he also attacked imperial territory both in the peninsula and in Gaul, besieging Clermont in 472 and seizing Arles and Marseille in 473. In 475, the emperor Julius Nepos acknowledged Euric's control of Provence and also transferred Clermont to him. As a result, Sidonius, who had been elected bishop of the city in c. 470/2 was sent into exile. He was not the only Catholic bishop to experience such a fate, but he was soon allowed to return. Euric's so-called persecution was short-lived and was largely tied up with the military expansion that he pursued [2: STROHEKER 1937; 11: GHELLER 2017].

Alaric II   Euric and his son and successor Alaric II, who ruled over the Visigoths from 484 to 507, seem not to have regarded themselves as imperial agents, as Theodoric the Ostrogoth and his Burgundian contemporaries did. Nevertheless, their government was still essentially Roman, as one can see in Sidonius' account of Euric's court. Moreover, Sidonius, like many other members of the Gallic senatorial aristocracy, managed to collaborate with the new Gothic court. The greatest achievement of this early period of independent Visigothic history was the promulgation of the *Breviary of Alaric* at Aire-sur-l'Adour in 506 [12.3: ROUCHE/DUMÉZIL 2009]. This was an edited version of the *Theodosian Code*, which was carefully tailored to the needs of the new kingdom. Almost at the same time as the promulgation of the Breviary, a major Church council was held at Agde under the leadership of Caesarius of Arles. Although Alaric himself was Arian, he approved the holding of the council, which in turn prayed for him. The Visigothic kingdom was independent, but it was still modelled on the Empire.

In 507, however, war broke out between the Visigoths and the Franks. There had been tension between the two peoples for several years, although at least one treaty had been negotiated, which apparently involved payments from the Goths. The seventh-century chronicle of Fredegar adds some puzzling information, saying that Alaric became Clovis' *patrinus*, which ought to mean that he stood as his godfather. If true, Clovis must initially have been baptised as an Arian, prior to his baptism as a Catholic – comments by Avitus of Vienne certainly support the idea that he was for a time inclined towards Arianism. Despite his treaty with Alaric, Clovis decided to attack the Visigoths, according to Gregory of Tours for religious reasons, although contemporary evidence suggests that the cause of the conflict was economic [12.3: Bourgeois 2010; Mathisen/Shanzer 2012]. The Gothic king was killed in battle at Vouillé, outside Poitiers. His son, Amalaric, was too young to take over his father's throne, but the boy was supported by his grandfather, the Ostrogoth Theodoric, who intervened. By 511, the Ostrogothic king had largely driven the Franks out of the Visigothic territory that they had occupied. For a while the Visigoths were ruled from Ravenna, since Theodoric appointed as governors first the Roman Liberius and then his shield-bearer Theudis, who claimed the Visigothic throne himself when Amalaric was killed in 531 [12.3: Collins 2004]. By that time, the centre of Visigothic power had moved from Gaul to Spain – although the chronology of the settlement of the Visigoths in the Iberian peninsula is by no means clear; and indeed they never constituted more than a small elite minority of the population [12.3: Arce 2020].

Alaric and Clovis

The battle of Vouillé

Ostrogothic rule

10.5 Vandals

The Vandals arguably played a greater role in breaking the West Roman Empire than did any other barbarian group. Valentinian III conceded much of Numidia and Mauretania to Gaiseric in 435, and subsequently, after the Vandal seizure of Carthage, he handed over

Africa Proconsularis. This provided the Vandals with the opportunity to expand their power through much of the western Mediterranean, so that at the fullest extent the Vandal kingdom also included Sicily, Sardinia, Corsica, Malta and the Balearic islands. This effectively constituted what Christian Courtois termed the Empire of Corn, *l'empire du blé* [2: COURTOIS 1955]. Control of the seaways in the central Mediterranean had a major impact on the economy of Rome, which had depended since 146 BC on Carthaginian corn. Control of the sea also allowed the Vandals to sack Rome in 455.

The Vandal persecutions

However, our main source for the first half-century of the Vandal kingdom, Victor of Vita's *History of the Vandal Persecution*, written apparently in the late 480s, concentrates on the religious aspect of the rule of Gaiseric and his successors. The Vandals were Arian, and at times aggressively so. The persecution of the Catholic Church began as part of the settlement of the Vandals: Gaiseric ordered the transfer of some Catholic churches to Arians as early as 435, exiling those bishops who refused to obey. He did the same again in 439 following the capture of Carthage. Thereafter there were moments when he adopted a more conciliatory attitude, notably in 454, when he reinstated a Catholic bishop in Carthage at the time that he was negotiating a marriage between his son Huneric and Eudocia, the daughter of Valentinian III [12.4: HEATHER 2007; SCHWARCZ 2008; MERRILLS/MILES 2010; 7: WHELAN 2014, 2018].

Despite the fact that he did marry Eudocia, Huneric, who succeeded his father Gaiseric in 477, was responsible for the most extreme period of persecution in Vandal history, in the year from 483 until his death in 484. This supposedly led to the exile of 5,000 Catholic bishops and clergy and to large-scale seizure of Catholic churches. With his death the persecution seems to have eased under his nephew and successor Gunthamund (484–96), but it resumed under Thrasamund (496–523). For this final period of Vandal persecution, we no longer have Victor of Vita as our guide, but instead we have a very considerable dossier of theological material, largely associated with bishop Fulgentius of Ruspe, who was the leading Catholic apologist and who was exiled to Sardinia from 502 to 515, and again from 520 to 523, along with numerous other clergy [7: WHELAN 2018].

Thrasamund's persecution would seem to have differed from those of Gaiseric and Huneric in that it was apparently driven by theological conflict, at least according to the *Life of Fulgentius*. The bishop's surviving works certainly indicate that he was involved in considerable doctrinal debate. By contrast, Gaiseric seems to have persecuted principally in order to be able to endow the Vandal Church with buildings and income. Huneric's persecution was at least in part political. Gaiseric's will had stated that the succession should pass through each of his heirs in order of birth and that the same rule of inheritance should apply to all following generations. From Huneric's point of view, not only did this mean that he might be succeeded by a brother, rather than his own son, but even that descendants of his brothers would succeed before one of his own children – which is indeed what happened. Huneric, however, tried to subvert his father's will, not least by the murder and execution of close relatives [12.4: COURTOIS 1955]. At least some of the clergy who suffered in the Great Vandal Persecution were apparently exiled because of their unwillingness to oppose Gaiseric's will.

Despite the brutality, and especially the religious brutality of much Vandal rule, the Hasding rulers were also concerned to establish connections with the Empire, both before and after 476 [12.4: MERRILLS/MILES 2010]. This was in part diplomatic necessity. Ricimer fought against the Vandals in Sicily in 456, and Majorian planned a campaign against Africa. Although the campaign never materialised, Gaiseric did negotiate a new treaty with the Eastern emperor Leo in 461/2, which led to the return of those members of the imperial family who had been taken captive at the time of the Vandal sack of Rome, except for Eudocia, who had married Huneric. Further campaigns, however, were launched against the Vandals: Marcellinus attacked Vandal Sardinia in c. 466, and a major expedition was launched by the Byzantines against Africa in 468, which failed, but nevertheless resulted in the temporary capture of Tripoli. A new treaty was signed between Byzantium and the Vandals in 476 which recognised Hasding authority in Africa and the western islands of the Mediterranean. Thereafter, Byzantium and Carthage remained on relatively good terms until 529. There was some conflict between the Vandals and the Ostrogoths following Theodoric's arrival in Italy, especially in Sicily, which had passed out of Vandal hands. Some attempt at a diplomatic solution was made with the marriage of Thrasamund to Theodoric's sister Amalafrida in 500.

The Vandals and the Empire

When Gaiseric died, Huneric made much of the fact that he had married a daughter of Valentinian, which perhaps conferred

Huneric and his successors

greater distinction on him and his children than could be claimed by any other western leader [12.4: MERRILLS/MILES 2010]. It neverthe-less counted for nothing in terms of the Vandal succession, which followed the line laid down by Gaiseric. Huneric was succeeded in turn by two nephews, Gunthamund and Thrasamund. Only with Thrasamund's death in 523 did a son of Huneric, and thus a grand-son of Valentinian, succeed to the Vandal throne. Not only was Hilderic a descendent of an emperor; he had also spent time in Con-stantinople, where he seems to have formed close contacts with Jus-tinian. As a result, when he was deposed by his cousin Gelimer in 530, the Byzantines used Hilderic's Roman descent and his connec-tions with Constantinople as an excuse for intervening in Vandal politics. At least in most of its later years, the Vandal kingdom had established a working relationship with Byzantium, despite its com-mitment to Arianism.

10.6 Franks

The relations between the Merovingian kingdom of the Franks and the Byzantine world have been regularly debated. On the one hand, the Frankish kingdom has been seen as having its roots in Ger-manic tradition, on the other it has been seen as being essentially Roman. Unlike the other barbarian peoples, the Franks were in-volved in no great migration. They later claimed to be descendants of Trojans, and they also asserted that they had come from Pan-nonia, like St Martin. In fact, the Franks were a relatively new con-federation of peoples, all of whom had been established on the re-gion of the lower Rhine for centuries, many of them even within the Roman Empire. To some extent the Frankish kingdom rose out of the numerous groups of federate soldiers who had been in the pay of the Roman State [12.7: ZÖLLNER 1970; JAMES 1988; GEARY 1988;12.6: GEUENICH 1998]. The Merovingian family itself may have originated slightly further east, and some of the high-status Frank-ish burials which have been uncovered, most obviously the grave of Childeric, have material that is best paralleled with Thuringian and Gothic finds [12.7: QUAST 2015]. The first Merovingian for whom we have any detailed evidence, Chlodio, fought against Romans somewhere in Artois. His son Childeric, however, fought alongside the Roman general Aegidius against the Visigoths in c. 463, and subsequently against the same enemy with the *comes* Paulus in c. 469. In other words, the Franks were deeply involved in the military activities of the last West Roman generals. Childeric's authority would seem to have developed out of what was essentially the career of a Roman federate. It is possibly in this military context that we should place the origins of the earliest Frankish law code, the *Pactus Legis Salicae*. Although it has traditionally been seen as legislation issued by Clovis, the earliest elements in the code seem to be an agreement drawn up in the course of Frankish expansion, at a time when the people were still pagan [12.7: MAGNOU-Nortier 1977; 11: UBL 2017]. However, the text as we have it, or rather the texts, because it survives in numerous different recensions, can only be dated by the date of its manuscripts [12.7: COUMERT 2023]. As for Childeric himself, it is possible that he spent some time in Byzantium. According to Fredegar, as a result of sexual indiscretion he was forced into exile for a period, spending time in Constantinople. Whether or not this is true, the hoard of Byzantine coins found in his grave in 1653 suggests that he had direct contact with the East Roman court.

Although he had fought alongside Aegidius, after 476 the two men were rivals, as were their sons, Syagrius and Clovis. Having succeeded to his father's position in c. 481, Clovis turned against Syagrius, defeating him at Soissons, probably in 486. Unfortunately for the chronology of Clovis' reign we are almost entirely dependent on the account of Gregory of Tours, which places the major events of the reign at 5- or 10-year intervals [12.7: WOOD 1985]. Thus, according to the traditional chronology for the reign, Clovis became king in 481: he defeated Syagrius in 486 and the Thuringians in 491. Five years later (following a small number of manuscripts of Gregory's *Histories*), he defeated the *Alamanni*, and this victory provided the occasion for his conversion to Catholicism. In 500 (a date provided by Marius of Avenches) he defeated the Burgundians, then in 506 (following some manuscripts of Gregory's *Histories*) he defeated the Visigoths. He died in 511 [5b: Meier and Patzold 2014].

Unfortunately, the only secure date in the whole of this chronology is that given by Marius for the Burgundian war, and some of Gregory's dates are provably wrong. The victory over the Visigoths at Vouillé certainly took place in 507. There was a victory over the *Alamanni* (perhaps not the same as that in Gregory's *Histories*) in 506, which is attested in Cassiodorus' *Variae*. In addition,

Childeric

Lex Salica

Clovis and Syagrius

The chronology of Clovis' reign

the dating of the conversion and baptism of Clovis is highly debated
[12.7: Wood 1985; 12.8: Shanzer 1998; Becher 2011]. The one contemporary source for the baptism, a letter from bishop Avitus of Vienne,
seems to date to 508, although it should be stressed that Clovis' conversion may have happened some time before his baptism. As already noted, a reconstruction of events is complicated by the hints
in Avitus, and in the later chronicle of Fredegar, that Clovis was initially converted to Arianism, apparently with Alaric II acting as godfather.

Clovis' baptism

For Gregory, it was important to place Clovis' conversion and
baptism early in the reign because his adherence to the Catholic
faith supposedly explained his successes. Moreover, Gregory effectively presents Clovis' war against Alaric as an anti-Arian crusade.
We can, however, be certain that this was not the case, since the
Franks were supported in their campaigns against the Visigoths by
the Arian Gundobad [12.3: Wood 2010, 2012].

Clovis and the Church

It is, therefore, necessary to exercise caution in interpreting the
reign of Clovis, but there are some points that are clear from contemporary sources. By the end of his reign, Clovis was energetically
supporting the Catholic Church. This is indicated by his actions in
favour of the shrine of St Martin at Tours, as he marched towards
the battle of Vouillé, and it is apparent from the Council of Orleans,
which he summoned in 511, shortly before his death. Moreover,
whatever the date of the king's baptism, it took place at the same
time as Clovis received some sort of imperial recognition, as Avitus
states. This may be the same as the consulship that Gregory states
was conferred by the emperor Anastasius, apparently in 508. The
exact nature of the title actually conferred is much debated, but it is
clear that Clovis received considerable recognition from the emperor Anastasius – perhaps even a title senior to those of his barbarian contemporaries, the *magistri militum* and *patricii* Theodoric
and Gundobad. The Franks were never as closely tied to the Empire
as were the Visigoths, the Burgundians, the Ostrogoths, or even the
Vandals. Nevertheless, their kingdom grew out of the military organisation of the Roman provinces of Belgica and Germania, and it
was recognised by Anastasius.

Clovis and the Empire

After the death of Clovis, Frankish power receded for quarter
of a century. The king had four sons, one, Theuderic, by an un-
named woman, and three by Chrotechildis, the daughter of the Burgundian Chilperic. Of these four children, only Theuderic was of an

The sons of Clovis

age to rule when Clovis died. Clovis' kingdom was divided between all the children. Since there is no reason for thinking that such a division was traditional in 511, it may be that Chrotechildis used her influence to ensure that not all power passed to her stepson [6: WOOD 1977]. That three of Clovis' successors were children may suggest that the acceptance of minority rule in the Later Empire had been noted among the Franks. One result of the period of minority rule, however, was that the Franks lost the territories they had taken from the Visigoths in Aquitaine. In 524, when the eldest of Chrotechildis' children, Chlodomer, invaded Burgundian territory, he was defeated and killed at Vézeronce. Merovingian expansion would only resume again in the 530s.

10.7 Britons and Anglo-Saxons

The process of kingdom formation in Britain differed from that of the successor states on the continent, in the case of both the British and the Anglo-Saxon kingdoms. The British kingdoms were formed by leaders of the indigenous population, and they grew out of strategies of survival following the loss of imperial support. As late as the 440s, the council governing the Roman province, led by Vortigern, appealed to Aetius for help against the Picts and Scots. When the Romans were unable to help, the council resorted to the importation of Saxon federates from east of the Rhine. The federates, however, revolted, on the grounds that the British had not paid them as promised, and seized a substantial area of territory. After a period of Saxon expansion, a Roman named Ambrosius Aurelianus led the British resurgence, which seems to have been remarkably successful. Gildas, who provides us with the only narrative of events, says that the Saxons were almost driven out of the island, which is surely an exaggeration. But Constantius of Lyon, writing in c. 470, states that the island of Britain was peaceful in his day. However, by the time that Gildas was writing, probably in the late 530s, there had been dramatic changes. The Saxons had established themselves in the South-East, while in the West a number of separate British kingdoms had emerged: Gildas names the leaders of five of them, based in Wales (in Dyfed and Gwynedd) and in the South-West of England (in Devon). There were certainly other British kingdoms in what had been the northernmost zone of Ro-

The emergence of the British kingdoms

man Britannia, most notably in Rheged, at the western end of Hadrian's Wall, and in Elmet, to the west of York [12.10: CHARLES-ED-WARDS 2013].

In these British kingdoms it is clear that we are dealing with small polities led by warlords. They preserved little of the Roman past, but in any case much of the territory that they occupied had been on the fringes of Roman civilian culture anyway. Wales, the south-west of Britain and the northern part of the Roman province (north of York) had been dominated by the Roman military. There is some slight evidence of continuing habitation in urban centres, even in the North, notably in York and Carlisle. But more important were the forts; and there, archaeology points to radical reorganisation and decline. Our best evidence, from Birdoswald on Hadrian's Wall, suggests that individual forts were turned into strongholds for local chieftains [10: WILMOTT 2014; 11.1: DARK 1992].

Britain and the Mediterranean

At the same time, contact between western Britain and the Mediterranean world continued. This is most obvious from the finds of fragments of amphorae, which reveal continuing import of wine, and probably of oil and corn, above all to Cornwall, along the Welsh coast, and up to Galloway in Scotland [9: CAMPBELL 2007]. And, extraordinarily, in the mountains of North Wales there is an inscription that uses Byzantine consular dating. It is also clear that Christianity survived in the West and that churchmen maintained some contacts with the continent, especially with ascetics in Gaul. In other words, this was a world that was attempting to preserve its Roman traditions in very difficult circumstances [12.10: FAFINSKI 2021]. The circumstances would get worse from the late 530s onwards, when environmental disaster would seem to have added to the problems facing the British kingdoms.

Anglo-Saxons and Byzantium

Unlike the British kingdoms or the successor states of the continent, the Anglo-Saxon kingdoms did not belong to a world that looked to Byzantium, although it is clear from coin finds in the Baltic region, and also from the development of military architecture at sites such as Eketorp on Öland, that barbarians did travel to the Greek East, where they probably served as mercenaries. Justinian apparently offered the territory of Britain to the defeated Ostrogoths, while the Merovingians of the mid to late seventh century thought that they had some authority over some peoples in England.

The origins of the Anglo-Saxon kingdoms differed greatly from those established in Italy, Gaul, Spain and Africa [12.10: BASSETT 1989]. According to tradition, recorded by Bede in the eighth century and in the *Historia Britonum* and the *Anglo-Saxon Chronicle* in the ninth, they had their origins in the migration of Angles, Saxons and Jutes across the North Sea. These sources relate that the Angles then established kingdoms in East Anglia, the Saxons in Sussex and Wessex, and the Jutes in Kent. Although from the archaeology of early Anglo-Saxon cemeteries, and from the abandonment of settlement sites on the North Sea coast of Germany it is clear that there was some migration, these are no more than origin legends. There had been Germanic people on the island of Britain for centuries [12.10: OPPENHEIMER 2006]. Certainly, the Romans had brought troops from the Rhineland to man the Hadrian's Wall border against the Picts, but it is also likely that some of the indigenous population of eastern Britain was Germanic. There was also a long tradition of Germanic piracy in the Channel and the North Sea.

The Anglo-Saxon power blocks in the island of Britain, however, developed out of the revolt of the Saxon federates who had been employed against the Picts and Scots in the 440s. After their initial successes they seem to have lost ground to the Britons, but they must have been joined by further migrants at the end of the fifth century and the beginning of the sixth, as is indicated by the evidence of cemetery archaeology. The legends related by Bede, the *Historia Britonum* and the *Anglo-Saxon Chronicle* place the origins of the kingdoms at this moment, but we do not have any firm evidence for their existence before the second half of the sixth century. After Gildas, who talks of British but not of Anglo-Saxon kingdoms, the next detailed information relates to the arrival of the mission of Augustine sent to the English by Gregory the Great in 596. By that time, it is clear that kingdoms had been established in Kent, Sussex, Essex and East Anglia. In the North there was a kingdom of the *Deiri* (in the modern region of York) and a kingdom of the *Bernicii* (in the region of Hadrian's Wall), but the origins of these may have differed from those of the south-eastern kingdoms. Unlike the kingdoms of Sussex, Kent, and Wessex, the Northumbrian kingdoms have no migration story, and it may be that they developed out of the military organisation of the late Roman Empire [8: WOOD 2018].

The Christian mission of Augustine, aimed at the conversion of the English in 597, and a later mission from Ireland are a clear indi-

Bede and the Anglo-Saxon migration

The origins of Anglo-Saxon kingdoms

cation that there was a much greater caesura in Britain than there was on the continent. We should, however, not ignore the indications that some aspects of Anglo-Saxon rulership seem to have drawn on the Roman past. Some of the symbolic objects found in the great Mound One grave at Sutton Hoo have clear links with Byzantium and with Roman insignia, and some of the claims made by the Northumbrian rulers in the seventh century suggest that not all memories of Rome had been lost.

11 The Continuance of Roman Culture

11.1 Friendship Letters after Sidonius

Avitus of Vienne, Ruricius of Limoges and Ennodius of Pavia

Although Sidonius was the last western author before 476 to gather his letters into a collection, he remained a model for subsequent generations. Two bishops who composed letters that have survived, Avitus of Vienne [12.8: SHANZER/WOOD 2002] and Ruricius of Limoges [13: MATHISEN 1999], were even related to him. Other letter writers of the late fifth and early sixth century include Ennodius of Pavia. All of these authors continued the practice of writing friendship letters, following the model set out by Sidonius, and before him Symmachus, and in the distant past, Pliny. In one respect, however, the letter collections of Avitus, and Ennodius, and possibly Ruricius, differ from that of Sidonius: they were not put together by their authors, and indeed two of the collections actually seem to have been made in the late eighth century [8: WOOD 2018]. In the case of the works of Ennodius, which include speeches and poems as well as letters, it appears that the collection was made by the author of the *Historia Langobardorum*, Paul the Deacon [12.9: KENNELL 2000]. What these works point to is the existence of archives in which letters were kept. This is also suggested by a collection of letters known as the *Epistolae Austrasicae*, which includes 43 letters by bishops (including Remigius of Reims) which were apparently discovered in Trier in the Carolingian period [13: BARRETT/WOUDHUYSEN

The *Epistolae Austrasicae*

2016]. The last of the letters of the *Epistolae Austrasicae* dates to c. 590. This, however, was not the end of the letter-writing tradition in Francia [13: TYRRELL 2019]. A collection of letters written by Desiderius of Cahors (630–55) also survives; again, it seems to have been put together in the Carolingian period. And there is also a

Desiderius of Cahors

small group of letters written in the mid seventh century by Chrodobert of Tours and Importunus of Paris which survive in a manuscript of formulae [13: WALSTRA 1962]. Letters, in other words, continued to be written and preserved throughout the early medieval period in Francia, even though authors did not usually gather their letters into collections. They attest to the continuing use of ancient norms of communication and social exchange among the aristocracy and senior clergy, right through to the Carolingian period. The same would also seem to be true of Visigothic Spain, where twenty letters survive from the late sixth and early seventh centuries.

One Frankish collection of letters, however, was put together by its author in the sixth century [12.7: REYDELLET 1994–2004]. The Italian poet Venantius Fortunatus, who spent most of his career in the late sixth century in Francia, where he eventually became bishop of Poitiers, collected his verse letters into books [12.7: WILLIARD 2022]. These poems differ slightly from the surviving prose letters of the period, and not just because they are in verse. As a foreigner, Fortunatus was a man in search of a patron, and his poems reflect his dependence on the kings, queens, aristocrats and bishops of Merovingian Gaul. In other words, they shed light on the function of letter writing outside the world of the post-Roman senatorial aristocracy.

Venantius Fortunatus

11.2 Ostrogothic Italy

Venantius Fortunatus was born and educated in Italy. He illustrates the education available in Ravenna even towards the end of the Ostrogothic War. He would have no successors. Rather, he comes at the end of a line of impressive Italian writers. The great figures of the early part of the century from whom we have a substantial amount of writing are Ennodius, Boethius and Cassiodorus, but there were clearly plenty of other writers and scholars, including geographers, whose work is little known or has not survived.

Cassiodorus' early career provides a clear illustration of political and cultural continuity from late imperial to Ostrogothic Italy. He held the posts of *quaestor sacri palatii*, consul and *magister officiorum*. As *magister officiorum* he was in charge of the governmental writing office. His work is best seen in the collection of official

Cassiodorus

letters he made while effectively in exile in Constantinople some-time after 538: the *Variae*. These are a goldmine of information, not just for the government of the Ostrogoths, but also for the Later Empire as a whole, for it is assumed that the duties of officials had changed little between 476 and the period in which Cassiodorus held office. We should not, however, accept the collection as a simple compilation of letters from the archive of a *magister officiorum*. It has been shown that Cassiodorus edited them for political purposes, in order to justify his own work as well as the rule of Theodoric [6: Bjornlie 2013]. In addition to the *Variae*, works from the earlier part of his life include a fragmentary panegyric which, like that of Ennodius, shows the continuation of the panegyric tradition in Italy.

Boethius Also belonging to the Ostrogothic period are the writings of Boethius, the senator who was executed alongside his father-in-law Symmachus for supposed collusion with Byzantium, shortly before Theodoric's death in 526. Boethius was an intellectual polymath, writing works of theology (the so-called *Opuscula sacra*, devoted to the Trinity and to the heresies of Eutyches and Nestorius) as well as treatises on mathematics and music (both of which reflect Aristotelian thought) [13: Chadwick 1981]. His most famous work, written while he was awaiting execution, is the *Consolation of Philosophy*, which is generally regarded as the last great work of classical philosophy.

Papal letters After the execution of Boethius and the death of Theodoric, the evidence that we have for Italian culture is very largely ecclesiastical. Apart from the *Variae*, the letters that survive are largely papal: many are included in the *Collectio Avellana*, compiled between 556 and 561 [7: Lizzi Testa/Marconi 2019]. There is also a collection of the letters of Pope Pelagius I (556–61) [14.2: Neil 2015], but above all there is the *Register* of Gregory the Great (590–604), although like the sixth-century Frankish collections, and that of Ennodius' works, this was actually put together in the eighth century [14.2: Martyn 2004].

Cassiodorus' religious writings Cassiodorus' own writings after his return from Italy were also predominantly ecclesiastical. He founded a monastery, the *Vivarium*, on an estate in Calabria, where he gathered a significant library. And he set out his notion of appropriate Christian learning in the *Institutes*, which would become a basic handbook for the Middle Ages [14.3: Halporn/Vessey 2004]. In addition, he wrote a major exegetic work, the *Expositio Psalmorum*. The shift in Cassiodorus' career illustrates a significant change in western culture, which was increasingly dominated by the Church and by the bishops and the concerns of Christian religion [14.3: O'DONNELL 1979].

One other significant aspect of the culture of Ostrogothic Italy is its architecture. Throughout the fourth and fifth centuries rulers and aristocrats had erected churches. A few from the Constantinian period and later survive, in Rome and in the Holy Land. One of the most substantial clusters of surviving late antique architecture is to be found in Ravenna, where there is an uninterrupted sequence of foundations from the reign of Honorius, when buildings were funded by Galla Placidia (including her so-called Mausoleum), through to that of Justinian in the 550s (including the churches of Sant'Apollinare in Classe and San Vitale). From the reign of Theodoric, we have the court church of Sant Apollinare Nuovo and the Arian baptistery as well as Theodoric's own mausoleum, which constitute the most significant court monuments of the early successor states [5: DEICHMANN 1969–76; 5.2: VERHOEVEN 2011; DELIYANNIS 2010]. Ravenna

11.3 Vandal Africa

The majority of writing to have survived from North Africa from the fourth century onwards is, of course, ecclesiastical, above all because of the scale of the output of Augustine. Religious writing also dominates the Vandal period, not least because of the persecutions and the Catholic response to the Arians. Our major narrative is Victor of Vita's *History of the Persecution* [12.4: MOORHEAD 1992; LANCEL 2002; VÖSSING 2011], and in addition we have theological works by Fulgentius of Ruspe and Ferrandus [12.4: FRAIPONT 2004].

The poet Dracontius wrote religious works, most notably the *De Laudibus Dei* and the *Satisfactio ad Gunthamundum*. But in addition he wrote works of secular poetry which look back to classical mythology [15.7/Dracontius: MOUSSY/CAMUS/BOUQUET/WOLFF 2002]. Among these there is an extended 1,000-line poem on the tragedy of Orestes. His minor poems include short pieces reflecting the life and culture of Carthage. This is also the case for the 91 works of the poet Luxorius, preserved, along with numerous other minor poems, in the *Latin Anthology*. Although they are not highly rated as poetry, Dracontius Luxorius they do provide a remarkable illustration of the rather erotic literary tastes of the reading classes of Vandal Africa [8: Kay 2006].

Corippus   Our evidence for the culture of Africa largely comes to an end with the Justinianic Conquest. One major poet of African origin, Corippus, did, however, continue to write secular verse, but he did so in Constantinople. He wrote two lengthy poems that survive. The first, the *Johannides*, or *De bellis Libycis*, is an account of the campaigns directed against the Moors by the general John Troglita, after the Byzantine take-over of Vandal Africa, culminating in 548 [13: Diggle/Goodyear 1970; Goldlust 2015; 12. 4: Merrills 2023]. The second is the panegyrical *In laudem Iustini Minoris* which describes the death of Justinian and the accession of Justin II in Constantinople in 565 [6: Cameron 1976a]. Although Corippus' output was directed towards an audience in Constantinople, his initial education was surely in Africa and confirms the continuing classical culture of the Vandal kingdom.

11.4 Historical Writing in the Sixth-century West

As we have already seen, the writing of history underwent considerable change already in the fourth century. In Latin, Ammianus and the *Historia Augusta* effectively mark the end of the classical tradition, although Orosius did set about adapting Roman history-writing to the defence of Christianity. Most western historical writing of the fifth century, however, had followed the Chronicle tradition established by Eusebius of Caesarea, for example the Chronicles of Prosper and Hydatius and the Chronicle of 452. Such annalistic writing continued through the sixth century down to the Middle Chronicle writing   Ages. Among the sixth-century continuators of Eusebius-Jerome one may note Marius of Avenches as well as the African Victor of Tunnuna and the Spaniard John of Biclaro [12.3: Cardelle de Hartmann 2001]. Victor of Tunnuna died in Constantinople under arrest because of his opposition to Justinian's condemnation of the so-called Three Chapters, the authors Theodore, Theodoret and Ibas. His surviving work is a continuation of the Chronicles of Eusebius-Jerome and Prosper, running down to the year 566. It includes important information on Vandal Africa, but also on Monophysitism and the Three Chapters. It was continued to 590 by the Spaniard, John of Biclaro, who himself spent time in Constantinople. Isidore of Seville also contributed to the genre. And in later centuries copyists of some of these chronicles made their own additions, inserting further annals.

But different traditions of historical writing were already emerging. They have been categorised as 'Barbarian Histories', but the term has been rightly attacked by Walter Goffart, who has also shown that they can scarcely be categorised as a single genre [11: GOFFART 1988]. Goffart singled out for discussion the historical writings of Jordanes, Gregory of Tours, the Venerable Bede and Paul the Deacon: that is, two authors from the sixth and two authors from the eighth century.

If we take surviving historical writings of the late fifth and sixth centuries, we should begin with Victor of Vita's *History of the Vandal Persecution* [12.4: MOORHEAD 1992; LANCEL 2002; VÖSSING 2011] and then turn to Gildas' *De Excidio Britonum*, his account of the collapse of Britain in the post-Roman period which begins with a narrative of fifth-century events [10: LAPIDGE/DUMVILLE 1984; 12.10: GEORGE 2009]. In fact, Gildas' work is really a work of moral theology, prefaced by a short historical introduction. What it shares with Victor of Vita, apart from its strident Christian message, is its concentration on a single region of what had been the Roman West. This was an essentially new development in historical writing.

Quite different from these are the histories written by Jordanes, his *Romana* and his *Getica* [8: VAN NUFFELEN/VAN HOOF 2020]. The *Romana* is essentially an epitome of early authors. The *Getica* is more complex. It used to be assumed that it was an abridged version of Cassiodorus' lost *Gothic History*, which Jordanes says he had read. But it is clear from the differences between what Cassiodorus and Jordanes have to say about individual Gothic leaders that he can at best have remembered the general outline of the *Gothic History*. Cassiodorus seems to have provided Jordanes with the idea of presenting the history of the Goths as essentially that of two families, the Amals and the Balts. The detail, however, Jordanes provided himself, in part from the traditions of his own family, but largely by scouring earlier authors (biblical, Greek and Latin) for any information that might help reconstruct the past of the Ostrogoths and Visigoths [11: CHRISTENSEN 2002]. Many of the details that he introduced were not, in fact, relevant for the history of the Goths – but some were based on genuine information, as has been shown by the recent discovery of fragments of the third-century historian

Barbarian histories

Victor of Vita

Gildas

Jordanes

Dexippus which refer to figures mentioned by Jordanes [11: Martin/ Grusková 2014]. The *Getica* was written c. 550, at approximately the same time as Cassiodorus was compiling the *Variae* and while Procopius and Marcellinus Comes were also writing. It should be seen as contributing to a debate on how Justinian should deal with the Ostrogoths after their defeat.

Historical writings of Cassiodorus

Although we lack Cassiodorus' own version of Gothic history, we do have the references to the Gothic past contained in the *Variae* (which are probably a more reliable guide to the contents of the history than is the *Getica* of Jordanes), his *Chronicle* and also the translation of the *Historia Tripartita* made for him by Epiphanius. The original text of this last work had been compiled by Theodorus Lector in Constantinople in the mid fifth century. It drew on the fifth-century Greek ecclesiastical historians Sozomen, Socrates Scholasticus and Theodoret of Cyrrhus to create a single Church history [8: Mazza 1984].

Gregory of Tours

More important for the historian of the sixth-century West are the *Ten Books of Histories*, written by Gregory of Tours between 576 and 594. There has been some debate over the chronology of the work's composition: it is clear that Gregory was writing over a period of years, since there are various references to very recent events and matters of specific concern, but it is possible that the text as a whole was subject to revision at the end of the author's life. It used to be thought that Gregory regarded his work as a *History of the Franks*, but this is an interpretation that has been rightly discarded [11: Goffart 1988; Reimitz 2015]. His own title appears to have been the *Ten Books of Histories*, or simply *Histories*. Although the Franks, and the Merovingians in particular, do come to dominate the narrative, that is only because Gregory was living under Frankish rule. There is no attempt to provide a coherent history of the Frankish people. But nor is there any attempt to write a history of Rome or its empire. Unlike Jordanes, Gregory was not interested in the Roman past except for the fact that it provided the context for certain anecdotes to do with the Church. It is the history of the Church, and more particularly of the Church in Gaul, and even more precisely of those dioceses with which the author's family had connections, that is at the heart of Gregory's concerns. He looks back to Eusebius-Jerome and to Orosius, and not to Ammianus, although he was aware of Sallust's *Catalina*. He did know of some fifth-century historical writings by Renatus Profuturus Frigeridus and Sulpicius Alexander, which were apparently secular in outlook but unfortunately have not survived. But while Gregory did look back to fourth and fifth century writers, in one crucial respect he differed from them. For him the Roman Empire was a world with which he had no affinity. It was a past age, and because of its persecution of Christians, it was not one that was commendable (a view that he shared with Gildas). His ecclesiastical interests are even more apparent when one adds to the *Histories* Gregory's books of miracles, which are explicitly cross-referenced.

Gregory, in other words, was writing a type of Church history, and not a Barbarian History. And it was a history that, despite his knowledge of certain classical authors, did not look back to the Roman past. It would be revised in various ways by its early medieval editors who removed some of the elements most closely connected with his family, and some of its revisions did indeed make it a *History of the Franks*. Crucially, however, Gregory's writings mark a shift from the early years of the sixth century. Although he was a friend of Venantius Fortunatus, and although the latter can be used to illustrate the continuation of certain aspects of the classical tradition, Gregory belonged to a world in which Rome and the Roman past was no longer a central point of reference.

12 The Failure of the Commonwealth

12.1 Justinian's Interventions: Vandal Africa

For a period of over half a century many of the regions of the old Western Empire, now divided up into petty kingdoms, continued to look up to the emperor in Constantinople. Ostrogothic Italy, the Burgundian lands of the basin of the Rhône and Saône, the Franks of north-eastern Gaul, and even the Vandals in Africa saw themselves as subject to Byzantium [12.8: WOOD 2018]. All this was to change in the 530s [12.9: MEIER 2004; 6: LEPPIN 2007; O'DONNELL 2009; 11.1: HEATHER 2018]; and it changed not so much because the successor states wanted to break out of a world dominated by the emperor but because of the aspirations of Justinian, pressurised at least in part by the old senatorial aristocracy, for they, more than any group other than the West Roman court, had suffered with the establishment of

The fate of the senatorial aristocracy

the successor states. The break-up of West Rome had rendered impossible the vast, Mediterranean-wide pattern of aristocratic estate-holding that had characterised the fourth century and the first decade of the fifth. The new political divisions made it dangerous, if not impossible, to hold property throughout the old Roman world. And there had been significant dispossession, as we have already seen in the case of Paulinus of Pella and as we can also see in the evidence for aristocratic refugees, above all from Africa, to be found in Justinian's Constantinople and elsewhere in the Byzantine East [11.1: HERRIN 2018].

Hilderic and Gelimer

Of course, some barbarian rulers were very much more closely connected with the imperial court than were others. The Vandal king Hilderic, as the son of Huneric and Eudocia, was the grandson of Valentinian III [12.4: MERRILLS/MILES 2010]. Moreover, he had spent time in Constantinople, where he had been a guest of Justinian before his accession to the throne in 523. On succeeding to the throne, Hilderic pursued a religious policy that was notably more friendly towards the Catholics than that of his predecessors had been. Otherwise, however, he was relatively inactive, and, already aged well over 50, he was no military leader. As a result, in 530 he was challenged by his cousin Gelimer, who deposed him and seized the throne. This gave Justinian an excuse to intervene in Africa. Equally important in Justinian's calculations, however, were the circumstances in Constantinople itself, and not merely the pressure put on him by aristocratic exiles from the West.

The Nika riot

In January 532, a riot had broken out in Constantinople, following the arrest for murder of a number of members of the Blue and Green chariot-racing factions, who were a dominant element in the life of the city where, as elsewhere in the Byzantine world, the Hippodrome was a focus of political as well as sporting activity [6: CAMERON 1976]. It soon took on wider political significance [6: GREATREX 1997;12.9: MEIER 2004]. The first six years of Justinian's reign had not been popular, above all because of his financial and legal reforms. The rioters demanded the removal of John the Cappadocian, who was in charge of the collection of taxes, which were all the heavier because Justinian had been involved in a war with Persia since 527. They also demanded the removal of Tribonian, whom Justinian had charged with reforming the law and who would ultimately be the chief architect of the *Corpus Iuris Civilis*, the great compilation of law which effectively superseded the *Codex Theo-*

dosianus [6: Honoré 1978]. And one group of senators wanted to see the removal of Justinian himself and the elevation in his place of Hypatius, the nephew of his predecessor but one, the emperor Anastasius.

Faced with a massive uprising, which caused enormous destruction in the city, Justinian himself effectively collapsed. He was saved by the determination of his wife, Theodora, and the loyalty of his leading generals, notably Narses and Belisarius, who massacred the rebels in the Hippodrome. Significantly the decision to attack Africa followed swiftly upon the suppression of the riot. Justinian could present himself as the avenger of Valentinian's grandson, Hilderic – who had been deposed all of three years before. A successful campaign against the Vandals might go some way to repair the damage of the Nika Riots and their suppression. So, having concluded his Persian Wars with the Perpetual Peace of 532, he directed Belisarius against Gelimer [6: O'Donnell 2009; 11.1: Heather 2018, 2019].

In the summer of 533, Belisarius landed on the African coast and marched on Carthage. Although Gelimer had prepared an ambush, he was defeated ten miles outside the Vandal capital, which soon fell to the Byzantine army. After a further defeat Gelimer surrendered at the beginning of 534. Belisarius returned to Constantinople with substantial booty, and he was granted a public triumph. Gelimer was sent into exile. Justinian broadcast the restoration of Africa to Roman rule in a law issued in 535 (*Corpus Iuris Civilis* I, 27), and he did so in a way that glossed over the opportunistic origins of the African campaign. This was the first public statement of an ideology of reconquest.

Belisarius in Africa

The collapse of the Vandal kingdom had been remarkably quick, although the conquest of the territory of Roman North Africa took very much longer because of the incursions of Berbers from the mountainous regions to the south. There was a major uprising in 546–8, which was suppressed by John Troglita, whose exploits are recorded by the poet Corippus [12. 4: Merrills 2023]. Although John managed to restore peace to Africa, the archaeological evidence suggests that the Byzantine province was always under threat from Berber raids.

The Berber threat

12.2 Justinian's Interventions: The Impact on Italy, 526–568

Amalasuntha and Theodohad

Gelimer had provided Justinian with a perfect excuse for intervening in North Africa. In Ostrogothic Italy, Theodohad did much the same. When Theodoric died in 526, his nearest male heir was his grandson, Athalaric, the son of his daughter Amalasuntha and the Spanish Goth Eutharic, who may have been the Ostrogoth's intended successor. Eutharic, however, died in 522, four years before Theodoric, thus leaving a ten-year old boy as the heir to the Ostrogothic throne. There was, of course, Roman imperial (although probably not Gothic) precedent for this, in the tradition of Child Emperors initiated by Valentinian I. Amalasuntha took the position of regent [12.9: Vɪᴛɪᴇʟʟᴏ 2017], but she was thought to be bringing Athalaric up in too Roman a manner, with the result that members of the Gothic nobility took over his education, which supposedly led to him living a debauched life, resulting in his early death in 534. Amalasuntha was then pressured by the Gothic nobility to accept her cousin, Theodohad, a son of Theodoric's sister, as joint ruler [12.9: Vɪᴛɪᴇʟʟᴏ 2014]. Both cousins had received a thoroughly Roman education, but Amalasuntha seems also to have been deeply committed to contact with Byzantium, and she is even said to have wished to move to Constantinople, taking the Gothic treasure with her. Not surprisingly, Theodohad ordered her incarceration, and soon after she was murdered. This, however, provided Justinian with a reason for intervening in Italy, much as the deposition of Hilderic had justified his intervention in Africa.

Procopius

As in the case of Justinian's Vandal wars, so too in that of the emperor's wars in Italy, and indeed those against the Persians, we have the remarkable account written by Procopius, who, as sometime secretary to Belisarius, was an eyewitness to some of the campaigns he records. As a result, we can follow some aspects of the Gothic wars in minute detail [11.1: Hᴇᴀᴛʜᴇʀ 2018].

Belisarius in Italy

Following the defeat of Gelimer, Justinian already had troops stationed in Africa. Belisarius therefore returned from Constantinople and then crossed with his army to Sicily, which he quickly conquered. Theodohad initially indicated that he would cede Sicily and accept the overlordship of Justinian in Italy, but following some Gothic successes against the Byzantines in Dalmatia, he ended negotiations. As a result, Belisarius crossed to mainland Italy, captured Naples and then took over Rome. Furious at the inactivity of

Theodohad, the Goths deposed him and elected Witigis in his place. Witigis
The new king then married Matasuntha, the daughter of Amalasuntha, before marching to Rome, which he besieged without success for a year in 537/8. In the meantime, Justinian sent reinforcements from Constantinople to support the Italian war-effort: the most important being an army under the eunuch Narses, who arrived in 538. At the same time Witigis called on the Franks for help, which they provided. Subsequently, however, in 539, the Franks under Theudebert intervened entirely for their own benefit, causing problems for both Goths and Byzantines. Witigis also appealed to the Persians, inciting them to renew their attacks on the East Roman Empire. But before anything could come of this, Belisarius turned against Ravenna, where the besieged Witigis was tricked into capitulating in 540. Belisarius returned to Constantinople, this time with the defeated Witigis.

The Goths had not yet been completely defeated, and indeed, Totila
once they realised that Belisarius had tricked Witigis, they turned on the remaining Byzantine troops. Having removed two lacklustre leaders, the Goths elevated Totila as their king in 541. A year later the Persian shah Khosrau I invaded Mesopotamia. Justinian was, therefore, also faced with a war in the East, which continued, despite truces in 545 and 557, down to the Fifty-Year Peace of 562. This gave Totila the opportunity to reverse the losses of 539/40. He succeeded in retaking Naples in 542 and Rome in 546. The Eternal City, however, fell once again to Belisarius, who was soon recalled to Constantinople, leaving Rome open to the Goths one more time in 549. Between 549 and 551, Totila recaptured most of Italy, only to be defeated by a new army led by Narses, who had been sent by Justinian. Narses defeated and killed the Gothic king at the battle of *Taginae* in 551. Totila's successor, Teia, was defeated by Narses at *Mons Lactarius* in 552/3.

The Gothic war had lasted from 535 to 554, and even then, pockets of Goths held out until 562. After the speedy success of the war in Africa, Justinian had badly underestimated the capacity of the Goths to resist. He had also been hamstrung by the renewal of the Persian War, which posed a threat to the Eastern Empire itself and thus had to take priority in any overall military strategy.

In addition, the war was fought against the background of The plague
plague, which was first noted in the Egyptian city of Pelusium in 541 and spread through much of the Mediterranean world in the

following years [9: MEIER 2016; HARPER 2011]. Plague was to recur regularly down to the mid eighth century. Its impact can only be guessed at and is much debated. However, it surely had an impact on Justinian's ability to field armies – not just because of its direct impact on manpower, but also because population decline meant a decrease in tax revenue. It is, therefore, likely to have been a factor in the length of the war.

The decline of Italy   The effect of twenty years of war was to bring to an end the classical period in Italy, which had continued throughout the reign of Theodoric [6: O'DONNELL 2009]. Certainly there had been destruction in the course of the fifth century, not least the Sack of Rome itself, but much of the damage had been made good during the periods of rule by Odoacer and Theodoric. The sieges and battles of the Gothic Wars damaged the infrastructure on a greater scale and more permanently. The destruction of water supplies and of drainage systems meant an overall decline in living standards. The presence of armies, and the impact of the plague on the population, rendered agriculture increasingly difficult. In other words, despite the rhetoric of his Pragmatic Sanction of 554, which proclaimed that Italy was now a Byzantine province (albeit in slightly more muted tones than had been employed to mark the capture of Africa in 535), far from restoring Italy to the Empire, Justinian helped ensure its decline. Most of the great Italian cities had been badly hit. The aristocratic exiles in Constantinople who had urged the conquest of the West had effectively ensured the destruction of the cosmopolitan life that they championed and which had played a key role in the late Roman economy [12.9: DEY 2024].

12.3 The Arrival of the Lombards

Moreover, the victories of Narses did not mean the end of war in Italy. In the course of the campaigns of 551–3, the Byzantine general had allied with the Lombards of Pannonia, using them as federates at the battle of *Taginae*. They were the last of the barbarians of the *Völkerwanderungszeit* to enter the territories of the old Roman Empire. By the late fifth century they had settled on the north bank of the Danube, taking over territory which had previously been occupied by the *Rugi*, a people who are best known from their appearance in the *Vita Severini*, where they are a source of trouble for the

population of Pannonia and Noricum [12.11: POHL/ERHART 2005]. However, they had been utterly defeated by Odoacer in 487.

The Rugi

Slightly to the east of Rugian territory was a Herule kingdom,
which had emerged after the death of Attila and the collapse of the
Hunnic empire. In Procopius we hear that the Herules were defeated by the Lombards, who then came into conflict with another
of the peoples that had emerged after the fall of the Huns, the
Gepids, whose kingdom is not well known from the written sources
but may be represented in the great gold finds from Szilágysomlyó.
Rather against the odds the Lombards under Audoin inflicted a defeat on the Gepids in 551/2. Subsequently, in 567 Alboin, Audoin's
successor, allied with the newly arrived nomadic Avars, and together they destroyed the Gepid kingdom [12.12: POHL 2002; 11: POHL
2018].

Herules and Gepids

The Avars would come to pose a very considerable threat to the
Byzantine East in the seventh century, and the Lombards seem to
have realised that they were dangerous neighbours. They apparently conceded their territory in Pannonia to them on diplomatic
terms, choosing to move across the Alps. Lombard troops had already been active in Italy as federates of Narses, and they may well
have known that the Byzantines were in no position to defend the
peninsula. There were even rumours that Narses, feeling that he
had not been adequately rewarded by Justinian, actually encouraged them to enter Italy, which they did in 568. Within a year they
had taken Friuli and Milan, and in 572 they took Pavia. The arrival
of the Lombards confirmed the fact that Italy was no longer part of
the classical world. Their seizure of the Lombard Plain, of Tuscany,
Spoleto and Benevento, seems to have been brutal. Thereafter there
was an uneasy division within Italy of Lombard and Byzantine territory, with the Byzantines continuing to hold on to the exarchate,
around Ravenna, Rome, Naples and Sicily [12.11: CHRISTIE 1995].

The Avars

The Lombard entry
into Italy

12.4 Justinian's Interventions: The Impact on Spain

The narratives of Justinian's wars in Africa, Italy, and on the Persian frontier are well known, above all because they are recorded
in Procopius' histories. A fourth area of conflict, in Spain, which is
not covered by the Byzantine historian, is very much less well understood [11.1: RIPOLL LOPEZ 2001; 12.3: ARCE 2020; CASTELLANOS 2020]. As

in the case of Africa and Italy, however, Justinian responded to a crisis among the barbarians themselves. After the death of Alaric II at the battle of Vouillé, the Ostrogoth Theodoric intervened to protect the Visigothic kingdom. In 522, he elevated Amalaric, the son of Alaric and Theodoric's daughter Theodegotha, to the throne. Amalaric then married Chrotechildis, the daughter of the Frankish king Clovis, but his mistreatment of her led her brothers to attack Spain. In the course of the subsequent conflict in 531, Amalaric was killed, and the throne was seized by Theudis, who was not a member of the Balt dynasty which had ruled over the Visigoths since the late fourth century. In fact, he was an Ostrogoth who had been one of the governors sent to administer Spain by Theodoric. Theudis avoided taking sides over Justinian's reconquest of Africa, but he may have taken advantage of the Vandal collapse to seize Ceuta, on the south side of the Straits of Gibraltar. This, however, was a short-lived success, and Belisarius soon took over the whole of what had been Roman Mauretania. Theudis was murdered in 548, as was his successor Theudigisel a year later, when Agila seized the throne. His reign was marked by a series of revolts, the most important of which was that of Athanagild in 551. It was the conflict between Agila and Athanagild that offered Justinian the opportunity to intervene [12.3: Collins 2004].

Theudis

Agila and Athanagild

Unfortunately, our sources are in direct conflict over what happened. According to Jordanes, Agila appealed to Justinian for help, whereas according to the seventh-century bishop and historian Isidore of Seville, it was Athanagild who turned to the Byzantine emperor. As a result, Justinian, who already controlled Mauretania, sent an army in 552. In the conflict that followed Agila was killed, and in 554 Athanagild became sole ruler of the Visigoths, while the Byzantines took advantage of the situation to establish their own province of Spania in southern Spain [12.3: Wood 2010].

Byzantine Spania

Just as the narrative of Justinian's intervention in Spain is unclear, so too is the extent of the territory that he seized [11.1: Ripoll Lopez 2001; 12.3: Wood 2010]. Historians are agreed that Cartagena and Malaga were under Byzantine control, as probably were Medina Sidonia and Sagontia (Castillo de Gigonza) in the province of Cadiz. It used to be thought that Justinian also controlled Cordoba and the Valley of the Guadalquivir, but this is no longer accepted. In other words, the Byzantine province of Spania seems to have been essentially a coastal enclave, which limited Visigothic access to the sea and in particular protected the Balearic Islands and North Africa, which Justinian had taken from the Vandals.

Justinian's Reconquest is perhaps best seen as a series of oppor- *Justinian's legacy* tunistic moves taken against the Vandals, the Ostrogoths and the Visigoths when they were weakened by internal crises. The rhetoric of a renewed Empire seems to have followed the successes in Africa and Italy. In the event, the reconquest destroyed more than it restored. The wars themselves, particularly those in Italy, were destructive, and, because of the onslaught of the plague, they coincided with a period of environmental disaster. Rather than restore the Empire, Justinian left the old Roman West in a state of greater decay than it had been in 530. What had, for a short while, been a functioning commonwealth was now a set of kingdoms that had little regard for the emperor in Byzantium.

13 The Environmental Crisis of the 530s

13.1 Environmental Problems

Late Antiquity was a period of environmental decline, which may well have lain behind many of the changes that took place in the course of the third to sixth centuries. What has been termed the Roman Climatic Optimum had ended around 150 AD. What followed was an age of generally cooler and drier weather, although there was considerable variation in the changes around the Mediterranean and thus in the impact on agriculture. It is, however, likely that overall there was a decline in economic productivity and also in the size of the population, which was always under threat from disease [3: HARPER 2011]. There would seem to have been a plague epidemic in the third century, although its scale and impact is questionable, but there was no major outbreak in the fourth and fifth centuries. Before 540, disease was not enough to cause major disruption, but it was enough to put additional stress on imperial resources, especially on the manpower needed to keep the army up to strength and on the tax-yield needed to pay the soldiers and the administration.

But the end of the Climate Optimum was only one element in *Seismic activity* the steady environmental decline of the Roman world. Comments on the changing climate are few and far between in our sources, no doubt because the changes were too long-term to be noticed on a year-by-year basis. Outbreaks of plague and earthquakes (which could, of course, help trigger plague) were much more apparent to contemporaries. Late Antiquity seems to have been a period of considerable seismic activity. Constantinople was hit by numerous earthquakes in the fifth and sixth centuries [12.9: Croke 2005]. One that destroyed the walls of the city in 447 very nearly left it exposed to the forces of Attila, but disease forced him to withdraw his army. In the eastern Mediterranean, a tsunami, which was surely related to seismic activity, is recorded for 541.

There is very much less evidence for seismic activity in the West, which is no doubt a reflection of the differing geological environments [9: Galladini/Ricci/Falcucci/Panzieri 2018]. But the authorities in the West were fully aware of earthquakes, and they took a keen interest in them. Thus, the *Ravenna Annals*, for which we have entries for 20 years, list two earthquakes, in 429 and 443. They are illustrated with a repeated image of a water god – a reference to Neptune as the supposed author of earthquakes [5.2: Bischoff/Koehler 1939]. The *Liber Pontificalis* and Agnellus' account of the bishops of Ravenna also note the occurrence of earthquakes. In the fifth century earthquakes are known to have hit Rome in 408 and 443, and a massive earthquake is known to have struck the city at some point between 484 and 508. An inscription at the Colosseum notes the generosity of Decius Marius Venantius Basilius in restoring buildings after earthquakes that had occurred between 443 and 484. A further earthquake is recorded for 618. In addition, major floods are recorded in Rome in 398, 411, 555, 570 and 589. This last flood destroyed the city's grain stores, which led to famine and an outbreak of plague, one of whose victims, in 590, was Pope Pelagius II [9: Squatriti 2010; Tsiamis/Poulakou-Rebelakou/Marketos 2013; Galli/Molin 2014]. The catastrophic impact of these floods on the city of Rome is visible in the remarkable excavations of the Crypta Balbi, the lower levels of what had been a theatre built by Balbus in the first century BC, which has shed extraordinary light on the state of part of Rome at the end of Antiquity and the start of the Middle Ages.

Natural disasters were, of course, a fact of life in Late Antiquity, but their frequency threatened a world that was already suffering from a downturn in the climate. Not surprisingly they prompted liturgical responses in the East [9: Croke 1981]. In the West, Mamertus of Vienne instituted a three-day liturgy in response to an earthquake that had shaken his city and destroyed some of its official buildings [14.1: Nathan 1998]. Public prayers had already been used by the Church in response to drought and to floods, but the Rogations instituted by Mamertus would become a model for one of the regular liturgical rituals of the ecclesiastical calendar.

13.2 The Volcanic Winters of 535/6 and 539/40 and the Coming of the Plague

Natural disasters were an ever-present threat to the delicate ecological balance of the Late-Antique World. But they were as nothing compared with the events of the late 530s and early 540s, which may have dealt a deathblow to the fragile sub-Roman world that had evolved in the second half of the fifth century [3: Harper 2011]. As yet, the precise chain of events is unclear; historians are dependent on the studies of scientists and historical geographers, whose findings are relatively recent and are constantly being updated. Essentially it appears that in 535/6 there was a major volcanic eruption, possibly in the Americas, Iceland, or somewhere in the modern Indonesian archipelago, and that such was the force of the eruption that the debris thrown into the atmosphere led to a year in which there was no summer. Extreme levels of acidic dust have   Volcanic eruptions been noted in deposits of this period in ice cores taken in Greenland and Antarctica, and tephra layers are now being detected in Britain and elsewhere. The weakness of the sun in 536 was recorded by Procopius. Gildas, writing in Britain, seems to refer to the same event [12.10: Woods 2010]. A second eruption, which had a similar meteorological impact, appears to have occurred four years later. In the British Isles the evidence of dendrochronology, the study of annual tree-growth, indicates that the weather remained unnaturally cool until the 550s [9: Baillie 1994; Gunn 2000; 12.10: Woods 2010]. An immediate result of the eruptions was crop failure, which in turn led to famine (which is recorded in the Irish Annals) and plague. Not only was the population hit by the absence of food, so too were animals, carrying the plague bacilli, forced to move out of their normal habitat and closer to human habitations. The result was a pandemic of what appears to have been a type of Bubonic plague and which is known as the Plague of Justinian [3: LITTLE 2007; 9: HARPER 2011].

Plague   In the Roman World the Plague was first recorded in 541, at the port of Pelusium on the Nile Delta, which is consonant with it having originated in East Asia. From there it moved to Palestine, Mesopotamia, and Asia Minor. It had reached Constantinople by early 542, where it may have killed half the population of 500,000; contemporary sources speak of 300,000 dead, although this figure is likely to be an exaggeration. If accepted, the mortality rate in Justinianic Constantinople would be comparable to that of the Black Death of the fourteenth century. Even if one does accept the figures for Constantinople, one should beware of assuming that all parts of the Mediterranean and of the post-Roman West suffered equally.

In the West our best written-evidence for the Plague is to be found in the writings of Gregory of Tours, who notes the arrival of the disease in 543. He recounts its spread to a number of cities, in particular Clermont, Trier and Reims, as well as to Narbonne, which was still in Visigothic hands [9: McCORMICK 2021]. Whether all cities in Gaul were equally affected is, however, unclear. Moreover, although Gregory of Tours claims that an outbreak of plague in 588 was caused by the arrival of a diseased ship from Spain, only a single marginal entry in the *Chronicle of Zaragoza* relating to 542/3 refers to an outbreak in the Spanish peninsula during the sixth century. Isidore does not mention it in his Chronicle, despite the fact that he discusses the nature of plague in other works. Nor does John of Biclaro refer to plague in Spain, even though he talks of its presence in Constantinople in the year 573. It has, however, been suggested that plague was a factor in the economic decline of the peninsula in the second half of the sixth century, but we have to wait until the Chronicle of 754 before we have clear documentary evidence of a major outbreak, which occurred in the reign of Egica (687–702) [9: KULIKOWSKI 2007]. It has also been noted that plague is referred to in a seventh-century Toledan homiliary. The plague seems to have reached Britain in 544, although the evidence is slight before the seventh and eighth centuries, when it certainly had a major impact [9: MADDICOTT 2007]. Its presence in Ireland is recorded in the Irish Annals for 576.

In fact, the recurrence of the Plague was just as important as its initial spread. Like the Black Death, once it was present in the landscape it was liable to break out again whenever the climatic conditions were most suitable (that is, in years when it is warm and wet, and usually in the late summer or autumn). The result was that the Plague was a regular feature from the late sixth century to the mid-eighth. Gregory of Tours records outbreaks in 543, 551, 571 and 588 [McCormick 2021]. There were recurrences throughout the seventh century. The pre-Carolingian period was beset with disease.

The scale of the impact of the Plague has, nevertheless, proved difficult to evaluate [3: Eisenberg/Mordechai 2019; Mordechai/Eisenberg et al. 2019]. Outbreaks of the disease are well recorded for certain specific places, but for others, even places for which we have evidence, there is no mention of plague. Uncertainty as to how widespread the plague was outside those places has allowed historians to minimise its impact and to see it as being confined to individual cities. That some cities and regions suffered very much less than others is perfectly likely, since that is also the case for plagues of the fourteenth century and of the early modern period. On the other hand, even though there seems to have been regional variation, archaeology is starting to suggest that the Justinianic Plague was widespread. Particularly important here has been the analysis of skeletons from early medieval cemeteries in Germany, and especially in Bavaria (Aschheim and Altenerding). So, too, the presence of black rats has been detected on non-urban archaeological sites. Evidence that the plague was present in rural areas, away from the main centres of communication and trade, which is where one would expect to find traces of the plague bacillus, suggests that over time a significant proportion of the early medieval West was affected. As yet, however, we have to acknowledge that the outbreaks of plague may have been regionally limited and spasmodic.

13.3 The Absence of Economic Revival

We have already noted the likely impact of the plague on Justinian's military projects. The campaign against the Vandals was the shortest and most effective of the emperor's wars, and it took place before the plague struck. During much of the period of the Gothic wars, Justinian also had to deal with a Persian threat, but his ability to raise and pay troops was certainly affected by the plague, and it is even possible that Shah Khosrau was encouraged to declare war by news of the difficulties experienced by the Byzantines – although, if this were the case, there is a question as to why Persia was not suffering from the same epidemic.

But it was not just military recruitment that suffered. High mortality would have affected the population at large, and, to judge by the evidence of Bavarian cemeteries, not just the urban population (although one should recognise that at present this evidence is exceptional). In other words, the plague is likely to have exacerbated, if not created, a general manpower crisis and a resulting decline in agricultural production and urban manufacturing.

Decline in Italy   This was surely a factor in the failure of any economic revival in Italy at the end of the Ostrogothic Wars. More than two decades of war had disrupted the economy of the Italian peninsula. The old aristocracy, who had dominated the landscape of imperial Italy, hardly survived the war, and certainly the wealth of those who remained had been destroyed, along with the economic value of their landed property. The additional mortality brought by the Plague may have rendered impossible any return to normality. There was simply not the manpower to restore the economy to the level that it had operated at even in the fifth century.

Gaul and Spain   It is possible that disruption elsewhere was not as extreme as it was in Italy. Certainly Gaul, Spain, and North Africa, which had suffered more than had Italy in the course of the fifth century, were not as badly damaged by war in the sixth. However, it is very clear from the narrative of Gregory of Tours that the impact of plague was considerable in a number of Merovingian cities [9: McCormick 2021]. Spain, at least away from the coast, may have been largely spared until the seventh century, but the late seventh-century laws may provide some evidence of a significant population decline: it has been suggested that the concern to hunt down runaway slaves in the Visigothic laws reflects the manpower shortage.

Britain and Ireland   In Britain, the evidence is equally fragmentary. Gildas recorded a period of unusual darkness which may have been the sunless summer of 535/6, which is also evidenced in the dendrochronological evidence from Ireland [9: Baillie 1994; Gunn 2000; 12.10: Woods 2010]. The Irish Annals also noted the subsequent famines. What is particularly problematic is the relationship between the plague and the expansion of Anglo-Saxon power. According to Gildas, the Britons still held the upper hand at the time he was writing, probably shortly after the sunless summer. When we next have significant evidence for Britain, the Saxons were dominant in most of England, except for parts of the West. It is not impossible that the Saxons were less affected by the plague than were their British enemies. Moors, Arabs and Turks seem to have been less affected than the majority of the Mediterranean population, although this might be explained by habitat and channels of communication rather than susceptibility to the disease. It is certainly possible that in the sixth century the disease was introduced into Britain along the sea-route that ran from the Mediterranean along the western coast of Spain to Ireland, Cornwall and Wales. By the late seventh century it was present among the Anglo-Saxons, to whom it may have been transmitted by a more easterly route.

Major problems of interpretation remain when one tries to integrate the history of the Plague into an overall narrative. No doubt further answers will come from the archaeologists and the scientists. It is, however, likely that the Justinianic Plague was a cause of significant decline and discontinuity in the late sixth century and throughout the seventh, and that it undermined the sub-Roman world that had emerged in the period between the end of the West Roman Empire and the Justinianic Wars. Ultimately it seems to have helped ensure that there could be no Justinianic restoration of the Roman World. But the effect of the Plague seems to have varied from region to region, and there is as yet no proof that the Justinianic Plague had as great an impact as did the Black Death.

14 The Successor States

14.1 Byzantium, Africa, and Italy after the Death of Justinian

The successor states had a new relationship with the Empire after the 530s. In the half century after 476, Western Europe had broken up into a group of regional states, most of which still paid lip-service to the emperor in Constantinople. In attacking Africa, Italy, and Spain, Justinian challenged this new political order [6: O'DON-NELL 2009]. While the conquered territory fell under the control of Constantinople, relations between the Empire and those successor states of the West that were not subject to Byzantium were also radically altered.

After 535 the old provinces of North Africa were subject to Constantinople, whereas before the Vandal conquest they had belonged

North Africa

to the Roman West. They would remain Byzantine down to the Arab expansion of the seventh century, but they were constantly under threat from the Berbers who lived on the southern fringes of the province.

Italy   For a brief period, the whole of the Italian peninsula was also a Byzantine province, and even after the arrival of the Lombards in 568 Ravenna, Rome, Naples and the far south of Italy continued to be subject to Constantinople, with Ravenna acting as the provincial capital and the seat of the Byzantine exarch, or governor. Despite its political subjugation to Byzantium, Rome was left largely to its own devices, which meant that the bishop – the title of pope had still not been established – had to take over political, social, and economic leadership in the city, which had been devastated by war and by the collapse of the local infrastructure [14.2: Richards 1979, 1980; Markus 1997; Neil 2015], although there is some evidence to suggest that the senate was of some importance into the sixth century [3: Salzman 2021]. Emperors did, however, intervene to ensure that papal doctrine was in line with that of Constantinople, most obviously over the issue of the Three Chapters, when Justinian condemned the writings of Theodoret, Theodore and Ibas to appease the moderate anti-Chalcedonians [14.3: Chazelle/Cubitt 2007; Price 2009].

The Lombards   The arrival of the Lombards led to the creation of a new state centred on the Po Valley, in particular on the cities of Pavia, Milan and Monza, and on the provinces of Friuli and Tuscany, with dependent duchies to the south in Spoleto and Benevento. The seizure of territory by the Lombards under the leadership of Alboin (d. 572) seems to have been unusually brutal [12.11: Christie 1995]. Our sources suggest that matters did not improve under his successor Cleph (572–4), while the ten-year interregnum that followed is thought to have been even worse for the indigenous population, and indeed for the neighbouring territories of the Frankish kingdom, which were raided in 574 and 575 [12.11: Dick 2005). According to Paul the Deacon, writing in the eighth century, even the dukes realised that the chaos of these years was not in their interests, not least because the Byzantines took advantage of the situation to reclaim territory. In 584/5 they agreed to restore the monarchy, under the leadership of Authari (584/5–90), who they also provided with

Authari   adequate resources to bring order to Lombard territory. Authari did bring some stability, introducing some aspects of Roman style to the kingship, as is apparent from the adoption of Roman titles and the importance of the royal palaces in Pavia and Milan, as well as Monza, which was set back slightly from the mosquito-infested Po Valley.

Relations between the Lombards and the Empire continued to be hostile, and there was frequent low-level military conflict between Pavia and Byzantine Ravenna. So too, the relations between the Lombards and the papacy were poor, for political and for religious reasons. Several Lombard kings clearly wished to take control of the city of Rome. For the popes, who often had to organise the defence of the city, the Lombards were a people to fear. But the threat was not just military: from the time of their arrival in Italy down to c. 680, the Lombards were more often than not Arian, although some individual rulers in that period were Catholic. From the point of view of the bishop of Rome the court of Pavia posed not only a political, but also a religious threat, which contributed to the image of them as the most wicked of all peoples, the *nefandissimus gens* [14.2: MARKUS 1997].

Yet despite the fears expressed by Gregory, relations between the papacy and the Lombard royal court in the period immediately after Authari's death were cordial. The king's successor, Agilulf, married Authari's widow, Theudelinda, who was the daughter of Garibald, duke of Merovingian Bavaria, and a Catholic. Not only was she on good terms with Gregory, who sent her several gifts which are still preserved in the cathedral treasury at Monza, but she also brought up her son, Adaloald, as a Catholic. He succeeded his father as king in 616 and ruled for ten years. Unfortunately, however, he lost the support of the Lombard nobility and was deposed, supposedly having gone insane. He was succeeded by his brother-in-law, Arioald, who was a staunch Arian, despite being married to Gundeperga, the Catholic daughter of Theodelinda.

Margin note: Arianism

Margin note: Relations with the papacy

14.2 Spain after Justinian

In Spain Justinian's intervention, and the formation of the Byzantine province of *Spania*, meant that relations between the Visigothic court and Constantinople were generally poor. Having secured the throne in 554, Athanagild attempted to win territory back from the Byzantines. His successor Leovigild succeeded in capturing Medina

Margin note: Leovigild and Reccared

Sidonia in the far south-west in 570. The Byzantines retaliated during the reign of Leovigild's son Reccared, which led to a new treaty demarcating the frontier. But later kings renewed their attacks on Byzantine *Spania*. By 624, the whole of the Byzantine province was in Visigothic hands, although the Balearics were still under the control of Constantinople [12.3: COLLINS 2004].

The Suevic kingdom   Leovigild and his son Reccared also put an end to the kingdom of the *Suevi* that had been established in the far north-west of Spain in 411 [2: THOMPSON 1982; 12.5: LÓPEZ QUIROGA/MARTÍNEZ TEJERA 2017; LÓPEZ QUIROGA 2018]. For the history of the Sueves down to the late 460s we have the remarkable testimony of bishop Hydatius [5.2: MUHLBERGER 1990; BURGESS 1993]. The image he gives of them, however, is extremely critical and stresses the barbarity of their annexation of the territory of Gallaecia. Certainly, the Sueves were almost constantly at war. And they showed no sign of wishing to integrate into the later Empire, unlike other barbarian groups. They displayed their independence, minting their own coins as early as 448. But this is also a mark of the extent to which they took Rome as a model.

Despite Hydatius' presentation of the *Suevi*, their king Rechiarius (448–58) converted to Catholicism, but the kingdom converted back to Arianism under pressure from the Visigothic king Theodoric II, who sent an Arian missionary, Ajax, in 466. By 561, however, when a Church council was held at Braga, they had adopted Catholicism once again, under the influence of the Pannonian Catholic Martin who became bishop of Braga in c. 550 and sur-
Martin of Braga   vived until 589. In its last years, before the Visigothic conquest, the Suevic kingdom of Gallaecia seems to have achieved a remarkable level of culture, to judge by the canons of the first two councils of Braga and the writings of bishop Martin as well as the architectural and archaeological evidence from Braga, Dumio and Polperra, which appears to indicate the existence of a culturally sophisticated centre of royal power. The evidence from excavations of the harbour area at Vigo suggests that the trade between the Mediterranean and the Suevic kingdom was considerable; presumably it was a nodal point in the maritime routes up to the British Isles [12.5: LÓPEZ QUIROGA 2018; LÓPEZ QUIROGA/MARTÍNEZ TEJERA 2017].

The kingdom of Gallaecia, however, was under constant threat from its more powerful southern neighbours, the Visigoths. To counter this, king Miro (570–83) attempted to ally with the Frankish king Guntram, and in 580 he also provided support for Hermenegild, the rebellious son of the Visigothic king Leovigild. On Miro's death, he was succeeded by his young son Eboric/Euric, who was deposed a year later by his stepfather, Audeca. At this point Leovigild intervened and incorporated the kingdom into his own Visigothic realm. There was a brief uprising in 590, led by *dux* Argimundus, before Reccared annexed the territory permanently [12.3: Barroso Cabrera/Morín de Pablos/Sánchez Ramos 2015].

Although the Visigoths themselves had been divided and had also been under threat from the Byzantines since the 540s, the last quarter of the century saw a remarkable change in their fortunes, in part because of the military successes of Athanagild and Leovigild, against the Byzantines, the Cantabrians, and finally against the Suevic kingdom of Gallaecia, but also because of the decision of the latter's son, Reccared, to abandon Arianism in favour of Catholicism.

Athanagild and Leovigild

After the death of Athanagild in 567, Liuva took over the kingship, which he divided with his brother Leovigild in 569 [2: Stroheker 1965]. On Liuva's death in 571/2, Leovigild took over the whole kingdom, raising his two sons Hermenegild and Reccared to being joint rulers. Ten years later, however, Hermenegild rebelled against his father. The prince had married a Frankish princess, Ingund, the Catholic daughter of the Merovingian Sigibert I and his Visigothic wife, Brunhild, who was the daughter of Athanagild. Hermenegild himself converted to Catholicism – the evidence is ambiguous as to whether his conversion antedated his rebellion or whether he converted when he was already in arms against his father, in order to secure additional support, perhaps from the Catholic Sueves. His conversion prompted his father to embark on a religious policy aimed at uniting Arians and Catholics [12.3: Collins 2004; Drews 2019]. In c. 581, Leovigild held a Church council that modified the doctrine of the Trinity, thus facilitating the conversion of Catholics to Arianism. Many Catholics, it would seem, were happy to accept this modified Arianism. Those who did not, and there was staunch opposition from some quarters, in particular from the bishop of Mérida, whose actions are recorded in the *Vitas Patrum Emeretensium*, found themselves the victims of persecution.

The revolt of Hermenegild

Hermenegild's rebellion failed in 584, when he surrendered. His widow and her son escaped to Byzantine territory. Following his victory, Leovigild turned against and conquered the Suevic king-

Reccared and the Third Council of Toledo

dom. Hermenegild was killed in 586, and Leovigild died shortly thereafter, leaving Reccared as his sole heir. The new king seems to have understood the sense of his father's desire to unite the kingdom's religious factions, but instead of promoting Arianism he opted to convert to Catholicism. A year after succeeding to the throne he himself became a Catholic, and in 589, with the help of Bishop Leander of Seville, he summoned the Third Council of Toledo, when Catholicism became the official doctrine of the kingdom. Fifteen more councils of the Visigothic Church would be held in the royal city of Toledo before the fall of the kingdom in 711. They would become a distinguishing feature of the Visigothic State.

14.3 The Merovingians and Byzantium

Frankish history followed a rather different path from that of Vandal North Africa, Ostrogothic Italy, or Visigothic Spain. There was no Byzantine invasion that affected the course of politics. Rather, Merovingian history, at a political level at least, was dominated by internal matters. The division of Francia between the four sons of Clovis set a precedent for the future. Theuderic, the eldest, ruled the north-eastern part of the Frankish kingdom from Reims; when he died in 533/4, he left one son, Theudebert, who ruled until 548, in turn leaving a son, Theudebald, who died in 555. As Theudebald had no heir, the kingdom of Reims passed back into the hands of Clovis' remaining sons, Childebert and Chlothar. Chlodomer, whose capital had been Orléans, had already died in battle against the Burgundians in 524. Like his brother Childebert, who ruled from Paris until 558, he left no son. As a result, the whole kingdom was reunited under Chlothar I, who had initially ruled from Soissons [12.7: Ewig 1976a; Wood 1994].

The Teilreiche

When Chlothar died in 561, the pattern was repeated. He left four sons: Charibert took over the kingdom of Paris, Guntram that of Orléans, Sigibert that of Reims, and Chilperic that of Soissons. Charibert died in 567, and his territory was divided between his surviving brothers. The relations between these three was almost consistently poor. There was an initial problem in that Chilperic had a different mother from his siblings. There was also a further complication in that his queen, the Spanish princess Galswinth who died in suspicious circumstances in 568, was the sister of Sigibert's queen

Brunhild. As a result, there was a period of intermittent civil war, down to the murder of Sigibert in 575. He was succeeded by his son Childebert II, who ruled until 595, when his kingdom was divided between his sons Theudebert II and Theuderic II. Chilperic, meanwhile, was murdered in 584, leaving a young son (whose parentage was questioned), Chlothar (II). Guntram, who had acted as guardian for the children of his brothers at various moments, died in 592. His territory was taken over by Theudebert II and Theuderic II, but disagreements between them led to civil war in 612, as a result of which Theudebert and his children were killed, but Theuderic died in 613, leaving the way open for Chlothar to reunite the kingdom once again.

The history of the sixth-century Merovingian kingdom tends to be told largely in terms of its internal politics. But it should still be considered within the larger history of the post-Roman World [12.1: Fischer/Wood 2014; 3: Esders/Fox/Hen/Sarti 2019; Esders/Hen/Lucas/Rotman 2019]. Francia did not suffer at the hands of Byzantine invaders. Instead, Justinian arranged an alliance with the Frankish king Theudebert against the Ostrogoths in 535, but in 538, after Witigis had ceded Provence to him, the Merovingian intervened on the side of the Goths, despite the fact that Frankish possession of Provence was reaffirmed by Constantinople. In 539, Theudebert of Austrasia again sent an army into Italy, but it had to withdraw following an outbreak of disease. Already before his death in 547 he was in disagreement with Justinian over regnal titles: the emperor and the Merovingian king each thought that the other was claiming too broad an area of authority. And it was not just titles that were claimed by Theudebert and his son Theudebald [12.7: Collins 1983]. The Austrasian Franks had conquered the province of Venetia by 552. It is not clear when they lost control of the region [11.1: Wood 1998].

Sigibert I sent another army into Italy at some point between the Lombard arrival 568 and his own death in 575. He was certainly involved in diplomatic negotiations with the Byzantines, probably in 568/9, when Radegund, the ex-wife of an earlier Frankish king, Chlothar I, negotiated the acquisition of a piece of the True Cross for her nunnery in Poitiers. We know of further attempts by the Byzantine emperor Maurice to involve Sigibert's son Childebert in his Lombard campaigns in 584, 585 and 590, despite the opposition of Childebert's uncle, Guntram king of Burgundy. In addition we

Contact with Byzantium

Theudebert I

Sigibert I and Childebert II

have evidence that the dowager queen Brunhild lobbied the Byzantine court, after her daughter, Ingund, the widow of Hermenegild, and her grandson Athanagild fell into their hands [11.1: GILLETT 2010).

The Franks, therefore, having been treated as imperial agents in the days of the emperor Anastasius and Clovis, emerged as potential allies of Constantinople, whose rights to large areas of Gaul were confirmed by Justinian's grant of Provence. Subsequently, and especially in the days of Theudebert, they asserted their status as near equals with policies of their own. At the same time, the Byzantines attempted to intervene in Frankish politics in the 570s and 580s by backing the claims of Gundovald, a supposed son of Chlothar II, as a rightful Merovingian king [11.1: GOFFART 1957, 12.7: GOFFART 2012; BACHRACH 1994].

14.4 The Roman Ideology of the Successor States

While the successor states increasingly asserted their independence, they retained a political ideology and an administrative infrastructure that was ultimately Roman, even if it was a pale reflection of what had been before. Continuity of political ideology and organisational practice is clearest for Italy under Theodoric, which is not surprising, for he effectively took over what had been the central imperial bureaucracy, as can be seen in the *Variae* of Cassiodorus. Other rulers inherited the administrative offices of West Roman provinces, together with the authority of military officials, although they also imitated the style of imperial rulership. The Burgundian Gibichungs, for instance, ruled primarily as *magistri militum* and *patricii*, and, as we have seen, their legislation was firmly based on Roman practice.

Imitiatio imperii   When the Merovingian Theudebert I set out his claims of rule in his letter to Justinian, he was essentially mimicking the rhetoric of Roman emperors. He also minted gold coins in his own name, as Theodoric the Ostrogoth had done. This was to claim what had been an imperial prerogative [12.7: COLLINS 1983]. Theudebert's son Theudebald held public horse races, as did Chilperic I, in imitation of the rituals of the Roman Hippodrome. The fullest expression of imperial-style ideology at the Merovingian court is to be found in the poetry of Venantius Fortunatus, and especially in his epithalamium to mark the marriage of Sigibert I to the Spanish princess Brunhild [13: REYDELLET 1981]. It is also likely that the very structure of the court, with offices such as the *maior palatii,* looked back to Roman models.

Although the evidence for late sixth-century Spain is less good than that for Merovingian Francia, we can see the same use of imperial political ideology. Leovigild, for instance, adopted the Roman title of Flavius as well as Roman-style insignia (including a throne and royal clothing), and like the Ostrogoths and Franks he issued gold coins [12.3: HILLGARTH 1966; 12.1: WOLFRAM 1967]. In addition, he revived the imperial tradition of naming urban foundations after members of his family; thus, Reccopolis was named after his son Reccared. Visigothic kings, like other rulers in most other kingdoms, issued law codes which were clearly modelled on the law-giving practices of the emperors. Not only did Alaric II base his *Breviary* of 506 on the *Codex Theodosianus,* but later rulers, especially Leovigild in the sixth century, and Chindaswinth, Recceswinth, Wamba, Erwig, and Egica in the seventh, issued revised compilations of Visigothic law. At the same time, the Councils of Toledo frequently echoed and, in some cases, modified secular law. The Visigoths were not alone in doing this; the Merovingian kings and the Frankish Church did the same [12.7: HALFOND 2009; 14.2: HALFOND 2019], but the secular and canon law of the Visigoths is the most substantial legal achievement of the post-Roman period. *(margin: Roman ideology in Spain)*

Lombard kings also issued laws from the middle of the seventh century onwards. The first to do so was Rothari, who issued a law book in 643, and further legislation was promulgated by Liutprand and his successors in the eighth century. The Lombard laws include more non-Roman tradition than do the laws of the Visigoths or of the Burgundians. But they were also keen to cultivate a style of rulership that was ultimately Roman. Like Leovigild, Rothari took the title of Flavius. A surviving piece of metal-work known as the visor of Agilulf (or Val di Nievole visor) presents an image of the ruler that is modelled on imperial iconography, such as one can see on the *Missorium* of Theodosius. Some doubts have been raised as to whether the name of the ruler which is cut into the metal is original, but it is unquestionable that we are dealing with a royal image that is based on a Roman prototype [12.11: LA ROCCA/GASPARRI 2010]. *(margin: Roman ideology among the Lombards)*

The ideology of the imperial past was very much less apparent in Britain, but it seems to have been present [12.10: FAFINSKI 2021]. *(margin: Roman ideology in Britain)*

Some of the most intriguing evidence comes from a later date: from genealogies of Welsh rulers who traced their origins back to the usurping fourth-century emperor Magnus Maximus. How early such claims circulated is hard to guess. But among the evidence we have for Anglo-Saxon rulers of the sixth and seventh centuries there are hints that Roman ideology and insignia mattered. Again, the issuing of law is important. The first Anglo-Saxon ruler to issue a code was Æthelberht (d. 616), who Bede says issued laws in the Roman manner (*more Romanorum*). Since his surviving code is in Old English and its provisions are unlike almost anything in Roman law, the general notion of issuing law and of gathering it into a collection, just as emperors had done, must have been what was regarded as Roman [6: WORMALD 1977]. Archaeology also points to Roman influence on the iconography of rulership. Among the objects found in Mound One at Sutton Hoo there is a large whetstone, which seems to have been inspired by symbols of office that are represented in the imperial *Notitia Dignitatum*.

In Britain it is unlikely that many elements of the Roman system of administration survived. In some successor states, however, there was considerable survival. The most obvious case is Ostrogothic Italy, where the *Variae* of Cassiodorus show the continuation of much of late imperial government. Elsewhere, too, institutions survived, although it was not the institutions of the old central government, but rather of provinces. But these institutions became increasingly irrelevant. The chief reason for this was the collapse of the Roman tax system.

Taxation   Since Constantine, the Romans had used a bipartite system of taxes, which involved taxation of land and individuals. In the course of the fifth and sixth centuries this system broke down, not so much as a result of any deliberate policy, but rather because the disruption of the period made tax assessment and the gathering of taxes difficult. Kings did try to reassert their rights to taxation in the sixth century [12.1: GOFFART 1974, 2008; CASTELLANOS 2003; 11: WICKHAM 1984, 3: WICKHAM 2005]. We hear of Merovingian kings drawing up lists of individuals liable for taxation, which surely indicates that they were attempting to levy the *capitatio*, even though some cities, and especially some ecclesiastical institutions, claimed exemption. Other taxes, especially those connected with transport and the transfer of goods, unquestionably continued though the sixth and seventh centuries. Ultimately, however, the income from taxation was not a major concern for the post-Roman rulers, for the simple reason that they no longer needed to pay for a standing army, which had been the chief raison d'être of Roman taxation.

14.5 The *civitas* and the Merovingian *Teilreiche*

Royal courts of the sub-Roman period looked back to the courts of emperors and of provincial governors. But the central building block of the new continental states was the *civitas*, the city with its dependent territory, which was often synonymous with the new episcopal see rather than the old province or secular diocese (which did, however, survive in Lombard Italy, most notably in the duchies of Spoleto and Benevento). The *civitas* had been at the heart of Roman local government, and it continued to be central to the kingdoms of the continental West – although again this is not the case in Britain, where earlier tribal divisions seem to have re-emerged.

The *comes civitatis* was usually the senior regional administrative figure [11: Claude 1964; Murray 1986; 6: Barnwell 1992], although there were higher, primarily military commands (*duces, patricii*) in Gaul, Spain, and the Lombard world [11: Zerjadtke 2019]. In Italy, the position equivalent to the *comes* was that of the *grafio* – a term which was also used in Francia. The origins of the office of *comes civitatis* are obscure. There is one reference to such an official in a city under imperial control in the fifth century, but it would appear that the notion that each city should have a *comes* only became fixed in the post-Roman period: the clearest expression that there should be a *comes* (or indeed two, one Roman and one Burgundian) in each town is stated in the *Liber Constitutionum* of the Gibichung Sigismund.

The *comes civitatis* was clearly the key figure in regional administration at the start of the sixth century. This situation changed, however, over the course of the following century. Bishops increasingly took over aspects of the role of the *comites*. This was not a simple development. It clearly depended a great deal on individuals [14.2: Durliat 1979]. Active and charismatic bishops intervened in local politics, but they could be challenged by energetic secular officials – as can be seen in the personal history of Gregory of Tours. From early in the seventh century, however, the bishop was usually the dominant figure in his *civitas* [14.2: Scheibelreiter 1983; Diefenbach

Urban administration

2013] The role of the *comes*, and of other secular officials such as the decurions, fade from the record. On occasion we do find evidence of the continuance of specific aspects of Roman administration. For instance, there are occasional references to the *gesta municipalia*, the official records of legal transactions in a city, but their continuing use seems to have been rare and confined to a small number of centres [11: BARBIER 2014].

The *Teilreiche*   The *civitas* was the basic division of sub-Roman kingdoms, and most especially of the Merovingian *Teilreiche*, the territorial divisions made to provide all the acknowledged sons of a Merovingian king with a kingdom [12.7: EWIG 1976a, 1976b]. When Clovis died in 511, his kingdom was divided between his four sons, probably because this was a way of ensuring that the sons of the dead king's widow could inherit part of his authority. These children (Chlodomer, Childebert I, and Chlothar I) were all juveniles, but Clovis had an older son, Theuderic I, who was already an active and successful warrior. The division of kingdoms does not seem to have been traditional before this date, but it was soon established as a tradition [6: WOOD 1977]. This made for an extremely complicated political history in Francia, but accidents of death determined that the whole of the Merovingian kingdom came into the hands of Clovis' longest-living son, Chlothar I, between 558 and his death in 561, when once again it was divided between four.

As we have seen, the Merovingian *Teilreiche* varied in number, according to the number of rulers at any one moment. Initially, the kingdoms seem to have been identified by their capital cities (Paris, Orleans, Soissons, and Reims), but from these four, three major units emerged: Neustria, Austrasia and Burgundy, with their respective capitals at Paris or Rouen, Reims or Metz, and Orléans. And for much of the seventh century the kingdoms of Neustria and Burgundy were combined. The boundaries of these kingdoms were determined by those of the *civitates* that belonged to them. However, Aquitaine, the whole of south-west Francia (to a large extent the territory south of the Loire and west of the Rhône, leaving aside the Visigothic enclave of *Septimania*), was treated separately. *Civitates* in this region were assigned to one of the northerly power centres. Behind the divisions there seems to have been some attempt to create strategic blocs, as well as an attempt to provide each Merovingian with a fair share of the overall kingdom.

14.6 The Erosion of the Distinction Between Military and Civilian

Apart from the fact that the successor states were mere fragments of the old Roman West, the main distinction between the structure of the post-Roman kingdoms and the Empire out of which they had been carved lay in the declining reliance on taxation, which was possible because there was no standing army to be paid, despite the fact that the royal office had partially developed out of Roman military command.

The Roman Empire depended on the existence of a large standing army. As we have already noted, the number of soldiers is debated. John Lydus, writing in the mid sixth century, talks of 389,704 soldiers and 45,562 sailors in the days of Diocletian; a slightly earlier author, Zosimus, refers to 581,000 troops involved in the civil wars of 312. A figure of between 400,000 and 600,000 men for the Late Roman army is generally accepted by modern historians [4.2: Tomlin 1988; 4.3: Southern/Dixon 1996; 3: Wood 2018]. From the early fourth century the soldiers were divided into frontier troops (*limitanei*) [4.2: Isaac 1988] and forces that were moved to where they were needed (*comitatenses*). The cost of the army was covered by taxation, above all by a tax on land; indeed, it was the major expenditure of the Empire.

The Roman army

The armies of the successor states, by contrast, were very different. In place of a standing army, there was a system of military obligation, which meant that landowners could be required to serve on campaigns, or to supply soldiers [12.1: Bachrach 1972; Halsall 2003; Goffart 2008]. The exact mechanism for summoning troops in the sixth and seventh centuries is unclear, but able-bodied males could be called upon to fight. This, however, did not mean an escalation in military activity. Although the successor states were thoroughly militarised and did not have an obvious division between soldier and civilian, the sub-Roman West of the seventh century was remarkably free from large-scale military conflict (though not from minor skirmishing).

The armies of the successor states

The shift from a standing army to an army of obligation is not easy to trace, and there was certainly an extensive period of overlap. For instance, Jordanes in his description of the imperial forces at the Battle of the Catalaunian Plains talks of one Roman squadron, the *Olybriones*, who were presumably still supported by the state, whilst the majority of fighters were barbarians following their leaders, who were presumably obliged to be present. That the state was finding it difficult to pay its troops, however, is apparent from two *Novellae* of Valentinian III [11: WICKHAM 1984]. The inability to collect tax because of the disruption caused by civil war and the passage of the barbarians and their settlement caused major difficulties when it came to the remuneration of troops. Some soldiers, particularly the followers of *magistri militum* like Ricimer or Odoacer, must still have been paid in kind, in coin, or in accommodation and the necessities of life, and in some cases payment may have continued beyond 476. An anecdote in the *Vita Severini* (20) by Eugippius, talking of the province of Noricum apparently in the years immediately after the deposition of Romulus Augustulus, relates how the frontier forces disbanded when their pay failed to reach them [2: THOMPSON 1982].

Retainers and *buccellarii*   At the same time, personal bands of retainers were also becoming increasingly normal in the later Empire. Roman generals themselves started employing forces known as *buccellarii* ('biscuit eaters') [4.1: SOUTHERN/DIXON 1996]. The word, which was Greek in origin, is attested in the *Codex Euricianus* (supposedly the laws of the Visigothic king Euric), and Gregory of Tours talks of a *buccellarius* of Aetius. Meanwhile, Roman aristocrats started to create their own military following, especially when the *Lex Iulia de vi publica* was overridden to allow self-defence against the barbarian threat [12.1: LENSKI 2009]. We find aristocrats organising the defence of their estates in the course of the invasion of Spain by the Vandals, Alans and Sueves, and we also see Ecdicius, the brother-in-law of Sidonius Apollinaris, creating his own private army to save Clermont from the Visigoths in 471/4. The lifting of the ban on the bearing of arms and the emergence of private armies essentially blurred the distinction between soldier and civilian, which had been a central feature of Roman society. As for the barbarians settled within the Empire from 376 onwards, it is likely that they had always carried arms, regardless of whether the *Lex Iulia* was officially in force or not. There is said to have been an attempt to disarm the *Tervingi* as they crossed the Danube, but it was clearly unsuccessful.

Weapon burials   The presence of armed men throughout the fifth-century West, and in all the successor states, is also attested in the existence of weapon burials. Men, and occasionally women and children, were sometimes buried with weapons. Not every male, however, was buried with weapons, and the range of arms placed in the grave would seem to provide an indication of the status of the dead man or woman – or perhaps the status that those organising the burial wished to confer on them [9: JAMES 1989; HÄRKE 2014]. In addition, we should not conclude from the presence of armed men everywhere, or from the fact that this was essentially a militaristic society, that it was more bellicose than the Roman Empire had been. Although there was plenty of low-grade conflict throughout the seventh century, after the establishment of the Lombards in Italy there were comparatively few major wars until the arrival of the forces of Islam first in North Africa in the 640s and the Berber invasion of Spain in 711 [3: WOOD 2018]. There were no conflicts in the early medieval West on the scale of the Roman campaigns against Persia or indeed against the Goths or Huns.

The relatively low level of military activity after the initial establishment of the successor states perhaps explains the fact that churches were able to claim exemption from the provision of soldiers for the royal armies. Whether or not they really were granted such exemptions is unclear, but kings did not push their demands for troops from ecclesiastical institutions until it became necessary in the eighth century, when Church land suddenly became the subject of intense interest and kings in both Francia and England insisted on the supply of men to carry out military obligations.

Ecclesiastical exemptions from military obligations

The ending of a military system paid for by public taxation and the substitution of a system of military obligation radically altered the structure of the state. Taxation, which was central to the structure of the Roman Empire, was no longer a major concern, even though kings regretted the loss of revenue. Of course, some taxes, most especially tolls on the transport of goods, continued. But the taxation of land, which had been a central feature of imperial government, dwindled, and in its place, landowners were faced with a different type of levy: the fulfilment of obligations to the State.

15 The Triumph of the Church

15.1 The Failure of the Empire

Between the restoration of the Empire by Diocletian and the death of Justinian, the Roman World had changed irrevocably. In place of the Western Empire there were now a group of successor states, and however much they tried to preserve the structures of the past, in almost every way they were an impoverished version of what had previously existed. The great bureaucratic edifice of the Later Empire had more or less vanished, and above all the collection of taxes, and therefore the maintenance of a standing army, had gone. In purely fiscal terms the breakdown of the Roman administration had led to the ending of the supply of gold *solidi* which had enriched the aristocracy, as it had also paid the wages of bureaucrats and soldiers [3: Banaji 2001, 2016]. At the same time, the late Roman aristocracy, which had held estates across the Mediterranean, had been reduced to regional landowners, and with it the literary, artistic and architectural culture they had supported had declined. So too, the trans-regional economy that they had supported had weakened and, in some places, collapsed. The result was an impoverished world. At the level of the ordinary population, however, there was perhaps less change.

The immediate cause of the break-up of the Western Empire had been the arrival of the barbarians, but given their numbers, they ought to have been a manageable problem. That the Empire failed to cope with them was the result of conflict within the ruling classes and a failure at the heart of government to understand the seriousness of the situation. The regular appearance of usurpers and the almost constant rivalry between generals, and also between the military and the court, meant that the barbarian problem was inadequately addressed. But there were also problems that were outside the control of the imperial court. Decline from the climatic optimum of the early Empire had meant slow environmental decay, while the famine years of the late 530s and the plague that began in the 540s and affected Europe and the Mediterranean through to the eighth century caused disruption, perhaps major disruption, from the mid-sixth century onwards.

15.2 The Formation of 'the Church'

Against this general tale of decline there is one major success story: the rise of the Church in its numerous and varied forms. Most obviously there is the Christianisation of the Roman Empire [3: Brown 1996, 2003]. Although the spread of Christianity was already well under way by the end of the third century, it was the fourth century that saw its adoption as the state religion and its acceptance by the majority of the population, although even as late as the Altar of Victory controversy, in 384, Symmachus could claim that most of the senatorial aristocracy was still pagan. In hagiographical accounts we still hear of individual pagans in the fifth and even in the sixth century. But for the most part, the Roman World, at least in the West, was Christianised in the century and a half following Constantine's conversion.

The result of this process is usually categorised for simplicity's sake as 'The Church'. Certainly, the term works well as a shorthand, although it is important to remember that this should not imply uniformity, even in the Latin West. Despite the growing authority of the bishops of Rome and the first glimmerings of a notion of papal primacy, this was still a world of what has been termed 'Microchristendoms' [7: BROWN 1996, 3: BROWN 2013]. Each region had its own particular traditions: they had different foundation stories, which were often legendary; they had different liturgies, different church calendars (which determined the date on which Easter was celebrated), and different theological traditions – some of which would have been regarded as heretical in other regions – thus some Pelagian ideas survived longer in Ireland than elsewhere. The structures of dioceses also varied. The balance between each bishop and his city varied. And the monastic life of each diocese varied considerably, not least because there was as yet nothing like a generally accepted monastic rule: the triumph of the Rule of St Benedict dates to the ninth century at the earliest. It is, therefore, important to bear in mind the fact that the Church was not a monolithic institution, even if one makes use of the term.

Clearly the new religion answered the spiritual needs of the population in general. Its basic doctrine of salvation was welcome, and individuals and communities could find solace in its rituals. It also attracted the intelligentsia. Although historians of Rome's fall tend to say little about the details of Christian doctrine, one should not underestimate the intellectual quality of Christian thought in the fourth, fifth and sixth centuries. This was the high point of the Patristic Age: in the East it could boast figures of the stature of Athanasius, Basil of Caesarea, Gregory Nazianzus and John Chrysostom, and in the West Hilary of Poitiers, Ambrose, Augustine, and Gregory the Great, with Jerome moving between the two halves of the Empire. Nor should one forget the amount of energy expended

Microchristendoms

The Patristic Age

in religious debate, in the meetings of the Ecumenical Councils, and in the definition of orthodoxy [3: PELIKAN 1987]. In the fifth century, this is an almost exact counterpoint to the failing of the Western Empire: the Council of Chalcedon took place at precisely the moment that Attila invaded Gaul.

The decline of secular culture   By the mid sixth century intellectual life was almost entirely religious. A tradition of non-religious letter-writing continued especially in Gaul. So did the composition of secular poetry, down to the time of Corippus in the second half of the sixth century. The last major work of secular philosophy was Boethius' *Consolation of Philosophy* of 524. Some secular history writing continued, most notably that of Procopius and Agathias, but thereafter histories, and especially chronicles, which set events within the scheme of Christian salvation, were usually religious works or at least written by clerics.

The Church thus came to dominate religious, intellectual and cultural life, and while political and military activity continued, it also came to influence an ever-increasing portion of social life, especially among the aristocracy. A career in the Church became a possible substitute for a career in the service of the Empire, as the opportunities for holding secular office dried up and the *cursus honorum* ceased to be available to aspiring aristocrats. One should be wary of making too much of this: we know of the family origins of only a small proportion of senior ecclesiastics in the fifth, sixth and seventh centuries, and by no means all of those whose origins are known came from an aristocratic background [14.2: PATZOLD 2010, 2014]. We should probably conclude that the majority of bishops were not aristocrats – although they did monopolise episcopal office in a handful of significant dioceses. Some notable families readily encouraged some of their members to follow a career in the Church. And churches certainly offered plenty of opportunities.

15.3 Quantifying the Change

The numbers of ecclesiastics (including bishops, priests, deacons, monks and nuns) around the year 600 was probably equivalent to the number of men in the army three centuries earlier, at least as a proportion of the overall population. By the end of the seventh century the Church may well have held approximately a third of the land of Western Europe [2: Wood 2013]. The same was not true of the Byzantine World, but perhaps only because of the expansion of Islam from the 630s onwards. In other words, while the story of Late Antiquity is the story of the failure of the West Roman Empire, the *Völkerwanderung* and the establishment of the successor states, it is equally the story of the rise of Western Christendom. The precise stages of this development are difficult to chart, but certain points are clear enough.

Any calculation of the numbers of ecclesiastics depends on the number of dioceses, and then on what can only be estimates of the number of clergy in each diocese, as of the number of monasteries and of their inmates. There would appear to have been around 1,800 dioceses in the Later Roman Empire, of which around 250 were in Italy, 500 in Africa, 130 in Francia, and at least 80 in Spain [8: Wood 2018]. Most of these were established in the course of the fourth century. For the numbers of clerics in each diocese we have to turn to sixth- and seventh-century evidence, and it is probably fair to assume that there had been a steady increase in numbers throughout the period. In some individual dioceses in the late sixth century, we can be sure that there were at least 90 priests and deacons, but the provision of clergy elsewhere was clearly lower. With regard to monks and nuns there were huge regional differences. Already in fourth-century Egypt and Palestine there were large numbers of them, with some communities housing as many as 200 persons [7: Wipszycka 2018]. In the fifth century we can trace a major expansion of numbers of monks in Constantinople, where 265 monasteries have been listed for the period before 850, some of them again holding 300 monks [14.5: Hatlie 2007]. In the West, there were few monastic communities in the fourth and early fifth centuries, but numbers increased throughout the fifth and sixth centuries, and there was a massive escalation in the seventh. Our best evidence comes from Francia where around 220 monasteries have been identified as being in existence by 600, rising to 550 by the early eighth century [14.5: Atsma 1976]. Again, some of these communities housed monks in their hundreds.

A separate issue was the endowment of ecclesiastical institutions [9: Wood 2013, 2022]. Here it is important to distinguish between gifts of treasure and gifts of land. Both were donated by Constantine. We know most about his gifts to the Church of Rome, although the lists provided by the *Liber Pontificalis* are highly

Numbers of clergy

Monastic numbers

Ecclesiastical wealth

questionable [5.5: Wood 2022]. For the rest of the fourth and fifth centuries we hear most about gifts of treasure, as for instance in the case of the donations of Melania and Pinian, who sold off their property to endow churches. Our knowledge of gifts of land becomes much stronger in the sixth century. In Italy, the charter evidence begins with the Ravenna papyri, but the largest body of evidence comes from Francia, where the earliest authentic charters date from around 600. Recently some sixth-century Spanish charters have also attracted attention. The lack of earlier charters may, of course, be no more than a question of survival. However, the histories of the dioceses of Auxerre, Le Mans and Reims, which were written down in the Carolingian period, suggest that the acquisition of land by the Church became important in the sixth century, not earlier. All we can say is that the surviving evidence suggests that initial endowments tended to be of treasure and that from the sixth century onwards gifts of property came increasingly to predominate. It is important to note the distinction between treasure and property: a landowner who donated treasure to a church could make good his loss in subsequent years; by contrast, the donation of land implied a more permanent alienation – although we know that the family of a donor often maintained an interest in the church that had been endowed. From the Church's point of view, of course, a gift of land meant steadier future income, which would have been all the more welcome as there was an increase in the number of churchmen who had to be provided for. In its need for endowment, and especially for a regular supply of income for the clergy, the Christian Church differed radically from the pagan religions of the High Empire.

The Church's awareness of the need for endowment is apparent in the reactions to the distribution of wealth by Melania and Pinian. On the one hand we hear of churches avidly hoping for gifts from the couple, but on the other hand we have Augustine's comments on the need for more sustained endowment. And by the end of the fifth century, we hear of the expectation that a bishop would donate his property to his church on his death – and to judge by some of the episcopal wills of the seventh century (notably that of Bertram of Le Mans), this could have meant the conveyance of sizeable amounts of property to the Church. We also have the so-called *Quadripartum*, the papal ruling on how bishops should allocate the oblations of the faithful: the funds should be divided into four, to be

The *Quadripartum* and church expenditure

split evenly between the bishop himself, the clergy, the poor, and the Church fabric. Admittedly, this ruling was not universally accepted; in Spain there was a three-fold division of income, and no mention was made of the poor [9: Wood 2022]. Despite the differences, the fact of Church landholding and wealth is incontrovertible.

15.4 A New Mentality

The amount of wealth given to the Church or rather to churches, especially in the sixth century, is important, but so too are the reasons for the donations. Piety and reverence for the Christian God were, of course, present from the start. Increasingly, however, we find that donors were concerned for their own souls [3: Brown 2012; 7: Brown 2015, 2016]. A gift to the Church was intended to facilitate the passage of the soul to heaven. This becomes explicit in so-called *pro anima* donations, where the wording of a charter explains that the gift is made for the wellbeing of the donor's soul [14.3: Angenendt 2008; 14.1: Magnani 2009].

Pro anima donations

Concern for the soul points to general anxiety, and here the calls to repentance that are to be found in sermons from the late fourth century onwards, and in the literature written in response to the arrival of the barbarians, the poetry of Prosper, Orientius and Paulinus, and the diatribes of Salvian, are relevant. According to the moralists of the fifth century the sins of the Roman population were prompting expressions of divine displeasure, and not just the barbarian invasions, but also the intermittent natural disasters. From the late 530s onwards there was downright cataclysm, first with famine and then with the plague.

Fears that the Empire was about to come to an end were already present in the early fifth century: a Sibylline oracle had implied that Rome would last for twelve centuries. Since the city had been founded in 753 BC, or thereabouts, depending on which calculation one used, its end could be expected in the mid fifth century. At the same time, there were Christians who believed that the Last Days of the world had come. Orthodox theologians knew that the time of the end of the world was unknown, as Christ himself had said, but there were many, including Gregory the Great, who believed that the Last Days were imminent, even if the time of their

The Last Days

coming was unknown [14.2: Markus 1997]. The sense of the Last Days may well have encouraged pious donation and entry into the religious life. Some donors may even have seen in their donations a means of protecting their property in an uncertain world: monasteries which remained under the control of their founding families provided places where unmarried members of the family might retire in safety.

Columbanus   At the end of the sixth century, the Irish monk Columbanus moved from Bangor in Ireland first to Brittany, then to the Vosges, and finally, having spent a short while in Bregenz, to Italy. Monasticism in the decades immediately prior to Columbanus' arrival on the continent is often portrayed as being in a state of decay, and as requiring a new injection of religious enthusiasm. In fact, monasticism in Francia was not in a state of decline [14.5: Wood 1981, 2018]. Nor was the monasticism promoted by Columbanus of a new kind: Irish monasticism was a direct development from the continental monasticism of the late fourth and early fifth centuries. In certain respects, it was, as a result, old fashioned. Poor communication meant that the Irish still accepted some doctrines that had been condemned, and they were following an out-dated method of calculating the date of Easter.

But Columbanus did promote monasticism in an area of Francia – the Vosges – that had been relatively untouched by asceticism. He also attracted benefactors from families that seem not to have been involved in monasticism previously [12.7: Fox 2014]. In addition, he promoted religious practices that, although not entirely new, had previously been relatively insignificant on the continent; above all the use of handbooks of penance (which had been developed within the British Church). The result was an energised monastic movement, and more generally an emphasis on penance and personal salvation, in the east of Francia, which came to influence the Merovingian kingdom as a whole and subsequently the Lombard kingdom. As a result, although almost all the elements in Columbanian monasticism were already in existence in Gaul before the arrival of the Irish saint, the impact of his foundations pointed forwards to the massive expansion of monasticism in the seventh century [2: Prinz 1965].

15.5 The Church and Social Crisis

Quite apart from personal salvation there were other prosaic reasons for supporting the Church. Although the barbarian migrations had not caused disruption everywhere, there were areas where they caused a temporary breakdown in social organisation, and on occasion it was churchmen, and most especially bishops, who stepped in to help organise the defence of their cities and to arrange for the ransom of captives [14.2: KLINGSHIRN 1983; 7: ALLEN/NEIL 2013; SALZMAN 2019, 9: SALZMAN 2017]. Since they were expected to provide for the poor, and for widows and orphans, this was a simple extension of their pastoral duty [7: LIZZI TESTA 1989; 9: NERI 1998]. That the population of a diocese looked to religion during periods of personal or general crisis is reflected in the evidence for the cult of the saints [7: BROWN 1981; HOWARD-JOHNSTON/HAYWARD 1999; WIŚNIEWSKI 2019]. Moreover, bishops were endowed with a certain amount of judicial power, by both canon and secular law [7: HUMFRESS 2011; SIRKS 2013].

This picture of ecclesiastical take-over can, however, be pushed too far. Some bishops exercised considerable authority over their dioceses. Historians have talked of *Bischofsherrschaft*, but not every bishop dominated his city. In some cities secular authority continued to be considerable [14.2: HEINZELMANN 1976; KAISER 1981; JUSSEN 1995; DIEFENBACH 2013]. Sometimes the *comes civitatis* remained more influential than the bishop. Precise circumstances (not least the influence of individual families) were important [14.2: DURLIAT 1979]. Yet, even if the exercise of *Bischofsherrschaft* was not universal, the emergence of the Church as a dominant force in the Mediterranean and European West was at least as significant a development as the *Völkerwanderung* and the Fall of the Western Empire.

A military empire had come to an end, and a world of kingdoms dominated by the Church had taken its place. The coming of the barbarians had played a role in the collapse of the Roman West, but it was failure of the emperor, his generals, and senatorial society to cope with them, because they were too wrapped up in their own conflicts and concerns, that allowed the establishment of the successor states. Not that the barbarians had wished to destroy Rome or its civilisation, and indeed the successor states preserved a great deal of classical culture and ideology. But above all they had taken on the new religion of the Roman state. The period from 300 to 600 essentially witnessed the foundations of Western Christendom.

II State of the Art

1 Introduction: Late Antiquity

The history of Europe from the late third to the late sixth centuries has been interpreted in various radically different ways, which, in part, are determined by the transitional nature of the period, which covers the end of Antiquity and the start of the Middle Ages. As a result it has been discussed by classicists and by medievalists. The classicists have not surprisingly concentrated on questions relating to the destruction of the Roman Empire in the West and on the survival of classical civilisation. The medievalists, by contrast, have tended to look rather more at the role played by the barbarians and at the changes that would lead to what has been termed feudal society. A distinct, but equally significant tradition has concerned itself primarily with the Eastern Mediterranean and the development of Byzantium. In addition, religious historians have studied the period with regard to the institution of the Church, the rise of Christendom, and to the religious and cultural importance of the Patristic period. All these approaches have their origins at least as far back as the eighteenth and nineteenth centuries.

More recently, and particularly since the 1970s, there has been a move towards seeing the period in question as an entity in its own right, and not simply as the tail end of the Classical World or the beginning of the Middle Ages. There are now several journals that are devoted solely to the Late Antique period, which is also the subject of entire encyclopaedias, as well as receiving substantial coverage in other handbooks, such as *Der Neue Pauly*, and the *Lexikon des Mittelalters*, and, for religious matters, the *Lexikon für Theologie und Kirche* and the *Biographisch-bibliographisches Kirchenlexikon*. In addition the period has been the focus of major collaborative research projects, and of the volumes they have produced. Publishers have dedicated complete series to Late Antiquity. Especially valuable for the student of the period are the prosopographies of the leading figures of the Empire and of the Church [1.2: JONES/MARTINDALE/MORRIS 1971–92; MANDOUZE 1982; PIETRI/PIETRI/DESMULIEZ 1999–2000; DESTEPHEN 2008; PIETRI/HEIJMANS 2013].

Equally important has been the extraordinary increase in the number of high-quality editions and translations of early medieval

Editions of sources

https://doi.org/10.1515/9783110352658-002

texts, often with very considerable commentary. Already before the 1970s there were major collections of source material, most obviously in the *Monumenta Germaniae Historica*, the *Corpus Scriptorum Ecclesiasticorum Latinorum*, and the *Corpus Christianorum* of patristic texts, many of them dating from Late Antiquity. For individual works there is the collection in *Sources Chrétiennes*, founded in 1942, many of the volumes of which boast valuable introductions as well as translations. Among other series of translations, the Liverpool *Translated Texts for Historians*, the first volume of which appeared in 1988, is dedicated exclusively to works of the Late Antique and Early Medieval periods. An extensive list of the source material is included in chapter 15 of the bibliography.

The world of
Late Antiquity

The book that was most influential in leading to the establishment of Late Antiquity as a period in its own right was Peter Brown's *The World of Late Antiquity* of 1971, but the term *Spätantike* had already been used by the art-historian Alois Riegl in his *Spätrömische Kunstindustrie* of 1901, while *antiquité tardive* was an expression current in France after 1945 [1.2: BROWN 1971; MARROU 1977; CAMERON 1998; GIARDINA 1999; CARRIÉ 1999; LIEBESCHUETZ 2001, 2004; VERA/CRACCO RUGGINI/FENTRESS et al. 2002; JAMES 2008; SCHULZ 2008; MEIER 2012, 2017; SARDELLA 2013; HUMPHRIES 2017]. Although the concept of Late Antiquity is now well established (even if there is disagreement over its extent [1.2: LIZZI TESTA 2017; for Britain: COLLINS/GERRARD 2004]), and despite the explosion of writing on the period since 1971, it is useful to look back to earlier discussions of the fourth, fifth and sixth centuries – many of them examined by Alexander DEMANDT in *Der Fall Roms*, published initially in 1984, when he estimated that 210 reasons had been put forward to explain the Fall of Rome, a figure which had already increased by the time the book was reissued in 2014 [1.2: DEMANDT 1984]. Eighteenth-, nineteenth-, and early twentieth-century readings of the end of Antiquity and the start of the Middle Ages form the bedrock of much recent discussion, and an examination of the changing trends in approach explains why certain lines of study are dominant in the field and why some have fallen out of fashion.

2 The Development of Historiography on the Early Middle Ages before 1970

All historical writing is conditioned by its context, but sometimes the context of writing is more important than it is at others. In the case of the transitional period between Antiquity and the Middle Ages, the context in which it was and is being discussed has often been of extreme significance in determining the concerns of historians and the interpretations that they have put forward [2: Wood 2013]. Political developments from the eighteenth century onwards have both influenced and been influenced by the study of the period.

The relationship between modern politics and the writing of the history of the third to seventh centuries has sometimes been so close that one cannot understand the interpretations of the period from the end of the third to the start of the seventh century without paying some attention to the contexts in which they emerged. The historiography of the Late Roman and early Medieval periods has been the subject of research in recent years [2: Wood 2013]. There has been notable work examining the historiography of the Roman Empire, which stretches into the fourth and fifth centuries. But equally important for certain aspects of the period, and especially for the historiography of the *Völkerwanderung*, has been the growing study of the history of archaeological research, which only emerged as a discipline in the nineteenth century [2: Fehr 2010; 12.7: Effros 2003]. Also of significance for understanding the interpretation of the *Völkerwanderung* has been the study of its representation in maps [2: Goffart 2003; 11.2: Goffart 2006], which have unquestionably propagated an overly simplistic idea of the movement of the barbarian peoples.

The later Roman Empire was seen as providing models for understanding Bourbon autocracy under the *ancien régime* in eighteenth-century France, and it was later regarded as a cautionary tale for imperial Britain [2: Hingley 2000]. The role played by the barbarians was a significant point of debate in the emergence of the new states of a united Germany, where the study of the history of Germanic tribes was an aspect of the creation of a new national identity [2: Wiwjorra 2006]. In nineteenth-century France and Italy, by contrast, the barbarians were seen by some as unwelcome in-

Scholarship under the ancien régime

Nineteenth- and twentieth-century debates

comers who oppressed an older Roman or Gallic population [2: GRACEFFA 2009]. Complementary to this line of argument was the question of Roman survival, especially in Italy. In the twentieth century the role of the *Germanen* was an important element in Nazi ideology, while the reaction against the 1939–45 war was a key influence on the historiography of the following twenty-five years.

Spanish historiography

It is significant that for a long time Spain was the one major country in western Europe that had little to offer on the history of the fall of the Empire and the coming of the barbarians. For Spanish scholars the important moment in the early Middle Ages was not the Fall of Rome, or even the arrival of the Visigoths, but rather the acceptance of Catholicism by Reccared in 587, and, even more significant, the defeat of the Visigoths by the Berbers in 711 [among the few exceptions is Orlandis Rivera, see 2: CASTILLO LOZANO 2014–15]. It was only in the 1990s that a major tradition of scholarship on the fourth to sixth centuries emerged in the Iberian peninsula.

The abbé Du Bos and his critics

Initially the interpretation of the fourth and fifth centuries was dominated by French readings of the Fall of Rome that emerged from two opposed political positions at the turn of the eighteenth century [2: WOOD 2013]. On the one hand, for the abbé Du Bos, there was a steady evolution of Roman institutions into those of the early medieval world, especially in France, and on the other there was a view exemplified by Boulainvilliers, Montesquieu and Mably, that the Roman Empire was a corrupt autocracy which could be compared with the absolutist rule of the Bourbons of their time. In his *opus magnum The Decline and Fall of the Roman Empire* (1776–

Gibbon

1789), the British historian Edward Gibbon, in part, reacted to this view, as was made clear in the numerous volumes that were produced at the bicentenaries first of the publication of the first volume of his work and then that of his death (1794) [2: BOWERSOCK/CLIVE/ GRAUBARD 1977; MCKITTERICK/QUINAULT 1996]. For the critics of the Bourbons, the incoming barbarians, who in their view overthrew the Empire, were the torchbearers of liberty. This was a view which naturally attracted the revolutionaries of 1789. Not all French scholars of the time, however, accepted this reading of the barbarians; they were seen not only as the champions of liberty, but also as conquerors who oppressed the native population. This second interpre-

Thierry

tation was the view of Augustin Thierry (1795–1856), who applied it to the Franks, and it was taken up in Italy by Alessandro Manzoni

Manzoni

(1785–1873) with regard to the Lombards.

In Germany the barbarians, naturally, were not seen as oppressors. Rather, during the first half of the nineteenth century they were drawn on by idealists who wished to see the creation of a German Reich. Already in 1726/37, J. J. Maskov had written about the migration of peoples, but in the aftermath of the Napoleonic intervention in Germany, the history of those peoples became central to the self-definition of the region. It was at this moment, in 1819, that the Freiherr vom Stein founded the *Gesellschaft für Deutschlands ältere Geschichtskunde*, which soon embarked on the publication of the *Monumenta Germaniae Historica* – and the history of the editing of original texts is a fundamental aspect of the development of the study of the early Middle Ages [2: Bresslau 1921; Fuhrmann 1996]. At the same time, Eichhorn embarked on the study of Germanic law [2: Eichhorn 1808]. The Germanic languages also attracted a great deal of attention, most obviously from Jacob Grimm [2: Wyss 1979]. The study of the *Völkerwanderungszeit* and of the culture of the barbarians was thus intimately related to the development of a new German self-consciousness.

Maskov and migration

MGH

The editions of the *Monumenta* included Roman as well as 'Germanic' texts, and the greatest of the editors was, indeed the great classical historian Theodor Mommsen (1817–1903). Although he never published a late-antique volume in his *Römische Geschichte* (the *Römische Kaisergeschichte* was published from his notes in 1992 by Barbara and Alexander Demandt [2: Mommsen 1992]), his editions of fourth-, fifth-, and sixth-century authors have been basic to all later study of the period, as has his edition of the Theodosian Code. It should, however, be noted that these editions are not above criticism. Mommsen sought to establish *Ur-Texts* of the works he was editing. In the case of the *Chronica Minora*, in particular, this led him to underestimate the value for the historian in understanding the differences between manuscript readings. What they often indicate is not more or less accurate copying, but rather scribal input and a different set of authorial concerns. A recent trend has been to pay much more attention to the manuscripts themselves.

Mommsen

It was for different reasons, however, that Mommsen was criticised by some of his scholarly contemporaries. Above all, Numa Denis Fustel de Coulanges (1830–1889) took exception to his work, more because of Mommsen's hostility to French foreign policy in Italy in the 1860s than because of his scholarly ability, although Fustel attacked the notion that German historical methodology was su-

Fustel de Coulanges

perior to that of the French [2: Hᴀʀᴛᴏɢ 2001]. Despite his patriotic bias, the Frenchman was himself one of the great interpreters of the late- and post-Roman periods. For him, the barbarians changed little in the Roman World; rather, in his interpretation, there was a steady social evolution, from Roman patronage to feudalism, while he saw the Germanic kings of the fifth and sixth centuries as would-be Roman functionaries. In this he was effectively restating the view that had already been set out by Du Bos in the 1730s, in a work that had initially been well received, but had subsequently been seen as a defence of the Bourbon monarchy and had thus fallen out of favour. The context in which Fustel was arguing for continuity was, of course, radically different from that in which Du Bos had been writing 150 years earlier. After the defeat of the French at the hands of Bismarck in 1871, the downgrading of the significance of the Germans inevitably had new political overtones.

Seeck

Although Mommsen never published his own account of the Later Empire, his contemporary Otto Sᴇᴇᴄᴋ provided a somewhat gloomy account in his *Untergang des Römischen Reiches* (1895–1920). For him, the Empire had essentially degenerated, as a result of mongrelisation following Caracalla's extension of citizenship to all, a view that had its origins in the Social-Darwinism of the nineteenth century. Like Mommsen, however, Sᴇᴇᴄᴋ was also a distinguished editor of late antique texts – in particular the *Notitia Dignitatum*, the list of offices compiled at the end of the fourth and the beginning of the fifth century [2: Sᴇᴇᴄᴋ 1966], which constitutes one of our major sources for the organisation of the Empire.

Dahn

Despite their political hostility, Fustel and Mommsen had more in common with each other intellectually than either of them had with the Germanists of their time. Of these perhaps the most impressive was Felix Dᴀʜɴ. Although he is best known for his fanciful novel on the fate of Ostrogothic Italy, *Ein Kampf um Rom*, Dahn published remarkable studies of sources, and above all in his eleven-volume *Könige der Germanen* he provided a model of Constitutional History (*Verfassungsgeschichte*) [2: Dᴀʜɴ 1861–1910]. He clearly wanted to be able to present the barbarian kings of the fifth, sixth and seventh centuries as true *Germanen*, but he consistently found that the evidence was lacking. To his credit, he stuck tightly to the evidence, putting the interpretation that he would have liked to advance into his literary works [2: Wᴏᴏᴅ 2012].

The nationalism of Fustel, Mommsen and Dahn was insignificant by comparison with that of the next generation. One of the most extreme examples is to be found in the work of Gustaf Kossinna (1858–1931), who combined linguistics and archaeology to determine the original homeland of the *Germanen*. Before 1914, this could be seen as justifying the Kaiser's expansionist policies. After 1918, Kossinna deployed his archaeological interpretations to argue against the Treaty of Versailles and to demand the return of land (above all in the east) that he regarded as quintessentially German [2: Kossinna 1911, 1919].

Kossinna

Kossinna was by no means the only scholar to use early medieval history to argue for a redrawing of the boundaries of Europe. Another was the cultural historian Karl Lamprecht (1856–1915), who understood the modern territory of Belgium to be German [2: Wood 2013]. This surprised many of his Belgian contemporaries, among them his friend Henri Pirenne (1862–1935) from whom he had even commissioned a history of Belgium. Although he was initially an enthusiast for German scholarship, Pirenne's interpretation of the barbarian invasions was much closer to that of Fustel. In the aftermath of the 1914–18 war, he elaborated a view of the fourth to seventh centuries in which the Germanic barbarians had little impact on the Roman World, which in his view was really destroyed by the coming of Islam and the consequent break-up of the unity of the Mediterranean.

Lamprecht and Pirenne

Pirenne, like Gibbon, is a historian who has attracted a very considerable amount of scholarly interest [2: Pirenne 1937; Havighurst 1958; Violante 1997; Hodges/Whitehouse 1983; Delogu 1998]. His thesis is all the more eye-catching because it has been reduced to a single aphorism – 'without Mahommed Charlemagne would never have existed'. Although he died before publishing *Mahomet et Charlemagne*, which only appeared in 1937, two years after his death, the basic idea was set out in a number of articles published in the 1920s. In many ways it provides a narrative account that runs parallel to the work of Fustel and also to that of Pirenne's own contemporary, the great Austrian historian Alfons Dopsch (1868–1953), who stressed steady development, rather than catastrophe, in his presentation of the socio-economic history of Late Antiquity [2: Dopsch 1918–20].

Mahomet et charlemagne

Dopsch

There were others, including the French historian Ferdinand Lot (1866–1952), who saw the barbarians in a rather less peaceful

Lot light [2: Lot 1935]. Equally important, there were a number of historians and archaeologists in Germany who were pursuing the sorts of views that had been expressed by Kossinna and Lamprecht, and they were supported by the foundation of several major research institutes that were largely devoted to studying the Germanic past in the Rhineland and eastern France [2: Arnold 1990; Härke 2000; Junker 1998; Maischberger 2002]. Among the historians were Franz

Steinbach and Petri Steinbach (1895–1964) and Franz Petri (1903–1993). Working in Italy was the archaeologist Siegfried Fuchs (1903–1978) [2: Fröhlich 2008]. The extent to which archaeology was contaminated by Nazism in the 1930s, and indeed the use made of archaeology by the Third Reich, has become a major subject of research and debate [2: Arnold 1990; Härke 2000]. Equally committed to the Nazi cause were a num-

MGH Leges ber of editors of Germanic laws, most importantly Franz Beyerle (1885–1977) and Karl Eckhardt (1901–1979).

Of course, German study of the Roman Empire did not come to an end entirely [2: Marchand 1996], but the scholars involved were belittled as *Römlingers*. The most important German-language study of the Later Empire in this period was the first volume of Ernst Stein's *Geschichte des spätrömischen Reiches*, which was published in Vienna in 1928; the second volume, however, only appeared in

Stein French in 1949 [2: Stein 1928, 1949]. The shift of language, and of place of publication, reflects the problems that Stein faced as a Jew and his displacement from Berlin to Belgium, France, Switzerland, and finally back to Belgium.

Seen against the close association of the study of the Germanic barbarians and Nazi ideology, it is scarcely surprising that the post-Roman period fell out of favour as an area of research in much of western Europe after 1945. Among the few German scholars to con-

Ewig tinue to work on the Merovingian period was Eugen Ewig, who had personally helped to ensure the preservation of the archives of Metz in 1945 and was appointed the first director of the *Deutsches Historisches Institut* in Paris in 1958. Ewig's books and articles are almost all very tightly focussed on specific aspects of the Merovingian world – its political geography and its ecclesiastical institutions; they are the basis of all modern study of the early Frankish kingdom [2: Ewig 1976–2009]. Equally focussed are the works of K. F.

Stroheker Stroheker [2: Stroheker 1948], whose analysis of the senatorial aristocracy of Gaul remains fundamental, as do his readings of Euric and Leovigild [2: Stroheker 1937, 1939].

However, several major German-language works that were much broader in approach appeared in the 1960s. Reinhard WENSKUS' *Stammesbildung und Verfassung* is a remarkable reconsideration of the nature of the barbarian peoples of the late antique period, and it was one that avoided many of the difficulties caused by the Nazi appropriation of the *Germanen* by seeing tribes as groups defined not by blood, but by tradition, and especially by core traditions (*Traditionskern*) propagated by the leading families [2: WENSKUS 1961]. Friedrich PRINZ's *Frühes Mönchtum im Frankenreich*, published in 1965 (and revised in 1988), provided an exceptional account of the spread of monasticism in the Merovingian World [2: PRINZ 1965]. One short book that is surprisingly little remembered is Franz Georg MAIER's study of change in the Mediterranean World, which was published in 1968 [2: MAIER 1968]. The Czech historian František GRAUS combined Marxism and the methodology of the French *Annales* School to explore the relationship between religion and society through a study of Merovingian hagiography in his *Volk, Herrscher und Heiliger* [2: GRAUS 1965].

In England, the medievalist Michael WALLACE-HADRILL was almost a lone voice in studying the barbarians [2: WALLACE-HADRILL 1952; id. 12.1; 1971]. Like his contemporaries he was deeply affected by the events of 1939–45, but it prompted him to search for traces of what he called 'nobility of the mind' in the post-Roman centuries. Equally important, he was among the first to turn to anthropology to develop an understanding of the early-medieval feud. Among his contemporaries, the most important of those to consider the barbarians was the ancient historian Edward THOMPSON who approached the period as a Marxist and a Romanist, writing initially about Ammianus Marcellinus before turning to Attila and then to the Goths [2: THOMPSON 1947, 1948, 1966, 1982].

The one region where the barbarians were a key focus of attention in the post-war period was Italy, where Mussolini had championed Rome rather than Goths or Lombards. As a result, the subject of the barbarians was not contaminated by the experience of Fascism or war. This allowed the foundation of the *Centro di Studi sull'Alto Medioevo* in Spoleto in 1952. The proceedings of the annual conferences held at the Centro have ever since been a staple of the diet of early medievalists. The 1950s and 60s, above all, witnessed a golden age of writing on the Lombards, dominated by Gian Piero Bognetti. There was, of course, some significant Italian scholarship

Wenskus and the Traditionskern

Prinz

Graus

Wallace-Hadrill

Thompson

Italy

Spoleto

that concentrated on Late Rome rather than the barbarians. Above all Santo MAZZARINO, who had already published on Stilicho in 1942, presented a series of historiographical studies in *La fine del mondo antico* in 1959, and he would return to the age of Constantine two decades later. As a Marxist, for him it was decadence that was at the heart of the Fall of Rome [2: MAZZARINO 1942, 1959, 1974–1980].

Mazzarino

French scholarship

Studies of the barbarians from the post-war period in the French-speaking world are not numerous, but they include some important works. Above all there was Christian COURTOIS' study of the Vandals [2: COURTOIS 1955]. But all too often interpretation of the Germanic invaders of the fourth and fifth centuries was influenced by the experience of the presence of the armies of the Third Reich. Famously, André PIGANIOL announced that the Roman Empire had been assassinated by the barbarians [2: PIGANIOL 1947]. Despite this pessimistic assessment there was notable work on the Latin writing of the fourth and fifth centuries – including that of Pierre COURCELLE, most obviously in his study of the *Histoire littéraire des grandes invasions* [2: COURCELLE 1948], but also by André LOYEN in his studies of Sidonius Apollinaris, whose works he also edited [2: LOYEN 1942, 1943]. Later in date is the work of the Swiss scholar François PASCHOUD, *Roma Aeterna*, a study of 'Roman patriotism' in the period of the invasions, which remains of value [2: PASCHOUD 1967].

Perhaps the most enduring work on the Later Empire, however, was published in England: the monumental study by A. H. M. JONES which appeared in 1964 and provided a detailed account of practically all aspects of the Empire's history from 284–602 [2: JONES 1964; GWYNN 2008]. This was unquestionably a milestone in the study of the Later Empire, but there was already a notable tradition of Anglophone writing on the period. For a narrative, J. B. Bury's two studies published in 1889 and 1923 were (and still are) extraordinarily reliable, but as a thematic analysis of the Empire Jones' work became the standard point of departure. More controversial, but also seminal, was Mikhail ROSTOVTZEFF's study originally issued in 1926, but reissued in a revised form in 1957. Perhaps as a result of the author's own early experiences in Russia, this emphasised the rigidity of the Later Roman State [2: ROSTOVTZEFF 1926]. Equally critical of the internal weaknesses of Rome, but stressing above all the issue of social inequality, was F. W. WALBANK's *The Decline of the Roman Empire in the West*, a Marxist reading which saw the collapse as

Jones

Bury

Rostovtzeff

Walbank

coming already in the third century [republished as 2: WALBANK 1969].

Like the Romanist study of the late imperial period, the writing of ecclesiastical history had avoided political contamination in the two decades before 1945. One of the best-received books of the 1930s, Christopher DAWSON's *The Making of Europe* [2: DAWSON 1932] continued to be popular in the 1950s and beyond. Dawson accepted that the barbarians had destroyed Rome, but he went on to argue that Europe was saved by the Church. In DAWSON's view, although civilisation on the continent collapsed, it was revived by monks from Ireland, and subsequently from England. This was, in fact, not a new argument. It had been put forward in the 1840s by Frédéric OZANAM and by Charles Forbes René de MONTALEMBERT, who saw the insular monastic movement as providing the salvation of Europe – just as they hoped that the revival of Catholicism in contemporary Ireland would kick start a movement of reform in the continental Church of their own day [2: OZANAM 1845, 1849; MONTALEMBERT 1860– 77].

Dawson

More important than DAWSON for the emergence of Late Antique studies was the work of ecclesiastical historians, above all Henri-Irenée MARROU. MARROU published a major study entitled *Saint Augustin et la fin de la culture antique* in 1938 [2: MARROU 1938]. It offered a remarkably bleak assessment of late Roman culture, even of one of the greatest of the Church Fathers. This was a decadent and sterile world, drained of vitality by the traditions of Late Roman education, on which MARROU had also written [2: MARROU 1948]. In 1949, however, MARROU revisited his work and published a *Retractatio* in which he reversed his previous opinion. What he had observed as decadence he now saw as an emergent new culture. This was an observation that was key to the development of the understanding of Late Antiquity as a period in its own right.

Marrou

MARROU's observation was most dramatically taken up and transformed in Peter BROWN's *The World of Late Antiquity* in 1971 [1.2: BROWN 1971, see also the debate 'The World of Late Antiquity revisited' in *Symbolae Osloenses* 72 (1997); 2: ROUSSEAU/PAPOUTSAKIS 2009; KREINER/REIMITZ 2016]. Brown presented the period from Marcus Aurelius to Mahommed as a single unit. In doing so he prioritised religion and culture, with the result that the Germanic barbarians are of secondary importance. Not everyone has adopted the same priorities, but the publication of *The World of Late Antiquity* effectively

Brown

marks the starting point for much subsequent study of the late and post-Roman centuries.

3 General Assessments of the Late Antique Period from 1970 to the Present

Brown's *The World of Late Antiquity* set out the case for treating the period from the third to the sixth century as a vibrant time of cultural and religious innovation, centred on the continuing importance of the Mediterranean. It also looked eastwards, towards Sasanian Persia, and ultimately towards early Islam. As Brown himself later noted, the book pays little attention to the West. This was an issue that he addressed subsequently in *The Rise of Western Christendom* [3: Brown 1996], which added the world of Gregory of Tours, and then, when dealing with the seventh and eighth centuries, the influence of the Irish and the Anglo-Saxons. Subsequently, Brown returned to many of the same themes, most notably in *Through the Eye of a Needle: Wealth, the Fall of Rome, and the Making of Christianity in the West, 350–550 AD* [3: Brown 2012]. Although the title of this last book suggests concern with economic history, the focus is on the spiritual economy, that is, with religious *mentalités* rather than production and distribution.

Marks   Equally concerned with the socio-religious history of the period is Robert Markus' study of *The End of Ancient Christianity*, which examines the shift in religious culture between the early fourth century and the age of Gregory the Great, placing particular stress on the cult of the martyrs, notions of sacred time and space, and the rise of monasticism [3: Markus 1990]. Rather more concerned with the Christian ideology of the Empire, and responding directly to Gibbon's religious reading of the Fall of Rome, is Jaroslav Pelikan's Pelikan *The Excellent Empire* [3: Pelikan 1987]. Gibbon also provides a point of departure for Ian Wood's *The Transformation of the Roman West*, which sees the rise of the Church in terms of the numbers of its dioceses, clergy and monks, and of its endowments [3: Wood 2018] More recently he has examined the same developments in the light of the concept of the Temple Society [3: 2022], which is also the subject of a fascicule of Early Medieval Europe published in 2021.

Brown's interpretation of the period privileges socio-religious and cultural issues, but others have emphasised different aspects of the late antique period, although more usually defining it as the Later Roman Empire or the Early Middle Ages. In addition to the detailed coverage of the Later Roman Empire by A. H. M. Jones [2: 1964], there are the last three volumes of the *Cambridge Ancient History*, which between them cover the period between 193 and 600 AD [3: Bowman/Cameron/Garnsey 2005; Cameron/Garnsey 1998; Cameron/Ward-Perkins/Whitby 2000], and also a number of books dedicated to the fourth, fifth and sixth centuries in a series covering the entirety of Roman history. Among the most valuable are two volumes by Averil Cameron, which together cover the period from 284 to 600 [3: Cameron 1993, 1993a], as well as three volumes of the *Edinburgh History of Ancient Rome* [3: Ando 2012; Harries 2012; Lee 2012]. A collection edited by Simon Swain gathers together studies of numerous aspects of the change from the Early to the Late Roman Empire [10: Swain/Edwards 2004]. There is also a great deal to be learnt from historical atlases, including that produced by Tim Cornell [3: Cornell/Matthews 1982]. For an overview of the archaeology one can turn to Neil Christie's study of the *Fall of the West Roman Empire* [3: 2011], and to Simon Esmonde Cleary's consideration of the Roman West from 200–500 [3: 2013]. For the archaeology of late-antique Spain there is a volume edited by Javier Martínez Jiménez, Isaac Sastre de Diego and Carlos Tejerizo García [3: 2018].

The period has been presented primarily in terms of the internal political divisions of the Empire and of its fall in the West by a number of recent scholars, including Christine Delaplace [3: 2015] and Henning Börm [3: 2018] – and this is an interpretation which also underlies recent studies of civil war in the fourth and fifth centuries [3: Wardman 1984; Omissi 2018] and of the so-called *Generalissimos* of the later Empire [3: O'Flynn 1983]. James O'Donnell – himself a notable Church historian [3: O'Donnell 1985] – has likewise placed the blame for the Fall of Rome firmly at the door of the Romans, insisting that the barbarian incomers did not destroy the Empire but rather that it was the choices made above all by Justinian that were the ultimate cause of the breakdown [3: O'Donnell 2009]. Michael Kulikowski's *The Tragedy of Empire* [3: 2019] also emphasises the failure of Rome itself.

Division within the Empire

Others, by contrast, have insisted on the role played by the Germanic barbarians. For Peter Heather, it was the pressure put on the

The barbarians

Germanic peoples by the Hunnic steppe nomads that overwhelmed the Empire [3: HEATHER 2005, 2009]. Even more dramatic in pointing the finger of blame at the barbarians is Bryan WARD-PERKINS' account of the Fall of Rome: their destruction was such that he labelled it 'the End of Civilization' [3: WARD-PERKINS 2005]. Equally concerned with the barbarians, but offering a more complex reading of their relationship with the Empire before and after the migrations is Herwig WOLFRAM's *Das Reich und die Germanen. Zwischen Antike und Mittelalter* [3: WOLFRAM 1990]. It appeared in a significantly revised version as *Das Römerreich und seine Germanen*, which includes a substantial new introductory section dealing with historiographical and conceptual issues [3: WOLFRAM 2018]. A collection of articles dealing with the relations between Rome and the barbarians is edited by Evangelos CHRYSOS and Andreas SCHWARCZ [3: 1989]. Another nuanced assessment of the significance of the *Völkerwanderung*, which carefully balances archaeology and military history within a broader historical narrative, is to be found in Guy HALSALL's study of the *Barbarian Migrations and the Roman West* [3: 2007].

The Mediterranean and the Roman economy

While the failure of the western Empire and the settlement of the barbarians undoubtedly had an impact on the economy of the region, the socio-economic history of the period has concentrated on rather different issues. For several of these studies the Mediterranean is a central factor – as it is for BROWN. Behind almost all of them lies the influence of Fernand BRAUDEL's *La méditerranée et le monde méditerranéen à l'époque de Philippe II*, the first volume of which provides an overview of the historical importance of the region's geography. First published in 1949, it attracted a good deal more interest among medievalists after its translation into English [3: BRAUDEL 1949]. In 2000, Peregrine HORDEN and Nicholas PURCELL reaffirmed the centrality of the Mediterranean, but they modified the description offered by Braudel, placing a good deal more stress on variety, in a work spanning three millennia from 1500 BC to 1500 AD [3: HORDEN/PURCELL 2000]. The Mediterranean is also a central feature of Michael McCormick's *Origins of the European Economy* [3: 2001].

Land and production

Less concerned with the Mediterranean itself, but nevertheless with an eye on all the regions that border it, is Chris WICKHAM's *Framing the Early Middle Ages* [3: 2005]. Here the focus is rather on changes in land, and in production, with strong emphasis on regional variation. Wickham's reformulation of the socio-economic history of the period has prompted considerable discussion, not least because of its combination of written and archaeological material, its emphasis on the peasantry, and the wide scale of his analysis [3: BANAJI 2016; HALDON 2008; WOOD 2007]. For a different view of the situation of the peasantry one may consult D. P. KEHOE's account of *Land and the Rural Economy in the Roman Empire* [3: 2007]. With regard to the topic of slavery, Kyle HARPER has argued against the prevailing view to assert a deep difference between the situation in the Later Roman period and that in the early Middle Ages, in which it was the collapse of the Empire rather than a slow development associated in part with Christianisation, that ended Roman slavery [3: HARPER 2011]. This history of slavery in the immediately post-Roman period is covered by Alice RIO [3: 2009] and also by Lukas BOTHE in an article dealing with Merovingian legislation on the issue [3: BOTHE 2019].

The one striking omission in WICKHAM's coverage is the Church, although he devotes a little more attention to religion in a subsequent volume [3: WICKHAM 2009]. The same absence is apparent in Jairus BANAJI's analyses of agrarian change, and more generally of the late antique economy. BANAJI's approach is firmly economic, placing considerable emphasis on the numismatic evidence and above all on Constantine's introduction of the *solidus*, access to which he sees as fundamental to the role of the aristocracy in driving the economy [3: BANAJI 2007, 2016].

A new focus in the consideration of the period is the question of environmental change and crisis. Here recent discoveries are continually being brought to bear. Analysis of ice cores from both the Arctic and Antarctic has provided significant evidence on climate, while the examination of traces of disease has changed awareness of the significance of plague. Kyle HARPER's study of *The Fate of Rome* argues that the crisis of the third century was caused largely by environmental problems (the ending of the climatic optimum and the outbreak of the so-called Plague of Cyprian), and that the Justinianic Plague was a central factor in the subsequent sixth-century crisis [3: HARPER 2017]. A number of other authors had already argued for the significance of the plague for the end of the Classical World [3: LITTLE 2007; McCORMICK 2015, 2016]. HARPER's wider thesis has, however, been sharply criticised in a multi-authored article by John HALDON, Hugh ELTON et al. [3: 2018]. While not denying the probable importance of plague or of natural disasters, the au-

Environmental history

thors have called into question much of the evidence and many of the statistical analyses offered by HARPER. Further critique of HARPER's argument has come from Lee MORDECHAI and Merle EISENBERG [9: 2019, 2020; also MORDECHAI/EISENBERG et al. 2019]. Certainly environmental factors need to be borne constantly in mind – and this is especially true when considering the mid sixth century (where dendrochronological evidence and the evidence of ice cores shows unequivocally the impact of volcanic activity on the climate) – but they need careful assessment.

4 The Fourth-century Emperors and their Reigns

4.1 The Third-Century Crisis and the Tetrarchy

Soldier emperors

Even though his argument needs modification, HARPER's work raises important questions for the causes of the third-century crisis, as do the criticisms levelled against it by Haldon and his fellow critics. Among recent work on the crisis the two volumes on *Die Zeit der Soldatenkaiser*, edited by Klaus-Peter JOHNE, together with Udo HARTMANN and Thomas GERHARDT [4a: 2008], provides an up-to-date examination of almost all aspects of the topic, including a full discussion of the sources, many of which are problematic.

The *Historia Augusta*

Our main narrative account is the *Historia Augusta*. The most recent edition is that of François PASCHOUD [4.1: 2002–11], who was also joint editor, along with Giorgio Bonamente, of proceedings of conferences on the text held in Geneva [4.1: BONAMENTE/PASCHOUD 1994, 1999]. The work is unquestionably not a series of near-contemporary biographies written by several different authors as the text claims. The latest computational study of the text by Justin STOVER and Mike KESTEMONT [4.1: 2016] has strengthened the case for a single author. The question of the work's date was reopened by Ronald SYME [4.1: 1968, 1971], who argued that the work was contemporary with that of Ammianus. SYME's view has, however, been challenged by Adolf LIPPOLD [4.1: 1998], who has argued for a Constantinian date, and by André CHASTAGNOL [4.1: 1997], who has argued for a date of c. 400, an argument which has been taken further by Bruno POTTIER [4.1: 2006]. Ronald SYME's argument for a date in the last decades of the fourth century has, however, been generally accepted. At the same time, there is a growing awareness that the author made use of genuine earlier sources which have not survived [4.1: Barnes 1978; Rohrbacher 2013]. His vocabulary suggests that he may have been a lawyer working in the imperial service [4.1: Honoré 1987].

In addition to Johne's two volumes [4a: Johne/Hartmann/Gerhardt 2008], there is also a major reassessment of the third century in the new *Cambridge Ancient History* vol 12, *The Crisis of Empire, AD 193–337* [4.1: Bowman/Cameron/Garnsey 2005]. As with the other volumes of the new *Cambridge Ancient History* [4.1: Cameron/Garnsey 1997; 3: Cameron/Ward-Perkins/Whitby 2001], this is a valuable guide to the *status quaestionis* of the major themes of the period at the time of publication. Despite the existence of these vast compendia there is much to be gained from Ramsey MacMullen's *Roman Government's Response to Crisis, AD 235–337* [4.1: 1976], which still provides a useful account of the major political, military and economic issues, though it has less to offer on social problems. The main recent French discussion of the period, which offers a thematic reading, is that by Jean-Michel Carrié and Aline Rousselle [4.1: 1999]. John Drinkwater's study of the Gallic Empire provides a detailed examination of one western region that played a significant role in the crisis [4.1: Drinkwater 1987]. The eastern breakaway region, Palmyra, is the subject of a monograph by Udo Hartmann [4.1: 2001].

Much of our evidence for Diocletian's reign is extremely hostile towards the emperor, coming from the pens of the Christians Eusebius of Caesarea [4.1: Barnes 1981; Johnson/Schott 2013; Corke-Webster 2019] and Lactantius [4.1: Barnes 1973], who had witnessed the Great Persecution at first hand. More positive views are to be found in the two fourth-century epitomators Aurelius Victor [4.1: Bird 1984, 1994; Rohrbacher 2002: Stover/Woudhuysen 2023] and Eutropius [4.1: Bird 1993], and there is also valuable information on two of Diocletian's Tetrarchic colleagues, Maximian and Constantius, in the Latin Panegyrics gathered together by Pacatus in c. 390 [4.1: Nixon/Rodgers 1994]. For some important aspects of Diocletian's reign we are dependent on the material evidence of coins, sculpture and of inscriptions (which provide our main evidence for the Price Edict).

The basic information for Diocletian's reign (and indeed for that of Constantine) was gathered by Tim Barnes in *The New Empire of Diocletian and Constantine* [4.1: 1982]. The main sources and the major controversies are outlined by Wolfgang Kuhoff [4.1: 2001] and by Roger Rees [4.1: 2004] in their handbooks on Diocletian and the Tetrarchy. There is a recent biography of the emperor by Umberto

The third-century crisis

Diocletian and the Tetrarchy

ROBERTO [4.1: 2014], and there is a monograph on the reign by Stephen WILLIAMS [4.1: 1985]. A collection of articles edited by Alexander DEMANDT, Andreas GOLTZ, and Heinrich SCHLANGE-SCHÖNINGEN [4.1: 2004] includes a survey of current scholarship as well as studies of the legislation issued by the tetrarchs. DEMANDT [1: 2018] offers a précis of his interpretation of the reign in *Die Spätantike*, while Alan BOWMAN [4.1: 2005] provides a useful overview in a contribution to the *Cambridge Ancient History*. Diocletian is also considered in some detail by Hartwin BRANDT [4.1: 1998] in his study of the Empire from 284 to 363. The journal *Antiquité Tardive* devoted two volumes to the history and archaeology of the Tetrarchy [*Antiquité Tardive*, 2–3, 1993].

The nature of Diocletian's government has been analysed by Frank KOLB [4.1: 1987] in his study of the First Tetrarchy and by Simon CORCORAN [4.1: 2000]. For the ideology of Diocletian's reign, William SESTON's work published in 1946 is still valuable [4.1: SESTON 1946]. Also stimulating, albeit questionable in several respects, is H. P. L'ORANGE's *Art Forms and Civic Life if the Later Roman Empire* [4.1: 1965]. Much more recent is Frank KOLB's discussion of imperial ideology throughout Late Antiquity [4.1: 2001].

The *Panegyrici Latini*   The Latin Panegyrics have received a great deal of attention in recent years. Although none of them is devoted to Diocletian himself, one is concerned with the Tetrarchy as a whole, two are devoted to Maximian and one to Constantius. Among recent work there is the commentary on the panegyrics by Ted NIXON [4.1: 1994], and a monograph by Adrastos OMISSI [3: 2018], which uses the whole collection to examine the construction of imperial legitimacy in the face of attempted usurpation between 284 and 395. A collection of essays edited by Diederick BURGERSDIJK and Alan ROSS [4.1: 2019] on the literary depiction of emperors draws extensively on the panegyrics.

The construction of a non-dynastic succession and its failure is discussed by Olivier HEKSTER within the broader history of Roman rule [4.1: HEKSTER 2015; see also BÖRM 2015]. Among the usurpers to challenge the Tetrarchs, the most important, Carausius and Allectus, are the subject of a monograph by P. J. CASEY [10: 1995], while the increasing evidence for Carausius, including relatively recent coin finds, is examined by Hugh WILLIAMS [4.1: 2004]. For the last years of Diocletian and for the subsequent reign of Galerius there is a useful study by William Lewis LEADBETTER [4.1: 2009].

It is not always easy to distinguish between the military re-   Military reform
forms instituted by Diocletian and those carried out by Constantine.
As a result, the majority of studies concerned with the army cover
the reigns of both emperors and indeed the whole of the late third,
fourth and early fifth centuries. Warren TREADGOLD's study takes as
its chronological range the years from 284 to 1081 [4.1: TREADGOLD
1995]. In fact, much of our information for the Roman army comes
from the *Notitia Dignitatum* [4.1: IRELAND 1999; HOFFMANN 1969–70],
compiled at the end of the fourth century, and probably still being
revised in the early fifth, a point which raises questions about its
reliability as a source [4.1: GOODBURN/BARTHOLEMEW 1976; KULIKOWSKI
2000]. There is an online bibliography for works published on the
Notitia between 1976 and 2000 [notitiadignitatum.org]. Two of the
most interesting texts commenting on the army, the *De re militare*
by Vegetius [4.1: MILNER 1993, 2011] and the anonymous *De rebus bellicis* [4.1: IRELAND 1979; THOMPSON 1952; BRANDT 1988] also date from the
late fourth century. Of specific importance for an understanding of
barbarian federate troops employed by the Empire is a fragment
preserved in the Digest of Justinian [4.1: LANIADO 2015]. For the numbers of troops in the age of Diocletian and Constantine, we are dependent on figures given by the sixth-century authors Zosimus and
John Lydus. The second half of volume 2 of *The Cambridge History
of Greek and Roman Warfare* is dedicated entirely to the Later Empire [4.1: SABIN/VAN WEES/WHITBY 2007]. Still useful is Pat SOUTHERN and
Karen DIXON's study of *The Late Roman Army* [4.1: 1996].

The religious persecution of Diocletian's reign has received con-   The Great Persecution
siderable attention in all the major handbooks, and it is often cov-
ered in the opening sections of works on Constantine. There is a
useful overview of Roman paganism in Wolfgang LIEBESCHUETZ's
study of Roman religion [4.1: 1979] and in the two-volume survey
edited by Mary BEARD, John NORTH and Simon PRICE [4.1: 1998], while
the material evidence is covered in *The Archaeology of Late Antique
Paganism*, edited by Luke LAVAN and Michael MULRYAN [4.1: 2011].

There are variant views on the spread of Christianity before   The spread of
Christianity
the start of the fourth century, albeit not so much on the numbers
of Christians as on the sections of society to which they belonged.
The evidence is inevitably patchy, with some centres, like Rome, being well represented. There, it is possible to trace the emergence of
a Christian community and of a degree of ecclesiastical organisation
and episcopal authority [4.1: CURRAN 2000; RIVES 1997]. Although Rod-

ney STARK [4.1: 1996] has argued that the early Christians were usually members of the middle class or of the world of Hellenistic Judaism, following the arguments of Thomas ROBINSON [4.1: 2017] there is a case for thinking that the early spread of Christianity was less urban than has been assumed and that a significant number of its adherents, which perhaps amounted to 10 per cent of the population, were rural and marginal members of society. As for the appeal of Christianity, Ramsay MACMULLEN [4.1: 1984] pointed to the influence of the miraculous: but perhaps the most significant factor was the care shown by Christians for members of their community [4.1: STARK 1996]. The proceedings of a conference on Christianisation, which include regional and general studies, have been edited by Hervé INGLEBERT [4.1: 2010].

On the persecution itself the old study of martyrdom by William H. C. FREND [4.1: 1967] remains influential, as does the study of pagans and Christians by Robin LANE FOX [4.1: 1986]. Among the Western sources, the Roman martyr acts (which largely date from the period from 425 to 675) have recently been translated into English by Michael LAPIDGE [4.1: 2017].

4.2 Constantine

The sources   The central narrative for the reign of Constantine is provided by Eusebius, in his *Ecclesiastical History* (which was later translated into Latin and continued by Rufinus), his *Vita Constantini*, his *Chronicle* (which was continued by Jerome) and his Tricennial orations [4.2: DRAKE 1976; CAMERON/HALL 1999]. Apart from the narrative sources there is, again, valuable information in the *Panegyrici Latini*, five of which are devoted to Constantine [4.1: NIXON/RODGERS 1994]. In addition, some of Constantine's legislation survives in the *Codex Theodosianus* and in the *Corpus Iuris* of Justinian [4.2: DILLON 2012]. For the Church councils, we have the conciliar acts from Arles 314 [4.2: MUNIER 1963, pp. 9–13], although not for the Council of Nicaea, which, however, is described in numerous ecclesiastical histories (for instance those of Socrates, Sozomen and Theodoret, as well as the *Chronicon Paschale*) and is referred to in the writings of such theologians as Athanasius of Alexandria [4.2: PIETRAS 2016]. On the representation of the Christian Empire in Socrates, Sozomen, and Theodoret, there is a significant study by Hartmut LEPPIN [4.2: 1996].

There are recent French editions in the *Sources Chrétiennes* series of Socrates [4.2: MARAVAL 2004–7], Sozomen [4.2: GRILLET/SABBAH 1983–2008], and Theodoret [4.2: BOUFFARTIGUE/CARNIVET et al. 2006–9]. For Socrates there is a study by Theresa URBAINCZYK [4.2: 1997].

The major overview of the sources is to be found in two studies by BARNES, *The New Empire of Diocletian and Constantine* [4.1: 1982], and *Constantine and Eusebius* [4.1: 1981]. A good deal of the material evidence of the reign is discussed in the catalogues of exhibitions held in Rimini, York, and Trier, to mark the centenary of Constantine's usurpation in 306 [4.2: DONATI/GENTILI 2005; HARTLEY/HAWKES/HENIG/MEE 2006; DEMANDT/ENGEMANN 2007]. In addition to the general handbooks, Constantine has been the subject of a *Companion to the Age of Constantine*, edited by Noel LENSKI [4.2: 2006]. There have also been numerous general assessments of the reign, especially since the anniversary celebrations of 2006, including those by Charles ODAHL [4.2: 2004], Hartwin BRANDT [4.2: 2006], Elisabeth HERMANN-OTTO [4.2: 2007], Raymond VAN DAM [4.2: 2007], Klaus ROSEN [4.2: 2013], Tim BARNES [4.2: 2011], and David POTTER [4.2: 2012].

Many aspects of Constantine's reign, including his military, financial and legal reforms, are most frequently considered with the broader history of the Later Empire. There is a chapter by Hugh ELTON on 'Warfare and the Military' in the *Cambridge Companion to the Age of Constantine* [4.2: 2006], and the same author also deals with the Constantinian reforms in his study of warfare in Roman Europe [4.2: ELTON 1996]. There is a substantial discussion in A. H. M. JONES' *The Later Roman Empire* [2: 1964], and there are valuable chapters on the army in volumes 12 and 13 of the *Cambridge Ancient History* by Brian CAMPBELL [4.2: 2005] and A. D. LEE [4.2: 1998]. So too, there is R. S. O. TOMLIN's survey of the late Roman army [4.2: 1988]. Edward LUTTWAK [4.2: 1976] discusses the changes in military strategy under Constantine in the context of his arguments in favour of a Roman strategy of defence in depth. His gathering of information is highly regarded, although many historians have not been entirely convinced by the strategic reading of the evidence.

The army

Constantine's government, which is best represented by legislation preserved in the *Theodosian Code*, has been examined by John DILLON [4.2: 2012]. DILLON's emphasis is on the emergence of a bureaucracy that was needed to cope with the expansion of state power that began in the days of Diocletian. As a result, in DILLON's view, the state from the days of Constantine became somewhat more proac-

Government

tive than it had been. The administration of the Empire in the second half of the fourth century is considered by Robert ERRINGTON [4.2: 2006], while there is an analysis covering a longer time-span by Christopher KELLY who, however, takes as his point of departure the work of the sixth-century Byzantine John Lydus [4.2: KELLY 2004]. The importance of Constantine's monetary policy, which was based on the gold *solidus*, is examined by Jairus BANAJI [3: 2001] who presents the new coinage as playing a fundamental role in the emergence of a new social hierarchy in which those with access to it (notably those involved in government) benefitted considerably.

Maxentius For the period before Constantine achieved sole power, there is a study of Maxentius by Hartmut LEPPIN and Hauke ZIEMSSEN [4.2: 2007] and also the more controversial study of the memory of the Battle of the Milvian Bridge by Raymond VAN DAM [4.2: 2011] which places a good deal of emphasis on the defeated emperor. Constantine's victory is a central issue for anyone trying to understand the complex question of his conversion. The main sources are gathered

Constantine's conversion by Volkmar KEIL [4.2: 1995]. Recent guides include Ekkehard MÜHLENBERG [4.2: 1998] and Klaus Martin GIRARDET [4.2: 2006, 2010]. More far-reaching is H. A. DRAKE's study of *Constantine and the Bishops*, which puts the emperor's conversion and his subsequent need to negotiate with the episcopate at the very heart of a reading of the reign [4.2: DRAKE 2000].

A religious emphasis is equally present in Noel LENSKI's analysis of the emperor's dealings with the cities [4.2: LENSKI 2016]. Here consideration of Constantine's use of iconography and of his responses to urban petitions (working within the model of the reactive nature of imperial rule set out by Fergus MILLAR [4.2: 1977]) leads to discussion of the furthering of Christianity. Constantine's conversion is also a dominant element in Jonathan BARDILL's study of the emperor, which is primarily concerned with the iconography of the reign and with the surviving archaeological evidence [4.2: BARDILL 2012].

Rome The emperor's dealings with Rome, which were central to Andreas ALFÖLDI's once influential reading of the emperor's relations with the aristocracy [4.2: ALFÖLDI 1948], are dealt with in the course of J. R. CURRAN's study of the city from the age of the Tetrarchy to 410 [4.1: CURRAN 2000]. There is further discussion by Bruno BLECKMANN [4.2: 2015] in his contribution to a collection of essays edited by Johannes Wienand, which also contains an essay by Noel Lenski [4.2: LENSKI 2015] on Constantine and the Tyche of Constantinople. The archaeological evidence for Constantinian Rome is presented by Ross Holloway [4.2: 2004]. Richard Westall [4.2: 2015], however, has noted that some finds indicate that Old St Peter's was built in the main not by Constantine, but by his son Constantius. Richard Krautheimer's *Three Christian Capitals* deals not just with Rome, but also with Constantinople and Milan in the Late Antique period [4.2: Krautheimer 1983]. On Rome and Milan there is also the collection of essays edited by Therese Fuhrer [4.2: 2012].

For the history of the Church itself a good point of departure remains Jean Gaudemet's general overview [4.2: Gaudemet 1958]. There is extensive discussion of the Councils of Arles and Nicaea in the major handbooks, including the conciliar history of Hefele-Leclerq [4.2: 1907] as well as Jaroslav Pelikan's study of the Christian Tradition [4.2: 1973] and J. N. D. Kelly's accounts of early Christian Creeds and early Christian doctrine [4.2: 1958]. On the conciliar process there is a slim but instructive volume of Ramsay MacMullen [4.2: 2006]. With regard to the question of Donatism there is a collection of essays edited by Richard Miles [4.2: 2016]. There is also the much older, but extremely influential work of William H. C. Frend on the Donatist Church [4.2: 1952], although this is concerned largely with Donatism as it developed in the later fourth century and beyond. Maureen Tilley [4.2: 1996] has translated and commented on the Donatist martyr acts of the third and fourth centuries. A collection of documents relating to the Council of Nicaea, with valuable discussion, has been published by Henryk Pietras [4.2: 2016], and the council and its legacy is also examined from a theological point of view by Lewis Ayres [4.2: 2004]. Jörg Ulrich [4.2: 1997] has examined the lack of Western involvement in the council. As regards Arius, who was condemned at Nicaea, there is a biography by Rowan Williams [4.2: 1987]. For the Arian debate as it continued through to 381 there is a survey by R. P. C. Hanson [4.2: 1988].

The Church under Constantine

4.3 The House of Constantine

With the death of Constantine there is a change in the surviving evidence. But, although Eusebius' information ends in 339, the other Church historians Socrates, Sozomen and Theodoret continue the story, as does Rufinus in his continuation of Eusebius' *Ecclesiastical History*. In addition, there is considerable documentary evidence

The sources

relating to the ecclesiastical figures who dominate the period after Constantine's death, most notably Athanasius of Alexandria. For the non-religious aspects of the reign of Constantius II there is the narrative of Ammianus Marcellinus, whose history originally covered the history of Rome from Nerva to the death of Valens; the surviving portion of the text, however, begins in 353 [4.3: MATTHEWS 1989; BARNES 1998; DRIJVERS/HUNT 1999; KELLY 2008]. For Ammianus there is a massive bibliography, for which there is a guide by Fred JENKINS [4.3: 2017]. Although Constantius II is not covered by any of the panegyrics included in the *Panegyrici Latini*, he is the subject of orations by his nephew, fellow emperor, and successor, Julian [4c: WRIGHT 1913, Orations 1 and 3], Libanius [4.3: NORMAN 1989, Oration 59], and Themistius [4.3: HEATHER/MONCUR 2001, Orations 3 and 4]. The significance of panegyric in the period running from the reign of Constantius to that of Theodosius is considered by VANDERSPOEL [4.3: 1995]. In addition to being the subject of panegyric, Constantius was also the butt of invectives by Athanasius of Alexandria, Hilary of Poitiers, and Lucifer of Cagliari [4.3: FLOWER 2016]. As with other emperors of the fourth century, some of Constantius' legislation is preserved in the Theodosian Code.

Constantius II and his brothers
    Although there is a valuable collection of essays on the sons of Constantine, edited by Nicholas BAKER-BRIAN and Shaun TOUGHER [4.3: 2020], which covers most aspects of the period, in general the secondary literature relating to Constantius II and his brothers is much less substantial than that for their father. Some discussions relating to the earlier reign (as for example that by ODAHL [4.3: 2004]) continue on into that of Constantius. The bloodbath that followed the death of Constantine is considered by Richard BURGESS [4.3: 2008], while Constantius' intellectual formation is the subject of an article by Nick HENK [4.3: 2001]. Representation of the emperor's style of rule, as exemplified by a famous passage in Ammianus Marcellinus relating to his visit to Rome, is discussed by Richard FLOWER [4.3: 2015]. The visit to Rome has also been analysed by Mark HUMPHRIES [4.3: 2019].

The Church in the time of Constantius II
    Otherwise, most studies concentrate on the question of the Church – even when setting out the biography of Constantius himself, as in the case of Pedro BARCELÓ's monograph [4.3: 2004]. Among works that deal with the development of a *Reichskirche* under Constantius, there are a book by Richard KLEIN [4.3: 1977] and a lengthy

article by Steffen Diefenbach [4.3: 2012]. The emperor's dealings with the pagans is the subject of an article by Hartmut Leppin [4.3: 1999].

Constantius was faced with a good deal of hostility from some of the leading bishops of the period because of his support for the homoeans. The criticism to which he was subjected is analysed in a study of episcopal invective by Richard Flower [4.3: 2013] and in an article by Mark Humphries [4.3: 1997]. The career of Athanasius and its importance for the reign of Constantius is painstakingly reconstructed by Tim Barnes [4.3: 1993] in a volume that continues the analytical approach used for the reign of Constantine in his previous work. The major western figure to oppose Constantius was Hilary of Poitiers, whose early years were studied with an eye on the Gallic episcopate by J. Doignon [4.3: 1971], while his most significant theological works have been placed firmly within the context of his career and especially his exiles [4.3: Beckwith 2009]. Another opponent, Hosius of Cordoba, is the subject of an older biography by V. C. de Clercq [4.3: 1954]. In addition, Constantius also came into conflict with the bishop of Rome, Liberius, appointing Felix II in his place. The history of Liberius is considered by Samuel Cohen [4.3: 2018] in an article. It is worth noting that Constantius was largely preoccupied with the conflict between Liberius and Felix in the course of his visit to Rome, although Ammianus makes no reference to the fact. This would seem to have been the context of the emperor's building work at St Peter's, noted by Richard Westall [4.2: 2015]. There is a general overview of Constantius' exiling of bishops by Walt Stevenson [4.3: 2014].

Among the few studies that do not concentrate on the Church is Muriel Moser's analysis of the relations between Constantius and the senatorial aristocracies of both Constantinople and Rome [4.3: Moser 2018]. Most other aspects of Constantius' rule are covered by the major handbooks in the general context of fourth-century history. For the military aspects of Constantius' reign, however, we have the evidence of Ammianus Marcellinus, which covers the last eight years of Constantius' reign. Ammianus' account of the campaigns of Constantius and Julian is the subject of an article by Moyses Marcos [4.3: 2015], while the more general question of Ammianus as a military historian is the subject of a rather older monograph by Gary Crump [4.3: 1975].

The aristocracy

The army

4.4 Julian

The sources For the emperor Julian, the primary sources and the secondary literature are much richer than they are for Constantius. In addition to Ammianus' narrative, we have the writings of Julian himself, which have been the subject of recent discussion [4.4: BAKER-BRIAN/ TOUGHER 2012], as well as the letters and orations of Libanius and a panegyric by Claudius Mamertinus, included in the *Panegyrici Latini*. There are also the hostile comments of Julian's Christian critics, notably Gregory Nazianzen, and the Church historians, Socrates, Sozomen and Theodoret.

Biographies of Julian   Among recent biographies there is one by Klaus BRINGMANN [4.4: 2004] and another by Klaus ROSEN [4.4: 2006]. *Antiquité Tardive* devoted a complete volume of the journal to Julian [*Antiquité Tardive* 17, 2009]. There is, however, much to be gained from older works, including that of Joseph BIDEZ [4.4: 1930]. Glen BOWERSOCK's study [4.4: 1978] remains a useful point of departure. So too does Polymnia ATHANASSIADI's much more personal, imaginative, and therefore more controversial study [4.4: 1981]. The cultural world of Julian is at the heart of Jean BOUFFARTIGUE's book [4.4: 1992].

Julian and religion   These works necessarily deal with Julian's paganism and his religious policies among other topics, but the subject is the sole focus of an article by Klaus ROSEN [4.4: 1997] and of monographs by Theresa NESSELRATH [4.4: 2013] and Rowland SMITH [4.4: 1995]. Most recently there is H. C. TEITLER's account of Julian's 'war against Christianity', which presents a much more nuanced view of his anti-Christian policies, presenting them rather as a reversal of Constantine's support for the Church and stressing the extent to which the apostate emperor was at odds with traditional paganism [4.4: TEITLER 2017]. One of the few studies that does not concentrate on Julian's biography or his religious ideas and policies is Raphael BRENDEL's study of the emperor's law-giving [4.4: 2017].

4.5 Valentinian, Valens, Gratian and Valentinian II

The sources With the accession of Valentinian the documentary evidence declines once more, although there are still the narratives of the Church historians and chroniclers and of Ammianus Marcellinus who saw the reigns of Valentinian and Valens as marking a decline in political culture, as argued by J. W. DRIJVERS [4.5: 2012]. The evidence provided by Ammianus for the period after Julian is assessed in a collection edited by Jan DEN BOEFT, Jan Willem DRIJVERS, Daniël DEN HENGST and Hans C. TEITLER [4.5: 2007], which includes a number of studies of Valentinian I. In addition there is a considerable body of legislation preserved in the *Theodosian Code*, which has been the subject of a monograph by Sebastian SCHMIDT-HOFNER [4.5: 2008], where he studies the laws of Valentinian as an illustration of late Roman rule. In a subsequent article he has approached the emperor's early legislation in the context of the change of dynasty from the house of Constantine to that of Valentinian [4.5: SCHMIDT-HOFNER 2015].

For the reigns of Gratian and Valentinian II, however, we are better served. Ausonius provides information on Gratian, as he had acted as his tutor and had also been appointed consul by the young emperor. The writings of Ambrose of Milan, and most especially his letters and his funerary oration on Valentinian II, are central to an understanding of the reigns of both of Valentinian's sons. Relations between Ambrose and Gratian are charted in a study by Tim BARNES [4.5: 2000], which applies the approach he adopted in his studies of Constantine and Eusebius and of Constantius and Athanasius. In addition, the letters and orations of Symmachus provide information on the senatorial aristocracy and on the conflict over the Altar of Victory [4.5: BARROW 1973]. For this episode, in addition to the works of AMBROSE [4.5: LIEBESCHUETZ 2005] and Symmachus we have the poetry of Prudentius [4.5: TRÄNKLE 2008].

For Valentinian and his successors there is a useful overview by A. D. LEE [4.5: 2012] in his volume for the *Edinburgh History of Ancient Rome*. Valentinian is not the subject of a modern biography; the massive study which constituted Roger TOMLIN's doctoral thesis [4.5: 1974] was never published, although it is possible to obtain a copy of the thesis itself. Valens, however, has been the subject of an important biography by Noel LENSKI [4.5: 2002] which provides a detailed analysis of the emperor's military activities on the eastern front and in the Balkans as well as a consideration of his imperial administration. Valens' policy towards the barbarians is discussed in all the major studies that cover the history of the Goths in the fourth century: most notably Herwig WOLFRAM [4.5: 2009], Peter HEATHER [4.5: 1991], Thomas BURNS [4.5: 1995], Guy HALSALL [3: 2007], and Michael KULIKOWSKI [4.5: 2007].

Valentinian I
and Valens

Child emperors   Following an ominous bout of ill-health, Valentinian raised his son Gratian to be co-emperor in 367, although he was only eight years old. The appointment of children to imperial office, a policy initially introduced in order to secure the succession, has been the subject of attention since the publication of Meaghan McEvoy's study of child-emperorship, covering the youthful rule of Gratian, Valentinian II, Honorius and Valentinian III [4.5: McEvoy 2013]. McEvoy draws a distinction between the appointment of Gratian by his father, in order to secure the survival of the dynasty, and the elevation of the even younger Valentinian III by the members of a small military and governing clique intent on furthering their own careers.

Ambrose   For Ambrose, and more generally for the imperial city of Milan in his day, there is a biography by Neil McLynn [4.5: 1994] and the study of the bishop's exploitation of heresy by Michael Stuart Williams [4.5: 2017]. More traditional is the old biography by Homes Dudden [4.5: 1935] which is still of value. A more theological approach is offered by Ernst Dassmann [4.5: 2004]. Ambrose's impact on the city of Milan is considered, in parallel to that of Damasus on Rome, in a study by Markus Löx [4.5: 2013]. In addition, for the court of Gratian and its connections with the senatorial aristocracy of

The senatorial aristocracy   Gaul there is Hagith Sivan's biography of Ausonius [4.5: 1993], while the poet's family is the subject of a study by Altay Coşkun [4.5: 2012]. John Matthews [4.5: 1975] places the relation between the court and the aristocracy, most particularly that of Gaul, at the centre of the history of the period from 364 to 425. The senatorial aristocracy is also the focus of a monograph by M. W. T. Arnheim [4.5: 1972].

5 From Theodosius I to the Deposition of Romulus Augustulus

5.1 Theodosius I

Sources   Ammianus's history ends with the aftermath of the Battle of Hadrianople. As a result, for Theodosius' reign, Church historians once again become our main narrative source, though to Socrates, Sozomen, and Theodoret one may add Orosius' *History against the Pagans* and also the Chronicle of Sulpicius Severus. The Chronicle is available in a new French edition [5.1: DE SENNEVILLE-GRAVE 1999]. For Orosius, there is a French edition [5.1: ARNAUD-LINDET 1990–1] as well as a recent English translation [5.1: FEAR 2010]. There is a major study of Orosius by Peter VAN NUFFELEN [5.1: 2012] and an analysis of the geographical chapters in the *History* by Andy MERRILLS [5.1: 2005]. In addition, there is the pagan history of Zosimus, who for this section of his narrative used the now-lost account of Eunapius. For Zosimus, there is an edition and French translation by François PASCHOUD [5.1: 1971].

Important aspects of Theodosius' reign are covered in the writings of Ambrose and also in Augustine's *De Civitate Dei*. The last of the *Panegyrici Latini*, that by Pacatus, who also gathered the collection together, is devoted to Theodosius. In addition, the emperor is also the subject of a panegyric by Themistius. Claudian, the panegyrist of Honorius and Stilicho, offers some retrospective comments on Theodosius.

Among recent accounts of Theodosius' reign there are biographies by Bertrand LANÇON [5.1: 2014] and Hartmut LEPPIN [5.1: 2003], both written with the general public in mind, but also of value to the scholar. The same is true of the study by Pierre MARAVAL [5.1: 2009]. The slightly older narratives by Stephen Williams and Gerry FRIELL [5.1: 1994] and by Jörg ERNESTI [3: 1998] are still valuable. A. D. LEE's overview of the period is also useful [5.1: LEE 2012]. A collection of essays on the government and reform of the Empire, edited by Umberto ROBERTO and Laura MECELLA [5.1: 2015], includes several essays on Theodosius. The Theodosian Empire is the subject of a volume of *Antiquité Tardive* [vol. 16, 2008].

Theodosius I

Theodosius' relations with the western Church are dealt with in Neil McLYNN's slightly iconoclastic study of Ambrose [4.5: 1994]. The emperor is also central to Fabian SCHULZ's discussion of Ambrose's views of Christian lawgiving [5.1: 2014]. Theodosius' reign saw an escalation of anti-pagan legislation and also of more general anti-pagan activity (often prompted by individuals, or carried out by gangs of monks), which is considered in the broader context of pagan-Christian relations by Frank TROMBLEY [5.1: 1993–4]. The notion that there was a significant pagan revival in Theodosius' reign, however, is firmly rebutted by Alan CAMERON in his study of *The Last Pagans of Rome* [5.1: 2011]. François PASCHOUD's *Roma Aeterna* [5.1: 1967], which considers attitudes towards the idea of Rome in the late

Theodosius, the Church and the pagans

fourth and early fifth centuries, and especially those held by pagans, nevertheless remains valuable.

Theodosius and the Goths

Theodosius' dealings with the barbarians (essentially his restoration of peace in the Balkans following the disaster of Hadrianople), for which we have relatively slight evidence, are reconstructed in the course of the studies of the Goths by Wolfram [4.5: 2009], Heather [4.5: 1991], Burns [4.5: 1994], Halsall [3: 2007], Kulikowski [4.5: 2007], and Gerd Kampers [5.1: 2008].

5.2 Honorius

The death of Theodosius in 395 led to the division of the Empire into East and West – a division from which it never recovered. As a result, the history of the Western Empire and of Late Antiquity in the West tends to be studied separately from that of the Greek East. The documentation for the two halves of the Empire also begins to diverge.

Sources

The church historians (Socrates, Sozomen, Theodoret, and Orosius) are still of value, as is the pagan Zosimus. To the Church histories one can add the additions to the *Chronicle of Jerome* [5.2: Burgess/Kulikowski 2013; Muhlberger 1990] and the fragmentary, but intriguing, *Ravenna Annals*, whose main interest seems to be civil war and natural disaster [5.2: Bischoff/Koehler 1939]. For Constantinople the works of John Chrysostom are of vital importance. For the first decade of Honorius' rule (effectively the period of Stilicho's dominance), the most important contemporary information comes from the poet Claudian, who was identified as Stilicho's propagandist by Alan Cameron [5.2: 1970] and who provides hostile information on Rufinus and Eutropius at the court of Arcadius.

Church historians and theologians (among them Augustine, Jerome and Pelagius) provide important reactions to the sack of Rome [5.2: Lipps/Machado/von Rummel 2013; Meier/Patzold 2010; de Bruyn 1993]. So too, there is material relating to the damage caused by the barbarians in a number of works of poetry from the period, all discussed by Pierre Courcelle in his *Histoire Littéraire des Grandes invasions* [5.2: 1964], a work which was obviously written in the aftermath of the 1939–45 conflict but remains valuable, despite changing views of the chronology and authorship of some of the texts involved. One pagan poet, Rutilius Namatianus, describes his journey north from Rome to Gaul, six years after the Gothic withdrawal from the Italian peninsula [5.2: Doblhofer 1972–77].

395 saw the start of a new period of child emperorship, with the appointment of the eighteen-year-old Arcadius in the East and the ten-year old Honorius in the West. The elevation of the two is considered in the context of child-emperorship by Meaghan McEvoy [4.5: 2013]. McEvoy has described the adult Arcadius as a 'jellyfish emperor' [5.2: 2020]. The court of Arcadius, and especially the influence of the barbarian military, is the subject of a study by Alan Cameron and Jacqueline Long [5.2: 1993]. Wolfgang Liebeschuetz [5.2: 1991] considers not only the barbarians, but also the importance of John Chrysostom. Child emperors

For Honorius there is a recent biography by Chris Doyle [5.2: 2018]. Henning Börm's study of the Western Empire from Honorius to Justinian provides a valuable assessment, and also contextualisation, of the reign, looking back to the Tetrarchs [3: Börm 2018]. Stilicho, who was the subject of a study by Santo Mazzarino [5.2: 1942] and is at the heart of Émilienne Demougeot's discussion of the period between 395 and 410 [5.2: 1951], is also the subject of a much more recent monograph by Tido Janssen [5.2: 2004]. As the focal point of Claudian's poetry, Stilicho is also central to Alan Cameron's study of the poet [5.2: 1970]. He is one of the leading figures in John O'Flynn's study of the generalissimos of the Later Roman Empire [5.2: 1983]. Wolfram [4.5: 2009], Heather [4.5: 1991], Burns [4.5: 1994] and Kulikowski [4.5: 2007] cover his dealings with the barbarians in the course of their histories of the Goths. For his fall there is a study by Jeroen Wijnendaele [5.2: 2018]. Stilicho

In terms of Gothic history, 410 and the sack of Rome has been the subject of a good deal of discussion, especially as a result of various commemorations of the event in 2010. The event itself prompted works by Jerome, Augustine, Orosius, and Pelagius. There are three substantial collections of essays, the first edited by A. D. Berardino, G. Pilara and L. Spera [5.2: 2010], the second by Henriette Harich-Schwarzbauer and Karla Pollmann [.2b: 2013], and the third by Johannes Lipps, Carlos Machado, and Philipp von Rummel [5.2: 2013], all of them subject to a discussion in a review article by Peter van Nuffelen [5.2: 2015], which points to the relative insignificance of the event. There is an acute discussion, directed primarily at the general public, in a volume by Mischa Meier and Steffen Patzold [5.2: 2010]. The year 410 was of less significance for the Roman province 410

of Britannia than it was for Italy, but this phantasy date for the end
of Roman Britain was also the subject of a number of conferences,
whose papers were gathered into a volume edited by F. K. HAARER
[5.2: 2014]. Relations between Romans and barbarians in Spain during the reign of Honorius and throughout the fifth century are covered by Javier ARCE, who has also provided the most recent biography of Alaric [5.2: ARCE 2005, 2018].

Constantius III and   For the years after 410, the dominant figure is the *magister mil-*
Galla Placidia   *itum* Constantius who was to become co-emperor with Honorius in
421, only to die shortly after his elevation. There is one modern
study dedicated to him, by Werner LÜTKENHAUS [5.2: 1998], but there
is also useful discussion in Michael O'FLYNN's [3: 1983] study of the
West Roman Generalissimos. Galla Placidia, the sister of Honorius
as well as the wife first of Athaulf and then of Constantius and a
major influence in the reign of her son Valentinian III, is the subject
of a biography by Hagith SIVAN [5.2: 2011], which replaces the previous works on the subject, although it does so largely by reconstruct-
ing the major stages of the life of an imperial princess. The hostile
relationship between Galla Placidia and Constantius and its impact
on politics in 421 is analysed by Geoffrey DUNN [5.2: 2020].

Ravenna and Rome   Friedrich Wilhelm DEICHMANN's study of Ravenna [5.2: 1969–76],
which often served as the imperial capital under Honorius, remains
valuable, but there are new ideas in Mariëtte VERHOEVEN's study [5.2:
2011] of the early Christian monuments, while Deborah DELIYANNIS
[5.2: 2010] provides a useful introduction to the city. In recent years
there has been a growing awareness that Honorius also spent a
good deal of time in Rome, and it was there that he was buried. His
mausoleum is the subject of Meaghan MCEVOY's contribution to a
volume on Old St Peter's edited by Rosamond MCKITTERICK, John OS-
BORNE, Carol RICHARDSON and Joanna STORY [5.2: 2013].

5.3 Valentinian III

Sources   For the narrative of the reign of Valentinian III we are dependent
on the Latin chronicles: Prosper, Hydatius, the *Chronicle of 452*, and
the Constantinopolitan *Chronicle* of Marcellinus Comes. There is
also some information in the fragmentary Greek historians of the
period. In addition, there are fragments of panegyrics written by
Flavius Merobaudes, who seems to have acted for Aetius as Clau-

dian had done for Stilicho [5.3: Clover 1971]. The *Theodosian Code*, which was issued jointly by Theodosius II and Valentinian, contains laws issued by the Western emperor. And there are additional novels of the emperor [5.3: Mommsen/Meyer 1905].

Valentinian has been the subject of one recent biography, in Italian by Febronia Elia [5.3: 1999]. The reign is covered in some detail by Henning Börm [3: 2018] and also by McEvoy in her study of child Emperors [4.5: 2013]. His interests in the city of Rome are well charted by Mark Humphries [5.3: 2012]. For the first part of the reign, Galla Placida was still a force to be reckoned with, so the biography of her by Hagith Sivan [5.2: 2011] is useful. The major military figures of the reign are covered by O'Flynn [3: 1983] in his study of the Generalissimos. The most important of them, Flavius Aetius, is the subject of a detailed biography by Timo Stickler [5.3: 2002], as well as a French thesis by D. Coulon [5.3: 2003]. There is also a study of the great rival of Aetius' early years and supporter of Galla Placidia, Bonifatius, by Jeroen Wijnendaele, which has also appeared in an Italian translation with a preface by Umberto Roberto [5.3: Wijnendaele 2005].

Valentinian III and Aetius

5.4 The Last Western Emperors

Following the murder of Valentinian III in 455, there was a quick succession of emperors. For the rapidly changing events of the period there are fewer chronicle sources than there are for the reign of Valentinian III; the *Chronicle of 452* ends in c. 452 (although that was certainly not the date of its composition) [5.4: Burgess 2001; Kötter/Scardino 2017] and that of Prosper in 455 (although there is a continuation in one manuscript) [5.2: Muhlberger 1990]. That of Hydatius, however, which focuses on Spain, runs on to 468 [5.4: Burgess 1933]. The main chronicle that covers the whole period is that of Marcellinus Comes [5.4: Croke 1995], and there are some valuable entries in the sixth-century Chronicle of Marcellinus' contemporary Cassiodorus. In addition, there are some important pieces of information in the fragmentary Greek historians [15.1: Blockley 1983]. In general, however, our narrative sources for the period are slight. To some extent there is compensation in the writings of Sidonius Apollinaris, whose letters, which are above all important for an understanding of the Gallic senatorial aristocracy, are particularly

Sources

valuable for events around the year 474. Even more useful are his panegyrics, which deal with the emperors Avitus, Majorian and Anthemius. For Majorian we also have some novels which are preserved alongside the *Breviarium Alarici* of 506 in some manuscripts. There is a website detailing publications on Sidonius [sidonapol. org] as well as a handbook edited by Gavin Kᴇʟʟʏ and Joop ᴠᴀɴ Wᴀᴀʀ-ᴅᴇɴ [5.4: 2020], and a complete volume of the *Journal of Late Antiquity* has been dedicated to him [5.4: *Late Antiquity* 2020].

The emperors and the *magistri militum*   There is a detailed study of events by Dirk Hᴇɴɴɪɴɢ [5.4: 1999] and a useful overview by Henning Böʀᴍ [3: 2018] in his account of the period from Honorius to Justinian. Among the last emperors, Majorian has been the subject of a biography by Fabrizio Oᴘᴘᴇᴅɪsᴀɴᴏ [5.4: 2013], who carefully reconstructs his career from the scattered source material and provides a detailed examination of his legislation. The reign of Anthemius is discussed by Umberto Rᴏʙᴇʀᴛᴏ [5.4: 2015] in a volume on the governance of the Roman Empire in its last century of existence. In addition, the (expanded) proceedings of a conference on Anthemius have been edited by Fabrizio Oᴘᴘᴇᴅɪsᴀɴᴏ [5.4: 2020]. A number of the other successors of Valentinian are covered in O'Fʟʏɴɴ's study of Generalissimos [3: 1983]. A further study of the military figures of the last quarter century of the Western Empire is that of Penny MᴀᴄGᴇᴏʀɢᴇ [5.4: 2002]. There is also a full-scale biography of the most powerful of these generals, Flavius Ricimer, by Friedrich Aɴᴅᴇʀs [5.4: 2010]. A collection of articles edited by John Dʀɪɴᴋᴡᴀᴛᴇʀ and Hugh Eʟᴛᴏɴ considers the state of Gaul in the fifth century [5.4: 1992].

5.5 The Year 476

The end of the West Roman empire   The question of the importance of the year 476 has at times been a major subject of debate. In 1967, Marinus Antony Wᴇs [5.5: 1967] put forward the argument that the importance of the year was constructed by Quintus Aurelius Memmius Symmachus. Six years later, Arnaldo Mᴏᴍɪɢʟɪᴀɴᴏ [5.5: 1973] argued that the event had passed almost unnoticed. In 1983, Brian Cʀᴏᴋᴇ argued that the turning point was a construct, but pointed towards circles in Constantinople, and especially to Marcellinus Comes, as promoting the idea [5.5: Cʀᴏᴋᴇ 1983]. All of which is to say that there were a variety of opinions, even in the late fifth and early sixth centuries, on whether the deposition of Romulus Augustulus was a matter of any importance [5.5: Wood 2022].

One source that has attracted a good deal of attention in the context of the end of the Empire is the *Vita Severini* by Eugippius which describes the last years of Roman Noricum. The most recent edition of the text by Philippe Régerat in the *Sources Chrétiennes* series [5.5: 1991] largely follows an earlier edition by Rudolf Noll, adding relatively little to it, although it does take account of the political reading of Severinus' career advanced by Friedrich Lotter [5.5: 1976]. The problems of the textual readings adopted by Régerat have been discussed by Clare Stancliffe [5.5: 1994]. There is a close historical reading of Eugippius' text by Edward Thompson [5.5: 1982]. The most substantial recent discussion of the *Vita Severini* is to be found in a volume edited by Walter Pohl and Maximilian Diesenberger [5.5: 2001].

Eugippius

More recently there has been emphasis on the extent to which the successor states of the late fifth and early sixth centuries saw themselves as heirs of Rome. Henning Börm [3: 2018] has analysed the period up until Justinian's conquest of Africa and Italy in those terms. Ian Wood [5.5: 2018] has described the same period as a Byzantine Commonwealth. Studies of individual kingdoms have argued the same case.

Heirs of Rome

6 Government and Law

The sources for Roman government in the fourth and fifth centuries are remarkably rich, above all because of the great legal collections of the *Codex Theodosianus* [5.3: Mommsen/Meyer 1905] and the *Corpus Iuris Civilis* of Justinian [6: Krüger/Mommsen/Schnoell/Kroll 1877–92], which includes some laws left out of the earlier compilation as well as legislation issued prior to the reign of Constantine and after 438. There are also some fifth-century novels issued by emperors after the promulgation of the *Codex*, including legislation by Valentinian III and Majorian; and there is the much debated collection known as the *Sirmondian Constitutions* which was certainly put together in the sixth century but which seems to have involved a certain amount of rewriting [6: Huck 2004; Esders/Reimitz 2019]. In addition to this information, there is a handbook for magistrates, written by the early sixth-century administrator John Lydus [6: Carney

The laws

Administrative sources 1965]. Christopher KELLY [6: 2004] has taken this as a point of departure for studying the government of the Later Roman Empire. Also from the sixth century is the *Variae* of Cassiodorus which, despite relating to the Ostrogothic kingdom rather than the Empire itself, sheds a good deal of light on the governmental offices of the Later Empire [6: VIDÉN 1984]. Although Cassiodorus clearly edited the letters he wrote as *magister officiorum* [6: BJORNLIE 2013], it is probable that his description of the duties of individual officials provides an accurate picture of their function during the last years of the Empire. For Cassiodorus' own political career there is a biography by Andrea GIARDINA [6: 2006]. In addition, the careers of individuals shed considerable light on the practice of government; here modern prosopographies are invaluable [1.2: JONES/MARTINDALE/MORRIS 1971–92].

The Theodosian Code The *Codex Theodosianus* and its compilation has received considerable attention in recent years. A new French translation with extensive commentary is in progress [15.4: Codex Theodosianus]. Among numerous recent studies there are works by the ancient historian John MATTHEWS [6: 2000] and the legal historians Boudewijn SIRKS [6: 2007] and José Maria Coma FORT [6: 2014]. The Code is also central to Jill HARRIES' examination of the functioning of late Roman Law [6: 1999]. In addition there are collections of essays dedicated to the Code, edited by Jill HARRIES and Ian WOOD [6: 1993] as well as two separate collections edited by Sylvie CROGIEZ-PÉTREQUIN and Pierre JAILLETTE, the first of which is very closely focussed on the text and on specific laws within it, while the second looks more generally at what it reveals about the late Roman World and its administration [6: CROGIEZ-PÉTREQUIN/JAILLETTE 2009, 2012]. Fergus MILLAR's study of the reign of Theodosius II [6: 2006] has put the Code as well as the theological developments of the period firmly into context. The laws of some individual emperors have been studied separately: Simon CORCORAN [6: 2000] has considered the legislation of the Tetrarchic period (most of which is not contained in the *Codex Theodosianus*, which only covers legislation issued between the years 312 and 438). There is also a study of Julian's legislation by Raphael BRENDEL [4.4: 2017] and of Valentinian I's by Sebastian SCHMIDT-HOFNER [4.5: 2008]. The novels of Majorian are discussed by Fabrizio OPPEDISANO [4.4: 2013].

The administration SCHMIDT-HOFNER takes up a major line of approach to imperial administration that is most firmly set out by Fergus MILLAR [4.2: 1977]:

that government was largely reactive. The fullest analysis of late Roman administration is that of Christopher Kelly [6: 2004], who takes as his point of departure the work of the early sixth-century Byzantine administrator John Lydus. Like Kelly, Daniëlle Slootjes [6: 2006] draws on evidence from the East (Libanius, Menander Rhetor and Basil of Caesarea) rather than the West in her study of Late Roman governors. Provincial governors are the subject of a volume of *Antiquité Tardive* [1998]. The office of praetorian prefect and its origins in the period between 282 and 337 are dealt with by Pierfrancesco Porena [6: 2003]. The development of imperial rule is the subject of a collection of articles resulting from a conference held at Konstanz and edited by Johannes Wienand [6: 2015]. The importance of the imperial court is explored in a collection of essays edited by Kamil Cyprian Choda, Maurits Sterk de Leeuw and Fabian Schulz [6: 2020]. The imperial court is also considered by Paul Barnwell in the first of two volumes that provide a survey of late- and post-Roman government [6: Barnwell 1992].

The legislation of the imperial court is very much less controversial than is the problem of the law to be found outside that of the classical jurists. To describe this, Ernst Levy used the term 'Vulgar Law', which had been coined by Heinrich Brunner to describe the laws of the successor states. Levy applied it specifically to the law of property [6: Levy 1951] and to the law of obligation [6: Levy 1956]. In order to reconstruct 'Vulgar Law' (which is not a term used by the Romans themselves), Levy combined Roman and post-Roman material, and in so doing pointed to the Roman origins of much that is contained in the so-called 'Germanic' law codes. A useful discussion of the problems of 'Vulgar Law' is that of Detlef Liebs in a volume edited by Boudewijn Sirks [6: Liebs 2008]. *(margin: Vulgar law)*

Others have approached the day-to-day legal practices of the Empire from different points of view, stressing the regional practice of law. Some of the best evidence comes from Egypt, which is studied by Bernard Palme in the volume edited by Sirks [6: Palme 2008]. Egyptian papyri also provide the material for a detailed analysis of dispute settlement by Traianos Gagos and P. van Minnen [6: 1994]. What is unclear is the extent to which one can apply the model that is suggested by the Egyptian evidence to the rest of the Empire. The question of military law has emerged increasingly as a subject of significance, not just for the Empire itself, but also for the successor *(margin: Legal practice)* states. On this there is a volume edited by Fabio Bᴏᴛᴛᴀ and Luca Lᴏsᴄʜɪᴀᴠᴏ [6: 2015].

The *Notitia Dignitatum*   A key source for the military organisation of the later Empire is the *Notitia Dignitatum*, a list of officials which seems to have achieved its final form in the early fifth century. On the *Notitia* there is a recent Spanish edition with commentary [15.4: Notitia dignitatum 2005] and a somewhat older collection of articles edited by J. C. Mᴀɴɴ, Roger Gᴏᴏᴅʙᴜʀɴ and P. Bᴀʀᴛʜᴏʟᴏᴍᴇᴡ [6: 1976]. There is also a substantial study of the evidence of the *Notitia* for the Late Roman army by Dietrich Hᴏꜰꜰᴍᴀɴɴ [6: 1969–70]. Studies of the late Roman army inevitably make much use of the *Notitia*. Among the most useful monographs devoted to the army are those of Warren Tʀᴇᴀᴅɢᴏʟᴅ [4.1: 1995], Pat Sᴏᴜᴛʜᴇʀɴ and Karen Dɪxᴏɴ [6: 1996], Hugh Eʟᴛᴏɴ [4.2: 1996], and Martijn J. Nɪᴄᴀsɪᴇ [6: 1998].

The *Tabula Peutingeriana*   The *Tabula Peutingeriana*, a map of itineraries stretching across the Roman Empire which only survives in a much later copy, is now thought by some scholars to be a work of propaganda, extolling the peaceful nature of the Empire, rather than a useful guide for travellers. Richard Tᴀʟʙᴇʀᴛ [6: 2010] has argued that it is a product of the Tetrarchy, although some of its source material would seem to belong to the early Empire, as argued by Glenn Bᴏᴡᴇʀsᴏᴄᴋ [6: 1994] in his study of Roman Arabia. By contrast Emily Aʟʙᴜ [6: 2014] has argued for a Carolingian origin, making use of Roman written material.

7 The Western Church in the Late Fourth and Fifth Centuries

The documentation of heresy   By comparison with the evidence for secular history, that for some aspects of the history of the Church is very considerable. Certainly, for most of the major theological debates the views of the victors are better known than are those of the losers. The Donatist and Arian controversies which began in the time of Constantine continued through the fourth and fifth centuries, and the Arian controversy would be transformed through the adoption of homoean doctrine by some barbarian groups – a point to which we will return. For Priscillianism we now have the translation and discussion of Priscillian's own writings by Marco Cᴏɴᴛɪ [7: 2009]. There is an extremely extensive bibliography in a Spanish study by Andrés Olivares Guillem [7: 2004]. There are a handful of Pelagian letters which have been edited and discussed by B. R. Rees [7: 1998]. The most recent study of Pelagianism, by Ali Bonner [7: 2018], argues somewhat controversially that the heresy was a fiction invented by Augustine.

The documentation for the Nestorians and the Monophysites is more complex, although it impinges less on the history of the Western Church. Despite the condemnation of Nestorius at the Council of Ephesus in 431, the Nestorians survived, largely outside the Empire, with the result that some of the most important evidence for their ideas is preserved in texts from Central Asia. The Monophysites survived in the Levant, where they proved a very disruptive force for the Empire in the late fifth to the early seventh century [7: Frend 1972]. Both theologies would be debated in the West, but with practically no understanding. Western reactions to the theological developments in the East are discussed by Henry Chadwick in his overview of relations between the eastern and western churches [7: 2003] and in much greater detail in the relevant volume of the *Geschichte des Christentums*, edited by Jean-Marie Mayeur, Luce Pietri and André Vauchez [7: 2005].

For the major Church councils we usually have good source material, almost all of which was edited by Eduard Schwartz and Johannes Straub [7: 1914–71] and all of which is discussed in the great handbook of Hefele-Leclerq [7: 1907–52]. However, we lack the canons of the pro-homoean councils of Seleucia (359), Rimini (Ariminum) (359) and the 360 Council of Constantinople, just as we lack the official records of Nicaea I. For the Councils of Sardica (343) [7: Barnard 1958], Ephesus, and Chalcedon, on the other hand, we have excellent documentation in terms of the canons promulgated as well as related documentation and narratives recorded in Church histories. Recent studies include translations of the canons of Ephesus, Chalcedon, and Constantinople together with extensive commentary by Richard Price [7: 2005; Price/Whitby 2009]. In addition to the œcumenical councils, we have important collections of provincial councils from Africa [7: Munier 1974], Spain [7: Vives 1963], and Gaul [4.2: Munier 1963], all of which are available in scholarly editions [see 15.2]. *The Church councils*

From the fourth century onwards, there are many works of theology, sermons as well as religious tracts, especially those written by the Church Fathers – most of which are edited in the *Corpus* *Editions of works of theology*

Scriptorum Ecclesiasticorum Latinorum or the *Corpus Christiano-rum* series. Among the most important collections for the study of the West are those of Hilary, Ambrose, Jerome, and Augustine. Of these, the last three are the subjects of very extensive bibliography; recent biographies provide useful points of departure [7: McLYNN 1994; CAIN/LÖSSL 2009; FUHRER 2004; O'DONNELL 2005; ROSEN 2015; LANE FOX 2015]. Augustine is also the subject of handbooks in both German and English [7: STUMP/KRETZMANM 2001; GEERLINGS 2002; DRECOLL 2007].

Less significant theologians, for instance Chromatius of Aquileia [7: LEMARIÉ 1969, 1971; TESTI 1989; McEACHNIE 2014] and Maximus of Turin, are represented in the sermon literature. A recent volume of studies of sermon literature provides an overview of late antique and early medieval preaching [7: DIESENBERGER/HEN/POLLHEIMER 2013]. Individual sermons are to be found in many manuscripts, and most collections of sermons, including that of Augustine, have been put together by modern scholars. One sixth-century collection known under the name of *Eusebius Gallicanus* has been studied by Lisa Karen BAILEY [7: 2010] in the light of what it has to tell us about the entrenchment of Christianity in fifth-century Gaul. BAILEY has also explored the piety of the laity in a more recent publication [7: 2017].

Christian epistolography
For some leading theologians and churchmen, we also have considerable numbers of letters. There are sizeable collections from Ambrose, Jerome, Augustine, and Paulinus of Nola as well as collections of papal letters together with small collections and individual letters from other bishops. The Christian epistolography of Late Antiquity is the subject of several volumes of collected essays [7: SOGNO/STORIN/WATTS 2017; NEIL/ALLEN 2015].

Christian poetry
The volume of Christian poetry is also a notable feature of the late fourth and fifth centuries. Most obviously there is the poetry of Prudentius, not least the *Peristephanon* [7: PALMER 1989; ROBERTS 1993] and the *Psychomachia* [7: FRISCH 2020]. Among the most recent studies of Prudentius is that of Paula HERSHKOWITZ [7: 2017]. A major feature of poetry of the period was the composition of Biblical epic, as for instance in the works of Claudius Marius Victorinus and Avitus of Vienne, who versified part of the Old Testament, and Juvencus and Sedulius, both of whom versified the New Testament. This tradition has been studied by Michael ROBERTS [7: 1985] and by Daniel NODES [7: 1993]. There is also the substantial autobiographical *Eu-*

charisticos of Paulinus of Pella [15.7/Paulinus of Pella: Moussy 1974; Lucarini 2006]. At the end of the fifth century, Dracontius wrote a verse account of the Creation story in his *Hexameron*, which forms the first part of his *De Laudibus Dei* [7: Moussy/Camus 2002]. This has attracted less attention than has Prudentius, although there is a study of Dracontius's use of allegory by Roswitha Simons [7: 2005; Castagna 1997].

From the first half of the fifth century there are a number of religious poems which offer comment on the state of the Empire, which attracted the attention of Pierre Courcelle, whose monograph retains much of its value [7: 1964], although some poems have been re-edited and reconsidered. For instance, the *De Providentia Dei* ascribed to Prosper of Aquitaine is the subject of study by Miroslav Marcovich [7: 1989]. Among other poetry, from the mid fourth century there are the short pieces written by pope Damasus in his promotion of the cults of Roman martyrs [7: Trout 2015].

Most of the martyr acts that have survived date from subsequent generations, even though they may purport to be eye-witness accounts [4.1: Lapidge 2018]. In the West, although there is little hagiography from before 400, we have numerous texts from the fifth century onwards. The multi-volume survey of hagiography, begun by Guy Philippart in 1994, is a useful starting point for studying the genre [7: 1994]. The development of the study of early hagiographical texts is surveyed by K. Staat [7: 2019]. Particularly important is the recent emphasis on the rewriting of works of hagiography, which was undertaken in the early Middle Ages and Carolingian periods [7: Goullet/Heinzelmann/Veyrad-Cosme 2010]. This has transformed what used to be a rather simplistic debate about authenticity and forgery. The early stages of the western tradition are considered by M. S. Williams [7: 2008], but for the fourth- and fifth-century texts the starting point is almost always with recent editions, especially those published in *Sources Chrétiennes*, not least Jacques Fontaine's edition of the *Vita Martini* by Sulpicius Severus [7: 1967–69]. *The Life of Martin* by Sulpicius Severus has attracted additional attention, for instance from Clare Stancliffe [7: 1983]. In addition we have a few accounts of journeys to the Holy Land, notably those of the Bordeaux pilgrim, from c. 333/4, and of Egeria (c. 381–6) [7: Hunt 1984].

Apart from the written sources, there is a sizable corpus of archaeological material, both in terms of objects and in terms of sites

Martyr acts and hagiography

Church archaeology

excavated, relating to the Church. The major compendium of information on ecclesiastical archaeology relates specifically to Gaul and is to be found in the *Topographie chrétienne de l'ancienne Gaule* [10: Topographie 1972–2014]. For Italy, there is an archaeological survey by Neil Christie [7: 2006] which covers ecclesiastical as well as secular sites. The early churches of Sardinia have been studied by Mark Joseph Johnson [7: 2013]. The North African churches are discussed by Isabelle Gui, Noël Duval, and Jean-Pierre Caillet in a two-volume survey from 1992 [7: 1992], and Duval [7: 2006] has subsequently provided an overview of the developments of art and architecture in the region in a contribution to *Antiquité Tardive*. The Christian archaeology of Spain is surveyed by Kim Bowes [7: 2005], and there are also relevant chapters in the overview of Spanish archaeology by Javier Martínez Jiménez, Isaac Sastre de Diego and Carlos Tejerizo García [3: 2018].

The spread of Christianity   The spread of Christianity following the conversion of Constantine has been much debated. The assumption that the religion was most widespread among the lower orders of society has been abandoned. Much recent work, notably by Kate Cooper, has concentrated on the history of the family as the locus for Christianisation [7: Cooper 2007; Cooper/Hillner 2007; Sessa 2012]. At the same time, the view that among aristocratic families it was the women who converted first has been strongly challenged by Michele Salzman [7: 2002].

The Church in secular legislation   For the development of the Church as an institution, there is a considerable body of law contained in Book XVI of the Theodosian Code – which, one might note, is much more exclusive in its definition of acceptable religion than pagan legislation had been, despite the earlier condemnation by pagan emperors of Christians, Jews, and Manichees. On legislation against heretics there is the study of Ferdinando Zuccotti [7: 1992].

Diocesan history   About some other aspects of Church development we are less well informed. The establishment of individual dioceses, which were usually based on the old blocks of city administration, the *civitates*, is rarely attested. Rather, we have to note episcopal lists from Church councils and references in letters and in works of hagiography. The information from these sources is gathered in the volumes of *Prosopographie chrétienne*.

For the functioning of the dioceses, in addition to the information of the *Theodosian Code* and of the Church canons, papal and episcopal letters are often extremely informative. Much of this material, especially that relating to the fourth and fifth centuries, above all in the East, has been studied by Claudia Rapp [7: 2005]. For episcopal crisis management in the fifth and sixth centuries there is a valuable survey by Pauline Allen and Bronwen Neil [7: 2013]. An equally illuminating study of a particular region is Rita Lizzi Testa's examination of the ecclesiastical structures of *Italia Annonaria* [7: 1989]. The question of a bishop's legal jurisdiction, and in particular the functioning of the *episcopalis audientia*, is complex and a matter of debate, not least because of changes in the relevant legislation. The current understanding is examined by Baudewijn Sirks [7: 2013], who emphasises the bishop's role as mediator. The *episcopalis audientia* is also examined by Caroline Humfress [7: 2011].

The development of papal authority did not, of course, follow exactly the same trajectory as did that of the authority of other bishops. Its establishment was slow and uneven. Kristina Sessa [7: 2012] has recently demonstrated that the papacy modelled its pastoral activities on traditional senatorial household management. In addition, individual bishops of Rome often took advantage of moments of conflict and dispute to extend their authority. This holds true for the development of the papal authority in the Church – for instance, pope Celestine responded to the Nestorian crisis by commissioning Cyril of Alexandria to proceed against Nestorius, while pope Leo was involved in the negotiations at the Council of Chalcedon, to which he directed his Tome. At a more local level, disputed elections – for instance those of Liberius and Felix II, Damasus and Ursinus, and Symmachus and Laurentius – were a factor in the development of papal authority within the city of Rome itself. Recent work on pope Damasus has stressed his conflict with the Antipope Ursinus as a factor in his championing of the cults of the Roman martyrs [7: Reutter 2009; 4.5: Löx 2013]. And disputed elections also underlay the development of liturgical processions [7: Latham 2012].

Papal authority

Despite the significance of the fourth- and fifth-century popes there are few modern biographies, although there are lengthy entries in the major encyclopedias, in particular the *Biographisch-bibliographisches Kirchenlexikon* and the *Lexikon des Mittelalters*. Damasus, however, has recently attracted a good deal of attention. There is Dennis Trout's study of his poetry, while his role in developing the cult of the martyrs is most fully examined by Markus Löx

The bishop of Rome

[4.5: 2013]. On his pontificate there are valuable articles in a volume devoted to the *Collectio Avellana* [7: TESTA/MARCONI 2019]. Among other articles there is Neil McLYNN's [7: 2012] contribution to a volume on late-antique Rome and Milan edited by Therese FUHRER. There is a biography of Leo the Great by Bronwen NEIL [7: 2009], while the pope's theology is placed in its social and political context by Susan WESSEL [7: 2008]. Walter ULLMANN [7: 1981] analysed the pontificate of Gelasius, and especially the pope's political ideology, in terms of the shift from Late Antiquity to the early Middle Ages, while a more recent study of Gelasius is that of Bronwen NEIL and Pauline ALLEN [7: 2014] which uses the pope's letters as a way of examining his management of the Church. Useful indications of the precise contexts in which the bishops of Rome advanced their authority is to be found in a collection edited by Geoffrey DUNN [7: 2015].

Rome   A good deal of attention has been paid to the city of Rome itself and its ecclesiastical monuments. An important point of departure is the volume published following the excavation of the site of the *Crypta Balbi*, edited by Maria ARENA, Paolo DELOGU et al. [10: 2001]. There is still much of value in Richard KRAUTHEIMER's *Rome, Profile of a City* [10: 1980] and his *Three Christian Capitals* [4.2: 1983], but both need to be read in the light of more recent research. There are more recent accounts of the city by John CURRAN [10: 2000] and Bertand LANÇON [10: 2000], and by Hendrik DEY in his survey of medieval Rome [10: 2021]. The collection edited by Lucy GRIG and Gavin KELLY entitled *Two Romes* [7: 2012] provides articles on Rome and Constantinople, with interesting comparisons between the two cities. Rome and Milan are juxtaposed in a volume edited by Therese FUHRER [4.2: 2012]. For fifth-century Rome there are discussions of the art and liturgy in the volume edited by Ivan FOLETTI and Manuela GIANANDREA [7: 2017]. The early history of St Peter's is the subject of a collection of articles edited by Rosamond McKITTERICK, John OSBORNE, Carol RICHARDSON and Joanna STORY [5.2: 2013] which adds significantly to our understanding of the building, although it appeared too early to take account of Richard WESTALL's arguments that the building was largely the work of Constantius II [4.2: 2015].

The cult of saints   Central to the history of Rome in this period is the development of the cult of the martyrs. In addition to Michael LAPIDGE's translation of the Acts of the martyrs [4.1: 2018], there has been a major project on the Roman martyrs, some of the findings of which have been published by Kate Cooper and Julia Hillner [7: 2007]. The evidence for the catacombs, however, is highly problematic, as has been shown by Nicola Denzey Lewis [7: 2020].

The modern study of the shrines of the Christian martyrs can probably be said to begin with André Grabar's art-historical study *Martyrium* of 1943–6 [7]. Historical study of the cult of the saints gathered momentum with the work of Peter Brown; above all, there is a monograph from 1981 [7: 1981], while the articles where he first set out his ideas are included in a collection published in 1972 [7: 1972]. Some of the ideas have been extended or modified in the course of subsequent discussion, for instance in a volume edited by James Howard-Johnston and Paul Antony Hayward [7: 1999]. Most recently, there is a volume edited by Jean-Pierre Caillet, Sylvain Destephen, Bruno Dumézil and Hervé Inglebert [7: 2015] with contributions on the development of patron saints in cities of the Roman World, including Rome, and Lyon, as well as more general surveys of the development of saint cults in North Africa, Italy, Gaul and Spain. The fullest study of the origins of the cult of relics is by Robert Wiśniewski [7: 2019], who also joint edited, along with Raymond Van Dam and Bryan Ward-Perkins, the procedings of a conference devoted to the cult of saints [7: 2023].

Brown's contribution is not just limited to a study of the cult of the saints. His subsequent work has dealt with the rise of Western Christendom [3: 1996] as well as Christian attitudes to wealth [3: 2012; 7: 2016] and to the afterlife [7: 2015]. These works have also led to further discussion, for instance in volumes edited by Philip Rousseau and Manolis Papoutsakis [2: 2009] and by Jamie Kreiner and Helmut Reimitz [2: 2016].

The rise of Christendom

Brown's first monograph, however, was devoted to Augustine, and his biography of the Church Father provides an introduction not only to the man and his thought, but also to his Age [7: 1967]. For the significance of Augustine's writings, not just of their theological importance, but rather of what light they shed on the Late Antique World, the more recent biographies by J.J. O'Donnell [7: 2005] and Robin Lane Fox [4.1: 2015] are also valuable. Robert Markus' consideration of Augustine's notion of the world (*Saeculum*) remains central for anyone trying to understand fifth- and sixth-century Christianity, although, as Markus points out, even in his own day Augustine was misunderstood. [7: 1970] Aspects of Markus'

Augustine

ideas are elaborated on in the *Festschrift* edited by William KLING-SHIRN and Mark VESSEY [7: 1999].

Monks and holy men

Prior to his monograph on the 'Cult of the Saints', BROWN had drawn attention to the importance of living holy men, above all in an article from 1971 [7]. A good deal of attention has subsequently been paid to the ascetics and monks of the Holy Land and of Egypt. The most important of the early monastic founders, Pachomius, is the subject of a biography by Philip ROUSSEAU [7: 1985]. Knowledge of Egyptian monasticism has been steadily transformed as a result of archaeological findings. The most comprehensive survey to-date is that of Eva WIPSZYCKA [7: 2018].

Although a significant monastic tradition did not develop within the western Church until the end of the fourth century, news of the ascetic movement was brought back from Egypt and the Holy Land by pilgrims, whose histories have been traced by numerous scholars, including David HUNT [7: 1984].

The spread of monasticism

One additional factor in setting the scene for the development of monasticism in the West was the persecution of orthodox bishops by the homoean successors of Constantine, which spread information about Antony, in particular, to the West. The impact of this on Martin has been emphasised by Clare STANCLIFFE [7: 1983]. Philip ROUSSEAU [7: 1978] has noted the influence of ascetic ideas in his study of the age of Jerome and Cassian. The development of these issues through to the Age of Gregory the Great is mapped out by Conrad LEYSER [7: 2000], who has also examined the question of authority in the *Life of Fulgentius of Ruspe* [7: 2007]. The impact of asceticism on the Gallic episcopate in the fifth and sixth centuries is considered by Franca Ela CONSOLINO [7: 1979].

Lérins and its influence

The spread of monasticism in southern Gaul is closely associated with the community of Lérins – which, for Friedrich PRINZ [2: 1965], along with the Martinian communities of Ligugé and Marmoutier, provided the chief inspiration of the movement. Lérinian monasticism has received increasing attention in recent years, not least because of the (questionable) ascription of the *Regula Patrum* to the island by Adalbert de VOGÜÉ [7: 1982]. More secure is the hagiography associated with the island, notably the *Lives* of Honoratus and Hilary [7: VALENTIN 1977; CAVALLIN 1997]. A useful compendium of articles on the island is that edited by Yann CODOU and Michel LAUWERS [7: 2009]. The influence of the monastery on several generations of bishops (mainly of Arles) who were trained there is set out most fully by Ralph Mathisen [7: 1989], who also exposes the extent to which even the most ascetic bishops were involved in politics.

Ascetic and theological authors from the Lérins circle include Eucherius of Lyon and Faustus of Riez. Some sermons of Faustus survive in the collection known as *Eusebius Gallicanus*. Faustus also occasioned the writing of perhaps the most sophisticated work of theology to be written in fifth-century Gaul, the *De Statu Animae* of Claudianus Mamertus. The debate between the two theologians is best studied by E. L. Fortin [7: 1959]. Associated with Lérins, but based in Marseille, was John Cassian, whose influence has been studied by Philip Rousseau [7: 1978], Conrad Leyser [7: 2000], and most recently by Richard Goodrich [7: 2007].

The other major Gallic religious author of the fifth century, Sal- Salvian
vian of Marseille, provides the most vivid account of Gallo-Roman society. He is frequently referred to in overviews of the period, not least because of his sharp analysis of the evils of wealth [3: Brown 2012] which has become central to readings of the socio-economic as well as the religious history of the period. For study devoted exclusively to his works there is a monograph by Jan Badewien [7: 1980].

8 Late Roman Secular Culture

Many of the major literary works of Late Antiquity exist in recent, Sources
or well-regarded older, editions. The great collection of the *Monumenta Germaniae Historica* provides the secular equivalent to the religious collections of the *Corpus Scriptorum Ecclesiasticorum Latinorum*, *Corpus Christianorum Series Latina*, and *Sources Chrétiennes*. There is a useful companion volume to Late Antique Literature edited by Scott McGill and Edward Watts [8: 2018].

Marrou's studies of Augustine and the end of Ancient culture [2: Education
1938] and his subsequent study of Late Antique Education [2: 1948] remain important, despite their age. The period following that studied by Marrou is covered, albeit at a more prosaic level, in Pierre Riché's study of education in the barbarian world [8: 1962]. Among more recent studies of the grammarians is that of Robert Kaster [8: 1988]. Rhetoric is central to the works of the panegyrists and to the sermons of ecclesiastics, several of whom (most notably Augustine) had rhetorical training. Rhetorical training is also apparent in the

works of the fourth- and fifth-century letter writers (a number of whom were also rhetors). Alongside discussions of rhetoric, it is important to note the significance of the teaching of grammar. The grammatical texts of Late Antiquity present problems in terms of their date and their geographical origin [8: Law 1997]; they are, nevertheless, key works in the history of Late Antique culture.

The democratisation of culture

For Santo Mazzarino [8: 1974], one aspect of Christianisation was the democratisation of culture: a novelty of Christian culture was that it was not just addressed to the elite, but to the whole of the population, including the rural and urban poor. The idea that Christianisation led to the development of popular, as opposed to elite, culture was challenged in a seminal lecture by Arnaldo Momigliano [8: 1972], who denied the value of the concept of popular religious beliefs. The question of the democratisation of culture, however, is the theme of a volume of *Antiquité Tardive* [8: 2002].

Panegyrics

Christian religious texts occupy more pages in modern printed editions than do secular texts, but the fourth and fifth centuries could still boast a significant secular written culture. For the panegyrics there are the editions of the Latin sources by Brigitte Müller-Rettig [8: 2008–12] and by Ted Nixon and Barbara Rogers [4.1: 1994]. Symmachus' oratorical works are considered by R. H. Barrow [4.5: 1976]. Symmachus himself is a key figure in Alan Cameron's study of the last pagans of Rome [8: 2011]. Cameron [8: 1970] is also among the chief interpreters of the poet Claudian. For more general studies of the late antique tradition of panegyric, there is seminal work by Sabine MacCormack [8: 1981], together with Michael McCormick's examination of victory celebrations [8: 1986]. The architectural context of such ceremonies is examined by Hendrik Dey [8: 2015].

Secular poetry

The panegyrics of Claudian and Sidonius are in verse. Other major writers of secular verse include Ausonius, of whom there is a study by Hagith Sivan [4.5: 1993]. The remaining book of the *De Reditu Suo* by Rutilius Namatianus, along with the rediscovered fragments of Book Two, is edited and discussed by Ernst Doblhofer [8: 1972–7]. In addition to his religious work, notably the *De Laudibus Dei*, Dracontius also wrote an epic on the story of Orestes, together with numerous occasional pieces, including the *Satisfactio ad Gunthamundum* [7: Moussy/Camus 2002]. A substantial number of papers in a collection on the literature of Vandalic Africa, edited by Étienne Wolf [8: 2015], are dedicated to Dracontius' secular poems. Some works by contemporaries of Dracontius from North Africa are preserved in the Latin Anthology and have been the subject of commentary by N. M. Kay [8: 2006] and more recently by Wolfgang Fels [8: 2014].

Among philosophical works the individual books of Martianus Capella's *De Nuptiis Philologiae et Mercurii* have been the subject of considerable study by Danuta Shanzer [8: 1986]. Macrobius' *Saturnalia* has been recently re-edited by Robert Kaster [8: 2011]. In addition there are Augustine's Cassiciacum dialogues, of which the most recent study is by Erik Kenyon [8: 2018].

Philosophy

A distinctive feature of the culture of Late Antiquity is the cult of letters, which are usually written in extremely elevated and often obscure Latin [8: Schwitter 2015]. Of relevance here is André Loyen's study [8: 1943] of the Latin style of the fourth and fifth centuries, which he identified as the *stylum pingue atque floridum* and which was central to the writing of the upper classes. A more recent study that extends the discussion is that of Michael Roberts [8: 1989]. Several important letter collections survive, among them the letters of Symmachus and Sidonius, which were gathered together by their authors. The model for these two authors was Pliny. For recent studies of the genre of letters there are volumes of essays edited by Bronwen Neil and Pauline Allen [7: 2015], Cristiana Sogno, Bradley K. Storin and Edward J. Watts [7: 2017] and Gernot Michael Müller [8: 2018]. Alongside the Plinian model, a tradition of Christian letter-writing developed, as is apparent in the letters of leading ecclesiastics, including Ambrose, Jerome, and Augustine. Among the most distinctive writers of Christian friendship letters was Paulinus of Nola, whose notion of friendship was explored by Pierre Fabre in 1949 [8] and more recently by Catherine Conybeare [8: 2000] and Sigrid Mratschek [8: 2002]. There is a study of all Paulinus' works by Dennis Trout [8: 1999]. The church built by Paulinus, which is the subject of some of his writing, survives in large measure [8: Brandenburg/Ermini 2003].

Letter-writing

The other major area of literary activity in the period was that of history writing, which divides into several separate traditions. Among those adopting classical models were Ammianus Marcellinus, who continued the tradition of Tacitus and who has been the subject of study by John Matthews [4.3: 1989], Tim Barnes [4.3: 1998], and Gavin Kelly [4.3: 2008]. There is also a collection of essays edited by Jan Drijvers and David Hunt [4.3: 1999]. There is a full bibliography edited by Fred C. Jenkins [4.3: 2017]. Probably nearly con-

History writing

temporary with the work of Ammianus was the *Historia Augusta*, whose author took Suetonius as his model [8: MECKLER 1996].

In addition to histories in the style of Tacitus and Suetonius, Aurelius Victor and Eutropius continued the tradition of historical epitomes [4.1: BIRD 1984; ROHRBACHER 2002: STOVER/WOUDHUYSEN 2023]. Late Antiquity also boasted a significant number of Chronicle writers. The tradition of Chronicle writing, from the first century BC onwards, is the subject of detailed analysis by Richard BURGESS and Michael KULIKOWSKI [5.2: 2013]. Also of importance in understanding the late antique Chronicle tradition is the work of Michele SALZMAN on the Calendar of Philocalus [8: 1990], Stephen MUHLBERGER on the fifth-century chroniclers [5.2: 1990], and Brian CROKE on Marcellinus Comes [8: 2001]. The chronicle tradition stretches back into the late Republican era, but underwent a major change in reaction to the *Chronicle* of Eusebius, whose contribution to Late Antique culture is the subject of a collection of essays edited by Aaron JOHNSON and Jeremy SCOTT [4.1: 2013].

9 Economy and Society

Coinage The sources for the Late Antique economy are extremely varied. The laws are often useful, and the coinage is an invaluable resource. There are numerous catalogues of coin collections. A particularly valuable analysis of the late Antique imperial gold and silver coinage before 411 is provided by P. GUEST in his study of the Hoxne hoard from fifth-century Britain [9: GUEST 2005]. The major study of the post-imperial coinage is that by Philip GRIERSON and Mark BLACKBURN [9: 1986], although subsequent finds have inevitably meant that modifications are necessary. Some literary texts (for instance the letters of Symmachus, but also some historical and hagiographical narratives) cast light on the wealth of the aristocracy.

The Albertini Tablets and Pizarras Visigodas Unfortunately there is little detailed information about the lower levels of society for the West, although some light on life in one great domain in Vandal Africa is shed by the Albertini Tablets – 34 wooden writing tablets dating from 493–6 – which were edited in 1952 [10: COURTOIS/LESCHI/PERRAT/SAUMAGNE 1952]. There has recently been a study of the information they provide on legal issues [9: WESSEL 2003]. From Spain there are the *pizarras visigodas*, documents on slate, the earliest of which date to the sixth century [9: VELÁZQUEZ

Soriano 2004]. By comparison, however, papyri have allowed extremely precise analysis of the Egyptian economy (for example by Jairus Banaji [3: 2001]), which is suggestive when considering the economy of the rest of the Empire, but cannot be taken as providing an image of the norm, simply because of the unique geography of Egypt, dominated by the Nile, but surrounded by desert.

Egyptian papyri

Two very substantial books have relatively recently dealt with the Late Roman and early medieval economy. Michael McCormick's emphasis, as his subtitle states, is on communications and commerce [3: 2001]. In addition to looking at the state of the economy, McCormick pays attention to the evidence for travel and travellers, including pilgrims, ambassadors, traders, slaves and exiles, as well as the objects that were transported. Less concerned with trade, albeit paying some attention to networks, is Chris Wickham's study of Europe and the Mediterranean in the period from 200–800 [3: 2005]. Wickham's emphasis is on aristocrats and peasants, with a good deal of emphasis placed on regional variation. His conclusions, particularly with regard to the changing situation of the peasantry, have prompted a good deal of discussion, not least in review articles by John Haldon [3: 2008], Ian Wood [3: 2007], and Jairus Banaji [3: 2008]. Banaji's article originally appeared in a volume of the *Journal of Agrarian Change* which also included a study of aristocrats and peasants between 400 and 800 by Peter Sarris [9: 2008], again responding to Wickham. At the start of his more recent study of the two centuries from 500 to 700, Sarris discusses many of the same issues [9: 2011]. Kyle Harper [9: 2011], in a monograph on slavery, takes a different line from Wickham on the nature of Late Roman slavery, which he sees as extensive and ending only with the political breakdown of the fifth century.

General surveys of the economy

Jairus Banaji has himself offered a major reinterpretation of the Late Roman Economy in which considerable emphasis is placed on the coin reforms of Diocletian and Constantine, which benefitted those in the pay of the Empire (soldiers and senior bureaucrats) and allowed the accumulation of vast amounts of wealth in the hands of the top levels of the senatorial aristocracy [3: 2007, 2016]. This is clearly an observation of major importance for the whole Roman World in the fourth and fifth centuries. Thereafter, Banaji directs his attention essentially to the evidence from Egypt. The ending of the supply of gold coin in much of the West, as a result of

Monetary history

political breakdown, was surely a factor in the subsequent economic decline.

The plague

The Late Antique economy has also been the subject of radical reconsideration in recent years because of a growing awareness of environmental issues. For the Justinianic Plague of the sixth century there is important discussion in a volume edited by Lester Lɪᴛᴛʟᴇ [3: 2007]. Michael McCoʀᴍɪᴄᴋ has emphasised the significance of 'mass death' [3: 2015, 2016]. But the most far-reaching study of climate change and plague by Kyle Hᴀʀᴘᴇʀ [9: 2017] has been challenged in its detail by John Hᴀʟᴅᴏɴ, Hugh Eʟᴛᴏɴ et al. [3: 2018]. The scale of impact has been keenly questioned by Lee Moʀᴅᴇᴄʜᴀɪ and Merle Eɪsᴇɴʙᴇʀɢ in a series of articles [3: 2019, 2020; Moʀᴅᴇᴄʜᴀɪ/Eɪsᴇɴ-ʙᴇʀɢ/Nᴇᴡғɪᴇʟᴅ et al. 2019]. That some cities and regions were badly affected by the plague seems clear enough, but the overall impact of climate change and plague on the economy is still a point of discussion, rather than an issue that is fully understood.

The Church and the economy

These major discussions do not concern themselves with the impact of the Church on the economy, which remains an understudied area, although the significance of religious structures is alluded to by John Hᴀʟᴅᴏɴ in his discussion of the 'tributary mode of production' [9: 1993]. *Antiquité Tardive* [9: Association pour l'Antiquité Tardive 2006] is unusual in dedicating a complete volume to religion and the economy. Further articles dealing with Church property are also included in a volume concerned with the countryside [9: Association pour l'Antiquité Tardive 2013]. Even so, the extent of ecclesiastical landholding remains under-researched. The standard point of reference is still the work of Émile Lᴇsɴᴇ, originally published in 1910 [9: 1910]. A recent overview by Ian Wᴏᴏᴅ [9: 2013: 7: 2022] studies property donations to the Church up to the early eighth century, but for detailed consideration of property-holding one needs to turn to studies of specific regions, like that of the papal landholdings in Lazio by Federico Mᴀʀᴀᴢᴢɪ [9: 1998].

Rich and poor

More attention has been paid to ecclesiastical attitudes towards wealth and more especially towards poverty. Building on the work of Évelyne Pᴀᴛʟᴀɢᴇᴀɴ [9: 1977], Peter Bʀᴏᴡɴ [9: 2002] traced the rise of Christian concerns for the poor and their effect on the Church's authority. More recently, Bʀᴏᴡɴ has stressed the deployment of wealth by Christians, above all aristocratic Christians, in their search for salvation, thus highlighting what he has described as the spiritual economy [3: 2012, 7: 2016]. Poverty in the West is the subject of a study by Valerio Neri [9: 1998], who considers the poor alongside other marginal groups: the 'infames' and the criminals.

The aspect of social history that has attracted most attention has been that of the senatorial aristocracy. For a general survey there are an old study by M. T. Arnheim [9: 1972] and a more recent one by Beat Näf [9: 1995]. The role of the senatorial classes in government has been analysed by D. Schlinkert [9: 1996], who notes the counterbalancing role of the eunuchs. The relations of the senators with the court in the late fourth and early fifth centuries is the subject of a seminal monograph by John Matthews [4.5: 1975], which prompted an important review article by Patrick Wormald [9: 1976], spelling out the implications of Matthews' work for the early medievalist. The ideology of the senatorial aristocracy as represented in inscriptions has been studied by H. Niquet [9: 2000]. Michele Salzman [7: 2002] has analysed the conversion of the aristocracy, arguing that the established model, according to which aristocratic women converted before the men, is not supported by the evidence. From the late fourth century the Gallic aristocracy is particularly well evidenced, and influential, as noted by Matthews [9: 1975]. The origins of its influence are studied by Hagith Sivan [4.5: 1993] in the context of the career of Ausonius. Still of great value is the seminal prosopographical survey made by Karl Friedrich Stroheker [2: 1948]. The Italian senate is the subject of studies by André Chastagnol [9: 1966] (dealing with the reign of Odoacer) and Adolfo La Rocca and Fabrizio Oppedisano [9: 2016], who are concerned principally with the Ostrogothic senate, although their discussion is of importance for the previous century as well.

The senatorial aristocracy

10 Regional History

A high proportion of studies of the Later Empire and of the Late Antique period before 476 are concerned with the Empire as a whole. But the disintegration of the Empire meant that its different regions had significantly different histories. Everywhere there was some disruption, but the level differed, and the chronology varied. Italy suffered from the arrival of the barbarians in the first decade of the fifth century and briefly from the Huns in 452, and it was intermittently plagued by civil war, but it experienced relative peace at other times. There was more extensive fighting in Gaul and Spain, largely because of the arrival of the barbarians and their subsequent rivalries. North Africa suffered the shortest period of war in the period before the Justinianic Reconquest, but it was subjected to the harshest barbarian rule. Britain, arguably, was least affected by the barbarians initially, but subsequently experienced greater disruption than any other of the western provinces, except for those on the Danube frontier.

At the same time, the disintegration of the Empire is reflected in the increasing evidence for and discussion of the regions of the late antique West and East. As a result there are numerous studies focussed on individual provinces and geographical areas, reflecting both the importance of archaeological information (much of which is usefully covered by the annual periodical *Late Antique Archaeology*) and the fact that significant texts were written in the provinces during this period, so that we hear the voices of provincials to a new and unusual degree. However, the nature and extent of the evidence varies from region to region.

Italy   The history of Italy in the fourth and fifth centuries is, of course, dominated by the imperial court and to a lesser extent by developments within the city of Rome. But there are also regional and local aspects to the history of the peninsula. The letters of Ambrose in the fourth century, the writings of Paulinus of Nola in the fifth, and those of Cassiodorus, Ennodius and Gregory the Great in the sixth shed a remarkable amount of light on the culture, society and economy of the region as well as on religious matters. The sermons of Chromatius of Aquileia and Maximus of Turin are central to Rita Lizzi Testa's religious study of *Italia annonaria* [7: 1998]. For the very end of the fifth and the sixth century, the Ravenna papyri are revealing of landholding, and not just of the church of Ravenna or even of the secular landowners [10: Tjäder 1955–82].

In addition, there is a growing amount of archaeological evidence which is mainly published in Italian (but which is regularly covered in *Late Antique Archaeology*). There are general surveys by Neil Christie, both in a monograph [7: 2006] and in an article [10: 2016]. Urban public building in Northern and Central Italy is the focus of a work by Bryan Ward-Perkins [10: 1984], much of which inevitably concerns the building of churches, several of which, usefully for the historian, contain mosaics with inscriptions naming the donor [7: Lizzi Testa 1989].

The monograph on *Italia Annonaria* by Lellia CRACCO-RUGGINI [10: 1961] remains a good point of departure for the study of late antique northern Italy. For an overview of the peninsula as a whole there is a study by Chris WICKHAM [10: 1981]. For urban history there is a useful collection of papers covering Late Antiquity and the early Middle Ages from a conference held in Ravenna in 2004 [10: AUGENTI 2006]. For Rome itself there is a vast amount of work, partially inspired by the excavations at the Crypta Balbi. The obvious starting point are the huge volumes *Roma dall'Antichità al Medioevo. Archeologia e Storia, nel Museo Nazionale Romano Crypta Balbi* [7: ARENA/ DELOGU et al. 2001; 10: PAROLI/VENDITELLI 2004]. There is also the recent study by Michele SALZMAN [3: 2021]

Gaul has been the focus of considerable attention, above all be- Gaul
cause of the range of written material. One theological debate that is almost confined to Gaul, which has been erroneously entitled 'semi-Pelagianism' [10: BACKUS/GOUDRIAAN 2014], can best be traced in the works of Faustus of Riez and the reactions to them [10: FORTIN 1959; SMITH 1990; Weaver 1996; 3: MARKUS 1990]. There are also a small number of hagiographical texts from before the mid sixth century, notably Sulpicius Severus' *Life of Martin*, the *Lives* of Honoratus and Hilary, Constantius' *Life of Germanus of Auxerre*, *Life of the Jura Fathers*, and the *Life of Caesarius of Arles*, together with a cluster of Aquitanian Lives which present problems of chronology [10: FONTAINE 1967–9; 7: VALENTIN 1977; CAVALLIN 1997; 10: BORIUS 1965; MARTINE 1968; DELAGE/HEIJMANS 2010; WOOD 2023].

More striking for the fifth and early sixth centuries is the evidence of the letter collections (of Sulpicius Severus, Sidonius Apollinaris, Ruricius of Limoges and Avitus of Vienne). This has been fundamental for discussion of the senatorial aristocracy. Here the work of Karl Friedrich STROHEKER [2: 1948] remains valuable. Most of the senators dealt with by John MATTHEWS [4.5: 1975] and by M. T. W. ARNHEIM [9: 1972] were based in Gaul. The formation of the Gallic aristocracy is the focus of Hagith SIVAN's study of Ausonius [4.5: 1993]. For the world of Sidonius there are numerous studies, not least a biography by Jill HARRIES [10: 1994].

Also attracting attention from scholars has been the issue of so- *Bacaudae*
cial unrest, associated with the *bacaudae* or *bagaudae* – the spelling and etymology of the name has been the subject of debate [10: MINOR 1996]. The term has been seen by Marxist scholars as referring to a lower-class movement [10: THOMPSON 1952] and by others to

alienated members of regional society at odds with imperial government [10: VAN DAM 1985; 5.4: DRINKWATER 1992]. They are attested above all in Salvian's *De gubernatione Dei*, the Gallic Chronicles and Hydatius, and they are alluded to in the curious fifth-century Roman play, the *Querolus*. But they were not confined to Gaul: the name is applied to groups of dissidents in Spain and in the Alps. Moreover, although the *bacaudae* of the last century of the Roman West seem to reflect particular social developments, the name is also attested in other, earlier, periods. The evidence for the *bacaudae* is usefully gathered together by Juan Carlos SÁNCHEZ LÉON [10: 1996, 1996a].

Gallic culture and archaeology

A study of *bacaudae* is included in a collection of essays edited by John DRINKWATER and Hugh ELTON [5.4: 1992] which considers developments in Gaul in the face of the barbarian threat of the fifth century. The culture of late Roman Gaul (and on into the Merovingian period), with particular emphasis on the source material, is the subject of a collection of articles edited by Ralph MATHISEN and Danuta SHANZER [10: 2001]. The region's culture and its cities are covered in a volume edited by Steffen DIEFENBACH and Michael Gernot MÜLLER [10: 2013]. For the archaeology of the cities, the collection of *Topographie chrétienne de l'ancienne Gaule* [10: 1972–2014] is essential. The publications of the *Association française d'archéologie mérovingienne* frequently cover material relating to the fifth as well as to later centuries. There are numerous excavation reports dealing with individual villas. The archaeology of villas throughout the western Mediterranean world is covered in a volume edited by Alexandra CHAVARRIA, Javier ARCE and Gian Pietro BROGIOLO [10: 2000].

Spain

Late Roman Spain is less rich than Gaul in written evidence, despite the fact that Prudentius originated there and despite the importance of the *Chronicle of Hydatius* [5.4: BURGESS 1993; 5.2: MUHLBERGER 1990]. Discussion is, therefore, more focussed on the archaeological material, most (although not all) of it urban. The history of fourth- and fifth-century Spain is set out in two monographs by Javier ARCE [10: 2009; 5.2: 2005], while specific issues are addressed in a collection of articles edited by Kim BOWES and Michael KULIKOWSKI [10: 2005]. The peninsula's cities are discussed by Michael KULIKOWSKI [10: 2004]. The particular case of Tarragona is the subject of a monograph by Meritxell Pérez MARTINEZ [10: 2012]. The non-urban villas have been discussed by Alexandra CHAVARRÍA ARNAU [10: 2007], who has also written widely on other aspects of Spanish and

Italian archaeology in Spanish, Italian and English. The early medieval Spanish economy is the subject of a fascicule of the Journal Al-Masaq, edited by Jamie Wood, Merle Eisenberg and Paolo Tedesco [12.1: 2023].

A good deal of attention has been paid to Late Roman North Africa, in part because of an interest in Augustine, but also because of a long French archaeological tradition in Tunisia and Algeria, above all centred on urban sites. In addition the discovery of the Albertini Tablets shed light on rural society and the economy [10: Courtois/Leschi/Perrat/Saumagne 1952; 9: Wessel 2003]. For the interpretation of late Roman North Africa the dominant figure over the last half century has been Claude Lepelley, whose study of the cities of the region in the later Empire is fundamental [10: 1977–81]. Subsequent work by Lepelley includes a further monograph from 2001 [10]. There are also several important papers on North Africa (largely related to Augustine) in a collection of articles by Eric Rebillard [10: 2014]. More recently, Anna Leone [10: 2013] has published on the cities of North Africa, their changing religion, and their economy. There is also a study of medical practice and the transmission of medical knowledge by Louise Cilliers [10: 2019].

Despite the fact that we do have written evidence from the fifth century relating to Britain (notably the *Passio* of Alban, the *Life of Germanus of Auxerre* by Constantius, and the *Chronicle of 452*), as well as work written in Britain in the sixth century (above all the *De Excidio Britonum* by Gildas), the majority of our evidence is archaeological, and this is reflected in the scholarship. With regard to Gildas and the survival of some elements of Latin culture into the sixth century, as well as discussion of the British visits of Germanus, the volume edited by Michael Lapidge and David Dumville [10: 1984] remains an obvious point of reference. For the *Life of Germanus* there is also a monograph by Edward Thompson [10: 1984].

For an overview of Late Roman Britain, Simon Esmonde Cleary's study is still useful [10: 1989], but takes a very bleak view of the evidence. An attempt to place an equally bleak view of the decline of Britain within the context of the changes taking place throughout the wider Roman Empire is that of N. Faulkner [10: 2000]. A more positive approach, which argues for some elements of continuity, is that of Ken Dark [10: 1994]. In his recent study, James Gerrard [10: 2013] has also kept the wider picture in view, stressing the importance of the withdrawal of the Roman adminis-

North Africa

Britain

tration from the island province. Certainly, the transfer of troops out of Britain and the severance from imperial government must have meant a breakdown in the movement of gold coin into the province and a subsequent collapse in the monetary economy. There was some continuing activity in towns (only 17% of them have revealed no sign of life in the post-Roman period) [10: SPEED 2014]. In most areas, the rural economy seems to have been even less affected [10: HARRINGTON/WELCH 2014].

Hadrian's Wall   Archaeologically speaking, late Roman Britain has been divided into north and south. With regard to the north, discussion has centred on the fate of Hadrian's Wall and the Wall zone in general. Central here has been Tony WILMOTT's excavation of the fort of Birdoswald [10: 2014]. More recently work at Vindolanda has uncovered a remarkable series of Christian buildings [10: BIRLEY/ALBERTI 2021]. The Wall zone has been the subject of conference proceedings, including those published by Tony WILMOTT and P. R. WILSON [10: 2000] and by R. COLLINS and L. ALLASON-JONES [10: 2010]. The treasure from Traprain Law, just south of Edinburgh, has recently been the subject of reinterpretation by Fraser HUNTER [10: 2013].

Southern Britain   Discussion of the south of Britain has focussed on very different issues. Here the 'type site' has been the city of Wroxeter, excavated by Phil BARKER [10: WHITE/BARKER 1998]. In addition, the considerable number of villa excavations have attracted attention, above all in terms of their mosaics, which have been studied by Sarah SCOTT [10: 2000]. The growing number of gold and silver hoards, from Water Newton [10: PAINTER 1977], Mildenhall [10: PAINTER 1977], Thetford [10: JOHNS/POTTER 1983], and Hoxne [10: JOHNS 2010], has also directed attention towards the wealth of fourth-century Britain. With regard to coin hoards, new finds keep adding to the record. The inventory published by A. S. ROBERTSON in 2000 [10] is already out of date following the discovery of hoards at Frome in Somerset [10: MOORHEAD/BOOTH/BLAND 2010].

11 The Barbarians

The major narratives for the late fourth, fifth and sixth centuries all cover aspects of the arrival of the barbarians; the chronicles provide a chronology: Ammianus supplies a crucial narrative of the period between the arrival of the Huns north of the Black Sea and the battle of Adrianople. The Church historians touch on the barbarians in passing. It is important to note, however, that for most of these fourth- and fifth-century sources (with the exception of Ammianus' account of the entry of the Goths into the Empire), the barbarians are not a central issue. The fullest study of the documentation is by Mischa MEIER [11: 2019].

There are a number of (mainly sixth-century) works in which barbarians are central, notably the *Getica* of Jordanes, the *History of the Vandal Persecution* by Victor of Vita, the accounts of the Vandal and Gothic Wars by Procopius, the *History of the Goths* by Isidore, and that of the Lombards by Paul the Deacon. Gregory of Tours' *Histories* are usually classified along with these texts, but as Walter GOFFART [11: 1988] and Martin HEINZELMANN [11: 1994] have both emphasised, he did not call his History a *History of the Franks* but *Books of Histories*. More generally, GOFFART [11: 1988] has convincingly challenged the notion that there was a genre of 'Barbarian History'. The (largely seventh- and eighth-century) process by which Gregory's *Histories* were turned into a *History of the Franks* is the subject of a study by Helmut REIMITZ [11: 2015]. For Jordanes, one may turn to the thesis of Arne Søby CHRISTENSEN [11: 2002], although his argument needs some modification in the light of the discovery of fragments of the history written by the third-century historian Publius Herenius Dexippus, which have shown that some parts of Jordanes' narrative have a more factual basis than had been thought [11: MARTIN/GRUSKOWÁ 2014]. Jordanes' geography is analysed by Andy MERRILLS [5.1: 2005]. There is a new English translation and commentary by Peter VAN NUFFELEN and Lieve VAN HOOF [8: 2020].

The other major written sources for the barbarians are the law codes produced in the kingdoms of the successor states, which (with the exception of the *Breviary of Alaric*) were edited in the *Monumenta Germaniae Historica*. These fifth- and sixth-century codes include the Code of Euric, the *Breviary of Alaric*, the so-called *Antiqua*, contained in the *Leges Visigothorum*, the Burgundian *Liber Constitutionum* and *Forma et Expositio Legum*, the *Edictum Theodorici*, and the *Pactus Legis Salicae*, together with various additional enactments that were appended to it. The most recent overview of the early codes is to be found in Karl UBL's study of the *Pactus Legis Salicae* [12.7: 2017], although for *Lex Salica* itself one needs to consult Magali COUMERT [12.7: 2023]. Several of the major

Sources

Laws

themes in the study of post-Roman law are discussed in a volume edited by Gerhard Dilcher and Eva-Marie Distler [11: 2006].

Vulgar, provincial and military law

The legal collections of the successor states (leaving aside the Visigothic and Burgundian compilations of Roman Law) used to be classified simply as *Germanenrechte*. More recently, the question of whether they should be categorised as 'Germanic' has been raised. Although there are certainly some individual clauses in the laws (sometimes using non-Roman terminology) which represent traditions of barbarian incomers, the issuing of law was a sub-Roman practice, as noted by Michael Wallace-Hadrill [11: 1971], and many of the individual laws which were once thought to be 'Germanic' are now categorised more convincingly as Roman 'Vulgar Law' (a concept most fully elaborated by Ernst Levy [6: 1951, 1956]). A recent overview of the notion of Vulgar Law is that of Detlef Liebs [6: 2008]. Other categories of law that related to the post-Roman codes are municipal and provincial, although the recent surveys of provincial law have not considered the late Roman evidence [11: Czajkowksi/Eckhardt/Strothmann 2020]. More important has been consideration of the relevance of Roman Military Law, as noted in particular by Stefan Esders [11: 2015]. There is a useful survey of specific aspects of military law in the collection edited by Fabio Botta and Luca Loschiavo [6: Botta /Loschiavo 2015]. In addition, Loschiavo is the author of a volume which draws together many aspects of legal history in the Late Antique period [11: Loschiavo 2016]. Rather than being seen as examples of some early Germanic tradition, the Law Codes are much better understood as the products of individual sub-Roman kings and rulers, working within traditions of Roman law-giving, although sometimes drawing on individual customs of non-Roman groups, especially those relating to family and inheritance.

The continuity of administrative institutions

Related to the question of the Roman elements in sub-Roman law is that of the survival of Roman administrative institutions. In the *Variae*, Cassiodorus provides clear evidence for continuity. But the Ostrogothic kingdom, being based in Italy, was heir to the imperial administration. Other kingdoms had to rely on surviving elements of the provincial administration. And in Italy, after the fall of the Ostrogothic kingdom, what had survived of imperial government was not taken over by the Lombards. Rather, it passed to the Byzantine Exarchate. How much survived elsewhere has been a point of discussion: Jean Durliat [11: 1990] advanced a maximalist case for continuity through to the Carolingian period. Among the most effective criticism of the case has been that of Chris Wickham both in a review article dealing with Durliat's arguments [11: Wickham 1993] and in his own reconstruction of the history of the post-Roman West [3: Wickham 2005]. Nevertheless, some aspects of Roman administration did survive. The majority of secular offices in the sixth and seventh centuries had evolved from Roman origins, among them the *dux*, *comes* and *centenarius* [11: Claude 1964; Zerjadtke 1980, 1986; 6: Barnwell 1992]. Elizabeth Magnou-Nortier has restated the case for administrative continuity in a recent study of fiscality, although her arguments have not been widely accepted [11: 2012]. Certainly the *iugatio-capitatio* tax faded away, but the *siliquaticum* introduced by Valentian III survived [11: Wickham 1984]. The survival of other aspects of Roman administration was equally erratic and varied from place to place. In a few places, as Josianne Barbier [11: 2014] has demonstrated, local archives, the *gesta municipalia*, were used on occasion even in the ninth century.

The other major source for the barbarian groups is archaeological, although here again the simple association of particular types of artefacts, or particular styles, with individual 'ethnic' groups has been found to be misleading, as is clear from a volume on the archaeology of identity edited by Walter Pohl and Mathias Mehofer [11: 2010]. Certainly some customs and some styles seem to be associated with particular regions, but the identification of them as specifically 'Germanic' or even as 'Gothic', 'Frankish', 'Burgundian' or 'Lombard' has proven unsatisfactory. The ethnic interpretation of the post-Roman cemeteries has been sharply questioned by Sebastian Brather [11: 2004], and there is a succinct overview of the literature by Guy Halsall [11: 2011]. The archaeological debates about 'Germanen' and 'Romanen' in the Merovingian kingdom have been discussed by Hubert Fehr [2: 2010]. There is also valuable discussion of the archaeology, alongside the written evidence, in Edward James' overview of the barbarians from the third to the sixth century [11: 2009].

In other words, the term 'Germanic peoples' has come to be seen as distinctly problematic and unhelpful. Jörg Jarnut [11: 2006] has pleaded for the concept 'Germanisch' to be dropped from the vocabulary of the debate – although it is too well entrenched in public consciousness to be easily discarded. The Romans of the Late Antique period did not classify all the incomers as a single hostile force, and they scarcely ever used the term *Germani* – it is very oc-

Archaeology

Problems in categorising the barbarians

casionally applied to Franks and Alamans and sometimes used to refer to barbarians in the past. As has been pointed out by Ingo Wi-wjorra [2: 2006], the concept of the Germans was a construct of the nineteenth century. Modern awareness of the problem of classification can be traced back to Reinhard Wenskus' work of 1961, *Stammesbildung und Verfassung: Das Werden der frühmittelalterlichen Gentes* [2: 1961]. Crucially for Wenskus the barbarian groups (and he discussed both 'Celtic' and 'Germanic' groups) were not defined by blood, but by attachment to traditions associated with their leading families. Ever since Wenskus, there has been a general understanding that the barbarian peoples were not biologically defined, although there clearly were biological groups within them. This is perfectly compatible with the use of the term 'ethnic groups', since the word *ethnos* in Greek does not carry biological implications. These groups were primarily social constructs, as has been noted by numerous historians, perhaps most notably by Patrick Geary [11: 2002] and more recently by Walter Pohl [11: 2018], who has traced the historiography of the study of ethnogenesis since the publication of Wenskus' work. Andrew Gillett [11: 2002] edited a volume devoted to the question of barbarian identity. Pohl has further added to the study of identity (*Identitätsforschung*) [11: 2018] and has been involved in the publication of a series of volumes of essays on early medieval identity [11: Pohl/Heydemann 2013, 2013a]. Viola Gheller [11: 2017] has also revisited the subject, providing a useful survey of the theoretical issues involved. The continuing transformation of both Roman and barbarian identity is the subject of collections of essays edited by Ralph Mathisen and Danuta Shanzer [11: 2011] and by Gerda Heydemann and Helmut Reimitz [11: 2020]. A volume which covers a larger range and has more to say about groups other than the Germanic barbarians is edited by Stephen Mitchell and Geoffrey Greatrex [11: 2000]. The related question of how to define the Romans is also at the heart of a collection devoted to the transformations of Romanness, edited by Walter Pohl, Clemens Gantner, Cinzia Grifoni, and Marianne Pollheimer-Mohaupt [11: 2018].

Bearing in mind the fact that we are dealing first and foremost with social constructs and not biologically defined groups (although family units were obviously integrated within the socially constructed blocs, as is clear from a project on genome sequencing) [11: Amorim et al. 2018], the relatively fast formation, dissolution and, on occasion, reformation of individual peoples is not difficult to comprehend. The extent to which identification with a group is subjective has, however, been the subject of major disagreement. Patrick AMORY [11: 1997] has presented Ostrogothic identity as entirely constructed, while Herwig WOLFRAM [11: 1979] has placed greater weight on the traditions preserved by the Goths, at the same time acknowledging that they were subject to manipulation. Attempts to present most of those who have continued to employ such terms as 'Germanic' (often because of the demands of publishers) as reviving a pre-1945 understanding of the barbarians (as in some contributions to a volume edited by Andrew GILLETT [11: 2002]) have underestimated the extent to which almost all scholars take for granted the notion that groups are largely social constructs.

One issue that is often thought to be central to the self-identification of the barbarians is their commitment to Arianism, which stems from the significance of Ulfila in the process of the conversion of the Goths and from the fact that the Visigoths entered the Empire at the moment when the emperor, Valens, was a homoean. The religious affiliation of the other east Germanic groups is usually said to have been determined by that of Visigoths, following the arguments set out by Heinz-Eberhard GIESECKE [11: 1939] and Kurt Dietrich SCHMIDT in 1939 [11: 1939]. This is a major oversimplification, but the question of 'Germanic Arianism' has only recently been subject to proper scrutiny, as for example in the volume by Guido BERNDT and Roland STEINACHER [11: 2014]. The broader issue of homoean doctrine is considered within the context of a volume of essays edited by Uta HEIL [11: 2019]. The same author has also analysed the evidence for homoean belief among the Burgundians [11: HEIL 2011]. The development of the idea that Visigothic identity was related to their Arianism has been most fully explored by Viola GHELLER [11: 2017]. The representation of the Goths, which discusses the question of their presentation as Arian, is the subject of a monograph by Christian STADERMANN [11: 2017].

Arianism and the barbarians

11.1 Relations with Rome Before the Barbarian Settlements

The history of the barbarians prior to their entry into the Empire has been dealt with primarily in the context of frontier studies or in the context of war. As regards Frontier Studies, the German tradition of *Limesforschung* represented in the publications of the

Limesforschung/ frontier studies

Deutsche Limeskommission has concentrated largely on the period before Late Antiquity. The English-language equivalent, which also tends to focus on the High Empire, is the *International Congress on Roman Frontier Studies*. In the United States there is an annual conference on *Shifting Frontiers in Late Antiquity*, which takes a very much broader view of the notion of frontier and has also published volumes of proceedings, beginning in 1996 [11.1: MATHISEN/SIVAN 1996]. An equally broad understanding of the idea of frontier underlies a collection of essays edited by Walter POHL, Ian WOOD and Helmut REIMITZ [11.1: 2000] within the publications of the *Transformation of the Roman World* Project.

There are monographs on the Roman frontier by C. R. WHITTAKER [11.1: 1994], who has emphasised the importance of the frontier as a zone, and by A. D. LEE [11.1: 1993], who has examined Rome's foreign relations in the Later Empire. For the Danube frontier there is a study by Andrew POULTER [11.1: 2007]. An overview of relations between the Roman and barbarian worlds in which the relationship between the two groups is central is Herwig WOLFRAM's study *Das Römerreich und seine Germanen* [3: 2018] – a revised version of a work originally published in 1990 [3: 1990]. Among the works dealing with Rome's wars with the barbarians, Michael KULIKOWSKI [11.1: 2009] considers conflict with the Goths from the third century down to the early fifth, presenting the relations between Rome and the Goths as key to the creation of a Gothic identity. For the sources relating to the early Goths there is a valuable volume of translations with commentary by Peter HEATHER and John MATTHEWS [11.1: 1991]. There is also a monograph by Peter HEATHER [4.5: 1991] dealing with relations between Goths and Romans from 332 to 489. Thomas BURNS [4.5: 1994] has examined Rome's dealings with the barbarians, both within and outside the Empire, between c. 375 and 425.

Roman influence beyond the frontier

Some studies of the territory beyond the Roman frontier, for instance that of Lotte HEADEAGER [11: 1992], have placed a good deal of emphasis on relations with Rome. This is a topic which is in a state of constant change as a result of new archaeological finds, and above all because of the discovery of Roman coins as far north as Scandinavia. A good illustration of current debates is the volume on the Sösdala horsemen, edited by Charlotte FABECH and Ulf NÄSMAN, most notably in the contribution of Svante FISCHER [11.1: 2017].

'Germanic' kingship

The nature of 'Germanic' kingship prior to the settlement of the barbarians within the Empire is dealt with by Stephanie DICK [11.1:

2008], who emphasises interplay with Rome rather than any barbarian tradition. Dennis GREEN's study of the Germanic terminology of rulership [11.1: 1965], however, remains valuable.

11.2 Barbarian Numbers and Destruction

A central matter of debate in recent years has been the question of barbarian numbers. Previous assumptions about vast numbers were decisively questioned by Walter GOFFART in the first chapter of his study of the barbarian settlements [11.2: 1980] and subsequently in a monograph in which he revisited the matter [11.2: 2006]. Although many, including Peter HEATHER [3: 2005, 11.2: 2010], have seen GOFFART's assessments of the numbers of barbarians as being too low, the case for thinking that any single migration involved more than tens of thousands of barbarians has been radically undermined. Most Roman sources talk of tens of thousands, and since it is highly unlikely that they underestimated the barbarian threat, these figures should be regarded as maxima [11.2: WOOD 2019; 3: WOOD 2018].

Coupled with the notion of there being overwhelming numbers of barbarians is the argument that they were responsible for the destruction of the West Roman Empire. This idea has been most cogently stated in recent times by Bryan WARD-PERKINS [3: 2005], but it also underlies Peter HEATHER's interpretation of the collapse of the Roman West [3: 2005, 2009]. Others have seen the barbarians as peripheral to the crisis that overwhelmed Rome, placing the emphasis firmly on conflicts within the Roman leadership which effectively left the Western Empire in the hands of the incomers; the case has been argued forcefully by Christine DELAPLACE [3: 2015] and by Henning BÖRM [3: 2018]. In this reading, although there was decline throughout the Roman West (initiated by the civil wars that plagued the Empire, and perhaps, in places, by environmental change), the most severe devastation in Italy was that caused by Justinian, as a result of the lengthy wars against the Ostrogoths, a view accepted, for instance, by Mischa MEIER [11.2: 2003] and by Chris WICKHAM [3: 2005]. Yet more recent is the collection of essays edited by Hendrik DEY and Fabrizio OPPEDISANO [12.9: 2024]. Whether or not the Gothic Wars caused substantial destruction, they certainly broke the power of the senatorial aristocracy of Italy. The debate between the

Levels of destruction

two positions on the role of the barbarians in the Fall of Rome has been categorised by Guy Halsall [11.2: 1999] in a survey of the historiography prior to 1998 as one between movers and shakers.

11.3 Huns

Written and archaeological documentation

The documentary evidence for the Huns is relatively slight: there are references in the major chronicle sources and there is vital information provided by Priscus in his account of his 448/9 embassy to Attila [11.3: Blockley 1983; Gordon 1966]. For the Catalaunian Plains the chief source is the *Getica* of Jordanes. There are, however, useful archaeological surveys by István Bóna [11.3: 1991], and by Michael Schmauder [11.3: 2009]. The catalogues of three important exhibitions were edited by Wilfried Menghin, Tobias Springer, and Egon Warmers [11.3: 1987], by Falko Daim [11.3: 1996], and by Bodo Anke and Heike Externbrink [11.3: 2007].

Attila

Despite the relative lack of sources, there is a large body of writing devoted to the Huns, much of it directed primarily at the general public – like the studies by Klaus Rosen [11.3: 2016], Christopher Kelly [11.3: 2008], and Edina Bozoky [11.3: 2012]. Some old works are still well regarded. Edward Thompson's 1948 study of Attila was reissued in 1996, with a preface by Peter Heather [2: Thompson 1996]. Otto Maenchen-Helfen's unfinished study of the Huns [11.3: 1973] which was published posthumously in 1973 is also worth consulting. Heather himself has considered the Huns on numerous occasions, most directly in [11.3: 1995]. There are numerous valuable papers in the *Companion to the Age of Attila* edited by Michael Maas [11.3: 2014]. The current state of scholarship on Attila has been assessed by Mischa Meier [1: 2017]. Many of the studies on the Huns, however, do not take account of recent surveys of the landscape of the Hungarian Plain before the drainage-works of the nineteenth century. For this it is necessary to turn to an article on the Hungarian Danube basin by Katalin Szende [11.3: 2010] and especially to the map that she includes.

Asia

One significant trend in recent years (already apparent in the work of Maenchen-Helfen) is the emphasis placed on the Central Asian origins of the Huns. The Huns are the subject of several chapters in the *Cambridge History of Early Inner Asia* edited by Denis Sinor [11.3: 1990]. In addition, the Huns feature significantly in a volume edited by Nicola Dɪ Cosᴍᴏ and Michael Mᴀᴀs [11.3: 2018]. The importance of the Asiatic origins of the Huns is taken to an extreme by Hyun Jin Kɪᴍ [11.3: 2016].

11.4 Settlement

Also associated with the question of barbarian numbers is the means by which the incomers were settled within the Roman Empire. The general assumption, derived from the work of Ernst Theodor Gaupp in 1844, was that the barbarians were settled in accordance with a system of billeting. This was challenged by Walter Gᴏꜰꜰᴀʀᴛ [11.2: 1980], who argued instead that the barbarians received a tax allocation rather than property. Gᴏꜰꜰᴀʀᴛ unquestionably transformed the history of the barbarian settlement, and his argument prompted a considerable amount of discussion, not least in a volume edited by Herwig Wᴏʟꜰʀᴀᴍ, *Anerkennung und Integration* [11.4: 1988]. The fullest response is to be found in a volume edited by Pierfrancesco Pᴏʀᴇɴᴀ and Yann Rɪᴠɪᴇ̀ʀᴇ [11.4: 2013], in which different authors addressed the settlements of individual barbarian groups. The result is an emphasis on the difference between the various settlements, which seem usually to have involved the allocation of land, at least by the time that the surviving evidence was set down.

12 The Successor States

12.1 General Comments

The first years of the successor states that filled the vacuum left by the deposition of the last Western Emperor (whether he is taken to be Romulus Augustulus or Julius Nepos) have come to be understood as a continuation of the Empire itself. A volume from the project on the *Transformation of the Roman World*, edited by Hans-Werner Gᴏᴇᴛᴢ, Jörg Jᴀʀɴᴜᴛ, and Walter Pᴏʜʟ [12.1: 2003], provides separate studies of each of the new political units. The final volume of the *Cambridge Ancient History*, edited by Averil Cᴀᴍᴇʀᴏɴ, Bryan Wᴀʀᴅ-Pᴇʀᴋɪɴs and Michael Wʜɪᴛʙʏ [3: 2000], and the first volume of the *Cambridge Medieval History*, edited by Paul Fᴏᴜʀᴀᴄʀᴇ [12.1: 2005], also provide surveys of the barbarian groups and the successor states.

Henning Börm [3: 2018] has taken the history of 'Westrom' up to the reign of Justinian, and Ian Wood [5.5: 2018] has argued that the period down to the Ostrogothic wars of the mid sixth century can best be described as a Byzantine Commonwealth. Certainly relations between Constantinople and the Western kingdoms that were not conquered by Justinian continued to be of importance, as noted in a collection edited by Andreas Fischer and Ian Wood [12.1: 2014] and also in a collection edited by Stefan Esders, Yitzhak Hen, Pia Lucas and Tamar Rotman [12.1: 2019]. Andrew Gillett [12.1: 2003] has studied the diplomatic relations between the Roman and barbarian states down to 533. Among the more curious illustrations of diplomatic activity is a cookery book written by a Greek, Anthimus, who gave a copy of his work to the Frankish king Theuderic, the text of which is preserved in a Carolingian manuscript [12.1: Paolucci 2003]. It has been the subject of a recent article by Yitzhak Hen [12.1: 2006].

Staatlichkeit　There has been a good deal of discussion in German-language scholarship about the applicability of the terms 'Staat' and 'Staatlichkeit', a debate that originated in a disagreement between Johannes Fried and Hans-Werner Goetz [12.1: Jarnut 2006]. Most scholars, and particularly scholars from outside the German tradition of research, have worked with the concept of 'Staat' without worry, as is clear from the proceedings of two conferences held in Vienna [12.1: Airlie/Pohl/Reimitz 2006; 12.1: Pohl/Wieser 2009].

Kings and their capitals　Among older studies of rulership in the post-Roman World, Herwig Wolfram's examination of Latin titles [12.1: 1967] and J. M. Wallace-Hadrill's *Early Germanic Kingship* [11: 1971] are still useful. Paul Barnwell gathers together much of what can be said about royal office [6: 1992; 12.1: 1997]. Yitzhak Hen [12.1: 2007] has also argued strongly for seeing the courts of the early successor states as essentially Roman. Gideon Maier [12.1: 2005] engages more directly with older traditions of German scholarship. Several of the capital cities of the late antique and post-Roman world (including Constantinople, Rome, Ravenna, Carthage, Toulouse, Geneva, Lyon, Toledo and Braga) are surveyed, from a primarily archaeological point of view, in a volume edited by Gisella Ripoll and Josep Gurt [12.1: 2000].

Government　The government of the successor states seems largely to have been based on Roman provincial government, although Theodoric the Great in Italy inherited much of the governmental machinery of the Western Empire, as is clear from the *Variae* of Cassiodorus as studied by Shane BJORNLIE and Jonathan ARNOLD [6: BJORNLIE 2013; 12.1: ARNOLD 2014]. Ostrogothic government is discussed in several contributions to the *Brill Companion to Ostrogothic Italy*, edited by Jonathan ARNOLD, Shane BJORNLIE and Kristina SESSA [12.1: 2018], and it is also discussed by Paul BARNWELL in his study of *Emperors, Kings and Prefects* [6: 1992] and by Gideon MAIER in his interpretation of the institutions of the successor states [12.1: 2005]. The development of certain specific offices has received particular attention, most notably that of the *dux*, which has been examined by Michael ZERJADTKE [11: 2019], and that of *comes*, which is the subject of a seminal article by Dietrich CLAUDE [11: 1964] and also of a study by Alexander Callander MURRAY [12.1: 1986]. MURRAY has also examined the function of the lesser administrator, the *centenarius* [11: 1988].

The question of taxation and its survival in the post-Roman West is the subject of Walter GOFFART's *Caput and Colonate* [12.1: 1974]. There is an extensive discussion of the issue by Chris WICKHAM in an article on 'The other transition. From the Ancient World to Feudalism' alongside other discussions in a volume of collected essays [12.1: WICKHAM 1994]. WICKHAM 's subsequent assessment of the topic is to be found in his general survey of the Early Middle Ages [3. 2005]. GOFFART dealt more specifically with the Frankish evidence in two articles conveniently gathered into his collected essays [12.1: GOFFART 1989] and more recently in an article on 'Frankish military duty and the fate of Roman taxation' [12.1: GOFFART 2008]. Visigothic taxation is the subject of an article by Santiago CASTELLANOS [12.1: 2003]. The Ostrogothic evidence is discussed by Shane BJORNLIE [6: 2014]. The Italian evidence is also the subject of an article by Sam BARNISH [12.1: 1986], written in response to some aspects of GOFFART's work. More recent still is a joint article dealing with fiscal structures in post-Imperial Italy by Merle EISENBERG and Paolo TEDESCO [12.1: 2021]. Clearly taxation continued into the sixth century and beyond: lists of taxable individuals were still drawn up, and land was subject to taxation. There were also taxes on the transport of various goods. But cities and, above all, ecclesiastical institutions sought exemptions, and the revenue from taxation became increasingly insignificant for kings, who no longer had to pay for a standing army. *Taxation*

The related issue of the shift from Roman to post-Roman military organisation has been dealt with either in terms of the decline *Military organisation* of the Roman army or in terms of barbarian military organisation. With regard to the late Roman military, change in the employment of barbarian troops between 375 and 425 is studied by Thomas S. Burns [4.5: 1994]. Military developments in the fifth century are discussed in articles by Wolfgang Liebeschuetz [12.1: 1993], by Dick Whittaker in his study of late Roman warlords [12.1: 1993], and by Noel Lenski in his study of the use of armed slaves in the formation of private armies [12.1: 2009]. Luca Loschiavo has edited a more recent collection that deals with the continuing influence of Roman military tradition [11: 2024]. Frankish military organisation was explored by Bernard Bachrach in 1972 [12.1: 1972]. A more recent and more wide-ranging analysis is that of Guy Halsall [12.1: 2003], who has also analysed the evidence for the Ostrogothic army [12.1: 2016]. There are several relevant articles in a collection on the Roman army and the barbarians from the third to the seventh century edited by Françoise Vallet and Michel Kazanski [12.1: 1993]. The actual process of the shift from an army paid for by the state to an army of obligation is, however, difficult to trace.

12.2 Odoacer

Arguably the earliest of the successor states was that controlled by Odoacer after his deposition of Romulus Augustulus. The source material for Odoacer's reign is not rich, although the narrative histories of the period (including Marcellinus Comes, Jordanes, the Anonymus Valesianus, and the fragmentary Greek historians) do provide some information. Perhaps the most interesting information, however, is to be found in the inscriptions in the Colosseum, which form the core of André Chastagnol's study of Odoacer's relations with the senate [9: 1996]. The subsequent history of the senate is the subject of a work by Adolfo La Rocca and Fabrizio Oppedisano [9: 2016]. For Odoacer's constitutional position, A. H. M. Jones' article of 1962 is still useful [12.2], as is that of Michael McCormick from 1977 [12.2]. There is an overview of his rule by Maria Cesa [12.2: 1994]. Odoacer is also the subject of the final chapter of Penny MacGeorge's study of late-Roman warlords [5.4: 2002].

12.3 Visigoths

The most important documents for the Visigothic kingdom in the Sources period before 507 are the *Breviary of Alaric* and the canons of the Council of Agde. The *Breviary* is the subject of the proceedings of a conference held at Aire-sur-l'Adour, the place where the code was promulgated, in 2006 [12.3: Rouche/Dumézil 2009]. The Council of Agde is fully discussed by Bill Klingshirn in his study of Caesarius of Arles [12.3: 1994]. The *Life of Caesarius* is a particularly valuable work of hagiography for the historian, but there are also several hagiographical texts that shed light on the Visigothic court and have been examined most recently by Andrew Gillett [12.1: 2003] and by Christian Stadermann in his discussion of the Merovingian sources [11: 2017]. For the period between the death of Alaric II at Vouillé and the reign of Reccared, the chronicles of Victor of Tunnuna, John of Biclaro and of Saragossa [12.3: Cardelle de Hartmann 2001] as well as the *Chronicle* and *Historia Gothorum* of Isidore [12.3: Martín 2003; for the *Historia* there is the edition by Mommsen in *Monumenta Germaniae Historica, Auctores Antiquissimi* XI], provide the main chronological framework. Gregory of Tours is valuable for those moments when Visigoths and Franks interact. The most significant work of hagiography relating to Visigothic Spain is the *Vitas Patrum Emeretensium* [12.3: Sánchez 1992]. For the Church, the conciliar acts, especially those of Toledo III, are vital [7: Vives 1963]. For Visigothic history in general there is an exhaustive bibliography of the Visigoths and their kingdom that has been published by Alberto Ferreiro; together with the original edition from 1988, there are numerous volumes of updates [12.3: 1988, 2006, 2008, 2011, 2014, 2017].

For modern studies of the Goths, the natural point of departure Overviews is Herwig Wolfram's *Geschichte der Goten* [11: 1979], although there is also much of value in Edward Thompson's studies of the early Goths and of their descendants in Spain [2: 1966, 1969]. There is consideration of aspects of the archaeological material in a volume that resulted from a conference in San Marino, edited by Peter Heather [12.3: 1999]. Heather has also provided a painstaking monograph on the Goths between 332 and 489 [12.3: 1991]. There is a useful overview by Wolfgang Giese [12.3: 2004] and a fuller study by Gerd Kampers [5.1: 2008]. Contemporary understanding of the Goths in the sixth and seventh centuries is the subject of a monograph by Christian Stadermann [11: 2017]. The issue of Gothic identity in Visigothic

Spain has been examined by Manuel Koch [12.3: 2012]. For the question of the notion of a Gothic identity, its relationship to Arianism, and the historiography of the subject there is a study by Viola Gheller [11: 2017].

Euric and Alaric II

For the reign of Euric, Karl Stroheker's study published in 1937 still has value [2]. There is also a lengthy article dealing with the king's accession by Andrew Gillett [12.3: 1999]. Aspects of the reign are also discussed in works on Sidonius Apollinaris, for instance the biography by Jill Harries [12.3: 1994]. For the reign of Alaric II, apart from discussions of the *Breviary* and the Council of Agde, the chief focus of recent scholarship has been on the Battle of Vouillé, where the king was killed, with the result that the kingdom of Toulouse collapsed. This was the subject of a conference held to mark the 1500th anniversary of the battle, the proceedings of which were edited by Luc Bourgeois [12.3: 2010]. A selection of those papers were republished in English, together with additional contributions, in a volume edited by Ralph Mathisen and Danuta Shanzer [12.3: 2012].

The Goths in Spain

For the decades following the defeat of Alaric, and for the emergence of a Visigothic kingdom in Spain, in addition to the general works by Herwig Wolfram and Gerd Kampers, there is a study by Edward Thompson from 1969 [12.3], but the basic work on the Spanish kingdom is that of José Orlandis [12.3: 1988]. More recent are the studies by Roger Collins [12.3: 2004] and Javier Arce [12.3: 2011]. There is also a collection of articles edited by Sabine Panzram and Paolo Pachá which provides discussion of most of the major questions relating to the Iberian peninsula, not least the problem of the settlement of the Visigoths in Spain, the evidence for which is critically reviewed by Arce [12.3: 2020]. For the reign of Leovigild, Karl Stroheker's study [2: 1965] is still valuable. There is also an online series of conference proceedings from Visigothic symposia [visigothic-symposia.org].

12.4 Vandals

Sources

For the Vandal kingdom there is substantial documentation. Procopius' account of Justinian's Wars provides an account of the Vandal kingdom before the Reconquest, and Victor of Vita presents a narrative of the fifth-century persecutions of the Catholics – albeit one that is highly partisan [12.4: Vössing 2002; Lancel 2002; Moorhead

1992]. The story of persecution is continued with the *Life of Fulgentius of Ruspe* [12.4: Isola 2016] and by Fulgentius' own works [12.4: FRAIPONT 2004; WHELAN 2018]. The religious history is dealt with in a study of Victor by Tancred HOWE [12.4: 2007]. A different picture is supplied by the poets Dracontius and Luxuriosus [8: KAY 2013]. For agrarian history the Albertini Tablets are a precious resource [10: COURTOIS/LESCHI/PERRAT/SAUMAGNE 1952; 9: WESSEL 2003].

Until recently, the Vandals were poorly represented in modern scholarship. The outstanding study of the post-war period was that of Christian COURTOIS, published in 1955 [2]. The work, with its presentation of the Vandal kingdom as 'un empire du blé', is still worth consulting. There is also a valuable account by Hans-Joachim DIESNER [12.4: 1966]. In the years after the publication of Courtois' work, perhaps the most significant contributions to the study of the Vandals were to be found in the articles of Frank CLOVER, which were collected together in 1993 [12.4: 1993]. Fortunately, since 2000 there have been several significant studies and publications of article collections:

For a concise overview of Vandal history there is a volume by Helmut CASTRITIUS [12.4: 2007], and for the migration period and the development of Vandal ethnogenesis a monograph by Guido BERNDT [12.4: 2007]. For a more general history of the people there is a volume by Andy MERRILLS and Richard MILES [12.4: 2010] and a monograph by Konrad VÖSSING [12.4: 2018]. Much of the work that deals with the Vandal migration also covers the Vandal kingdom. The journal *Antiquité Tardive* devoted two volumes to Vandal Africa [12.4: Association pour l'Antiquité Tardive 2003–4], which is also the focus of the collection of articles edited by Guido BERNDT and Roland STEINACHER [12.4: 2006]. A collection of papers edited by A. H. MERRILLS [12.4: 2004] provides discussions of aspects of the culture of the Vandal kingdom in addition to considerations of the political and religious context. Arian-Catholic debates are the focus of a study by Robin WHELAN [12.4: 2018]. The issue of a continuing Roman identity in Africa is discussed by Jonathan CONANT [12.4: 2012].

The Berber hinterland, which impinged on Late Roman, Vandal, and Byzantine North Africa, is the subject of a study by Yves MODÉRAN [12.4: 2003]. It is also covered in a chronologically more wide-ranging volume by Michael BRETT and Elizabeth FENTRESS [12.4: 1996], together with a survey article by FENTRESS [12.4: 2006]. In addi-

Overviews

The Berbers

tion, the Berbers are central to the study of Corippus' *Iohannis* by Andy MERRILLS [13: 2023].

12.5 Alans and Sueves

Of the peoples who accompanied the Vandals into the Roman Empire in c. 406, the Alans have been most poorly served by modern scholarship, despite their importance in their eastern homelands in the Caucasus. A good point of departure for their history in Asia is the collection of sources made by Augusti Alemany [12.5: 2000]. The only monograph dealing with the Alans in the West is that by Bernard BACHRACH [12.5: 1973].

Sources   The Suevic migration has also received little attention, although the Suevic kingdom in north-western Spain has been the subject of recent discussion. The written sources are not substantial, consisting largely of the *Chronicle of Hydatius* [5.4: BURGESS 1993], the works of Martin of Braga [BARLOW 1950], and the canons of two Councils of Braga [7: VIVES 1963], apart from a few references in the Gregory of Tours *Histories* and hagiography, but the archaeology of the kingdom is rich, as can be seen in the catalogue of an exhibition held in Ourense in 2017 [12.5: LÓPEZ QUIROGA/MARTÍNEZ 2017]. Accompanying the catalogue is a volume of essays, edited by Jorge LÓPEZ QUIROGA [12.5: 2018].

Overviews   A full history of the Suevic kingdom is provided by Pablo DÍAZ [12.5: 2011]. The early years are discussed by Javier ARCE [5.2: 2005] in his study of fifth-century Spain. A substantial chapter of Andrew GILLETT's study [12.1: 2003] of late-antique envoys is concerned with the evidence supplied by Hydatius, who lived in the kingdom. Among older studies a series of articles on the Suevi by Edward THOMPSON [2: 1982] are collected in a volume on *Romans and Barbarians*. THOMPSON also published a study of the initial conversion of the the Sueves [12.5: 1980].

12.6 Alamans

The Alamans, like the Franks, were the subject of a major exhibition in the 1990s [12.6: FUCHS/KEMPA/REDIES 1997], the catalogue of which provides a useful starting point for considering the archaeological evidence. A much older volume by Reiner CHRISTLEIN [12.6: 1978] is still useful on the archaeology, as are the more recent studies by Frank SIEGMUND [12.6: 2000] (who considers the Alamans and Franks together) and Claudia THEUNE [12.6: 2004], whose focus is on barbarians and Romans in Alamannia. Among historical studies, there is a significant monograph on relations between Romans and Alamans by John DRINKWATER [12.6: 2007]. Alamans are considered alongside the Franks in volumes edited by both Dieter GEUENICH [12.6: 1998], and Ian WOOD [12.6: 1998]. Contacts between Alamannia and areas to the North are considered in a volume edited by Hans-Peter NAUMANN [12.6: 2004]. On the overlap between Alamans and Sueves there is an article by Hans HUMMER [12.6: 1998].

12.7 Franks

For the Franks of the fifth and sixth centuries we have the narrative provided by Gregory of Tours, together with the earliest of the Merovingian saint's *Lives*, edited by Bruno KRUSCH and Wilhelm LEVISON in the *Monumenta Germaniae Historia, Scriptores Rerum Merovingicarum*. Another source of value are the poems of Venantius Fortunatus [12.7: REYDELLET 1994–2004; 12.7: QUESNEL 1996] and the letter collection known as the *Epistolae Austrasicae*. One text that poses considerable problems, not least because of the debate over its origins, is the *Pactus Legis Salicae* [12.7: ECKHARDT 1962], of which there is an important discussion by Karl UBL [11: 2017], who has traced the development of Salic Law from its fifth-century origins down to the Carolingian period, while the manuscripts have been discussed by Magali COUMERT in a contribution which raises many new questions [12.7: 2023]. The Merovingian Church canons have been edited by Jean GAUDEMET and Brigitte BASDEVANT [12.7: 1989], and are the subject of a study by Odette PONTAL which has appeared in both German and (in a revised version) in French [12.7: 1986, 1989], and of a monograph by Gregory HALFOND [12.7: 2009]. *(margin: Sources)*

For the period before the establishment of the Merovingian kingdom the main evidence is archaeological; our chief literary source, Gregory of Tours, has little to say on the early years of the people. For an overview of the archaeology the catalogue from the vast exhibition on *Die Franken* staged in Mainz, Paris and Berlin in 1996/7 provides a good compendium of material even if more recent *(margin: Archaeology)* finds have added to our knowledge [12.7: Wieczorek/Périn/von Welck/ Menghin 1996/1997]. In addition there is an archaeological survey by Frank Siegmund [12.6: 2000]. The history of Frankish archaeology has been studied by Bonnie Effros [12.7: 2003]. There are valuable archaeologically-informed discussions by Edward James [12.7: 1988] and by Guy Halsall in his collected articles [12.7: 2010]. The problems of Frankish archaeology and of distinguishing between Franks and Romans are discussed, with full consideration of the historiography of the subject, by Hubert Fehr [2: 2010].

The early Franks   For an up-to-date survey of all aspects of Merovingian history there is a handbook edited by Bonnie Effros and Isabel Moreira [12.7: 2020]. The proceedings of a conference held in San Marino, edited by Ian Wood [12.7: 1988], discuss various aspects of Frankish history.

Until recently the majority of historians passed over the early history of the Franks to concentrate on the Merovingian kingdoms, but Erich Zöllner's account of Frankish history [12.7: 1970] only goes up to the mid sixth century. The opening chapter of Patrick Geary's *Before France and Germany* [12.7: 1988] also has an important discussion of the formation of the people. Recently, however, a number of centenaries have led to greater consideration of the reigns of Childeric and Clovis. These include the commemoration of the publication of the account of the discovery of Childeric's tomb in 1655, which involved an exhibition and catalogue edited by Dieter Quast [12.7: 2015] that provides a full discussion of the grave finds (our most valuable evidence for Childeric's reign).

Clovis   In addition, there were celebrations to mark 1500 years since Clovis' defeat of the Alamans and his conversion to Catholicism, which, following the narrative of Gregory of Tours, were traditionally dated to 496/8, although early sixth-century evidence make a date of 506 for the Alaman victory and 508 for the king's baptism more likely. The early chronology is argued for by Matthias Becher [12.7: 2011], and the late chronology by Ian Wood [12.7: 1985] and Danuta Shanzer [12.7: 1998]. The 496 celebrations were a *raison d'être* for the exhibition on *Die Franken* and also for a conference organised by Dieter Geuenich [12.7: 1998]. A yet more sizeable conference was held in Reims, organised by Michel Rouche [12.7: 1997]. The Frankish victory at Vouillé was celebrated by a conference and by two volumes of articles, the one edited by Luc Bourgeios [12.7: 2010], the other (which includes English versions of some of the articles in

the volume edited by Bourgeios] by Ralph Mathisen and Danuta
Shanzer [12.7: 2012]. Clovis' death in 511 was marked by Matthias
Becher's biography of the king [12.7: 2011] and by a conference and
volume of conference proceedings edited by Mischa Meier and Steffen Patzold [12.7: 2014].

The written documentation on the Franks is dominated by the
Histories of Gregory of Tours, who has been the focus of numerous
studies over the past generation, notably by Walter Goffart [11.
1988], Martin Heinzelmann [11. 1994/2001], Giselle de Nie [14.4: 1987],
Helmut Reimitz [11. 2015], Margarete Weidemann [12.7: 1982], and Ian
Wood [12.7: 1994]. Gregory's life and works are also covered by a
compendium edited by Alexander C. Murray [12.7: 2015]. One reason
for the spate of studies in the 1980s and 90s was the centenary of
Gregory's death in 594. This was the focus of a conference in Tours,
whose proceedings were edited by Nancy Gauthier and Henri Galinié
[12.7: 1997], and also of papers delivered at the 1994 *International
Medieval Congress* in Leeds, gathered together by Kathleen Mitchell
and Ian Wood [12.7: 2002].

For the Merovingian kingdom, the starting point remains the
seminal articles on the *Teilreiche* by Eugen Ewig [12.7: 1976, 1979,
2009]. Ewig also wrote a short, but perceptive, overview of Merovingian history [12.7: 1988]. There are other surveys by Reinhold Kaiser
[12.7: 1993], Martina Hartmann [12.7: 2003], and Sebastian Scholz [12.7:
2015]. Overviews in English include those by Pat Geary [12.7: 1988],
Edward James [12.7: 1988], and Ian Wood [12.7: 1944]. In French there
is a recent survey by Charles Mériaux [12.7: 2014]. Clovis' successors
have attracted less attention; the one substantial biography has
been that of Brunhild by Bruno Dumézil [12.7: 2008].

Gregory of Tours

The Teilreiche

12.8 Burgundians

The Burgundians have attracted some attention in recent years. In
terms of written evidence, the chief sources are the *Chronicle of
Marius of Avenches*, recently re-edited by Justin Favrod [12.8: 1993],
and the letters of Avitus of Vienne, together with the two legal
codes, the *Liber Constitutionum* and the *Forma et Expositio Legum*
[12.8: de Salis 1892], and the canons of the councils of Epaon and
Lyon I [12.7: Gaudemet/Basdevant 1989]. For the writings of Avitus of
Vienne there is the translation and commentary by Danuta Shanzer

Sources

and Ian Wood [12.8: 2002] as well as a more recent French edition and translation by Elena Malaspina [12.8: 2016]. Katalin Escher [12.8: 2005] has provided an invaluable compendium of all the relevant material, archaeological as well as literary. For the archaeology there are also useful articles in the collection deriving from a conference of held in Dijon, edited by Henri Gaillard de Semainville [12.8: 1995].

Overviews   There is a full, traditional study of the kingdom, with much useful detail, by Justin Favrod [12.8: 1997] as well as more modern, but briefer, overviews by Reinhold Kaiser [12.8: 2004] and Biagio Saitta [12.8: 2006]. There are also the proceedings of two conferences, one edited by Volker Gallé [12.8: 2008] and the other by Anne Wagner and Nicole Brocard [12h: 2018], which encompasses the history of the Burgundian region down to 1032. The nature of the Burgundian state has been considered by Wood [12.8: 2014], and by Merle Eisenberg [12.8: 2019], both of whom question whether the traditional model of a kingdom is appropriate.

The question of Burgundian ethnicity has been studied by Ian Wood [12.8: 1990] and, on two occasions, by Patrick Amory [12.8: 1993, 1994], stressing the non-biological nature of the group. The law-codes have been the subject of studies by David Frye [12.8: 1990], Wood [12.8: 2016, 2017] and Peter Heather [12.8: 2011]. They have also been discussed in a more general context of social and economic change by Matthew Innes [12.8: 2006].

12.9 Ostrogoths

Sources   The Ostrogoths, after their settlement in Italy, are the best evidenced of the barbarian peoples. Although Jordanes has little to say about the reign of Theodoric, for a narrative there is material in various chronicles, notably of Marcellinus Comes [5.4: Croke 1995] and Cassiodorus, and there is the short text known as the *Anonymus Valesianus* [12.9: König 1997]. Procopius provides an account of the Ostrogothic kingdom preceding his narrative of the Gothic War.

Equally valuable are the non-narrative sources, above all the *Variae* of Cassiodorus, for which there is now an Italian annotated edition [12.9: Giardina 2014–20], in addition to that of Mommsen in the *Monumenta Germaniae Historica*. Cassiodorus' intentions in putting together his collection of letters has been the subject of much discussion, and it is now thought that he edited them while in exile in Constantinople in order to present Theodoric and his successors in a particular light, as has been argued by Shane BJORNLIE [6: 2013]. For Theodoric's government there is also the *Edictum Theodorici* [12.9: KÖNIG 2013], which is now assigned to the Ostrogothic king with a fair degree of certainty by Sean LAFFERTY [12.9: 2013]. In addition to the work of Cassiodorus, there are the letters and speeches of Ennodius [12.9: GIOANNI 2006–10], including a panegyric on Theodoric [12.9: ROHR 1995]. The letters shed a great deal of light on the senatorial aristocracy of his day. For Ennodius himself there is a biography by S. A. H. KENNELL [12.9: 2000]. In addition, for papal history, there is the *Collectio Avellana* [12.9: GUENTHER 1895], which has been the subject of a recent collection of articles [7: TESTA/MARCONI 2019; 12.9: BLAIR-DIXON 2007]. Also vital for papal history in this period is the *Liber Pontificalis* [12.9: DUCHESNE 1886–92], which provides a particularly partisan account of the pontificate of pope Symmachus. The translation into English of the *Liber Pontificalis* by Raymond DAVIES [12.9: 1998–95] provides a useful introduction, while Rosamond McKITTERICK's study [12.9: 2020] of the text is the obvious point of departure for further study.

For the history of the Ostrogoths from the time of Attila down to the move to Italy the narratives provided by Herwig WOLFRAM [4.5: 2009] and by Peter HEATHER [4.5: 1991] are valuable. The question of Ostrogothic identity is raised by Patrick AMORY [11: 1997], who stresses its constructed nature. Amory's argument has been much debated in the context of studies of barbarian identity. A convenient survey of the arguments can be found in Brian SWAIN's contribution [12.9: 2006] to the *Companion to Ostrogothic Italy* edited by Jonathan ARNOLD, Shane BJORNLIE and Kristina SESSA. The volume itself provides an extensive overview of the major topics in the history of the peninsula under Ostrogothic rule [12.9: ARNOLD/BJORNLIE/SESSA 2006]. There is also a collection of articles edited by Sam BARNISH and Federico MARAZZI [12.9: 2007] that cover the main themes of Ostrogothic history.

Before and after the move to Italy

A new biography of Theodoric by Hans-Ulrich WIEMER [12.9: 2018] puts the king's life into the broader context of Ostrogothic history from the mid fifth century onwards. There is a convenient narrative of Theodoric's reign in Italy by John MOORHEAD [12.4: 1992]. Greater emphasis is placed on Theodoric as reviving the Empire in the West by Jonathan ARNOLD [12.1: 2004], while Henning BÖRM [3:

Theodoric

2013] considers Theodoric within the context of the later Empire. Theodoric's subsequent reputation is studied by Andreas GOLTZ [12.9: 2008]. The generation after Theodoric's death is covered by biographies of Amalasuintha [12.9: VITIELLO 2017] and Theodohad [12.9: VITIELLO 2014], which inevitably have more to say about the contexts of the two rulers than about the individuals themselves.

Theodoric's court and Ravenna For the ideology of Theodoric's court there is a volume by Massimiliano VITIELLO [12.9: 2006], while the importance of *civilitas* is the subject of an article by Marc REYDELLET [12.9: 1995]. The role of the senate in the Ostrogothic period is re-evaluated by Adolfo LA ROCCA and Fabrizio OPPEDISANO [9: 2016], in a work that is also of value for understanding the senate in the fifth century. The surviving monuments from the reign of Theodoric in Ravenna have been the subject of much discussion by art- and architectural historians, especially in the monumental study of Friedrich DEICHMANN [5.2: 1969–76], but more recently, and from a more historical point of view, by Deborah MAUSKOPF DELIYANNIS [12.9: 2010] and Mariëtte VERHOEVEN [5.2: 2011]. Although Rome has fewer surviving monuments from the Ostrogothic period, the city is the subject of a study by Massimiliano VITIELLO [12.9: 2005].

The Gothic wars The Gothic Wars receive detailed consideration from Mischa MEIER in the context of his study of Justinian's reign, which emphasises the catastrophic nature of the period [11.2: MEIER 2003; see also 11.3: MAAS 2014]. The biography of Belisarius by Ian HUGHES [12.9: 2009], although intended for a general audience, fills a gap in modern accounts. For the devastation caused by the Gothic Wars, there is an important discussion in WICKHAM's *Framing the Early Middle Ages* [3: 2005]. The most recent study of the impact of Justinian's wars is a volume by Hendrik DEY and Fabrizio OPPEDISANO [12.9.2024].

12.10 Anglo-Saxons

Sources The fifth- and sixth-century Anglo-Saxons present a particular set of problems, and indeed Britain from the late fifth century onwards tends to be ignored in discussions of the late-antique West. Most, although not all, of our written sources (above all Bede's *Ecclesiastical History*, the *Historia Britonum*, and the *Anglo-Saxon Chronicle*) date from the eighth century and later. Of the fifth- and sixth-century sources, the *Life of Germanus* by Constantius records a Saxon attack, but says it was repulsed [10: Borius 1964]. The *Chronicle of 452*, probably written not long after the *Life of Germanus*, however states that Britain was under Saxon control [12.10: Burgess 2001]. The significance of the work of Constantius for the history of Britain is explored in depth by Edward Thompson [12.10: 1984]. Gildas, writing in the sixth century (probably in the 530s), says that the Britons were still dominant in much of the island of Britain in his day, although he does talk of a major uprising by Saxon federates against their British employers, which scored considerable success for a while. A recent edition of the text of Gildas emphasises the literary and theological construction of the text [12.10: George 2009]. There is still much of value in the collection of articles dealing with Gildas edited by Michael Lapidge and David Dumville [10: 1984].

The archaeological, and particularly the cemeterial, evidence is our main source for the arrival of the Anglo-Saxons. This used to be interpreted in the light of Bede's statement that three groups, Angles, Saxons and Jutes, came to Britain. Each of these groups was thought to be identifiable in the archaeological record. More recently these identifications have been challenged, and the whole model of a triple migration has been understood to be oversimplified. This was already argued by Vera Evison [12.10: 1965] in a much-discussed book on the fifth-century migrations south of the Thames. Although migrants clearly did come from territories associated with the continental Angles, Saxons and Jutes, these were not their only points of departure, as is becoming increasingly clear from scientific analysis of the skeletal evidence [12.10: Budd/Millard et al. 2004]. Archaeology suggests connections with much of the southern North Sea region, and indeed with some areas further inland. Work on the Continental Saxons (for instance that edited by Dennis Green and Frank Siegmund [12.10: 2003]), has provided a background for the migration, as has recent work on Frisia, where our understanding of the landscape and the social structures associated with it is changing rapidly, as can be seen in the work of Johan Nicolay [12.10: 2014].

Archaeology

Moreover, the chronology of the migrations is now questioned. The invitation to Saxon federates, recorded by Gildas and repeated by Bede, who places it in the 450s, clearly did not mark the beginning of migration. In a controversial, but thought-provoking book, Stephen Oppenheimer [12.10: 2006] placed the linguistic influence of Germanic in Britain very much earlier than the Migration Period,

The chronology of migration

and this is supported by the work of Daphne Nash-Briggs [12: 2011]. Nor was the migration large-scale, at least before the late sixth century. Catherine Hills provided useful overview of the subject in 2003 [12.10: 2003]. Guy Halsall [12.10: 2013] has raised further questions about the Anglo-Saxon migration and the problems posed by both the literary and the archaeological material. It is only towards the end of the sixth century and the beginning of the seventh that the evidence is strong enough to form a relatively secure idea of the formation of the Anglo-Saxon kingdoms, for which the volume of papers edited by Stephen Bassett [12.10: 1989] remains a useful point of departure. The history of the period is told from a British point of view by Thomas Charles-Edwards in his volume on the History of Wales [12.10: 2013], which also deals with the history of Brittany in the late- and post-Roman period.

12.11 Lombards

Sources As in the case of the Anglo-Saxons, the earliest narrative account of the Lombards comes from the eighth century, with the *History* of Paul the Deacon, although there are numerous references in Procopius and Gregory of Tours as well as in the letters of Gregory the Great. Once again, therefore, the archaeology evidence is of crucial importance, especially in understanding the Lombards prior to and at the time of their entry into Italy. Although new finds are constantly changing the picture (not least because of the developments in genome sequencing) [11: Amorim 2018], the catalogue of an exhibition held in Bonn in 2008 provides a fine sample of material [12.11: Hegewisch 2008].

Archaeology An earlier overview of Lombard history and archaeology is that of Wilfried Menghin [12.11: 1985]. There is a slightly more recent monograph by Neil Christie [12.11: 1995]. For the migration into Italy there is a study by Panagiotis Antonopoulos [12.11: 2006] which concentrates almost entirely on the written sources, without consideration of the archaeology.

Overviews Several recent publications are primarily volumes of conference proceedings or of collected papers. From the same year as the Bonn exhibition, there is a volume of conference proceedings edited by Jan Bemmann and Michael Schmauder [12.11: 2008], which places the Lombards alongside the Avars and Slavs in their Central European context before their entry into Italy. Covering both the period before and after the move to Italy, there is a volume on Lombard lordship and identity edited by Walter Pohl and Peter Erhart [12.11: 2005]. Largely, but not exclusively concerned with the Lombards in Italy is a volume edited by Giorgio Ausenda, Paolo Delogu and Chris Wickham [12.11: 2009].

12.12 Avars

With regard to the sixth century, the Avars have usually been studied along with the Lombards and Slavs, as in the case of the Bonn conference, the proceedings of which were edited by Jan Bemmann and Michael Schmauder [12.11: 2008]. Their archaeology has also been presented alongside that of the Huns [11.3: Daim 1996]. The one substantial monograph is that by Walter Pohl, which originally appeared in German in 2002, but was issued in English in a substantially revised version in 2018 [both 12.12].

13 The Non-theological Culture of the Sixth-century West

The picture given by Pierre Riché [13: 1962] in his study of education and culture in the West from the sixth to eighth centuries is a largely depressing one. Over the past half-century there has been a greater appreciation of the creativity of the period – not least in Yitzhak Hen's evaluation of the culture of the Merovingian kingdom [13: 1995], to which may be added that of Ian Wood [13: 2017].

Certainly, it is true that the Latin language became less classi-　Linguistic change
cal, as noted above all by Michel Banniard [13: 1992] and Roger Wright [13: 1982]. But this is a matter of linguistic change and not linguistic degeneration. A useful regional overview is provided by Alex Mullen and George Woudhuysen [13: 2023]. And despite changing language, there was still an interest in grammar, which is apparent from the transmission of the works of Donatus and Priscian as well as the composition of the grammar of Asporius, whose origins are disputed between Burgundy and Ireland [8: Law 1997]. Good public speaking was still valued, as is clear from the reception of the ser-

mons of Caesarius of Arles and Avitus of Vienne in the early sixth century [13: Diesenberger/Hen/Pollheimer 2013].

Panegyric

There is some evidence that panegyrics (for instance those of Cassiodorus [13: MacCormack 1976]) were still delivered orally, although that by Ennodius may be too long to have been read out to a listening public [13: Rohr 1995]. From Byzantium we have some works of panegyric, including the poem in praise of Justin II by Corippus [13: Cameron 1976]. Some of Venantius Fortunatus' poems directed at kings and queens can certainly be categorised as panegyric [12.7: Reydellet 1989]. The continuance of the panegyric tradition in the West, even in contexts when a prose or verse text was not read out in public, is charted by Marc Reydellet, in his study of views of royalty [13: 1981].

Letter-writing

Another genre of writing which was popular in the Later Empire and continued into the sixth century was the writing of letters. There is, of course, the collection of official documents gathered together in Cassiodorus' *Variae*. In addition, there are other collections of official correspondence from Italy, notably the letters by popes, including the *Collectio Avellana*, the letters of Pelagius I and the *Register* of Gregory I [7: Sogno/Storin/Watts 2017].

But more indicative of the tradition of letter-writing is the continuing composition of friendship letters. Just as Sidonius looked back to earlier writers, including Pliny, a number of late fifth- and early sixth-century writers regarded Sidonius as a model, among them his relatives Ruricius of Limoges [13: Mathisen 1999] and Avitus of Vienne [12.8: Shanzer/Wood 2002], as well as Ennodius of Pavia [12.9: Gioanni 2006–10]. The tradition of letter-writing continued throughout the sixth century with the *Epistulae Austrasicae* [13: Barrett-Woudhuysen 2016; Tyrell 2019], and into the seventh with Desiderius of Cahors [13: Norberg 1961; Mathisen 2013]. The importance of letter-writing as a genre is mapped out in the contributions to collections edited by Klaus Herbers [13: 2017], Gernot Michael Müller [8: 2018], and Cristiana Sogno, Bradley Storin, and Edward Watts [7: 2017].

Boethius

Certainly, there is little in the way of philosophical writing from the period, but there is the *Consolation of Philosophy* by Boethius in addition to his other secular works. Henry Chadwick [13: 1981] considered his treatises on music and logic, alongside the *Consolation* and Boethius' theological works. Anja Heilmann [13: 2007] has discussed the relationship of the treatise on music with the

Quadrivium, while Joachim GRUBER has written a two-volume commentary on the *Consolatio* [13: 2006]. The major general assessment of Boethius is to be found in another two-volume work, by Luca OBERTELLO [13: 1974], but there is a shorter introduction by John MARENBON [13: 2003]. MARENBON has also edited a *Companion to Boethius* [13: 2009], and there are other collections of papers dedicated to the senator, edited by Margaret GIBSON [13: 1981], Manfred FUHRMAN and Joachim GRUBER [13: 1984], and Alain GALONNIER [13: 2003].

Much of the written material to survive from the sixth-century West is infused with Christianity, even when it is not theological. This is true, for instance, of much historical writing, including the *Histories* of Gregory of Tours, as shown decisively by Martin HEINZELMANN [11: 1994]. In that the chronicle-writers (who include Marius of Avenches, Victor of Tunnuna and John of Biclaro) were almost all continuing the chronicle of Jerome-Eusebius, either directly or indirectly, they too have a religious focus [5.2: BURGESS/KULIKOWSKI 2013]. *(margin: History writing)*

There are, however, a handful of historical writings that are more secular, notably Jordanes in both his *Historia Getica* and his *Historia Romana* [11: CHRISTENSEN 2002]. So, too, is Jordanes' exact contemporary, Procopius, a secular writer. Equally, there is the secular verse account of the campaigns of John Troglita in North Africa by Corippus [13: DIGGLE/GOODYEAR 1970; on Corippus see 13: GOLDLUST 2015; MERRILLS 2023]. All three of them, however, were writing in Constantinople and so scarcely illustrate Western culture, although the information contained in their works is crucial for Western History. For secular historical writing of the period from the Late Antique West it is necessary to turn to the so-called *Anonymus Valesianus* II [12.9: KÖNIG 1997].

There is little poetry from the West after the early years of the sixth century. Changes in language did not help: as Gregory of Tours noted, king Chilperic was unable to stress Latin properly, although he tried to write verse; his surviving hymn was edited by K. STREKER [13: 1923] and is discussed by Dag NORBERG [13: 1954]. Up until the mid-sixth century, however, the tradition of Biblical Epic had continued, as noted by Michael ROBERTS [7: 1985], Daniel NODES [7: 1993], and most recently by Roger GREEN [13: 2006]. Around the year 500, Avitus of Vienne wrote a version of the early books of the Old Testament in verse [13: HECQUET-NOTI 1999–2005], and Arator *(margin: Poetry / Biblical epic)* wrote a verse account of the Acts of the Apostles shortly thereafter [13: HILLIER 2020; SCHWIND 1990; GREEN 2006; SOTINEL 1989]. Dracontius in North Africa also wrote about the creation of the world, but most of his poems are more occasional pieces [7: MOUSSEY/CAMUS 2002]. In addition to his biblical epic, Avitus also wrote an extended poem on chastity and the virgins of his family as an exhortation to his sister [13: HECQUET-NOTI 2011]. From the late sixth century there are not so many writers of verse, but Venantius Fortunatus was able both to write occasional pieces, many of which are verse letters, and to compose panegyrics and religious works, including his *De Virginitate* and his verse *Life of St Martin*. A new edition, with French translation, provides commentary on the works of Fortunatus [12.7: REYDELLET 1994–2004; QUESNEL 1996], and there is also an edition and English translation by Michael ROBERTS [13: 2017], while Judith GEORGE [13: 1992] has provided a good biographical introduction to the poet.

14 The Western Church in the Sixth century

14.1 General

Most studies of sixth-century Christianity look back to the period of the conversion of Constantine. In *The Rise of Western Christendom* Peter BROWN [3: 1996] examines the period from 200–1000. He has focussed his attention more precisely on the sixth century in his study of the impact of Christian gift-giving in the creation of a 'spiritual economy' [3: BROWN 2012] and in his consideration of the relation of this to attitudes towards the afterlife [7: BROWN 2015]. Robert MARKUS [3: 1990] traces the in-depth Christianisation of the Roman World through the growth of Christian and specifically ascetic culture. Arnold ANGENENDT [14.1: 2001], whose account of Western Christianity begins in 400 and carries on to 900, places his emphasis firmly on matters of religiosity and of the significance of the Old Testament as a model for early-medieval churchmen.

With regard to more mundane aspects of the spiritual economy, Ian WOOD [14.1: 2013] has traced the donation of property to the Western Church in the pre-Carolingian era and has examined Church property holding within the context of the transformation of the Roman West: he has suggested that it is useful to consider the

Church-dominated world of the seventh century as conforming to
the model of a Temple Society [3: 2018; 2022].

14.2 The Structure of the Sixth-century Church

The development of ecclesiastical authority in this period is generally seen within a broader late-antique context. Conrad Leyser [7:
2000] places asceticism at the heart of his study of religious authority between Augustine and Gregory the Great, while Kristina Sessa
[7: 2012] emphasises the model of good household management in
her study of papal authority. Studies of the episcopate also consider
the period from the fourth century onwards, as in the case of the
monographs by Claudia Rapp [7: 2005] and by Pauline Allen and
Bronwen Neil [7: 2013] (who concentrate on the episcopal response
to crisis).

Religious authority

More specific to fifth- and sixth-century developments are the
studies of the (modern) notion of *Bischofsherrschaft*, including
those by Martin Heinzelmann [14.2: 1976] and Georg Scheibelreiter
[14.2: 1983], both of which build on the seminal work of Dietrich
Claude [14.2: 1963]. The debate over *Bischofsherrschaft* is usefully reviewed by Steffen Diefenbach [14.2: 2013]. The basic outlines of a
growth in episcopal power are clear enough, but detailed evidence
suggests that there was considerable variety and that the growth in
power was by no means straightforward. Studies of individual dioceses suggest that episcopal power depended to some extent on individuals – not just the bishops, but also those who might challenge
their power (especially the local *dux* or *comes*), as noted by Jean
Durliat [14.2: 1979] in his study of the seventh-century bishop
Desiderius of Cahors. The traditional view that by the end of the
fifth century episcopal positions were increasingly being taken over
by members of the aristocracy (which was supposedly a factor in
the development of episcopal authority) has been challenged by
Steffen Patzold [14.2: 2014, 2014a].

Bischofsherrschaft

The exercise of episcopal authority is perhaps best evidenced
by the official ecclesiastical letters of the period [7: Allen/Neil 2013].
The vast majority of these are papal. Above all there is the *Register*
of Gregory the Great [14.2: Ewald/Hartmann 1891–9; Norberg 1982;
Martyn 2004], but there is also a smaller collection of letters of
Pelagius I [14.2: Gasso/Batlle 1956], which is the subject of a study by

*Episcopal and
papal letters*

Bronwen NEIL [14.2: 2015]. Among collections of letters of several popes the most important is the *Collectio Avellana* (a collection of 248 papal and imperial documents from 367–553, apparently put together 556–61) [12.9: BLAIR-DIXON 2007], which is the subject of a recent volume of papers edited by Rita LIZZI TESTA and Giulia MARCONI [14.2: 2019]. Smaller collections which contain papal letters have been studied by Ralph MATHISEN [14.2: 1999] and by Geoffrey DUNN [14.2: 2015].

Papal history There are not many modern biographies of individual popes, despite the importance of the sixth century for the expansion of papal authority, which is reflected in the compilation of the *Liber Pontificalis*, as noted by Rosamond McKITTERICK [12.9: 2020]. The disputed pontificate of Symmachus and Laurentius is the subject of a monograph by Eckhard WIRBELAUER [14.2: 1993] and of an article by John MOORHEAD [14.2: 1978]. Pelagius I is studied in the context of the Tri-Capitoline schism by Florian BATTISTELLA [14.2: 2017]. Much greater attention has, inevitably, been paid to the pontificate of Gregory the Great. Robert MARKUS [14.2: 1997] provides valuable insight in his study of the pope, and there is much useful detail in the older biography by Jeffrey RICHARDS [14.2: 1980], which depends heavily on the pope's *Register*.

Bishops and priests The position of bishops has been considered by Greg HALFOND [14.2: 2019]. For studies of individual bishops there are William KLINGSHIRN's study of Caesarius of Arles [12.3: 1994] and Marie-Céline ISAÏA's study of Remigius of Reims [14.2: 2010]. Priests have been the subject of very much less attention than have bishops, but there is an invaluable collection of material by Robert GODDING [14.2: 2001], and a collection of articles edited by Carine VAN RIJN and Steffen PATZOLD [14.2: 2016]. Notions of priesthood in the works of Dionysius Exiguus are considered by Conrad LEYSER [14.2: 2019].

Church councils The most important council of the century was certainly that of Constantinople in 553. Although it was essentially a Byzantine affair, it had a considerable impact on the West because of its condemnation of the so-called Three Chapters [14.2: PRICE 2009]. In the West itself there were regional councils of significance in Africa [7: MUNIER 1974], Francia (discussed by Odette PONTAL [12.7: 1989] and Greg HALFOND [12.7: 2009]), Burgundy, the Suevic kingdom, and Visigothic Spain by Rachel STOCKING [12.7: 2001]. Moreover, at the end of the century one finds the first indications of the compilation of collections of canon law in a handful of manuscripts, as shown by

Ralph MATHISEN [14.2: 1999], and more systematically in the collection underlying the *Vetus Gallica*, studied by Hubert MORDEK [14.2: 1975].

Although most of Western Europe was no longer under the direct control of Byzantium after 476, Rome was subject to the Eastern Empire, following the Justinianic Reconquest, and this had a considerable impact on papal actions, as traced by Claire SOTINEL [14.2: 2005]. The impact of certain aspects of Justinian's *Kirchenpolitik* on ecclesiastical jurisdiction in the West was studied by Robert MARKUS [14.2: 1979].

14.3 Doctrine

Most of the doctrinal debates of the sixth century are continuations of earlier conflicts. Within the West, Arianism continued to pose a problem in the Vandal, Ostrogothic, and Visigothic kingdoms, and it would come to pose a problem in the Lombard kingdom. The topic of Arianism in this period is the subject of a useful collection edited by Guido BERNDT and Roland STEINACHER [11: 2014]. The last phase of the Vandal persecutions is distinguished by the works of Fulgentius [12.4: WHELAN 2018]. There is also a meticulous study of relations between Avitus of Vienne and homoeans in the Burgundian kingdom by Uta HEIL [14.3: 2011]. Visigothic Arianism lasted down to the conversion of Reccared and the Third Council of Toledo.

Nestorian and Monophysite issues also continued to be debated, not because either doctrine was important in the West, but rather because imperial religious policies had western repercussions. The considerable documentation for the Acacian Schism between Rome and Constantinople (caused by the Monophysite leanings of the patriach Acacius) was edited by Eduard SCHWARTZ [14.3: 1934]. This is also the context of Boethius' theological works, which have been discussed by Henry CHADWICK [13: 1981]. Active in Rome at the time of the Acacian schism, and playing an important part in the transmission of Eastern canons to the West, was the Scythian monk Dionysius Exiguus, who was also responsible for what was to prove to be the most important *computus* for the dating of Easter and for the promotion of the *Anno Domini* dating system [14.3: DE-CLERCQ 2002; 7: CHADWICK 2003]. The Schism has been examined in detail by Mischa MEIER in the context of his study of Anastasios [14.4: 2006].

Arianism

Nestorianism and Monophysitism

The Tri-Capitoline schism

From the middle of the century there are the canons of the oecumenical Council of Constantinople, which had considerable impact on the West because of its condemnation of the works of Theodore, Theodoret and Ibas, which led to the Tricapitoline Schism. The proceedings of the council and related documents have been translated by Richard Price [14.2: 2009]. For the history of the schism there is a collection of articles edited by Celia Chazelle and Catherine Cubitt [14.3: 2007]. For the ramifications of the Tri-Capitoline Schism for papal authority, there is a study by Florian Battistella [14.: 2007].

Cassiodorus' theological works

From the same period, we have the religious writings of Cassiodorus following his return to Italy from Constantinople after the end of the Gothic War. For Cassiodorus' views on Christian learning there is his *Institutiones*, for which the translation and commentary of James Halporn and Mark Vessey [14.3: 2004] provide a useful point of entry. And there is his *Commentary on the Psalms* [14.3: Astell 1999]. A volume of papers partly concerned with the culture of the Vivarium was produced by Sam Barnish et al. [14.3: 2008]. For the life of Cassiodorus there is a biography by James O'Donnell [14.3: 1979], and for a general survey of his significance there is a monograph by Franco Cardini [14.3: 2009; 6: GIARDINA 2006]

Gregory the Great

The theology of Gregory the Great has been the subject of much attention. Peter Eich has provided a useful historiographical survey of writings about the pope in his biography [14.3: 2016]. Alongside Markus' study [14.2: 1997], Carole Straw's monograph [14.3: 1988] provides a useful introduction. The importance of asceticism in Gregory's thought is underlined by George E. Demacopoulos [14.3: 2015]. There is much of value in two old volumes of conference proceedings, one from 1986, edited by Jacques Fontaine [14.3: 1986], and the other from 1995, edited by John Cavadini [14.3: 1995]. The most up-to-date discussions of Gregory are to be found in the collection of essays edited by Bronwell Neil and Matthew J. Dal Santo [14.3: 2013].

14.4 The Cult of the Saints

Hagiography

A genre of increasing importance in the sixth century is that of hagiography. Many of the Roman Martyr Acts were probably composed in this period [4.1: Lapidge 2017]. A handful of works of hagiography from the first half of the sixth century are known from Francia (including the *Life of Genovefa* [14.4: Krusch 1896; Heinzelmann/

POULIN 1986], the *Vita Patrum Iurensium* [14.4: MARTINE 1968], and the *Vita Abbatum Acaunensium* [14.4: KRUSCH 1920]). At the end of the century there is something of an explosion of hagiographical writing, with numerous texts from Gregory of Tours [14.4: KRUSCH 1885] and Venantius Fortunatus [14.4: KRUSCH 1885] as well as the *Dialogues* ascribed to Gregory the Great [14.4: DE VOGÜÉ 1978–80].

Following Peter BROWN's exploration of the cult of the saints [7: 1981], the subject has attracted a good deal of interest among scholars. Among the volumes of essays that have resulted from this is one edited by James HOWARD-JOHNSTON and Paul Antony HAYWARD [7: 1999]. Central to BROWN's argument are the hagiographical works of Gregory of Tours, which are also key to Raymond VAN DAM's study of saints and their miracles [14.4: 1993]. Among other works on the bishop of Tours there is a more psychologically focussed study by Giselle DE NIE [14.4: 1987]. Gallo-Roman hagiography of the fifth and sixth centuries is at the centre of a study of Christian charisma by Götz HARTMANN [14.4: 2006]. Apart from the *Miracula* of Gregory of Tours, the other major collection of miracle stories from the period before the seventh century is the *Dialogues*, whose ascription to Gregory the Great has been much debated in recent years. Matthew DAL SANTO's contribution to the long-standing debate on the authorship of the *Dialogues* [14: 2012] ascribes them firmly to Gregory the Great, and it situates the work in the context of Byzantine debates about the miraculous. The cult of saints is also the subject of a volume edited by Robert WIŚNIEWSKI, Raymond VAN DAM and Bryan WARD-PERKINS [7: 2023]. Closely related to the cult of the saints is that of relics, the origins of which are meticulously examined by WIŚNIEWSKI [7: 2019].

On the development of the notion of the saint as patron of the city in the early Middle Ages there is a collection of articles in French edited by Jean-Pierre CAILLET, Sylvain DESTEPHEN, Bruno DUMÉZIL, and Hervé INGLEBERT [7: 2016]. The papers respond directly to the work of Peter BROWN, who provides the concluding remarks to the volume.

Ann Marie YASIN [14.4: 2009] examines the archaeology of cult sites, particularly in the western Mediterranean, and most especially in North Africa. For North Africa there is also a survey by Stephen POTTHOFF [14.4: 2017] which can be supplemented by the work of Eric REBILLARD [10: 2014]. For the city of Rome there are archaeological and architectural surveys by Caroline GOODSON [14.4:

The cult of the saints

Religious archaeology

2014, 2007] together with a monograph by Maya Maskarinec [14.4: 2018]. Italy more broadly is covered by Gisella Cantino Wataghin [14.4: 2016] in the volume edited by Jean-Pierre Caillet et al. [14.4: 2016]. The remarkable Christian archaeology of Lyon is discussed by Jean-François Reynaud [14.4: 1998], the archaeologist who excavated many of the key sites.

14.5 Monasticism

The other major development within the western Church in the sixth century is the expansion of monasticism. There is a vast, and growing, bibliography, for which one can turn to the website 'Bibliography on the history of monasticism in Late Antiquity', set up by Albrecht Diem [www.earlymedievalmonasticism.org].

Monastic rules   There are two major blocks of written evidence: monastic rules [14.5: Diem and Rousseau 2020; Diem 2005] and the lives of monastic saints. The most famous monastic rule, that of Benedict [14.5: de Vogüé 1971–2], was not the earliest, nor did it become the predominant rule until the Carolingian period. From the fifth and sixth century West there are the Rules of Augustine [14.5: Verheijen 1967; Lawless 1990], Caesarius [14.5: Courreau/de Vogüé 1988–94], Aurelian [*Patrologia Latina* 68, cols. 385–408; 14.5: Schmidt 1975] and Ferreolus [14.5: Desprez 1982], as well the Rule of the Master [14.5: de Vogüé 1964–5], that ascribed to Eugippius [14.5: Villegas/de Vogüé 1976], and a collection of rules known as the *Regulae Patrum*, which Adalbert de Vogüé [7: 1982] associated with Lérins. The fullest discussion of the Rule of Eugippius as a monastic text is by Maximilian Krausgruber [14.5: 1996]. De Vogüé's argument that Benedict was dependent on the Master has been challenged by Marilyn Dunn, not altogether successfully, although her criticisms of his arguments deserve consideration [14e: Dunn 1990; de Vogüé 1992; Dunn 1992].

Monastic hagiography   Among the leading works of monastic hagiography to date from the early sixth century there are the *Vita Patrum Iurensium* [10: Martine 1968] and the *Vita Abbatum Acaunensium* [14.4: Krusch 1920]. There has been relatively little in the way of archaeology on monastic sites dating to the late fifth and sixth centuries, although the largely archaeological question of monastic space is considered in a volume edited by Hendrik Dey and Elizabeth Fentress [14.5: 2011].

For a general overview of monastic development in the West, there is a study by Marilyn Dunn [14.5: 2000]. The history of Italian monasticism before 604 is the subject of a classic monograph by Georg Jenal [14.5: 1995]. In terms of individual communities in Italy, the monastery of the *Lucullanum*, outside Naples, is considered in the context of its abbot Eugippius [5.5: Pohl/Diesenberg 2011]. In Spain the history of monasticism is hard to trace before the seventh century, although there are some interesting charters for the monastery of San Martín de Asán from the early sixth century [14.5: Tomás-Faci/Martín-Iglesias 2017; Tomás-Faci 2017]. For the archaeological evidence for early monasticism in the peninsula there are surveys by Moreno Martín [14.5: 2011] and by Jorge López Quiroga [14.5: 2016].

The major evidence for monasticism in this period, however, comes from Francia, for which the key study remains that of Friedrich Prinz [2: 1988], to which should be added articles by Hartmut Atsma [14.5: 1976, 1983]. Individual communities have been the subject of volumes of essays, for instance that edited by Yann Codou and Michel Lauwers on Lérins [14.5: 2009] and that edited by Nicole Brocard, Françoise Vannotti, and Anne Wagner on Agaune [14.5: 2011].

Columbanus

Studies of monasticism tend to distinguish the period after 590 from the previous century and a half, seeing the arrival on the continent of the Irishman Columbanus and his foundations at Luxeuil and Bobbio as marking a new beginning. However, Columbanus was grounded in late-antique monastic tradition as it had developed in Britain and had been transmitted to Ireland. But his foundations and those that were affiliated in some way or other look forward to developments of the seventh and eighth centuries, not least in the endowment of rural institutions. The arrival of Columbanus and of subsequent Irish saints can, therefore, reasonably be seen as marking a watershed between Late Antiquity and the Early Middle Ages. The proceedings of a conference on Columbanus held at Luxeuil, although largely concerned with the seventh century and beyond, also situates the Irish saint within the monastic culture of Francia at the time of his arrival in Gaul [14.5: Bully/Bully/Dubreucy 2018].

Peter Brown [14.1: 2006] has argued on a number of occasions that Late Antiquity stretches on through the seventh century and even into the eighth, but the establishment of the Columbanian

(margin note, first paragraph:) Monasticism and monasteries

communities on the continent, together with the reintegration of the island of Britain into the world of Western Europe, marks a plausible end to the Late Antique period.

III Bibliography

1 Introduction: Late Antiquity

1.1 Handbooks, Source Collections, Book Series, and Periodicals

Antigüedad y Cristianismo 1984-
Antiquité Tardive 1993-
Biographisch-bibliographisches Kirchenlexikon 1975-
Corpus Christianorum 1953-
Corpus Scriptorum Ecclesiasticorum Latinorum 1866-
Early Medieval Europe 1992-.
Jahrbuch für Antike und Christentum 1958-.
Journal of Late Antiquity 2008-.
Lexikon des Mittelalters 1980-99
Lexikon für Theologie und Kirche 1930-
Monumenta Germaniae Historica 1826-
Der Neue Pauly 1996-2003
Oxford Studies in Late Antiquity 2009-.
Revue des études tardo-antiques 2011-.
Romanobarbarica 1976-.
Sources Chrétiennes 1942-.
Studies in Late Antiquity 2017-.
The Transformation of the Classical Heritage, 54 vols. Berkeley 1981-.
The Transformation of the Roman World, 14 vols. Leiden 1997-.
Translated Texts for Historians 1988-.

1.2 Individual Works

R. Auty et al. (eds.), Lexikon des Mittelalters, 9 vols. Munich/Zurich 1980 ff.; Lexikon
    des Mittelalters Online. Turnhout 2009.
F. W. Bautz et al. (eds.), Biographisch-Bibliographisches Kirchenlexikon, 39 vols. to
    date. Hamm/Herzberg/Nordhausen 1975-.
G. Bowersock/P. Brown/A. Grabar (eds.), Late Antiquity. A Guide to the Post-Classical
    World. Cambridge Mass. 1999.
P. Brown, The World of Late Antiquity. London 1971.
A. Cameron, The Perception of Crisis, in: Settimane di Studio del centro italiano di
    studi sull'alto medioevo 45, 1998, 9–34.
J.-M. Carrié, Introduction. "Bas Empire" ou "Antiquité Tardive"?, in: 4.1 J.-M. Carrié/
    Rousselle, 9–25.
R. Collins/J. Gerrard (eds.), Debating Late Antiquity in Britain AD 300–700. Oxford
    2004.

https://doi.org/10.1515/9783110352658-003

A. Demandt, Der Fall Roms. Die Auflösung des römischen Reiches im Urteil der Nachwelt. Munich 1984, 2nd ed. 2015.

S. Destephen (ed.), Prosopographie chrétienne du Bas-Empire, vol. 3: Diocèse d'Asie (325–641). Paris 2008.

A. Giardina, Esplosione di tardoantico, in: Studi Storici 40, 1999, 157–80.

J. Hoops (ed.), Reallexikon der germanischen Altertumskunde, Straßburg 1911–19; 2nd ed.: H. Beck et al. (eds.), 35 vols. Berlin/New York 1973–2008; Germanische Altertumskunde Online. Berlin 2010.

M. Humphries, Late Antiquity and World History. Challenging Conventional Narratives and Analyses, in: Studies in Late Antiquity 1, 2017, 8–37.

E. James, The Rise and Function of the Concept "Late Antiquity", in: Journal of Late Antiquity 1, 2008, 20–30.

A. H. M. Jones/J. R. Martindale/J. Morris, The Prosopography of the Later Roman Empire, 3 vols. Cambridge 1971–92.

J. H. W. G. Liebeschuetz, Late Antiquity and the Concept of Decline, in: Nottingham Medieval Studies 45, 2001, 1–11.

J. H. W. G. Liebeschuetz, The Birth of Late Antiquity, in: Antiquité Tardive 12, 2004, 253–61.

R. Lizzi Testa (ed.), Late Antiquity in Contemporary Debate. Newcastle-upon-Tyne 2017.

A. Mandouze (ed.), Prosopographie chrétienne du Bas-Empire, vol. I: Prosopographie de l'Afrique chrétienne (303–533). Paris 1982.

H.-I. Marrou, Décadence romaine ou Antiquité tardive? Paris 1977.

S. McGill/E. Watts (eds.), A Companion to Late Latin Literature. Oxford 2018.

M. Meier, Ostrom–Byzanz, Spätantike–Mittelalter. Überlegung zum "Ende" der Antike im Osten des römischen Reiches, in: Millennium 9, 2012, 187–253.

M. Meier, Die Spätantike, zeitlich und räumlich neu gefasst. Eine Zwischenbilanz aktueller Suchbewegungen, in: HZ 304, 2017, 686–706.

J. Neusner/A. Avery-Peck (eds.), Encyclopedia of Religious and Philosophical Writings in Late Antiquity. Leiden 2012.

O. Nicholson (ed.), The Oxford Dictionary of Late Antiquity, 2 vols. Oxford 2018.

L. Pietri/C. Pietri/J. Desmuliez (eds.), Prosopographie chrétienne du Bas-Empire, vol. 2: Prosopographie de l'Italie chrétienne (313–694), 2 vols. Paris 1999–2000.

L. Pietri/M. Heijmans (eds.), Prosopographie chrétienne du Bas-Empire, vol. 4: La Gaule chrétienne (314–614), 2 vols. Paris 2013.

T. Sardella, La fine del mondo antico e il problema storiografico della Tarda Antichità. Il ruolo del cristianesimo, in: Chaos e Kosmos 14, 2013, http://www.chaosekosmos.it/pdf/2013_22.pdf (27.06.2024).

R. Schulz, Das neue Bild der Spätantike als Epoche der europäischen Geschichte, in: GWU 59, 2008, 323–35.

D. Vera/L. Cracco Ruggini/E. Fentress et al., Antico e tardoantico oggi, in: RSI 114, 2002, 349–79.

2 The Development of Early Medieval Historiography Before 1970

B. Arnold, The Past as Propaganda. Totalitarian Archaeology in Nazi Germany, in: Antiquity 64, 1990, 464–78.

G. W. Bowersock/J. Clive/S. R. Graubard (eds.), Gibbon and the Decline and Fall of the Roman Empire. Cambridge Mass. 1977.

H. Bresslau, Geschichte der Monumenta Germaniae Historica, in: Neues Archiv 14, 1921.

P. Brown, The World of Late Antiquity. London 1971.

J. Á. Castillo Lozano, Los forjadores de la Antigüedad Tardía. El padre Orlandis y su contribución a la historia visigoda, in: Antigüedad y cristianismo 31–32, 2014–2015, 325–36.

P. Courcelle, Histoire littéraire des grandes invasions germaniques. Paris 1948; 3rd ed. 1964.

C. Courtois, Les Vandales et l'Afrique. Paris 1955.

F. Dahn, Könige der Germanen, 13 vols. Leipzig 1861–1910.

C. Dawson, The Making of Europe 400–1000 A. D. London 1932; reprinted with an introduction by A. C. Murray. London 2006; French trans. Les Origines de l'Europe et de la civilisation européenne. Paris 1934; Le moyen âge et les origines de l'Europe des invasions à l'an 1000. Paris 1960; German trans. Die Gestaltung des Abendlandes. Leipzig/Frankfurt 1935.

P. Delogu, Reading Pirenne Again, in: R. Hodges/W. Bowden (eds.), The Sixth Century. Production, Distribution and Demand. Leiden 1998, 15–40.

A. Dopsch, Wirtschaftliche und soziale Grundlagen der europäischen Kulturentwicklung. Vienna 1918–20; 2nd ed. Vienna 1923–4; abridged English trans. The Economic and Social Foundations of European Civilization. London 1937.

K. F. Eichhorn, Deutsche Staats- und Rechtsgeschichte, vol. 1. Göttingen 1808.

E. Ewig, Spätantikes und fränkisches Gallien. Gesammelte Schriften, 3 vols. Munich/Ostfildern 1976–2009.

H. Fehr, Germanen und Romanen im Merowingerreich. Berlin 2010.

T. Fröhlich, The Study of the Lombards and the Ostrogoths at the German Archaeological Institute of Rome in: Fragmenta 2, 2008, 183–213.

H. Fuhrmann, "Sind eben alles Menschen gewesen". Gelehrtenleben im 19. und 20. Jahrhundert. Munich 1996.

W. Goffart, Historical Atlases. The First Three Hundred Years. Chicago 2003.

A. Graceffa, Les historiens et la question franque. Le peuplement franc et les Mérovingiens dans l'historiographie française et allemande des XIXe–XXe siècles. Turnhout 2009.

F. Graus, Volk, Heiliger und Herrscher. Studien zur Hagiographie der Merowingerzeit. Prague 1965.

D. Gwynn (ed.), A. H. M. Jones and the Later Roman Empire. Leiden 2008.

T. Hägg (ed.), The World of Late Antiquity Revisited. SO Debate, in: Symbolae Osloenses 72, 1997, 5–90.

H. Härke (ed.), Archaeology, Ideology and Society. The German Experience. Frankfurt am Main 2000.

F. Hartog, Le XIXe siècle et l'histoire. Le cas Fustel de Coulanges, 2nd ed. Paris 2001.

A. F. Havighurst (ed.), The Pirenne Thesis. Analysis, Criticism, and Revision. Boston 1958.

R. Hingley, Roman Officers and English Gentlemen. The Imperial Origins of Roman Archaeology. London 2000.

R. Hodges/D. Whitehouse, Mohammed, Charlemagne, and the Origins of Europe. Ithaca 1983.

A. H. M. Jones, The Later Roman Empire 284–602. A Social, Economic and Administrative Survey, 3 vols. Oxford 1964.

K. Junker, Research under Dictatorship. The German Archaeological Institute, 1929–45, in: Antiquity 72, 1998, 282–92.

G. Kossinna, Die Herkunft der Germanen. Zur Methode der Siedlungsarchäologie. Würzburg 1911.

G. Kossinna, Das Weichselland, ein uralter Heimatboden der Germanen. Danzig 1919.

J. Kreiner/H. Reimitz (eds.), Motions of Late Antiquity. Essays on Religion, Politics, and Society in Honour of Peter Brown. Turnhout 2016.

F. Lot, Les Invasions germaniques. La pénétration mutuelle du monde barbare et du monde romain. Paris 1935.

A. Loyen, Recherches historiques sur les panégyriques de Sidoine Apollinaire. Paris 1942.

A. Loyen, Sidoine Apollinaire et l'esprit précieux en Gaule aux derniers jours de l'Empire. Paris 1943.

F. G. Maier, Die Verwandlung der Mittelmeerwelt. Frankfurt am Main 1968.

M. Maischberger, German Archaeology during the Third Reich. A Case Study Based on Archival Evidence, in: Antiquity 76, 2002, 209–18.

S. L. Marchand, Down from Olympus. Archaeology and Philhellenism in Germany, 1750–1970. Princeton 1996.

H.-I. Marrou, Saint Augustin et la fin de la culture antique. Paris 1938, completely rev. ed. 1949.

H.-I. Marrou, Histoire de l'éducation dans l'Antiquité. Paris 1948.

S. Mazzarino, Stilicone. La crisi imperiale dopo Teodosio. Rom 1942.

S. Mazzarino, La fine del mondo antico. Le cause della caduta dell' Impero Romano. Milan 1959; German trans. Das Ende der antiken Welt. München 1961; English trans. The End of the Ancient World. London 1966.

S. Mazzarino, Il basso impero. Antico, tardoantico ed era costantiniana, 2 vols. Bari 1974–1980.

R. McKitterick/R. Quinault (eds.), Edward Gibbon and Empire. Cambridge 1996.

T. Mommsen, Römische Kaisergeschichte. Nach den Vorlesungs-Mitschriften von Sebastian Paul Hensel 1882/86, eds. B. Demandt/A. Demandt. Leipzig 1992.

C. F. R. Comte de Montalembert, Les moines d'Occident, 7 vols. Paris 1860–77.

A. F. Ozanam, Die Begründung des Christenthums in Deutschland und die sittliche und geistige Erziehung der Germanen. München 1845.

A. F. Ozanam, Études Germaniques pour servir à l'histoire des francs, vol. 2: La Civilisation chrétienne chez les francs. Paris 1849.

F. Paschoud, Roma Aeterna. Études sur le patriotisme romain dans l'Occident latin à l'époque des grandes invasions. Neufchâtel 1967.

A. Piganiol, L'Empire chrétien (325–395), 2nd ed. updated by A. Chastagnol. Paris 1972 (first published 1947).

H. Pirenne, Mahomet et Charlemagne, Paris 1937; English trans. Mohammed and Charlemagne, London 1939; German trans. Geburt des Abendlandes. Untergang der Antike am Mittelmeer und Aufstieg des germanischen Mittelalters. Amsterdam 1939.

F. Prinz, Frühes Mönchtum im Frankenreich. Kempten 1965.

M. Rostovtzeff, The Social and Economic History of the Roman Empire, 2 vols. Oxford 1926; 2nd ed. 1957; German trans. Gesellschaft und Wirtschaft im römischen Kaiserreich. Leipzig 1931; Italian trans. Storia economica e sociale dell'Impero romano. Florence 1933.

P. Rousseau/E. Papoutsakis (eds.), Transformations of Late Antiquity. Essays for Peter Brown. Farnham 2009.

O. Seeck, Geschichte des Untergangs der antiken Welt, 6 Bde. Stuttgart 1920–1923; new ed. 1966.

E. Stein, Geschichte des spätrömischen Reiches, vol. I: Vom römischen zum byzantinischen Staate (284–476 n. Chr.). Vienna 1928; vol. II: Histoire du Bas Empire. De la disparition de l'empire d'occident à la mort de Justinien (476–565), trans. J.-R. Palanque. Paris 1949.

K. F. Stroheker, Eurich, König der Westgoten. Stuttgart 1937.

K. F. Stroheker, Leowigild. Aus einer Wendezeit westgotischer Geschichte, in: Die Welt als Geschichte 5, 1939, 446–485; reprinted in: K. F. Stroheker, Germanentum und Spätantike, Zürich 1965, 134–91.

K. F. Stroheker, Der senatorische Adel im spätantiken Gallien. Reutlingen 1948.

E. A. Thompson, The Historical Work of Ammianus Marcellinus. Cambridge 1947; new ed. Groningen 1969.

E. A. Thompson, A History of Attila and the Huns. Oxford 1948; reissued as: The Huns, with a foreword by P. Heather. Oxford 1996.

E. A. Thompson, The Visigoths in the Time of Ulfila. Oxford 1966.

E. A. Thompson, Romans and Barbarians. The Decline of the Western Empire. Madison 1982.

C. Violante, La fine della "Grande illusione". Un storico europeo tra guerra e dopo guerra (1914–32). Per una rilettura della "Histoire de l'Europe". Bologna 1997; German trans. Das Ende der "großen Illusion". Ein europäischer Historiker im Spannungsfeld von Kriegs und Nachkriegszeit. Henri Pirenne (1914–1923) – Zu einer Neulesung der "Geschichte Europas". Berlin 2004.

F. W. Walbank, The Awful Revolution. The Decline of the Roman Empire in the West. Liverpool 1969.

J. M. Wallace-Hadrill, The Barbarian West, London 1952; 3rd ed. London 1967.

R. Wenskus, Stammesbildung und Verfassung. Das Werden der frühmittelalterlichen gentes. Köln/Graz 1961.

I. Wiwjorra, Der Germanenmythos. Konstruktion einer Weltanschauung in der Altertumsforschung des 19. Jahrhunderts. Darmstadt 2006.

I. N. Wood, Early Medieval History and Nineteenth-Century Politics in Dahn's "Ein Kampf um Rom" and Manzoni's "Adelchi", in: S. Patzold/A. Rathmann-Lutz/V. Scior (eds.), Geschichtsvorstellungen. Bilder, Texte und Begriffe aus dem Mittelalter. Vienna 2012, 535–57.

I. N. Wood, The Modern Origins of the Early Middle Ages. Oxford 2013.
U. Wyss, Die wilde Philologie. Jacob Grimm und der Historismus. Munich 1979.

3 General Assessments of the Late Antique Period from 1970 to the Present

P. Anderson, Passages from Antiquity to Feudalism. London 1974.
C. Ando, Imperial Rome AD 193–284. The Critical Century. Edinburgh 2012.
J. Banaji, Agrarian Change in Late Antiquity. Gold, Labour, and Aristocratic Domi-
    nance. Cambridge 2001.
J. Banaji, Exploring the Economy of Late Antiquity. Selected Essays. Cambridge 2016.
J. Banaji, Aristocracies, Peasantries and the Framing of the Early Middle Ages, in:
    Journ. of Agrarian Change 9, 2008, 59–91, reprinted in: 3: J. Banaji, Exploring
    the Economy, 143–177.
H. Börm, Westrom. Von Honorius bis Justinian. Stuttgart 2013; 2nd ed. 2018.
L. Bothe, Merovingian Homesick Blues. Human Trafficking in the Merovingian leges,
    in: 12.1: Esders/Hen/Lucas/Rotman, 79–91.
A. Bowman/A. Cameron/P. Garnsey (eds.), Cambridge Ancient History, vol. 12: The Crisis
    of Empire, AD 193–337. Cambridge 2005.
F. Braudel, La Méditerranée et le Monde Méditerranéan à l'Époque de Philippe II,
    vol. 1. Paris 1949; English trans. The Mediterranean World in the Age of Philip
    II, vol. 1. London 1972.
P. Brown, The Rise of Western Christendom. Triumph and Diversity A. D. 200–1000.
    Oxford 1996; 2nd ed. Oxford 2003; anniversary ed. Oxford 2013.
P. Brown, Through the Eye of a Needle. Wealth, the Fall of Rome and the Making of
    Christianity in the West, 350–550. Princeton 2012.
A. Cameron, The Later Roman Empire AD 284–430. London 1993.
A. Cameron, The Mediterranean World in Late Antiquity AD 395–600. London/New
    York 1993a.
A. Cameron/P. Garnsey (eds.), Cambridge Ancient History, vol 13: The Late Empire,
    337–425. Cambridge 1997.
A. Cameron/B. Ward-Perkins/M. Whitby (eds.), Cambridge Ancient History, vol 14: Em-
    pire and Successors, AD 425–600. Cambridge 2000.
H. Cancik/H. Schneider (eds.), Der neue Pauly. Enzyklopädie der Antike. Stuttgart/
    Weimar 1996–2003; engl. ed.: M. Landfester (ed.), Brill's New Pauly. Encyclopae-
    dia of the Ancient World. Leiden 2002–2010.
A. Chastagnol, L'évolution politique, sociale et économique du monde romain de Dio-
    clétien à Julien. Paris 1982.
N. Christie, The Fall of the West Roman Empire. An Archaeological and Historical Per-
    spective. London 2011.
E. K. Chrysos/A. Schwarcz (eds.), Das Reich und die Barbaren. Vienna/Cologne 1988.
S. E. Cleary, The Roman West AD 200–500, Cambridge 2013.
T. Cornell/J. Matthews, Cultural Atlas of the Roman World. London 1982.
C. Delaplace, La fin de l'Empire romain d'Occident. Rome et les Wisigoths de 382 à
    531. Rennes 2015.

S. Esders/Y. Fox/Y. Hen/L. Sarti (eds.), East and West in the Early Middle Ages in Mediterranean Perspective. Cambridge 2019.

J. F. Haldon, Framing Transformation, Transforming the Framework, in: Millennium 5, 2008, 327–51.

J. F. Haldon/H. Elton/S. Huebner/A. Izdebsk/L. Mordechai/T. Newfield, Plagues, Climate Change, and the End of an Empire. A Response to Kyle Harper's The Fate of Rome in: History Compass 2018, https://doi.org/10.1111/hic3.12508.

G. Halsall, Barbarian Migrations and the Roman West 376–568. Cambridge 2007.

K. Harper, Slavery in the Late Roman World AD 275–425. Cambridge 2011.

K. Harper, The Fate of Rome. Climate, Disease, and the End of an Empire. Princeton 2017.

J. Harries, Imperial Rome AD 284–363. The New Empire. Edinburgh 2012.

P. Heather, The Fall of the Roman Empire. A New History. London 2005.

P. Heather, Empires and Barbarians. Migration, Development and the Birth of Europe. London 2009.

P. Horden/N. Purcell, The Corrupting Sea. A Study of Mediterranean History. Oxford 2000.

D. P. Kehoe, Land and the Rural Economy in the Roman Empire. Ann Arbor 2007.

M. Kulikowski, The Tragedy of Empire. From Constantine to the Destruction of Roman Italy. Cambridge Mass 2019.

A. D. Lee, From Rome to Byzantium AD 363 to 565. Edinburgh 2012.

L. K. Little (ed.), Plague and the End of Antiquity. The Pandemic of 541–750. Cambridge 2007.

R. Markus, The End of Ancient Christianity. Cambridge 1990.

J. Martínez Jiménez/I. Sastre de Diego/C. Tejerizo García, The Iberian Peninsula between 300 and 850. An Archaeological Perspective. Amsterdam 2018.

M. McCormick, Origins of the European Economy. Communications and Commerce AD 300–900. Cambridge 2001.

M. McCormick, Tracking Mass Death During the Fall of Rome's Empire I, in: Journal of Roman Archaeology 28, 2015, 325–27.

M. McCormick, Tracking Mass Death During the Fall of Rome's Empire II: A First Inventory, in: Journal of Roman Archaeology 29, 2016, 1008–46.

L. Mordechai/M. Eisenberg/T. Newfield/A. Izdebski/J. Kay/H. Poinar, The Justinianic Plague. An Inconsequential Pandemic?, in: Proceedings of the National Academy of Sciences of the United States of America, vol. 116, no. 61, 2019, 25546–25554.

J. J. O'Donnell, Augustine. Saint and Sinner. A New Biography. London 2005.

J. J. O'Donnell, The Ruin of the Roman Empire. London 2009.

J. M. O'Flynn, Generalissimos of the Western Roman Empire. Edmonton 1983.

A. Omissi, Emperors and Usurpers in the Later Roman Empire. Civil War, Panegyric and the Construction of Legitimacy. Oxford 2018.

J. Pelikan, The Excellent Empire. The Fall of Rome and the Triumph of the Church, San Francisco 1987.

A. Rio, Slavery after Rome. 500–1000. Cambridge 2009.

M. R. Salzman, The Falls of Rome. Crises, Resilience, and Resurgence in Late Antiquity. Cambridge 2021.

S. Swain/M. Edwards (eds.), Approaching Late Antiquity. The Transformation from Early to Later Empire. Oxford 2004.

A. E. Wardman, Usurpers and Internal Conflicts in the Fourth-Century AD, in: Historia 33, 1984, 220–237.

B. Ward-Perkins, The Fall of Rome and the End of Civilization. Oxford 2005.

C. J. Wickham, Framing the Early Middle Ages. Europe and the Mediterranean, 400–800. Oxford 2005.

C. J. Wickham, The Inheritance of Rome. A History of Europe from 400–1000. London 2009.

H. Wolfram, Das Reich und die Germanen. Zwischen Antike und Mittelalter. Berlin 1990; 2nd ed. 1992; English trans. The Roman Empire and its Germanic Peoples. Berkeley 1997.

H. Wolfram, Das Römerreich und seine Germanen. Eine Erzählung von Herkunft und Ankunft. Vienna 2018.

I. N. Wood, Landscapes Compared, in: Early Medieval Europe 15, 2007, 223–37.

I. N. Wood, The Transformation of the Roman West. Leeds 2018.

I. N. Wood, The Christian Economy in the Early Medieval West: towards a Temple Society. Binghamton 2022.

4 The fourth-century emperors and their reigns

4.1 The Third-Century Crisis and the Tetrarchy

Association pour l'Antiquité Tardive (ed.), La tetrarchie (293–312). Histoire et archéologie, Antiquité Tardive, 2–3, 1993.

T. D. Barnes, Lactantius and Constantine, in: JRS 63, 1973, 29–46.

T. D. Barnes, The Sources of the Historia Augusta. Brussels 1978.

T. D. Barnes, Constantine and Eusebius. Cambridge Mass. 1981.

T. D. Barnes, The New Empire of Diocletian and Constantine. Cambridge Mass. 1982.

M. Beard/J. North/S. Price (eds.), Religions of Rome. 2 vols. Cambridge 1998.

H. W. Bird, Sextus Aurelius Victor. A Historiographical Study. Liverpool 1984.

H. W. Bird (ed.), Eutropius, Breviarium ab urbe condita. Liverpool 1993.

H. W. Bird (emccord.), Aurelius Victor, De Caesaribus. Liverpool 1994.

G. Bonamente/F. Paschoud (eds.), Historiae Augustae. Colloquium Genevense. Bari 1994, 1999.

H. Börm, Born to be Emperor. The Principle of Succession and the Roman Monarchy, in: 6: Wienand, 239–264.

A. Bowman/A. Cameron/P. Garnsey (eds.), Cambridge Ancient History, vol. 12: The Crisis of Empire, AD 193–337. Cambridge 2005.

A. K. Bowman, Diocletian and the First Tetrarchy, A. D. 284–305, in: 4.1: Bowman/Cameron/Garnsey, 67–89.

H. Brandt, Zeitkritik in der Spätantike. Munich 1988.

H. Brandt, Geschichte der römischen Kaiserzeit. Von Diokletian und Konstantin bis zum Ende der konstantinischen Dynastie (284–363). Berlin 1998.

H. Brandt, Erneute Überlegung zum Preisedikt Diokletians, in: A. Demandt/A. Goltz/H. Schlange-Schöningen (eds.), Diokletian und die Tetrachie. Aspekte einer Zeitenwende. Berlin 2004, 47–56.

D. Burgersdijk/A. Ross (eds.), Imagining Emperors in the Later Roman Empire. Leiden 2019.

A. Cameron/P. Garnsey (eds.), Cambridge Ancient History, vol 13: The Late Empire, 337–425. Cambridge 1998.

A. Cameron/B. Ward-Perkins/M. Whitby (eds.), Cambridge Ancient History, vol 14: Empire and Successors, AD 425–600. Cambridge 2000.

J.-M. Carrié/A. Rousselle, L'Empire Romain en mutation, des Sévères à Constantin, 192–337. Paris 1999.

A. Chastagnol, Constantinople et ombres chinoises dans l'Histoire Auguste, in: 4.1: Bonamente/Rosen, 85–96.

S. Corcoran, The Empire of the Tetrarchs. Imperial Pronouncements and Government AD 284–324. Oxford 1996, 2nd ed. 2000.

J. Corke-Webster, Eusebius and Empire. Constructing Church and Rome in the Ecclesiastical History. Cambridge 2019.

J. Curran, Pagan City and Christian Capital. Rome in the Fourth Century. Oxford 2000.

A. Demandt/A. Goltz/H. Schlange-Schöningen (eds.), Diokletian und die Tetrarchie. Aspekte einer Zeitenwende. Berlin 2004.

J. F. Drinkwater, The Gallic Empire. Separatism and Continuity in the North-western Provinces of the Roman Empire. Stuttgart 1987.

W. H. C. Frend, Martyrdom and Persecution in the Early Church. Oxford 1965.

R. Goodburn/P. Bartholemew (eds.), Aspects of the Notitia Dignitatum. Papers Presented to the Conference in Oxford December 13 to 15, 1974. Oxford 1976.

U. Hartmann, Das palmyrenische Teilreich. Stuttgart 2001.

O. Hekster, Emperors and Ancestors. Roman Rulers and the Constraints of Tradition. Oxford 2015.

D. Hoffmann, Das spätrömische Bewegungsheer und die Notitia Dignitatum, 2 vols. Düsseldorf 1969–70.

T. Honoré, Scriptor Historiae Augustae, in: JRS 77, 1987, 156–76.

H. Inglebert (ed.), Le problème de la Christianisation du monde antique. Paris 2010.

R. Ireland, De rebus bellicis. The Text. Oxford 1979.

R. I. Ireland (ed.), Notitia Dignitatum. Leipzig 1999.

K.-P. Johne/U. Hartmann/T. Gerhardt (eds.), Die Zeit der Soldatenkaiser. Krise und Transformation des Römischen Reiches im 3. Jahrhundert n. Chr (235–284). Berlin 2008.

A. Johnson/J. Scott (eds.), Eusebius of Caesarea. Tradition and Innovations. London 2013.

F. Kolb, Diocletian und die Erste Tetrarchie. Berlin 1987.

F. Kolb, Herrscherideologie in der Spätantike. Berlin 2001.

W. Kuhoff, Diokletian und die Epoche der Tetrarchie. Das römische Reich zwischen Krisenbewältigung und Neuaufbau (284–313 n. Chr.). Frankfurt am Main 2001.

M. Kulikowski, The "Notitia Dignitatum" as a Historical Source, in: Historia 49, 2000, 358–77.

R. Lane Fox, Pagans and Christians. Harmondsworth 1986.

A. Laniado, Ethnos et droit dans le monde protobyzantin, Ve–VIe siècle. Geneva 2015.

M. Lapidge, The Roman Martyrs. Introduction, Translations and Commentary. Oxford 2018.

L. Lavan/M. Mulryan, The Archaeology of Late Antique Paganism. Leiden 2011.

W. L. Leadbetter, Galerius and the Will of Diocletian. London 2009.

J. H. W. G. Liebeschuetz, Continuity and Change in Roman Religion. Oxford 1979.

A. Lippold, Die Historia Augusta. Eine Sammlung römischer Kaiserviten aus der Zeit Konstantins. Stuttgart 1998.

H. P. L'Orange, Art Forms and Civic Life in the Late Roman Empire. Princeton 1965.

R. MacMullen, Roman Government's Response to Crisis A. D. 235–337. New Haven/ London 1976.

R. MacMullen, Christianizing the Roman Empire (A. D. 100–400). New Haven/London 1984.

N. P. Millner (trans.), Vegetius, Epitome of Military Science. Rev. ed. Liverpool 2011.

C. E. V. Nixon/B. S. Rogers, In Praise of Later Roman Emperors. Berkeley 1994.

Notitia dignitatum, https://notitiadignitatum.org.

A. Omissi, Emperors and Usurpers in the Later Roman Empire. Civil War, Panegyric and the Construction of Legitimacy. Oxford 2018.

F. Paschoud (ed.), Histoire Auguste, 5 vols. Paris 2002–11.

B. Pottier, L'Histoire Auguste, le consul Aurelianus et la réception de la Notitia Dignitatum en Occident, in: Antiquité Tardive 14, 2006, 225–34.

R. Rees, Diocletian and the Tetrarchy. Edinburgh 2004.

J. B. Rives, Religion and Authority in Roman Carthage. From Augustus to Constantine. Oxford 1997.

U. Roberto, Diocleziano. Rome 2014.

T. A. Robinson, Who Were the First Christians? Dismantling the Urban Thesis. Oxford 2017.

D. Rohrbacher, The Historians of Late Antiquity. London 2002.

D. Rohrbacher, The Sources of the Historia Augusta Re-visited, in: Histos 7, 2013, 146–80.

P. Sabin/H. van Wees/L. M. Whitby (eds.), The Cambridge History of Greek and Roman Warfare, vol. 2: Rome from the Late Republic to the Late Empire. Cambridge 2007.

W. Seston, Dioclétien et la Tétrarchie. Paris 1946.

P. Southern/K. R. Dixon, The Late Roman Army. New Haven 1996.

R. Stark, The Rise of Christianity. A Sociologist Reconsiders History. Princeton 1996.

J. Stover/M. Kestemont, The Authorship of the "Historia Augusta". Two New Computational Studies, in: Bulletin of the Institute of Classical Studies 59, 2016, 140–57.

R. Syme, Ammianus and the Historia Augusta. Oxford 1968.

R. Syme, Emperors and Biography. Studies in the Historia Augusta. Oxford 1971.

E. A. Thompson (ed.), On Matters Military (De Rebus Bellicis). A Roman Reformer and Inventor. Oxford 1952.

W. Treadgold, Byzantium and Its Army, 284–1081. Stanford 1995.

H. P. G. Williams, Carausius. A Consideration of the Historical, Archaeological and Numismatic Aspects of his Reign. Oxford 2004.

S. Williams, Diocletian and the Roman Recovery. London 1985.

4.2 Constantine

A. Alföldi, The Conversion of Constantine and Pagan Rome. Oxford 1948, 1969.

L. Ayres, Nicaea and its Legacy. An Approach to Fourth-century Trinitarian Theology. Oxford 2004.

J. Banaji, Agrarian Change in Late Antiquity. Gold, Labour, and Aristocratic Dominance. Cambridge 2001.

J. Bardill, Constantine, Divine Emperor of the Christian Golden Age. Cambridge 2012.

T. D. Barnes, Constantine and Eusebius. Cambridge Mass. 1981

T. D. Barnes, The New Empire of Diocletian and Constantine. Cambridge Mass. 1982.

T. D. Barnes, Constantine. Dynasty, Religion and Power in the Later Roman Empire. Chichester 2011.

B. Bleckmann, Constantine, Rome and the Christians, in: 6: Wienand, 309–329.

H. Brandt, Konstantin der Große. Munich 2006.

J. Bouffartigue/P. Canivet/A. Martin/L. Pietri/F. Thelamon (eds.), Théodoret de Cyr, Histoire Ecclésiastique, 2 vols., SC 501, 530. Paris 2006, 2009.

A. Cameron/S. G. Hall (trans.), Eusebius, Life of Constantine. Oxford 1999.

B. Campbell, The Army, in: 4.1: Bowman/Cameron/Garnsey, 110–30.

J. Curran, Pagan City and Christian Capital. Rome in the Fourth Century. Oxford 2000.

A. Demandt/J. Engemann (eds.), Konstantin der Große. Imperator Caesar Flavius Constantinus. Mainz 2007.

J. N. Dillon, The Justice of Constantine. Law, Communication and Control. Ann Arbor 2012.

A. Donati/G. Gentili (eds.), Costantino il Grande. La civiltà antica al bivio tra Occidente e Oriente. Milan 2005.

H. A. Drake, In Praise of Constantine. A Historical Study and New Translation of Eusebius' Tricennial Orations. Berkeley 1976.

H. A. Drake, Constantine and the Bishops. The Politics of Intolerance. Baltimore 2000.

J. W. Drijvers, Helena Augusta. The Mother of Constantine the Great and the Legend of the Finding of the True Cross. Leiden 1992.

H. Elton, Warfare in Roman Europe, AD 350–425. Oxford 1996.

H. Elton, Warfare and the Military, in: 4.2: Lenski 2006, 325–346.

R. M. Errington, Roman Imperial Policy from Julian to Theodosius. Chapel Hill 2006.

W. H. C. Frend, The Donatist Church. A Movement of Protest in Roman North Africa. Oxford 1952.

T. Fuhrer (ed.), Rom und Mailand in der Spätantike. Repräsentationen städtischer Räume in Literatur, Architektur und Kunst. Berlin 2012.

J. Gaudemet, L'Église dans l'Empire romain (IVe–Ve siècles). Paris 1958.

B. Grillet/G. Sabbah/A. J. Festugière/ /L. Angleviel de la Beaumelle (eds.), Sozomène. Histoire Ecclésiastique, 4 vols., SC 306, 418, 495, 516. Paris 1983–2008.

K. M. Girardet, Die konstantinische Wende. Voraussetzungen und geistige Grundlagen der Religionspolitik Konstantins des Großen. Darmstadt 2006.

K. M. Girardet, Der Kaiser und sein Gott. Das Christentum im Denken und in der Religionspolitik Konstantins des Großen. Berlin 2010.

G. C. Hansen/P. Périchon/P. Maraval (eds.), Socrate de Constantinople, 4 vols., SC 477, 493, 505, 506. Paris 2004-7.

R. P. C. Hanson, The Search for the Christian Doctrine of God. The Arian Controversy 318–38. Edinburgh 1988.

E. Hartley/J. Hawkes/M. Henig/F. Mee (eds.), Constantine the Great. York's Roman Emperor. London 2006.

K. J. Hefele/H. Leclercq, Histoire des conciles, d'après les documents originaux, vol. 1. Paris 1907.

E. Herrmann-Otto, Konstantin der Große. Darmstadt 2007.

R. R. Holloway, Constantine and Rome. New Haven 2004.

V. Keil (ed. and trans.), Quellensammlung zur Religionspolitik Konstantins des Großen. Darmstadt 1995.

C. Kelly, Ruling the Later Roman Empire. Cambridge Mass. 2004.

J. N. D. Kelly, Early Christian Doctrines. London 1958.

J. N. D. Kelly, Early Christian Creeds, 2nd ed. London 1960.

R. Krautheimer, Three Christian Capitals. Topography and Politics. Berkeley 1983.

A. D. Lee, The Army, in: 4.1: Cameron/Garnsey, 211–237.

N. E. Lenski, The Cambridge Companion to the Age of Constantine. Cambridge 2006.

N. E. Lenski, Constantine and the Tyche of Constantinople, in: 6: Wienand, 330–352.

N. E. Lenski, Constantine and the Cities. Imperial Authority and Civic Politics. Philadelphia 2016.

H. Leppin, Von Constantin dem Großen zu Theodosius II. Das christliche Kaisertum bei den Kirchenhistorikern Socrates, Sozomenus und Theodoret. Göttingen 1996.

H. Leppin/H. Ziemssen, Maxentius. Der letzte Kaiser in Rom. Mainz 2007.

E. N. Luttwak, The Grand Strategy of the Roman Empire from the FirstCcentury AD to the Third. Baltimore 1976.

R. MacMullen, Voting about God in Early Church Councils. New Haven 2006.

R. Miles (ed.), The Donatist Schism. Controversy and Contexts. Liverpool 2016

F. Millar, The Emperor in the Roman World (31 BC to AD 337). London 1977.

E. Mühlenberg (ed.), Die Konstantinische Wende. Gütersloh 1998.

C. Munier (ed.), Concilia Galliae, a. 314–506, CCSL 148. Turnhout 1963.

C. E. V. Nixon/B. S. Rogers, In Praise of Later Roman Emperors. Berkeley 1994.

C. M. Odahl, Constantine and the Christian Empire. London 2004.

J. Pelikan, The Christian Tradition. A History of the Development of Doctrine, vol. 1: The Emergence of the Catholic Tradition, 100–600. Chicago 1973.

H. Pietras, Council of Nicaea (325). Religious and Political Context, Documents, Commentaries. Rome 2016.

D. Potter, Constantine the Emperor. Oxford 2012.

K. Rosen, Konstantin der Große. Stuttgart 2013.

M. Tilley (trans.), Donatist Martyr Stories. The Church in Conflict in Roman North Africa. Liverpool 1996.

R. S. O. Tomlin, The Army of the Late Empire, in: J. Wacher (ed.), The Roman World. New York 1988, 107–133.

J. Ulrich, Nicaea and the West, in: Vigiliae Christianae 51, 1997, 10–24.

T. Urbainczyk, Socrates of Constantinople. Ann Arbor 1997.

R. Van Dam, The Roman Revolution of Constantine. Cambridge 2007.

R. Van Dam, Remembering Constantine at the Milvian Bridge. Cambridge 2011.

R. Westall, Constantius II and the basilica of St Peter in the Vatican, in: Historia 64, 2015, 205–242.

R. Williams, Arius, Heresy and Tradition. London 1987.

4.3 The House of Constantine

N. Baker-Brian/S. Tougher (eds.), The Sons of Constantine AD 337–361. In the Shadow of Constantine and Julian. London 2020.

P. Barceló, Constantius II. und seine Zeit. Die Anfänge des Staatskirchentums. Stuttgart 2004.

T. D. Barnes, Athanasius and Constantius. Theology and Politics in the Constantinian Empire. Cambridge Mass. 1993.

T. D. Barnes, Ammianus Marcellinus and the Representation of Historical Reality. Ithaca 1998.

C. Beckwith, Hilary of Poitiers on the Trinity. From De Fide to De Trinitate. New York 2009.

R. W. Burgess, The Summer of Blood. The "great massacre" of 337 and the Promotion of the Sons of Constantine, in: Dumbarton Oaks Papers 62, 2008, 5–51; reprinted in: R. W. Burgess, Chronicles, Consuls, and Coins. Historiography and History in the Later Roman Empire. Farnham 2011, 5–51.

S. Cohen, Liberius and the Cemetery as a Space of Exile in Late Antique Rome in: D. Rohrmann/J. Ulrich/M. Vallejo Girvés (eds.), Mobility and Exile at the End of Antiquity. Berlin 2018, 141–60.

G. A. Crump, Ammianus Marcellinus as a Military Historian. Wiesbaden 1975.

V. C. de Clercq, Ossius of Cordova. Washington D. C. 1954.

S. Diefenbach, Constantius II. und die "Reichskirche". Ein Beitrag zum Verhältnis von kaiserlicher Kirchenpolitik und politischer Integration im 4. Jh., in: Millennium 9, 2012, 59–121.

J. Doignon, Hilaire de Poitiers avant l'exil. Recherches sur la naissance, l'enseignement et l'épreuve d'une foi épiscopale en Gaule au milieu du IVe siècle. Paris 1971.

G. Downey/A. F. Norman (eds.), Themistius, Orationes, 3 vols. Stuttgart 1965–74.

J. W. Drijvers/D. Hunt (eds.), The Late Roman World and its Historian. Interpreting Ammianus Marcellinus. London 1999.

R. Flower, Emperors and Bishops in Late Roman Invective. Cambridge 2013.

R. Flower, "Tamquam figmentum hominis". Ammianus, Constantius II and the Portrayal of Imperial Ritual, in: CQ 65, 2015, 822–835.

R. Flower (trans.), Imperial Invectives against Constantius II. Liverpool 2016.

P. Heather/D. Moncur, Politics, Philosophy and Empire in the Fourth Century. Selected Orations of Themistius. Liverpool 2001.

N. Henk, Constantius' "paideia", Intelletual Milieux and Promotion of the Liberal Arts, in: Cambridge Classical Journal 47, 2001, 172–187.

M. Humphries, "In nomine patris". Constantine the Great and Constantius II in Christological Polemic, in: Historia 46, 1997, 448–64.

M. Humphries, Narrative and Subversion. Exemplary Rome and Imperial Misrule in Ammianus Marcellinus, in: I. Repath/F.-G. Hermann (eds.), Some Organic Readings in Narrative, Ancient and Modern. Groningen 2019, 233–54.

F. Jenkins, Ammianus Marcellinus. An Annotated Bibliography, 1474 to the Present. Leiden 2017.

G. Kelly, Ammianus Marcellinus. The Allusive Historian. Cambridge 2008.

R. Klein, Constantius II. und die christliche Kirche. Darmstadt 1977.

H. Leppin, Constantius II. und das Heidentum, in: Athenaeum 87, 1999, 457–80.

M. Marcos, A Tale of Two Commanders. Ammianus Marcellinus on the Campaigns of Constantius II and Julian on the Northern Frontiers, in: AJPh 136, 2015, 669–708.

J. Matthews, The Roman Empire of Ammianus. London 1987.

M. Moser, Emperor and Senators in the Reign of Constantius II. Cambridge 2018.

A. F. Norman (ed.), Libanius. Selected Orations, vol. 1. Cambridge Mass. 1989.

C. M. Odahl, Constantine and the Christian Empire. London 2004.

W. Stevenson, Exiling Bishops. The Policy of Constantius II, in: Dumbarton Oaks Papers 68, 2014, 7–27.

J. Vanderspoel, Themistius and the Imperial Court. Oratory, Civic Duty, and Paideia from Constantius to Theodosius. Ann Arbor 1995.

R. Westall, Constantius II and the Basilica of St Peter in the Vatican, in: Historia 64, 2015, 205–42.

W. Wright (ed.), Julian. Orations, vol. 1. Cambridge Mass. 1913.

4.4 Julian

P. Athanassiadi, Julian and Hellenism. An Intellectual Biography. London 1981.

P. Athanassiadi, Julian. An Intellectual Biography, London 1988.

N. Baker-Brian/S. Tougher (eds.), Emperor and Authors. The Writings of Julian the Apostate. Swansea 2012.

J. Bidez, La vie de l'empereur Julien. Paris 1930; reissued 2012; German trans. Julian der Abtrünnige. Munich 1947.

J. Bouffartigue, L'empereur Julien et la culture de son temps. Paris 1992.

G. W. Bowersock, Julian the Apostate. London 1978.

R. Brendel, Kaiser Julians Gesetzgebungswerk und Reichsverwaltung. Hamburg 2017.

K. Bringmann, Julian. Darmstadt 2004.

T. Nesselrath, Kaiser Julian und die Repaganisierung des Reiches. Konzept und Vorbilder. Münster 2013.

K. Rosen, Kaiser Julian auf dem Weg vom Christentum zum Heidentum, in: JbAC 40, 1997, 126–46.

R. Smith, Julian's Gods. Religion and Philosophy in the Thought and Action of Julian the Apostate. London 1995.

H. C. Teitler, The Last Pagan Emperor. Julian the Apostate and the War against Christianity. Oxford 2017.

4.5 Valentinian, Valens, Gratian and Valentinian II

M. T. W. Arnheim, Vicars in the Later Roman Empire, in: Historia 19, 1970, 593–606.

T. D. Barnes, Ambrose and Gratian, in: Antiquité Tardive 7, 2000, 165–74.

R. H. Barrow, Prefect and Emperor. The Relationes of Symmachus, AD 384. Oxford 1973.

T. S. Burns, Barbarians within the Gates of Rome. A Study of Roman Military Policy and the Barbarians, c. 375–425, A. D. Indianapolis 1995.

A. Coşkun, Die gens Ausoniana an der Macht. Untersuchungen zu Decimius Magnus Ausonius und seiner Familie. Oxford 2002.

E. Dassmann, Ambrosius von Mailand. Leben und Werk. Stuttgart 2004.

J. den Boeft/J. W. Drijvers/D. den Hengst/H. C. Teitler (eds.), Ammianus after Julian. The Reign of Valentinian and Valens in Books 26–31 of the Res Gestae. Leiden 2007.

J. W. Drijvers, Decline of Political Culture. Ammianus Marcellinus' Characterisation of the Reigns of Valentinian and Valens, in: D. M. Delyannis/E. Watts (eds.), Shifting Cultural Frontiers in Late Antiquity. Farnham 2012, 85–97.

F. H. Dudden, The Life and Times of St Ambrose, 2 vols. Oxford 1935.

B. Gibson, Gratitude to Gratian. Ausonius' Thanksgiving for his Consulship, in: 4.1: Burgersdijk/Ross, 270–88.

G. Halsall, Barbarian Migrations and the Roman West 376–568. Cambridge 2007.

P. J. Heather, Goths and Romans 332–489. Oxford 1991.

M. Kulikowski, Rome's Gothic Wars. Cambridge 2007; German trans. Die Goten vor Rom. Darmstadt 2009.

A. D. Lee, From Rome to Byzantium AD 363 to 565. Edinburgh 2012.

N. E. Lenski, Failure of Empire. Valens and the Roman State in the Fourth Century. Berkeley 2002.

J. H. W. G. Liebeschuetz, Ambrose of Milan Political Letters and Speeches. Liverpool 2005.

M. Löx, Monumenta sanctorum. Rom und Mailand als Zentren des Christentums. Märtyrerkult und Kirchenbau unter den Bischöfen Damasus und Ambrosius. Wiesbaden 2013.

J. E. Matthews, Western Aristocracies and the Imperial Court A. D. 364–425. Oxford 1975.

M. McEvoy, Child Emperor Rule in the Late Roman West, AD 367–455. Oxford 2013.

N. McLynn, Ambrose of Milan. Church and Court in a Christian Capital. Berkeley 1994.

M. Raimondi, Valentiniano I e la scelta dell'Occidente. Alessandria 2001.

S. Schmidt-Hofner, Reagieren und Gestalten. Der Regierungsstil des spätrömischen Kaisers am Beispiel der Gesetzgebung Valentinians I. Munich 2008.

S. Schmidt-Hofner, Ostentatious Legislation. Law and Dynastic Change, AD 364–5, in: 6: Wienand, 67–99.

H. Sivan, Ausonius of Bordeaux. Genesis of a Gallic Aristocracy. London 1993.

R. S. O. Tomlin, The Emperor Valentinian I. Oxford D. Phil., 1974.

H. Tränkle (ed.), Prudentius Contra Symmachum. Gegen Symmachus. Turnhout 2008.

M. S. Williams, The Politics of Heresy in Ambrose of Milan. Community and Consensus in Late Antique Christianity. Cambridge 2017.

H. Wolfram, Die Goten. Von den Anfängen bis zur Mitte des sechsten Jahrhunderts. 5th ed. Munich 2009.

5 From Theodosius to the Deposition of Romulus Augustulus

5.1 Theodosius

M. Arnaud-Lindet (ed.), Orose. Contre les Païens, 3 vols. Paris 1990–1.

Association pour l'Antiquité Tardive (ed.), L'empire des Théodoses. Antiquité Tardive 16, 2008.

T. S. Burns, Barbarians within the Gates of Rome. A Study of Roman Military Policy and the Barbarians, c. 375–425 A. D. Indianapolis 1995.

A. Cameron, The Last Pagans of Rome. Oxford 2011.

G. de Senneville-Grave (ed.), Sulpice Sévère. Chroniques, SC 441. Paris 1999.

J. Ernesti, Princeps christianus und Kaiser aller Römer. Theodosius der Große im Lichte zeitgenössischer Quellen. Paderborn 1998.

A. T. Fear (trans.), Orosius. Seven Books of History against the Pagans. Liverpool 2010.

G. Halsall, Barbarian Migrations and the Roman West 376–568. Cambridge 2007.

P. Heather, Goths and Romans 332–489. Oxford 1991.

G. Kampers, Geschichte der Westgoten. Paderborn 2008.

M. Kulikowski, Rome's Gothic Wars. Cambridge 2007; German trans. Die Goten vor Rom. Darmstadt 2009.

B. Lançon, Théodose. Paris 2014.

A. D. Lee, From Rome to Byzantium AD 363 to 565. Edinburgh 2012.

H. Leppin, Theodosius der Große. Auf dem Weg zum christlichen Imperium. Darmstadt 2003.

P. Maraval, Théodose le grand, le pouvoir et la foi. Paris 2009.

N. McLynn, Ambrose of Milan. Church and Court in a Christian Capital. Berkeley 1994.

A. Merrills, History and Geography in Late Antiquity. Cambridge 2005.

F. Paschoud, Roma Aeterna. Études sur le patriotisme romain dans l'Occident latin à l'époque des grandes invasions. Neufchâtel 1967.

F. Paschoud (ed.), Zosime. Histoire Nouvelle. Paris 1971.

U. Roberto/L. Mecella (eds.), Governare e riformare l'impero al momento del sua divisione. Oriente, Occidente, Illirico. Rome 2015.

F. Schulz, Ambrosius, die Kaiser und das Ideal des christlichen Ratgebers, in: Historia 63, 2014, 214–242.

F. R. Trombley, Hellenic Religion and Christianization c. 370–529, 2 vols. Leiden 1993–94, repr. 2001.

P. Van Nuffelen, Orosius and the Rhetoric of History. Oxford 2012.

S. Williams/G. Friell, Theodosius. The Empire at Bay. London 1994.
H. Wolfram, Die Goten. Von den Anfängen bis zur Mitte des sechsten Jahrhunderts. 5th ed. Munich 2009.

5.2 Honorius

J. Arce, Bárbaros y romanos en Hispania 400–507 A. D. Madrid 2005.
J. Arce, Alarico (365/370–410 A. D.). La integración frustrada. Madrid 2018.
A. D. Berardino/G. Pilara/L. Spera, Roma e il sacco del 410. Realtà, interpretazione, mito. Atti della giornata di Studio (Roma 6. dicembre 410). Rome 2012.
B. Bischoff/W. R. W. Koehler (eds.), Eine illustrierte Ausgabe der spätantiken Ravennater Annalen, in: W. R. W. Koehler (ed.), Studies in Memory of A. Kingsley Porter. Cambridge Mass. 1939, 125–38.
H. Börm, Westrom. Von Honorius bis Justinian. Stuttgart 2013. 2nd ed. 2018.
R. W. Burgess/M. Kulikowski, Mosaics of Time. The Latin Chronicle Traditions from the First Century BC to the Sixth Century AD. Turnhout 2013.
T. S. Burns, Barbarians within the Gates of Rome. A Study of Roman Military Policy and the Barbarians, c. 375–425 A. D. Indianapolis 1995.
A. Cameron, Claudian. Poetry and Propaganda at the Court of Honorius. Oxford 1970.
A. Cameron/J. Long, Barbarians and Politics at the Court of Arcadius. Berkeley 1993.
P. Courcelle, Histoire littéraire des grandes invasions germaniques. Paris 1948; 3rd ed. 1964.
T. de Bruyn, Ambivalence within a "totalizing discourse". Augustine's Sermons on the Sack of Rome in: Journal of Early Christian Studies 1, 1993, 405–21.
F. W. Deichmann, Ravenna, Hauptstadt des Abendlandes, 5. vols. Wiesbaden 1969–76.
D. M. Deliyannis, Ravenna in Late Antiquity. Cambridge 2010.
É. Demougeot, De l'unité à la division de l'empire romain, 39–-410. Essai sur le gouvernement imperial. Paris 1951.
E. Doblhofer (ed.), Claudius Rutilius Namatianus. De reditu suo sive Iter Gallicum, 2 vols. Heidelberg 1972–77.
C. Doyle, Honorius. The Fight for the Roman West AD 395–423. London 2018.
G. D. Dunn, Constantius III, Galla Placidia, and Libanius the Magician. Olympiodorus of Thebes and the Reconstruction of Imperial Politics in Ravenna in 421, in: Journal for Late Antique Religion and Culture 14, 2020, 50–64.
F. K. Haarer (ed.), AD 410. The History and Archaeology of Post-Roman Britain. London 2014.
H. Harich-Schwarzbauer/K. Pollmann (eds.), Der Fall Roms und seine Wiederauferstehungen in Antike und Mittelalter. Berlin 2013.
P. Heather, Goths and Romans 332–489. Oxford 1991.
T. Janssen, Stilicho. Das weströmische Reich vom Tode des Theodosius bis zur Ermordung Stilichos (395–408). Marburg 2004.
M. Kulikowski, Rome's Gothic Wars. Cambridge 2007; German trans. Die Goten vor Rom. Darmstadt 2009.
J. H. W. G. Liebeschuetz, Barbarians and Bishops. Army, Church and State in the Age of Arcadius and Chrysostom. Oxford 1990.

J. Lipps/C. Machado/P. von Rummel (eds.), The Sack of Rome in 410 AD. The Event, its Context and its Impact. Wiesbaden 2013.

W. Lütkenhaus, Constantius III. Studien zu seiner Tätigkeit und Stellung im Westreich 411–421. Bonn 1998.

S. Mazzarino, Stilicone. La crisi imperiale dopo Teodosio. Rome 1942.

M. McEvoy, Child Emperor Rule in the Late Roman West, AD 367–455. Oxford 2013.

M. McEvoy, The Jellyfish Emperor. The Emperor Arcadius and Imperial Leadership in the Late Fourth Century, 395–408, in: E. Manders/D. Slootjes (eds.), Leadership, Ideology and Crowds in the Roman Empire of the Fourth Century AD. Stuttgart 2020, 181–97.

R. McKitterick/J. Osborne/C. Richardson/J. Story (eds.), Old St Peter's Rome. Cambridge 2013.

M. Meier/S. Patzold, August 410. Ein Kampf um Rom. Stuttgart 2010.

S. Muhlberger, The Fifth-century Chroniclers. Prosper, Hydatius and the Gallic Chronicle of 452. Leeds 1990.

J. M. O'Flynn, Generalissimos of the Western Roman Empire. Edmonton 1983.

H. Sivan, Galla Placidia. The Last Roman Empress. Oxford 2011.

P. Van Nuffelen, Not Much Happened. 410 and All That, in: JRS 105, 2015, 322–329.

M. Verhoeven, The Early Christian Monuments of Ravenna. Turnhout 2011.

J. W. P. Wijnendaele, "Dagli altari alla polvere". Alaric, Constantine III, and the Downfall of Stilicho, in: Journal of Ancient History 6, 2018, 260–77.

H. Wolfram, Die Goten. Von den Anfängen bis zur Mitte des sechsten Jahrhunderts, 5th ed. Munich 2009.

5.3 Valentinian III

H. Börm, Westrom. Von Honorius bis Justinian. Stuttgart 2013. 2nd ed. 2018.

F. M. Clover (ed.), Flavius Merobaudes. A Translation and Historical Commentary, in: TAPhA 61, 1971, 1–78.

D. Coulon, Aetius. Villeneuve d'Ascq 2003.

F. Elia, Valentiniano III. Catania 1999.

M. Humphries, Valentinian III and the City of Rome (AD 425–55). Patronage, Politics, and Power, in: 7: Grig/Kelly, 161–82.

M. McEvoy, Child Emperor Rule in the Late Roman West, AD 367–455. Oxford 2013.

Th. Mommsen/P. M. Mayer (eds.), Codex Theodosianus. Berlin 1905, new ed. 1954; trans: C. Pharr (ed.), The Theodosian Code. New York 1952.

J. M. O'Flynn, Generalissimos of the Western Roman Empire. Edmonton 1983.

H. Sivan, Galla Placidia. The Last Roman Empress. Oxford 2011.

T. Stickler, Aëtius. Gestaltungsspielräume eines Heermeisters im ausgehenden Weströmischen Reich. Munich 2002.

J. W. P. Wijnendaele, The Last of the Romans. Bonifatius – Warlord and comes Africae. London 2015; Italian trans. L'ultimo romano. Il generale Bonifacio e la crisi dell'impero d'Occidente. Palermo 2017.

5.4 The Last Emperors

F. Anders, Flavius Ricimer. Macht und Obermacht des weströmischen Heermeisters in der zweiten Hälfte des 5. Jahrhunderts. Frankfurt am Main 2010.

H. Börm, Westrom. Von Honorius bis Justinian. Stuttgart 2013. 2nd ed. 2018.

R. W. Burgess (ed. and trans.), The Chronicle of Hydatius and the Consularia Constantinopolitana. Oxford 1993.

R. W. Burgess (ed.), The Chronicle of 452. A New Critical Edition with a Brief Introduction, in: 10: Mathisen/Shanzer, 52–84.

B. Croke, The Chronicle of Marcellinus. A Translation and Commentary. Sydney 1995.

J. Drinkwater/H. Elton (eds.), Fifth-Century Gaul. A Crisis of Identity. Cambridge 1992.

H. Harich-Schwarzbauer/J. Hindergarten (eds.), Leisure and the Muses in Sidonius Apollinaris, in: Journal of Late Antiquity 13.1, Special Issue, 2020.

D. Henning, Periclitans res Publica. Kaisertum und Eliten in der Krise des Weströmischen Reiches 454/5–493 n. Chr. Stuttgart 1999.

G. Kelly/J. van Waarden, The Edinburgh Companion to Sidonius Apollinaris, Edinburgh 2020.

J. M. Kötter/C. Scardino (eds.), Gallische Chroniken. Paderborn 2017.

P. MacGeorge, Late Roman Warlords. Oxford 2002.

S. Muhlberger, The Fifth-century Chroniclers. Prosper, Hydatius and the Gallic Chronicle of 452. Leeds 1990.

J. M. O'Flynn, Generalissimos of the Western Roman Empire. Edmonton 1983.

F. Oppedisano, L'impero d'Occidente negli anni di Maioriano. Rome 2013.

F. Oppedisano, Procopio Antonio imperatore di Roma. Bari 2020.

U. Roberto, Politica, tradizione e strategie familiari. Antemio e la ultima difesa dell'unità del impero (467–72), in: 5.1: Roberto/Mecella, 163–96.

Sidonius Appollinarius Research Companion, https://sidonapol.org.

5.5 The Year 476

H. Börm, Westrom. Von Honorius bis Justinian. Stuttgart 2013. 2nd ed. 2018.

B. Croke, 476. The Manufacture of a Turning Point, in: Chiron 13, 1983, 81–120.

F. Lotter, Severinus von Noricum. Legende und historische Wirklichkeit. Stuttgart 1976.

A. Momigliano, La caduta senza rumore di un impero nel 476. d. C., in: RSI, 85, 1973, 5–21.

R. Noll, Eugrippius. Das Leben des heiligen Severin. Berlin 1963.

W. Pohl/M. Diesenberger (eds.), Eugippius und Severin. Der Autor, der Text und der Heilige. Vienna 2002.

P. Régerat (ed.), Eugippe. Vie de saint Severin, SC374. Paris 1991.

C. Stancliffe, Review of: P. Régerat, Eugippe. Vie de saint Séverin, in: Journal of Theological Studies 4, 1994, 351–3.

E. A. Thompson, The End of Roman Noricum, in: E. A. Thompson, Romans and Barbarians. The Decline of the Western Empire. Madison 1982, 113–33.

M. A. Wes, Das Ende des Kaisertums im Westen des römischen Reiches. The Hague 1967.

I. N. Wood, A Byzantine Commonwealth, 476–533, in: W. Pohl/M. Diesenberger/B. Zeller (eds.), Neue Wege der Frühmittelalterforschung. Bilanz und Perspektiven. Vienna 2018, 65–74.

I. N. Wood, When did the West Roman Empire Fall, in: W. Pohl/V. Wieser (eds.), Emerging Powers in Eurasian Comparison, 200–1100. Leiden/Boston 2022, 55–77.

6 Imperial Government and Law

E. Albu, The Medieval Peutinger Map. Roman Revival in a German Empire. Cambridge 2014.

Association pour l'Antiquité Tardive (ed.), Les gouverneurs de province dans l'Antiquité tardive, Antiquité Tardive 6, 1998.

P. Barnwell, Emperor, Prefects and Kings. The Roman West, 395–565. London 1992.

A. Baumann, Freiheitsbeschränkungen der Dekurionen in der Spätantike. Hildesheim 2014.

S. Bjornlie, Politics and Tradition between Rome, Ravenna and Constantinople. A Study of Cassiodorus and the Variae, 527–554. Cambridge 2013.

F. Botta/L. Loschiavo (eds.), Civitas, Iura, Arma. Organizzazioni militari, istituzioni giuridiche e strutture sociali alle origini dell'Europa (sec. III–VIII). Lecce 2015.

G. Bowersock, Roman Arabia. Cambridge Mass. 1994.

R. Brendel, Kaiser Julians Gesetzgebungswerk und Reichsverwaltung. Hamburg 2017.

A. Cameron, Circus Factions. Blues and Greens at Rome and Byzantium. Oxford 1976.

A. M. Cameron, The Early Religious Policies of Justin II, in: D. Baker (ed.), The Orthodox Churches and the West. Oxford 1976a, 51–67.

T. F. Carney, On the Magistrates of the Roman Constitution. Sydney 1965.

K. C. Choda/M. Sterk de Leeuw/F. Schulz (eds.), Gaining and Losing Imperial Favour in Late Antiquity. Leiden 2020.

S. Corcoran, The Empire of the Tetrarchs. Imperial Pronouncements and Government AD 284–324. Oxford 1996, 2nd ed. 2000.

S. Crogiez-Pétrequin/P. Jaillette (eds.), Le Code théodosien. Diversité des approches et nouvelles perspectives. Rome 2009.

S. Crogiez-Pétrequin (eds.), Société, économie, administration dans le Code Théodosien. Lille 2012.

H. Elton, Imperial Politics at the Court of Theodosius II, in: A. Cain (ed.), The Power of Religion in Late Antiquity. Aldershot 2009, 133–42.

H. Elton, Warfare in Roman Europe, AD 350–420. Oxford 1996.

S. Esders/H. Reimitz, After Gundovald, before Pseudo-Isidore. Episcopal Jurisdiction, Clerical Privilege, and the Uses of Roman Law in the Frankish Kingdoms, in: Early Medieval Europe 27, 2019, 85–111.

C. N. Faleiro, La notitia dignitatum. Nueva edición crítica y comentario histórico. Madrid 2005.

J. M. C. Fort, Codex Theodosianus. Historia de un texto. Madrid 2014.

T. Gagos/P. Van Minnen, Settling a Dispute. Towards a Legal anthropology of Late Antique Egypt. Ann Arbor 1994.

A. Giardina, Cassiodoro politico. Rome 2006.

G. Greatrex, The Nika Riot. A Reappraisal, in: JHS 117, 1997, 60–86.

W. Hagl, Arcadius Apis Imperator. Synesios von Kyrene und sein Beitrag zum Herrscherideal der Spätantike. Stuttgart 1997.

J. Harries, Law and Empire in Late Antiquity. Cambridge 1999.

J. Harries/I. Wood (eds.), The Theodosian Code. London 1993.

D. Hoffmann, Das spätrömische Bewegungsheer und die Notitia Dignitatum, 2 vols. Düsseldorf 1969–70.

K. G. Holum, Theodosian Empresses. Women and Imperial Dominion in Late Antiquity. Berkeley 1982.

T. Honoré, Tribonian. London 1978.

O. Huck, Encore à propos des Sirmondiennes. Arguments présentés à l'appui de la thèse de l'authenticité, en reponse à une mise en cause récente, in: Antiquité Tardive 11, 2004, 181–96.

B. Isaac, The Meaning of the Terms "Limes" and "Limitanei", in: JRS 78, 1988, 125–47.

A. H. M. Jones/J. R. Martindale/J. Morris, The Prosopography of the Later Roman Empire, 3 vols. Cambridge 1971–92.

C. Kelly, Ruling the Later Roman Empire. Cambridge Mass. 2004.

C. Kelly (ed.), Theodosius II. Rethinking the Roman Empire in Late Antiquity. Cambridge 2013.

P. Krüger/T. Mommsen/R. Schnoell/W. Kroll (eds.), Corpus Iuris Civilis. Berlin 1877–92.

Y. Le Bohec/C. Wolff (eds.), L'armée romaine de Dioclétien à Valentinien Ier. Lyon 2004.

H. Leppin, Justinian und die Wiederherstellung des Römischen Reiches. Das Trugbild der Erneuerung, in: M. Meier (ed.), Sie schufen Europa. Munich 2007, 176–94.

D. Liebs, Roman Vulgar Law in Late Antiquity, in B. Sirks (ed.), Aspects of Law in Late Antiquity. Dedicated to A. Honoré on the Occasion of the Sixtieth Year of his Teaching in Oxford. Oxford 2008, 35–53.

E. Levy, West Roman Vulgar Law. The Law of Property. Philadelphia 1951.

E. Levy, Weströmisches Vulgarrecht. Das Obligationsrecht. Weimar 1956.

J. C. Mann/R. Goodburn/P. Bartholomew (eds.), Aspects of the notitia dignitatum. Papers Presented to the Conference in Oxford December 13 to 15, 1974. Oxford 1976.

J. Matthews, Laying Down the Law. New Haven, 2000.

F. Millar, A Greek Roman Empire. Power and Belief under Theodosius II, 408–450. Berkeley 2006.

Th. Mommsen/P. M. Mayer (eds.), Codex Theodosianus. Berlin 1905, new ed. 1954; trans. C. Pharr (ed.), The Theodosian Code. New York 1952.

M. J. Nicasie, Twilight of Empire. The Roman Army from the Reign of Diocletian until the Battle of Adrianople. Amsterdam 1998.

J. J. O'Donnell, Liberius the Patrician, in: Traditio 37, 1981, 31–72.

F. Oppedisano, L'impero d'Occidente negli anni di Maioriano. Rome 2013.

B. Palme, Law and Courts in Late Antique Egypt, in: B. Sirks (ed.), Aspects of Law in Late Antiquity. Dedicated to A. Honoré on the Occasion of the Sixtieth Year of his Teaching in Oxford. Oxford 2008, 55–76.

P. Porena, Le origini della prefettura del pretorio tardoantica. Rome 2003.

B. Salway, The Publication and Application of the Theodosian Code, in: MEFRM 125, 2013, 204–11.

S. Schmidt-Hofner, Reagieren und Gestalten Der Regierungsstil des spätrömischen Kaisers am Beispiel der Gesetzgebung Valentinians I. Munich 2008.

B. Sirks, The Theodosian Code. A Study. Friedrichsdorf 2007.

D. Slootjes, The Governor and his Subjects in the Later Roman Empire. Leiden 2006.

P. Southern/K. R. Dixon, The Late Roman Army. New Haven 1996.

J. Szidat, Die Usurpation des Eugenius, in: Historia 28, 1979, 487–508.

R. J. A. Talbert, Rome's World. The Peutinger Map Reconsidered. Cambridge 2010.

R. S. O. Tomlin, The Legions of the Late Empire, in: R. J. Brewer (ed.), Roman Fortresses and their Legions. Papers in Honour of George C. Boon. London 2000, 159–181.

W. Treadgold, Byzantium and its Army, 284–1081. Stanford 1995.

G. Vidén, The Roman Chancery Tradition. Studies in the Language of the Codex Theodosianus and Cassiodorus. Gothenburg 1984.

C. Whately, Jordanes, the Battle of the Catalaunian Plains and Constantinople, in: Dialogues d'Historie Ancienne 8, 2012, 64–66.

J. Wienand (ed.), Contested Monarchy. Integrating the Roman Empire in the Fourth Century AD. Oxford 2015.

J. Wijnendaele, Ammianus, Magnus Maximus and the Gothic Uprising, in: Britannia 51, 2020, 330–5.

J. Wijnendaele, Stilicho, Radagaisus and the so-called "Battle of Faesulae" (406 CE), in: Journal of Late Antiquity 9, 2016, 267–84.

I. N. Wood, Kings, Kingdoms and Consent, in: P. H. Sawyer/I. Wood (eds.), Early Medieval Kingship. Leeds 1977, 6–29.

P. Wormald, Lex Scripta and Verbum Regis. Legislation and Germanic Kingship from Euric to Cnut, in: P. H. Sawyer/I. N. Wood (eds.), Early Medieval Kingship. Leeds 1977, 105–38; reprinted in: P. Wormald, Legal Culture in the Early Medieval West. Law as Text, Image and Experience. London 1999, 1–43.

7 The Western Church in the Late Fourth and Fifth Centuries

P. Allen/B. Neil, Crisis Management in Late Antiquity (410–590 CE). A Survey of the Evidence from Episcopal Letters. Leiden 2013.

M. Arena/P. Delogu/L. Paroli/M. Ricci/L. Sagui/L. Vendittelli (eds.), Roma dall'Antiquità al Medioevo. Archeologia e storia nel Museo Nazionale Romano Crypta Balbi. Milan 2001.

J. Badewien, Geschichtstheologie und Sozialkritik im Werk Salvians von Marseille. Göttingen 1980.

L. K. Bailey, Christianity's Quiet Success. The Eusebius Gallicanus Sermon Collection and the Power of the Church in Late Antique Gaul. South Bend 2010.

L. K. Bailey, The Religious Worlds of the Laity in Late Antique Gaul. London 2017.

L. W. Barnard, The Council of Serdica 343 A. D. Sofia 1983.

A. Barrett, Saint Germanus and the British Missions, in: Britannia 40, 2009, 197–218.

A. Bonner, The Myth of Pelagianism. Oxford 2018.

B. K. Bowes, "Une coterie espagnole pieuse." Christian Archaeology and Christian Communities in Theodosian Hispania, in: 10: Bowes/Kulikowski, 189–258.

P. Brown, Augustine of Hippo. A Biography. London 1967.

P. Brown, Religion and Society in the Age of Saint Augustine. London 1972.

P. Brown, The Rise and Function of the Holy Man in Late Antiquity, in: JRS 61, 1971, 80–101, reprinted in: P. Brown, Society and the Holy. London 1982, 103–52.

P. Brown, The Rise of Western Christendom, Triumph and Diversity, A. D. 200–1000. London 1996, 10th anniversary ed. 2006.

P. Brown, Through the Eye of a Needle. Wealth and the Fall of Rome and the Making of Christianity in the West, 350–550 AD. Princeton 2012.

P. Brown, The Cult of the Saints. Its Rise and Function in Latin Christianity. Chicago 1981; enlarged ed. 2015.

P. Brown, The Ransom of the Soul. Afterlife and Wealth in Early Western Christianity. Cambridge Mass. 2015.

P. Brown, Treasure in Heaven. The Holy Poor in Early Christianity. Charlottesville, 2016.

J.-P. Caillet/S. Destephen/B. Dumézil/H. Inglebert (eds.), Des dieux civiques aux saints patrons. IVe–VIIe siècle. Paris 2015.

A. Cain/J. Lössl, Jerome of Stridon. His Life, Writings, and Legacy. London 2009.

L. Castagna (ed.), Studi Draconziani (1912–1996). Naples 1997.

S. Cavallin (ed.), La vie d'Hilaire d'Arles. Paris 1997.

H. Chadwick, East and West. The Making of a Rift in the Church, from Apostolic Times until the Council of Florence. Oxford 2003.

N. Christie, From Constantine to Charlemagne. An Archaeology of Italy AD 300–800. Aldershot 2006.

Y. Codou/M. Lauwers (eds.), Lérins, une île sainte de l'Antiquité au Moyen Âge. Turnhout 2009.

F. E. Consolino, Ascesi e mondanità nella Gallia tardoantica. Naples 1979.

M. Conti, Priscillian of Avila. Complete Works. Oxford 2009.

K. Cooper, The Fall of the Roman Household. Cambridge 2007.

K. Cooper/J. Hillner (eds.), Religion, Dynasty, and Patronage in Early Christian Rome 300–900. Cambridge 2007.

P. Courcelle, Histoire littéraire des grandes invasions germaniques, 3rd ed. Paris 1964.

N. Denzey Lewis, The Early Modern Invention of Late Antique Rome. Cambridge 2020.

A. De Vogüé, Les règles des saints Pères. Introduction, texte, traduction et notes, 2 vols. Paris 1982.

M. Diesenberger/Y. Hen/M. Pollheimer (eds.), Sermo Doctorum. Compilers, Preachers and their Audiences in the Early Medieval West. Turnhout 2013.

V. H. Drecoll, Augustin-Handbuch. Tübingen 2007.

G. D. Dunn, The Bishop of Rome in Late Antiquity. Farnham 2015.

N. Duval, L'Afrique dans l'Antiquité tardive et la periode byzantine. L'évolution de l'architecture et de l'art dans leur environnement, in: Antiquité Tardive 14, 2006, 119–64.

S. Elm, New Romans. Salvian of Marseilles. On the Governance of God, in: Journal of Early Christian Studies 25, 2017, 1–28.

I. Foletti/M. Gianandrea (eds.), The Fifth Century in Rome. Art, Liturgy, Patronage. Rome 2017.

J. Fontaine (ed.), Sulpice Sévère. Vie de saint Martin, 3 vols. Paris 1967–9.

E. L. Fortin, Christianisme et culture philosophique au Ve siècle. La querelle de l'âme humaine en Occident. Paris 1959.

W. H. C. Frend, The Rise of the Monophysite Movement. Cambridge 1972.

M. Frisch, Psychomachia. Einleitung, Text und Kommentar. Berlin 2020.

T. Fuhrer, Augustinus. Darmstadt 2004.

T. Fuhrer (ed.), Rom und Mailand in der Spätantike. Repräsentationen städtischer Räume in Literatur, Architektur und Kunst. Berlin 2012.

W. Geerlings, Augustinus – Leben und Werk. Eine bibliographische Einführung. Paderborn 2002.

R. Goodrich, Contextualizing Cassian. Aristocrats, Asceticism, and Reformation in Fifth-century Gaul. Oxford 2007.

M. Goullet/M. Heinzelmann/C. Veyrard-Cosme (eds.), L'hagiographie mérovingienne à travers ses réécritures. Ostfildern 2010.

A. Grabar, Martyrium. Recherches sur le culte des reliques et de l'art chrétien antique, 2 vols. Paris 1943–6.

L. Grig/G. Kelly (eds.), Two Romes. Rome and Constantinople in Late Antiquity. Oxford 2012.

I. Gui/N. Duval/J.-P. Caillet, Basiliques chrétiennes de l'Afrique du Nord, 2 vols. Paris 1992.

A. O. Guillem, Prisciliano a través del tiempo. Historia de los estudios sobre el priscilianismo. Madrid 2004.

C. J. Hefele/H. Leclerq, Histoire des conciles d'après les documents originaux, 11 vols. Paris 1907–52.

P. Hershkowitz, Prudentius, Spain, and Late Antique Christianity. Cambridge 2017.

H. Hess, The Canons of the Council of Sardica, A. D. 343. A Landmark in the Early Development of Canon Law. Oxford 1958.

J. Howard-Johnston/P. A. Hayward (eds.), The Cult of the Saints in Late Antiquity and the Early Middle Ages. Essays on the Contribution of Peter Brown. Oxford 1999.

C. Humfress, Bishops and Law Courts in Late Antiquity. How (not) to Make Sense of the Legal Evidence, in: Journal of Early Christian Studies, 19, 2011, 375–400.

E. D. Hunt, Holy Land Pilgrimage in the Later Roman Empire AD 312–460. Oxford 1984.

J. M. Jiménez/I. Sastre de Diego/C. Tejerizo García, The Iberian Peninsula between 300 and 850. An Archaeological Perspective. Amsterdam 2018.

M. J. Johnson, The Byzantine Churches of Sardinia. Wiesbaden 2013.

J. N. D. Kelly, Jerome, his Life, Writings and Controversies. London 1975.

W. E. Klingshirn/M. Vessey (eds.), The Limits of Ancient Christianity. Essays on Late Antique Thought and Culture in Honour of R. A. Markus. Ann Arbor 1999.

J. Kreiner/H. Reimitz (eds.), Motions of Late Antiquity. Essays on Religion, Politics, and Society in Honour of Peter Brown. Turnhout 2016.

R. Lane Fox, Augustine. Conversions to Confessions. London 2015; German trans. Augustinus. Bekenntnisse und Bekehrungen im Leben eines antiken Menschen. Stuttgart 2017.

M. Lapidge, The Roman Martyrs. Introduction, Translations, and Commentary. Oxford 2018.

J. Latham, From Literal to Spiritual Soldiers of Christ. Disputed Episcopal Elections and the Advent of Christian Processions in Late Antique Rome, in: ChurchH 81, 2012, 298–327.

H. Lemarié (ed.), Chromace d'Aquilée, Sermons, 2 vols. Paris 1969, 1971.

C. Leyser, Authority and Asceticism from Augustine to Gregory the Great. Oxford 2000.

C. Leyser, "A wall protecting a city". Conflict and Authority in the Life of Fulgentius of Ruspe, in: A. Camplani/G. Filoramo (eds.), Foundations of Power and Conflicts of Authority in Late-antique Monasticism, Louvain 2007, 175–92.

R. Lizzi Testa, Vescovi e strutture ecclesiastiche nella città tardoantica (L'Italia Annonaria nel IV–V secolo d.C). Como 1989.

R. Lizzi Testa/G. Marconi (eds.), The Collectio Avellana and its Revivals. Cambridge 2019.

M. Löx, Monumenta sanctorum. Rom und Mailand als Zentren des frühen Christentums: Märtyrerkult und Kirchenbau unter den Bischöfen Damasus und Ambrosius. Wiesbaden 2013.

C. M. Lucarini (ed.), Paulinus Pellaeus: Carmina. Accedunt duo carmina ex Cod. Vat. Urb. 533. Munich 2006.

C. M. Lucarini (ed.), Paulinus Pellaeus. Poème d'action de grâces et prière. Paris 1974.

M. Marcovich, Prosper of Aquitaine, De Providentia Dei. Text, Translation and Commentary. Leiden 1989.

R. Markus, Saeculum. History and Society in the Theology of St Augustine. Cambridge 1970.

R. W. Mathisen, Ecclesiastical Factionalism and Religious Controversy in Fifth-century Gaul. Washington D. C. 1989.

J.-M. Mayeur/L. Pietri/A. Vauchez (eds.), Die Geschichte des Christentums. Altertum. vol. 3: Der lateinische Westen und der byzantinische Osten (431–642). Freiburg 2005.

L. M. McDonald, The Biblical Canon. Its Origin, Transmission and Authority. Grand Rapids 2011.

R. McEachnie, A History of Heresy Past. The Sermons of Chromatius of Aquileia, 388–407, in: ChurchH 83, 2014, 273–96.

J. McGuckin, St Gregory of Nazianzus, an Intellectual Biography. Crestwood 2001.

R. McKitterick/J. Osborne/C. Richardson/J. Story (eds.), Old Saint Peter's Rome. Cambridge 2013.

N. McLynn, Ambrose of Milan Church and Court in a Christian Capital. Berkeley 1994.

N. McLynn, Damasus of Rome. A Fourth-century Pope in Context, in: 7: Fuhrer 2012, 305–26.

J. Moorhead, Ambrose. Church and Society in the Late Roman World. London 2014.

C. Moussy/C. Camus, Dracontius, Œuvres, vols. 1–2: Louages de Dieu. Paris 2002.

C. Munier (ed.) Concilia Galliae a. 314–a. 506. Turnhout 1963.

C. Munier (ed.), Concilia Africae a. 345–525. Turnhout 1974.

B. Neil, Leo the Great. London 2009.

B. Neil/P. Allen, The Letters of Gelasius I (492–496). Pastor and Micro-Manager of the Church of Rome. Turnhout 2014.

B. Neil/P. Allen (eds.), Collecting Early Christian Letters. From the Apostle Paul to Late Antiquity. Cambridge 2015.

V. F. Nicolai/F. Bisconti/D. Mazzoleni, Catacombes chrétiennes de Rome. Turnhout 2000.

D. Nodes, Doctrine and Exegesis in Biblical Latin Poetry. Leeds 1993.

R. Nürnberg, Askese als sozialer Impuls. Monastisch-asketische Spiritualität als Wurzel und Triebfeder sozialer Ideen und Aktivitäten der Kirche in Südgallien im 5. Jahrhundert. Bonn 1988.

G. O'Daly, Augustine's City of God. A Reader's Guide. Oxford 1999.

J. J. O'Donnell, Augustine: Saint and Sinner. A New Biography. New York 2005.

A.-M. Palmer, Prudentius on the Martyrs. Oxford 1989.

G. Philippart (ed.), Hagiographies. Turnhout 1994.

R. Price/M. Gaddis, The Acts of the Council of Chalcedon, 3 vols. Liverpool 2005.

R. Price/T. Graumann, The Council of Ephesus of 431. Documents and Proceedings. Liverpool 2020.

R. Price/M. Whitby (eds.), Chalcedon in Context. Church Councils 400–700. Liverpool 2009.

F. Prinz, Frühes Mönchtum im Frankenreich. Kempten 1965.

C. Rapp, Holy Bishops in Late Antiquity. The Nature of Christian Leadership in an Age of Transition. Berkeley 2005.

S. Rebenich, Hieronymus und sein Kreis. Prosopographische und sozialgeschichtliche Untersuchungen. Stuttgart 1992.

S. Rebenich, Jerome. London 2002.

B. R. Rees, Pelagius, Life and Letters. Woodbridge 1998.

U. Reutter, Damasus, Bischof von Rom (366–384). Leben und Werk. Tübingen 2009.

A. M. Ritter, Das Konzil von Konstantinopel und sein Symbol. Göttingen 1965.

M. Roberts, Biblical Epic and Rhetorical Paraphrase in Late Antiquity. Liverpool 1985.

M. Roberts, Poetry and the Cult of the Martyrs. The Liber Peristephanon of Prudentius. Ann Arbor 1993.

K. Rosen, Augustinus. Genie und Heiliger. Wiesbaden 2015.

P. Rousseau, Ascetics, Authority and the Church in the Age of Jerome and Cassian. Oxford 1978.

P. Rousseau, Pachomius. The Making of a Community in Fourth-century Egypt. Berkeley 1985. 2nd ed. 1999.

P. Rousseau/M. Papoutsakis (eds.), Transformations of Late Antiquity. Essays for Peter Brown. Farnham 2009.

M. Salzman, The Making of a Christian Aristocracy. Social and Religious Change in the Western Empire. Cambridge Mass. 2002.

M. R. Salzman, The Religious Economics of Crisis. The Papal Use of Liturgical Vessels as Symbolic Capital in Late Antiquity, in: Religion in the Roman Empire 5–1, 2019, 125–41.

E. Schwartz/J. Straub, Acta Conciliorum Oecumenicorum, 4 vols. Berlin 1914–71.

K. Sessa, Domestic Conversions. Households and Bishops in the Late Antique "Papal Legends", in: 7: Cooper/Hillner, 79–114.

K. Sessa, The Formation of Papal Authority in Late Antique Italy. Roman Bishops and the Domestic Sphere. Cambridge 2012.

R. Simons, Dracontius und der Mythos. Christliche Weltsicht und pagane Kultur in der ausgehenden Spätantike. Munich 2005.

A. J. B. Sirks, The episcopalis audientia in Late Antiquity, in: Droits et cultures 65, 2013, 79–88.

C. Sogno/B. K. Storin/E. J. Watts (eds.), Late Antique Letter Collections. A Critical Intro-duction and Reference Guide. Oakland 2017.

S. Squires, The Pelagian Controversy. An Introduction to the Enemies of Grace and the Conspiracy of Lost Souls. Eugene 2019.

K. Staat, Late Antique Latin Hagiography: Truth and Fiction. Trends in Scholarship, in: AC 87, 2019, 209–24.

C. Stancliffe, St Martin and his Hagiographer. History and Miracle in Sulpicius Severus. Oxford 1983.

E. Stump/N. Kretzmann (eds.), The Cambridge Companion to Augustine. Cambridge 2001.

V. Toneatto, Les banquiers du Seigneur. Évêques et moines face à la richesse, IVe–début IXe siècle. Rennes 2012.

D. Trout, Damasus of Rome. The Epigraphic Poetry. Oxford 2015.

W. Ullmann, Gelasius I. (492–496). Das Papsttum an der Wende der Spätantike zum Mittelalter. Stuttgart 1981.

M.-D. Valentin (ed.), Hilaire d'Arles, Vie de saint Honorat. Paris 1977.

M. Vessey, Orators, Authors and Compilers. The Earliest Latin Collections of Sermons on Scripture, in: 7: Diesenberger/Hen/Pollheimer, 25–43.

J. Vives, Concilios Visigóticos e Hispano-Romanos. Barcelona 1963.

K. Vössing, Augustinus und Martianus Capella – ein Diskurs im spätantiken Karthago?, in: T. Fuhrer (ed.), Die christlich-philosophischen Diskurse der Spä-tantike. Texte, Personen, Institutionen. Stuttgart 2008.

S. Wessel, Leo the Great and the Spiritual Rebuilding of Universal Rome. Leiden 2008.

R. Westall, Constantius II and the Basilica of St Peter in the Vatican, in: Historia 64, 2015, 205–42.

J. Wetzel (ed.), Augustine's City of God. A Critical Guide. Cambridge 2012.

R. Whelan, Arianism in Africa, in: 11: Berndt/Steinacher, 239–55.

M. S. Williams, Authorised Lives in Early Christian Biography. Between Eusebius and Augustine. Cambridge 2008.

E. Wipszycka, The Alexandrian Church. People and Institutions. Warsaw 2015.

E. Wipszycka, The Second Gift of the Nile. Monks and Monasteries in Late Antique Egypt. Warsaw 2018.

R. Wiśniewski, The Beginnings of the Cult of Relics. Oxford 2019.

R. Wiśniewski/R. Van Dam/Ward-Perkins (eds.), Interacting with Saints in the Late An-tique and Medieval Worlds. Leiden 2023.

I. N. Wood, The Christian Economy of the Early Medieval West. Towards a Temple Society. Binghamton 2022.

F. Zuccotti, "Furor haereticorum". Studi sul trattamento giuridico della follia e sulla persecuzione della eterodossia religiosa nella legislazione del tardo impero romano. Milan 1992.

8 Late Roman Secular Culture

Association pour l'Antiquité Tardive (ed.), La démocratisation de la culture dans l'Occident Tardive, Antiquité Tardive 9, 2002.

T. Barnes, Ammianus Marcellinus and the Representation of Historical Reality. Ithaca, 1998.

J. W. Binns (ed.), Latin Literature of the Fourth Century. London 1974.

H. W. Bird, Sextus Aurelius Victor. A Historiographical Study. Liverpool 1984.

H. Brandenburg/L. Pani Ermini (eds.), Cimitile e Paolino di Nola. La tomba di S. Felice e il centro di pellegrinaggio. Trent'anni di riecherche. Vatican City 2003.

R. Burgess/M. Kulikowski, Mosaics of Time. Chronicle Traditions from the First Century BC to the Sixth Century AD, vol. 1. Leiden 2013.

A. Cameron, Claudian. Poetry and Propaganda at the Court of Honorius. Oxford 1970.

A. Cameron, The Last Pagans of Rome. Oxford 2011.

C. Conybeare, Paulinus noster. Self and Symbols in the Letters of Paulinus of Nola. Oxford 2000.

B. Croke, Count Marcellinus and his Chronicle. Oxford 2001.

H. Dey, The Aftermath of the Roman city: Architecture and ceremony in Late Antiquity and the Early Middle Ages. Cambridge 2014.

E. Doblhofer (ed.), Rutilius Claudius Namatianus. De reditu suo sive iter Gallicum, 2 vols. Heidelberg 1972–7.

J. Drijvers/D. Hunt (eds.), The Late Roman World and its Historian. Interpreting Ammianus Marcellinus. London 1999.

P. Fabre, Saint Paulin de Nole et l'amitié chrétienne. Paris 1949.

W.-Fels, Anthologia Latina mit den Vergil-Centonen. Eingel., übers. u. komm. Stuttgart 2014.

R. H. Barrow, Prefect and Emperor. The Relationes of Symmachus, AD 384. Oxford 1976.

C. Jacquemard-Le Saos (ed.), Querolus sive Aulularia. Paris 1994.

F. C. Jenkins, Ammianus Marcellinus. An Annotated Bibliography from 1474 to the Present Day. Leiden 2017.

A. Johnson/J. Scott (eds.), Eusebius of Caesarea. Tradition and Innovations. London 2013.

R. A. Kaster, Guardians of Language. The Grammarian and Society in Late Antiquity. Berkeley 1988.

R. A. Kaster (ed.), Macrobius, The Saturnalia. Cambridge Mass. 2011.

N. M. Kay, Epigrams from the Anthologia Latina. London 2006.

G. Kelly, Ammianus Marcellinus. The Allusive Historian. Cambridge 2008.

E. Kenyon, Augustine and the Dialogue. Cambridge 2018.

D. Lassandro/E. Romano, Rassegna bibliografica degli Studi sul Querolus, in: Bollettino di Studi Latini 21, 1991, 26–51.

V. Law, Grammar and Grammarians in the Early Middle Ages. London 1997.

A. Loyen, Sidoine Apollinaire et l'esprit précieux en Gaule aux derniers jours de l'Empire. Paris 1943.

S. MacCormack, Art and Ceremony in Late Antiquity. Berkeley 1981.

H.-I. Marrou, Histoire de l'éducation dans l'Antiquité. Paris 1948.

H.-I. Marrou, Saint Augustin et la fin de la culture antique. Paris 1938, 2nd ed. 1949.

J. F. Matthews, The Letters of Symmachus, in: J. W. Binns (ed.), Latin Literature of the Fourth Century. London 1974.

J. Matthews, The Roman Empire of Ammianus. London 1989.

M. Mazza, La Historia tripartita di Flavio Magno Aurelio Cassiodore senatore. Metodi e scopo, in: S. Leanza (ed.), Flavio Magno Aurelio Cassiodoro. Atti della settimana di Studi. Catanzaro 1984, 210–44.

S. Mazzarino, La "democratizzazione" della cultura nella tarda antichità, in: S. Mazzarino, Antico, Tardoantico ed era constantiniana, vol. 1, Bari, 1974, 74–98.

M. McCormick, Eternal Victory. Triumphal Rulership in Late Antiquity, Byzantium, and the Early Medieval West. Cambridge 1986.

S. McGill/E. Watts (eds.), A Companion to Late Latin Literature. Oxford 2018.

M. Meckler, The Beginning of the Historia Augusta, in: HZ 45, 1996, 364–75.

A. Momigliano, Popular Religious Beliefs and the Late Roman Historians, in: Studies in Church History 8, Popular Belief and Practice, 1972, 1–18.

C. Moussy/C. Camus, Dracontius, Œuvres, vols. 2–4. Paris 2002.

S. Mratschek, Der Briefwechsel des Paulinus von Nola. Göttingen 2002.

S. Muhlberger, The Fifth-Century Chroniclers. Prosper, Hydatius, and the Chronicler of 452. Leeds 1990.

G. M. Müller (ed.), Zwischen Alltagskommunikation und literarischer Identitätsbildung. Stuttgart 2018.

B. Müller-Rettig, Panegyrici Latini. Lobreden auf römische Kaiser. Lateinisch und deutsch, 2 vols. Darmstadt 2008–12.

B. Neil/P. Allen (eds.), Collecting Early Christian Letters. From the Apostle Paul to Late Antiquity. Cambridge 2015.

C. E. V. Nixon/B. S. Rodgers, In Praise of Later Roman Emperors. The Panegyrici Latini. Berkeley 1994.

R. Rees (ed.), Latin Panegyric. Oxford 2012.

P. Riché, Éducation et culture dans l'Occident barbare, VIe–VIIIe siècles. Paris 1962.

M. Roberts, The Jewelled Style. Poetry and Poetics in Late Antiquity. Ithaca 1989.

D. Rohrbacher, The Historians of Late Antiquity. London 2002.

M. R. Salzman, On Roman Time. The Codex Calendar of 354 and the Rhythms of Urban Life in Late Antiquity. Berkeley 1990.

R. Schwitter, Umbrosa lux. Obscuritas in der lateinischen Epistolographie der Spätantike. Stuttgart 2015.

D. Shanzer, A Philosophical and Literary Commentary on Martianus Capella's De Nuptiis Philologiae et Mercurii Book 1. Berkeley 1986.

H. Sivan, Ausonius of Bordeaux, Genesis of a Gallic Aristocracy. London 1993.

C. Sogno/B. K. Storin/E. J. Watts (eds.), Late Antique Letter Collections. A Critical Introduction and Reference Guide. Oakland 2017.

J. A. Stover/G. Woudhuysen, The Lost History of Sextus Aurelius Victor. Edinburgh 2023.

C. Trout, Paulinus of Nola, Life, Letters and Poems. Berkeley 1999.
P. Van Nuffelen/L. Van Hoof, Jordanes Romana and Getica. Liverpool 2020.
É. Wolff (ed.), Littérature, politique et religion en Afrique vandal. Paris 2015.
I. N. Wood, Why Collect Letters?, in: 8: Müller, 45–61.

9 Economy and Society

Ancient Coastal Settlements, Ports and Habours, https://www.ancientportsantiques.com/ (27.06.2024)
M. T. W. Arnheim, The Senatorial Aristocracy in the Later Roman Empire. Oxford 1972.
Association pour l'Antiquité Tardive (ed.), Économie et religion dans l'antiquité tardive, Antiquité tardive 14, 2006.
Association pour l'Antiquité Tardive (ed.), Mondes ruraux en Orient et en Occident, Antiquité tardive 21, 2013.
M. G. L. Baillie, Dendrochronology Raises Questions about the Nature of the AD 536 Dust-Veil Event, in: Holocene 4, 1994, 212–7.
J. Banaji, Agrarian Change in Late Antiquity. Gold, Labour and Aristocratic Dominance. Oxford 2007.
J. Banaji, Aristocracies, Peasantries and the Framing of the Early Middle Ages, in: Journal of Agrarian Change 9, 2008, 59–91, reprinted in 9: J. Banaji 2016, 143–77.
J. Banaji, Exploring the Economy of Late Antiquity. Selected Essays. Cambridge 2016.
J. Banaji, The Economic Trajectories of Late Antiquity, in: 9: J. Banaji 2016, 61–88.
G. P. Brogiolo/N. Gauthier/N. Christie (eds.), Towns and their Territories between Late Antiquity and the Early Middle Ages. Leiden 2000.
G. P. Brogiolo/B. Ward-Perkins (eds.), The Idea and Ideal of the Town between Late Antiquity and the Early Middle Ages. Leiden 1999.
P. Brown, Poverty and Leadership in the Later Roman Empire. Hanover, N. H. 2002.
P. Brown, Through the Eye of a Needle. Wealth, the Fall of Rome and the Making of Christianity, 350–550 AD. Princeton 2012.
P. Brown, The Ransom of the Soul. Afterlife and Wealth in Early Western Christianity. Cambridge Mass. 2015.
P. Brown, Treasure in Heaven. The Holy Poor in Early Christianity. Charlottesville 2016.
E. Campbell, Continental and Mediterranean Imports to Atlantic Britain and Ireland, AD 400–800. London 2007.
A. Chastagnol, Le senat romain sous le regne d'Odoacer. Recherches sur l'épigraphie du Colisée au 5ᵉ siècle. Bonn 1966.
K. Cooper, The Virgin and the Bride. Cambridge, Mass. 1996.
C. Courtois/L. Leschi/C. Perrat/C. Saumagne (ed.), Tablettes Albertini. Actes privés de l'époque Vandale (fin du Vᵉ siècle). Paris 1952.
B. Croke, Two Early Byzantine Earthquakes and their Liturgical Commemoration, in: Byzantion 51, 1981, 122–47.

F. Galladini/G. Ricci/E. Falcucci/C. Panzieri, Archaeoseismological Evidence of Past Earthquakes in Rome (Fifth to Ninth Century A. D.) used to Quantify Dating Uncertainties and Coseismic Damage, in: Natural Hazards 94, 2018, 319–48.

P. A. C. Galli/D. Molin, Beyond the Damage Threshold. The Historic Earthquakes of Rome, in: Bulletin of Earthquake Engineering 12, 2014, 1277–306.

J. Gunn, The Years without Summer. Tracing A. D. 536 and its Aftermath. Oxford 2000.

P. Grierson/M. Blackburn, Medieval European Coinage, vol. 1: The Early Middle Ages (5th–10th centuries). Cambridge 1986.

L. Grigg, Cities in the "long" Late Antiquity, 2000–2012. A Survey Essay, in: Urban History 40, 2013, 554–66.

P. Guest, The Late Roman Gold and Silver Coins from the Hoxne Treasure. London 2005.

H. Härke, Grave Goods in Early Medieval Urials. Messages and Meanings, in: Mortality 19, 2014, 1–21.

J. Haldon, The State and the Tributary Mode of Production. London 1993.

J. Haldon, Framing Transformation, Transforming the Framework, in: Millenium 5, 2008, 327–51.

J. Haldon/H. Elton/S. Huebner/A. Izdebski/L. Mordechai/T. Newfield, Plagues, Climate Change, and the End of an Empire. A Response to Kyle Harper's The Fate of Rome, in: Hist. Compass 2018, https://doi.org/10.1111/hic3.12508 (11.01.2023).

K. Harper, Slavery in the Late Roman World AD 275–425. Cambridge 2011.

K. Harper, The Fate of Rome. Climate, Disease, and the End of an Empire. Princeton/Oxford 2017.

E. James, Burial and Status in the Early Medieval West, in: TRHS 5th series 39, 1989, 23–40.

M. Kulikowski, Plague in Spanish Late Antiquity, in: 9: Little, 150–70.

A. La Rocca/F. Oppedisano, Il senato romano nell'Italia Ostrogotha. Rome 2016.

L. Lavan, The Late-Antique City. A Bibliographic Essay, in: L. Lavan (ed.), Recent Research in Late Antique Urbanism. Portsmouth, Rhode Island 2001, 9–26.

H. Leppin, The Richest Private Landowners of all Times. Anmerkungen zur Quellenlage für den Großgrundbesitz der Spätantike, in: R. Haensch/P. von Rummel (eds.), Himmelwärts und erdverbunden. Berlin 2021, 181–92.

É. Lesne, Histoire de la Propriété Ecclésiastique en France, vol. 1. Lille 1910.

L. K. Little (ed.), Plague and the End of Antiquity. The Pandemic of 541–750. Cambridge 2007.

J. Maddicott, Plague in Seventh-Century England, in: 9: Little, 171–214.

F. Marazzi, I "patrimonia sanctae Romanae ecclesiae" nel Lazio (secoli IV–X). Rome 1998.

J. Matthews, Western Aristocracies and Imperial Court AD 364–425. Oxford 1975.

R. W. Mathisen, Roman Aristocrats in Barbarian Gaul. Strategies for Survival in an Age of Transition. Austin 1993.

M. McCormick, Gregory of Tours on Sixth-century Plague and other Epidemics, in: Speculum 96, 2021, 38–96.

M. McCormick, Origins of the European Economy. Communications and Commerce AD 300–900. Cambridge 2001.

M. McCormick, Tracking Mass Death during the Fall of Rome's empire, in: Journal of Roman Archaeology, part I: 28, 2015, 325–7; part II: 29, 2016, 1008–46.

M. Meier, The "Justinianic Plague". The Economic Consequences of the Pandemic in the Eastern Roman Empire and its Cultural and Religious Effects, in: Early Medieval Europe 24, 2016, 267–92.

L. Mordechai/M. Eisenberg, Rejecting Catastrophe. The Case of the Justinianic Plague, in: P & P 244, 2019, 3–50.

L. Mordechai/M. Eisenberg, The Justinianic Plague. An Interdisciplinary Review, in: Byzantine and Modern Greek Studies 43, 2019, 156–80.

L. Mordechai/M. Eisenberg/T. Newfield/A. Izdbeski/J. Kay/H. Poinar, The Justinianic Plague. An Inconsequential Pandemic?, in: Proceedings of the National Academy of Sciences of the United States of America 116, 2019, https://www.pnas.org/doi/full/10.1073/pnas.1903797116.

L. Mordechai/M. Eisenberg, The Justinianic Plague and Global Pandemics, in: AHR 125, 2020, 1632–67.

B. Näf, Senatorisches Standesbewußtsein in Spätrömischer Zeit. Freiburg 1995.

V. Neri, I marginali nell'Occidente Tardoantico. Poveri, "infames" e criminali nella nascente società Cristiana. Santo Spirito 1998.

H. Niquet, Monumenta virtutum titulique. Senatorische Selbstdarstellung im spätantiken Rom im Spiegel der epigraphischen Denkmäler. Stuttgart 2000.

É. Patlagean, Pauvreté économique et pauvreté sociale à Byzance. 4e–7e siècles. Paris 1977.

J. Rich (ed.), The City in Late Antiquity. London 1992.

M. R. Salzman, From a Classical to a Christian City. Civic Euergetism and Charity in Late Antique Rome, in: Studies in Late Antiquity 1, 2017, 65–85.

M. Salzman, The Making of a Christian Aristocracy. Social and Religious Change in the Western Empire. Cambridge Mass. 2002.

P. Sarris, Empires of Faith. The Fall of Rome to the Rise of Islam, 500–700. Oxford 2011.

P. Sarris, Introduction. Aristocrats, Peasants and the Transformation of Rural Society, in: Journal of Agrarian Change 9, 2008, 3–32.

D. Schlinkert, Ordo senatorius et nobilitas. Die Konstitution des Senatsadels in der Spätantike. Stuttgart 1996.

H. Sivan, Ausonius of Bordeaux, Genesis of a Gallic Aristocracy. London 1993.

P. Squatriti, The Floods of 589 and Climate Change at the Beginning of the Middle Ages, in: Speculum 85, 2010, 799–826.

K. F. Stroheker, Der senatorische Adel im spätantiken Gallien. Tübingen 1948.

C. Tsiamis/E. Poulakou-Rebelakou/S. Marketos, Earthquakes and Plague during Byzantine Times. Can Lessons from the Past Improve Epidemic Preparedness, in: Acta medico-historica Adriatica 11, 2013, 55–64.

I. Velázquez Soriano, Las pizarras visigodas. Murcia 1989.

H. Wessel, Das Recht der Tablettes Albertini. Berlin 2003.

C. Wickham, Framing the Early Middle Ages. Europe and the Mediterranean, 400–800. Oxford 2005.

I. Wood, "Landscapes compared", Early Medieval Europe 15, 2007, 223–37.

I. Wood, Entrusting Western Europe to the Church, 400–750, in: Transactions of the Royal Historical Society 23, 2013, 37–73.

P. Wormald, The Decline of the Western Empire and the Survival of its Aristocracy, in: JRS 66, 1976, 217–26.

10 Regional History

J. Arce, Bárbaros y Romanos en Hispania (400–507 A. D.). Madrid 2005.

J. Arce, El último siglo de la España romana (284–409), 2nd ed. Madrid 2009.

J. Arce, España entre el mundo antiguo y el mundo medieval. Madrid 1988.

M. A. Arena/P. Delogu/L. Paroli/M. Ricci/L. Sagui/L. Venditelli (eds.), Roma dall'Antichita al Medioevo, vol. 1: Archeologia e Storia, nel Museo Nazionale Romano Crypta Balbi. Rome 2001.

M. T. W. Arnheim, The Senatorial Aristocracy in the Later Roman Empire. Oxford 1972.

A. Augenti (ed.), Le città italiane tra la tarda antichità e l'alto medioevo. Atti del convegno. Florence 2006.

I. Backus/A. Goudriaan, "Semipelagianism". The Origins of the Terms and its Passage into the History of Heresy, in: Journal of eccl. Hist. 65, 2014, 25–46.

A. Birley/M. Alberti, Vindolanda Excavation Report, Focusing on Post-Roman Vindolanda. Hexham 2021.

R. Borius (ed.), Constance de Lyon, Vie de saint Germain d'Auxerre. Paris 1965.

K. Bowes/M. Kulikowski, Hispania in Late Antiquity. Current Perspectives. Leiden 2005.

R. W. Burgess (ed. and trans.), The Chronicle of Hydatius and the Consularia Constantopolitana. Oxford 1993.

P. J. Casey, Carausius and Allectus. The British Usurpers. London 1995.

S. Cavallin (ed.), La vie d'Hilaire d'Arles. Paris 1997.

A. Chavarría Arnau, El final de las "villae" en "Hispania" (siglos IV–VIII). Turnhout 2007.

A. Chavarría/J. Arce/G. P. Brogiolo, Villas tardoantiguas en el Mediterráneo occidental. Madrid 2000.

N. Christie, From Constantine to Charlemagne. An Archaeology of Italy AD 300–800. Aldershot 2006.

N. Christie, Late Roman and Late Antique Italy. From Constantine to Justinian, in A. Cooley (ed.), A Companion to Roman Italy, Hoboken, 2016, 133–53.

L. Cilliers, Roman North Africa. Environment, Society and Medical Contribution. Amsterdam 2019.

S. E. Cleary, The Ending of Roman Britain. London 1989.

R. Collins/L. Allason-Jones (eds.), Finds from the Frontier. Material Culture in the 4th–5th Centuries. York 2010.

C. Courtois/L. Leschi/C. Perrat/C. Saumagne, Tablettes Albertini. Actes privés de l'époque vandale (fin du Ve siècle), 2 vols. Paris 1952.

L. Cracco-Ruggini, Economia e società nell'Italia Annonaria. Rapporti fra agricoltura e commercio dal IV al VI secolo d. C. Milan 1961.

J. Curran, Pagan City and Christian Capital. Rome in the Fourth Century. Oxford 2000.

K. Dark, Civitas to Kingdom. British Political Continuity 300–800. Leicester 1994.

M.-J. Delage/M. Heijmans (eds.), Vie de Césaire d'Arles, Sources Chrétiennes 536. Paris 2010.

H. Dey, The Making of Medieval Rome: a new profile of the city, 400–1420. Cambridge 2021.

S. Diefenbach/M. Gernot Müller, Gallien in Spätantike und Frühmittelalter. Kulturgeschichte einer Region. Berlin 2013.

J. Drinkwater, The Bacaudae of Fifth-century Gaul, in: 10: J. Drinkwater/H. Elton, 208–17.

J. Drinkwater/H. Elton, Fifth-century Gaul. A Crisis of Identity. Cambridge 1992.

J. Drinkwater, The Usurpers Constantine III (407–11) and Jovinus (411–413), in: Britannia 29, 1998, 269–98.

N. Faulkner, The Decline and Fall of Roman Britain. Stroud 2000.

J. Fontaine (ed.), Vie de saint Martin. Paris 1967–9.

E. L. Fortin, Christianisme et culture philosophique au Ve siècle. La querelle de l'âme humaine en Occident. Paris 1959.

J. Gerrard, The Ruin of Roman Britain. An Archaeological Perspective. Cambridge 2013.

J. Harries, Sidonius and the Fall of Rome. Oxford 1994.

S. Harrington/M. Welch, The Early Anglo-Saxon Kingdoms of Southern Britain AD 450–650. Oxford 2014.

M. W. C. Hassall, Britain in the Notitia Dignitatum, in: 6: Goodburn/Bartholemew, 103–7.

F. Hunter/K. Painter (eds.), Late Roman Silver. The Traprain Treasure in Context. Edinburgh 2013.

C. Johns, The Hoxne Late Roman Treasure. Gold Jewellery and Silver Plate. London 2010.

C. Johns/T. Potter, The Thetford Treasure. Roman Jewellery and Silver. London 1983.

R. Krautheimer, Rome. Profile of a City, 312–1308. Princeton 1980.

R. Krautheimer, Three Christian Capitals. Topography and Politics. Berkeley 1983.

M. Kulikowski, Late Roman Spain and its Cities. Baltimore 2004.

B. Lançon, Rome in Late Antiquity. Edinburgh 2000.

M. Lapidge/D. N. Dumville, Gildas. New Approaches. Woodbridge 1984.

C. Lepelley, Les cités de l'Afrique romaine au Bas-Empire, vol. 1: La permanence d'une civilisation municipale; vol. 2: Notice d'histoire municipal. Paris 1977–81.

C. Lepelley, Aspects de l'Afrique romaine. La cité, la vie rurale, le Christianisme. Bari 2001.

A. Leone, The End of the Pagan City. Religion, Economy and Urbanism in Late Antique North Africa. Oxford 2013.

R. Lizzi Testa, Vescovi e strutture nella città tardoantica. L'Italia annonaria nel IV–V secolo d. C. Como 1989.

R. Markus, The End of Ancient Christianity. Cambridge 1990.

F. Martine, Vie des Pères du Jura. Paris 1968.

M. P. Martinez, Tarraco en la Antigüedad tardía. Cristianización y organización eclesiástica (siglos III–VIII). Tarragona 2012.

J. Matthews, Western Aristocracies and Imperial Court AD 364–425. Oxford 1975.

R. W. Mathisen/D. Shanzer (eds.), Society and Culture in Late Antique Gaul. Revisiting the Sources. Aldershot 2001.

C. Minor, Bacaudae. A Reconsideration, in: Traditio 51, 1996, 297–307.

S. Moorhead/A. Booth/R. Bland, The Frome Hoard. London 2010.

S. Muhlberger, The Fifth-century Chroniclers. Prosper, Hydatius, and the Gallic Chronicler of 452. Leeds 1990.

K. Painter, The Mildenhall Treasure. Roman Silver from East Anglia. London 1977.

K. Painter, The Water Newton Early Christian Silver. London 1977.

L. Paroli/L. Venditelli (eds.), Roma dall'Antichita al Medioevo, vol. 2: Contesti tardoantichi e altomedievali. Rome 2004.

E. Rebillard, Christians and their Many Identities in Late Antiquity. North Africa, 200–450 CE, in: E. Rebillard (ed.), Transformations of Religious Practices in Late Antiquity. Farnham UK 2014.

A. S. Robertson, An Inventory of Romano-British Coin Hoards. London 2000.

J. C. Sánchez Léon, Les sources de l'histoire des bagaudes. Paris 1996.

J. C. Sánchez Léon, Los Bagaudas: Rebeldes, demonios, mártires. Revueltas campesinas en Galia e Hispania durante el Bajo Imperio. Jaén 1996a.

S. Scott, Art and Society in Fourth-century Britain. Villa Mosaics in Context. Oxford 2000.

H. Sivan, Ausonius of Bordeaux. Genesis of a Gallic Aristocracy. London 1993.

T. A. Smith, De Gratia. Faustus of Riez's Treatise on Grace and its Place in the History of Theology. South Bend 1990.

G. Speed, Towns in the Dark? Urban Transformations from Late Roman Britain to Anglo-Saxon England. Oxford 2014.

K. F. Stroheker, Der senatorische Adel im spätantiken Gallien. Tübingen 1948.

J.-O. Tjäder, Die nichtliterarischen lateinischen Papyri Italiens aus der Zeit 445–700, 2 vols. Lund 1955–82.

E. A. Thompson, Peasant Revolts in Late Roman Gaul and Spain, in: P & P 2, 1952, 11–23.

E. A. Thompson, Saint Germanus of Auxerre and the End of Roman Britain. Woodbridge 1984.

Topographie chrétienne des cités de la Gaule des origines au milieu du VIIIe siècle, 16 vols. Paris 1972–2014.

M.-D. Valentin (ed.), Hilaire d'Arles, Vie de saint Honorat. Paris 1977.

R. Van Dam, Leadership and Community in Late Antique Gaul. Berkeley 1985.

B. Ward-Perkins, From Classical Antiquity to the Middle Ages, AD 300–850. Oxford 1984.

R. H. Weaver, Divine Grace and Human Agency. A Study of the Semi-Pelagian Controversy. Washington D. C. 1996.

H. Wessel, Das Recht der Tablettes Albertini. Berlin 2003.

R. White/P. Barker, Wroxeter. Life and Death of a Roman City. Stroud 1998.

C. Wickham, Early Medieval Italy. Central Power and Local Society, 400–1000. London 1981.

T. Wilmott/P. R. Wilson (eds.), The Late Roman Transition in the North. Papers from the Roman Archaeology Conference, Durham 1999. Oxford 2000.

T. Wilmott, Birdoswald. Excavations of a Roman Fort on Hadrian's Wall and its Successor settlements, 1987–1992. London 2014.

I. Wood, The Development of the Visigothic Court in the Fifth and Sixth Centuries, in: J. Wood/D. Fernandez/M. Lester (eds.), Rome, Byzantium, and the Visigothic Kingdom of Toledo. Imitation, Reinvention, or Strategic Adoption? Amsterdam 2023, 53–72.

I. Wood, The Lives of episcopal saints in Gaul: models for a time of crisis, c. 470–550, in R. Wiśniewski/R. Van Dam/Ward-Perkins (eds.), Interacting with Saints in the Late Antique and Medieval Worlds. Turnhout 2023, 213–228.

11 The Barbarians

C. E. G. Amorim et al., Understanding 6th-century Barbarian Social Organization Through Paleogenomics, in: Nature Communications 9, article number 3547, 2018, https://www.nature.com/articles/s41467-018-06024-4 (05.06.2024).

P. Amory, People and Identity in Ostrogothic Italy, 489–554. Cambridge 1997.

J. Barbier, Archives oubliées du haut Moyen Âge. Les gesta municipalia en Gaule franque (VIe–IXe siècle). Paris 2014.

P. Barnwell, Emperor, Prefects and Kings The Roman West, 395–565. London 1992.

G. Berndt/R. Steinacher (eds.), Arianism. Roman Heresy and Arian Creed. Farnham 2014.

S. Brather, Ethnische Interpretationen in der frühgeschichtliche Archäologie. Geschichte, Grundlagen und Alternativen. Berlin 2004.

A. S. Christensen, Cassiodorus, Jordanes and the History of the Goths. Studies in a Migration Myth. Copenhagen 2002.

D. Claude, Untersuchingen der frühfränkischen Comitat, in: ZRG GA 81, 1964, 1–69.

K. Czajkowski/B. Eckhardt/M. Strothmann (eds.), Law in the Roman Provinces. Oxford 2020.

G. Dilcher/E.-M. Distler (eds.), Leges – Gentes – Regna. Zur Rolle von germanischen Rechtsgewohnheiten und lateinischer Schrifttradition bei der Ausbildung der frühmittelalterliche Rechtskultur. Berlin 2006.

J. Durliat, Les finances publiques de Dioclétien aux Carolingiens (284–889). Sigmaringen 1990.

S. Esders, Spätrömisches Militärrecht in der Lex Baiuvariorum, in: F. Botta/L. Loschiavo (eds.), Civitas, Iura, Arma. Organizzazioni militari, istituzioni giuridiche e strutture sociali alle origini dell'Europa (sec. III–VIII). Lecce 2015, 44–78. English version: S. Esders, Late Roman Military Law in the Bavarian Code, Clio@Themis, 10, March 2016, accessible via https://journals.openedition.org/cliothemis/1168 (04.06.2024).

H. Fehr, Germanen und Romanen im Merowingerreich. Berlin 2010.

P. Geary, The Myth of Nations. The Medieval Origins of Europe. Princeton 2002.

V. Gheller, "Identità" e "arianesimo gotico". Genesi di un topos storiografico. Bologna, 2017.

H.-E. Giesecke, Die Ostgermanen und der Arianismus. Leipzig/Berlin 1939.

A. Gillett (ed.), On Barbarian Identity. Critical Approaches to Ethnicity in the Early Middle Ages. Turnhout 2002.

W. Goffart, The Narrators of Barbarian History. Jordanes, Gregory of Tours, Bede, and Paul the Deacon. Princeton 1988.

G. Halsall, Ethnicity and Early Medieval Cemeteries, in: Arqueologia y territorio medieval 18, 2011, 15–27.

U. Heil, Avitus von Vienne und die homöische Kirche der Burgunder. Berlin 2011.

U. Heil (ed.), Das Christentum im frühen Europa. Diskurse, Tendenzen, Entscheidungen. Berlin 2019.

M. Heinzelmann, Gregor von Tours (538–594) "Zehn Bücher Geschichte". Historiographie und Gesellschaftskonzept im 6. Jahrhundert. Darmstadt 1994; English trans. Gregory of Tours, History and Society in the Sixth Century. Cambridge 2001.

G. Heydemann/H. Reimitz (eds.), Historiography and Identity 2, Post-Roman Multiplicity and New Political Identities. Turnhout 2020.

E. James, Europe's Barbarians. AD 200–600. London 2009.

J. Jarnut, Germanisch. Plädoyer für die Abschaffung eines obsoleten Zentralbegriffes der Frühmittelalterforschung, in: 11: Dilcher/Distler, 69–78.

E. Levy, West Roman Vulgar Law. The Law of Property. Philadelphia 1951.

E. Levy, Weströmisches Vulgarrecht. Das Obligationenrecht. Weimar 1956.

D. Liebs, Roman Vulgar Law in Late Antiquity, in: B. Sirks (ed.), Aspects of Law in Late Antiquity. Dedicated to A. Honoré on the Occasion of the Sixtieth Year of his Teaching in Oxford. Oxford 2008, 35–53.

L. Loschiavo, L'Étà del Passaggio. All'alba del diritto comune europeo (secoli III–VII). Turin, 2016.

L. Loschiavo, Personality of Law or ius speciale militum? Around the Origins of the leges barbarorum, in: 6: L. Loschiavo (ed.), The Civilian Legacy of the Roman Army: Military Models in the Post-Roman World. Leiden 2024, 413–45.

L. Loschiavo (ed.), The Civilian Legacy of the Roman Army: Military Models in the Post-Roman World. Leiden 2024.

E. Magnou-Nortier, Aux Origines de la fiscalité modern. Geneva 2012.

G. Martin/J. Grusková, "Scythica Vindobonensia" by Dexippus (?). New Fragments on Decius' Gothic Wars, in: Greek, Roman and Byzantine Studies 54, 2014, 728–54.

R. W. Mathisen/D. Shanzer (eds.), Romans, Barbarians and the Transformation of the Roman World. Cultural Interaction and the Creation of Identity in Late Antiquity. Farnham 2011.

M. Meier, Geschichte der Völkerwanderung. Europa, Asien und Afrika vom 3. bis zum 8. Jahrhundert. Munich 2019.

A. Merrills, History and Geography in Late Antiquity. Cambridge 2005.

S. Mitchell/G. Greatrex (eds.) Ethnicity and Culture in Late Antiquity. London 2000.

A. C. Murray, From Roman to Frankish Gaul. Centenarii and centenae in the Administration of the Merovingian Kingdom, in: Traditio 44, 1980, 59–100.

A. C. Murray, The Position of the grafio in the Constitutional History of Merovingian Gaul, in: Speculum 64, 1986, 787–805.

W. Pohl, Von der Ethnogenese zur Identitätsforschung, in: W. Pohl/M. Diesenberger/B. Zeller (eds.), Neue Wege der Frühmittelalterforschung. Bilanz und Perspektiven. Vienna 2018, 9–24.

W. Pohl/C. Gantner/C. Grifoni/M. Pollheimer-Mohaupt (eds.), Transformations of Romanness. Early Medieval Regions and Identities. Berlin 2018.

W. Pohl/G. Heydemann (eds.), Post-Roman Transitions. Christian and Barbarian Identities in the Early Medieval West. Turnhout 2013.

W. Pohl/G. Heydemann (eds.), Strategies of Identification. Ethnicity and Religion in
    Early Medieval Europe. Turnhout 2013a.
W. Pohl/M. Mehofer, Archaeology of Identity – Archäologie der Identität. Vienna
    2010.
H. Reimitz, History, Frankish Identity and the Framing of Western Ethnicity, 550–850.
    Cambridge 2015.
K. D. Schmidt, Die Bekehrung der Ostgermanen zum Christentum. Der ostgermanis-
    che Arianismus. Göttingen 1939.
C. Stadermann, Gothus. Konstruktion und Rezeption von Gotenbildern in narrativen
    Schriften des merowingischen Galliens. Stuttgart 2017.
K. Ubl, Sinnstiftungen eines Rechtsbuchs. Die Lex Salica im Frankenreich. Ostfildern,
    2017.
P. Van Nuffelen/L. Van Hoof, Jordanes, Romana and Getica. Liverpool 2020.
J. M. Wallace-Hadrill, Early Germanic Kingship in England and on the Continent. Ox-
    ford 1971.
R. Wenskus, Stammesbildung und Verfassung. Das Werden der frühmittelalterlichen
    Gentes. Köln, 1961.
C. Wickham, The Other Transition. From the Ancient World to Feudalism, in: P & P
    103, 1984, 3–36.
C. Wickham, La chûte de l'empire romain n'aura pas lieu, in: Le Moyen Âge 99, 1993,
    88–119; reprinted in L. K. Little/B. H. Rosenwein (eds.), Debating the Middle
    Ages. Oxford 1998, 45–57.
C. Wickham, Framing the Early Middle Ages. Europe and the Mediterranean, 400–
    800. Oxford 2005.
I. Wiwjorra, Der Germanenmythos. Konstruktion einer Weltanschauung in der Alter-
    tumsforschung des 19. Jahrhunderts. Darmstadt 2006.
H. Wolfram, Geschichte der Goten. Munich 1979. English trans. History of the Goths.
    Berkeley 1979.
M. Zerjadtke, Das Amt "Dux" in Spätantike und frühem Mittelalter. Der "Ducatus" im
    Spannungsfeld zwischen Römischem Einfluss und eigener Entwicklung. Berlin
    2019.

11.1 Relations with Rome Before the Barbarian Settlements

T. S. Burns, Barbarians within the Gates of Rome. A Study of Roman Military Policy
    and the Barbarians, ca. 375–425 AD. Bloomington 1994.
K. Dark, A sub-Roman Re-defence of Hadrian's Wall, in: Britannia 23, 1992, 111–20.
S. Dick, Der Mythos vom "germanischen" Königtum. Studien zur Herrschaftsorgani-
    sation bei den germanischsprachigen Barbaren bis zum Beginn der Völker-
    wanderungzeit. Berlin 2008.
S. Fischer, The Material Culture of Fifth-Century Returning Veterans, in: C. Fabech/U.
    Näsman (eds.), The Sösdala Horsemen and the Equestrian Elite of Fifth-Century
    Europe. Aarhus 2017, 313–27.

A. Gillett, Love and Grief in Post-imperial Diplomacy. The Letters of Brunhild, in: B. Sidwell/D. Dzino (eds.), Studies in Emotions and Power in the Late Roman World. Piscataway 2010, 127–65.

W. Goffart, Byzantine Policy in the West under Tiberius II and Maurice. The Pretenders Hermenegild and Gundovald (579–85), in: Traditio 13, 1957, 73–118.

D. Green, The Carolingian Lord. Semantic Studies on Four Old High German Words. Balder, Frô, Truhtin, Hêrro. Cambridge 1965.

P. J. Heather, The Crossing of the Danube and the Gothic Conversion, in: GRBS 27, 1986, 289–318.

P. J. Heather, Goths and Romans 332–489. Oxford 1991.

P. J. Heather, Rome Resurgent. War and Empire in the Age of Justinian. Oxford 2018; German trans. Die letzte Blüte Roms. Das Zeitalter Justinians. Darmstadt 2019.

P. J. Heather/J. Matthews, The Goths in the Fourth Century. Liverpool 1991.

L. Hedeager, Iron Age to State in Northern Europe, 500 BC to AD 700. Oxford 1992.

J. Herrin, Constantinople and the Treatment of Hostages, Refugees and Exiles during Late Antiquity, in: Constantinople réelle et imaginaire. Autour de l'œuvre de Gilbert Dagron. Travaux et mémoire. Paris 2018, 739–58.

M. Kulikowski, Barbarians in Gaul, Usurpers in Britain, in: Britannia 31, 2000, 325–45; German trans. in 4.5: Kulikowski.

M. Kulikowski, Rome's Gothic Wars. From the Third Century to Alaric. Cambridge 2007; German trans. Die Goten vor Rom. Darmstadt 2009.

A. D. Lee, Information and Frontiers. Roman Foreign Relations in Late Antiquity. Cambridge 1993.

R. W. Mathisen, Barbarian Invasions or Civil Wars? Goths as Auxiliary Forces in the Roman Army, in: F. Mitthof/G. Martin/J. Gruskova (eds.), Empire in Crisis. Gothic Invasions and Roman Historiography. Vienna 2020, 263–86.

R. W. Mathisen/H. Sivan (eds.), Shifting Frontiers in Late Antiquity. Papers from the First Interdisciplinary Conference on Late Antiquity. Aldershot 1996.

W. Pohl/I. Wood/H. Reimitz (eds.), The Transformation of Frontiers. From Late Antiquity to the Carolingians. Leiden 2000.

A. G. Poulter, The Transition to Late Antiquity on the Danube and Beyond. Oxford 2007.

G. Ripoll Lopez, On the Supposed Frontier between the Regnum Visigothorum and Byzantine Hispania, in: 11.1: Pohl/Wood/Reimitz, 95–116.

C. R. Whittaker, Frontiers of the Roman Empire. A Social and Economic Study. Baltimore 1994.

H. Wolfram, Das Reich und die Germanen. Berlin 1990.

H. Wolfram, Das Römerreich und seine Germanen. Eine Erzählung von Herkunft und Ankunft. Vienna 2018.

I. N. Wood, The Frontiers of western Europe. Developments East of the Rhine in the Sixth Century, in: R. Hodges/W. Bowden (eds.), The Sixth Century. Production, Distribution and Demand. Leiden 1998, 231–53.

11.2 Barbarian Numbers and Destruction

H. Börm, Westrom. Von Honorius bis Justinian. 2nd edition. Stuttgart 2018.

C. Delaplace, La fin de l'Empire romain d'Occident. Rome et les wisigoths de 382 à 531. Rennes 2015.

W. Goffart, Barbarians and Romans, A. D. 418–584. The Techniques of Accommodation. Princeton 1980.

W. Goffart, Barbarian Tides. The Migration Age and the Later Roman Empire. Philadelphia 2006.

G. Halsall, Movers and Shakers. The Barbarians and the Fall of Rome, in: Early Medieval Europe 8, 1999, 131–45.

P. Heather, The Fall of the Roman Empire. A New History of Rome and the Barbarians. Oxford 2005.

P. Heather, Empires and Barbarians. Migration, Development and the Birth of Europe. London 2009.

P. Heather, Empires and Barbarians. The Fall of Rome and the Birth of Europe. Oxford 2010.

M. Meier, Das andere Zeitalter Justinians. Kontingenzerfahrung und Kontingenzbewältigung im 6. Jahrhundert n. Chr. Göttingen 2003.

B. Ward-Perkins, The Fall of Rome and the End of Civilization. Oxford 2005.

C. Wickham, Framing the Early Middle Ages. Europe and the Mediterranean, 400–800. Oxford 2005.

I. Wood, The Transformation of the Roman West. Leeds 2018.

I. Wood, Responses to Migration and Migrants in the Fifth- and Sixth-Century West, in: Settimane di Studio, 66, Le migrazioni nell'alto medioevo. Spoleto 2019, 177–203.

11.3 Huns

B. Anke/H. Externbrink (eds.), Attila und die Hunnen. Stuttgart 2007.

R. Blockley, The Fragmentary Classicising Historians of the Later Roman Empire, vol. 2. Liverpool 1983.

I. Bóna, Das Hunnenreich. Budapest 1991.

E. Bozoky, Attila et les Huns. Vérités et legends. Paris 2012.

F. Daim (ed.), Hunnen und Awaren. Reitervölker aus dem Osten. Eisenstadt 1996.

N. Di Cosmo/M. Maas (eds.), Empires and Exchanges in Eurasian Late Antiquity. Rome, China, Iran, and the Steppe, ca. 250–750. Cambridge 2018.

C. D. Gordon, The Age of Attila. Fifth-Century Byzantium and the Barbarians. Ann Arbor 1966.

P. Heather, The Huns and the End of the Roman Empire in Western Europe, in: EHR 110, 1995, 5–41.

C. Kelly, Attila the Hun. Barbarian Terror and the Fall of the Roman Empire. London 2008.

H. J. Kim, The Huns. New York 2016.

J. Linn, Attila's Appetite. The Logistics of Attila the Hun's Invasion of Italy in 452, in: The Journal of Military History 83-2, 2019, 325–46.

M. Maas (ed.), The Cambridge Companion to the Age of Attila. Cambridge 2014.

O. J. Maenchen-Helfen, The World of the Huns. Studies in Their History and Culture. Berkeley 1973.

M. Meier, Die Spätantike, zeitlich und räumlich neu gefasst. Eine Zwischenbilanz aktueller Suchbewegungen, in: HZ 34, 2017, 686–706.

W. Menghin/T. Springer/E. Warmers, Germanen, Hunnen und Awaren. Die Archäologie des 5. und 6. Jahrhunderts an der mittleren Donau und der östlich-merowingische Reihengräberkreis. Schätze der Völkerwanderungszeit. Nürnberg 1987.

K. Rosen, Attila. Der Schrecken der Welt. Munich 2016.

M. Schmauder, Die Hunnen. Ein Reitervolk in Europa. Darmstadt 2009.

D. Sinor (ed.), The Cambridge History of Early Inner Asia. Cambridge 1990.

K. Szende, Stadt und Naturlandschaft im ungarischen Donauraum des Mittelalters, in: F. Opil/C. Sonnlechner (eds.), Europäische Städte im Mittelalter. Innsbruck 2010, 365–400.

E. A. Thompson, A History of Attila and the Huns. Oxford 1948, reissued: The Huns, Oxford 1996.

11.4 Settlement

W. Goffart, Barbarians and Romans, A. D. 418–584. The Techniques of Accommodation. Princeton 1980.

P. Porena/Y. Rivière (eds.), Expropriations et confiscations dans les royaumes barbares. Rome 2013.

H. Wolfram/A. Schwarcz (eds.), Anerkennung und Integration. Zu den wirtschaftlichen Grundlagen der Völkerwanderungszeit, 400–600. Vienna 1988.

I. N. Wood, The Barbarian Invasions and First Settlements, in: 4.1: Cameron/Garnsey, 516–37.

12 The Successor States

12.1 General Comments

S. Airlie/W. Pohl/H. Reimitz (eds.), Staat im frühen Mittelalter. Vienna 2006.

J. Arnold/S. Bjornlie/K. Sessa (eds.), The Brill Companion to Ostrogothic Italy. Leiden 2018.

J. J. Arnold, Theodoric and the Roman Imperial Restoration. Cambridge 2014.

B. S. Bachrach, Merovingian Military Organisation, 481–751. Minneapolis 1972.

S. Barnish, Taxation, Land and Barbarian Settlement in the Western Empire, in: Papers of the British School at Rome 54, 1986, 170–95.

P. Barnwell, Emperors, Prefects and Kings. The Roman West, 395–565. London 1992.

P. Barnwell, Kings, Courtiers and Imperium. The Barbarian West, 565–725. London 1997.

M. S. Bjornlie, Politics and Tradition between Rome, Ravenna and Constantinople. Cambridge 2013.

M. S. Bjornlie, Law, Ethnicity and Taxes in Ostrogothic Italy. A Case for Continuity, Adaptation and Departure, in: Early Medieval Europe 22, 2014, 138–70.

H. Börm, Westrom. Von Honorius bis Justinian, 2nd ed. Stuttgart 2018.

T. S. Burns, Barbarians within the Gates of Rome. A Study of Roman Military Policy and the Barbarians, ca. 375–425 A. D. Bloomington 1994.

A. Cameron/B. Ward-Perkins/M. Whitby (eds.), The Cambridge Ancient History, vol. 14: Late Antiquity, Empire and Successors, A. D. 425–600. Cambridge 2000.

S. Castellanos, The Political Nature of Taxation in Visigothic Spain, in: Early Medieval Europe 12, 2003, 201–28.

D. Claude, Untersuchungen zum frühfränkischen Comitat, in: ZRG GA 81, 1964, 1–79.

M. Eisenberg/P. Tedesco, Seeing the Churches like the State: Taxes and Wealth Distribution in Early Medieval Italy, in: Early Medieval Europe 29, 2021, 505–34.

S. Esders/Y. Hen/P. Lucas/T. Rotman (eds.), The Merovingian Kingdoms and the Mediterranean World. Revisiting the Sources. London 2019.

A. Fischer/I. Wood (eds.), Western Perspectives on the Mediterranean. Cultural Transfer in Late Antiquity and the Early Middle Ages. London 2014.

P. Fouracre (ed.), The New Cambridge Medieval History, vol. 1: c. 500–c. 700. Cambridge 2005.

A. Gillett, Envoys and Political Communication in the Late Antique West, 411–533. Oxford 2003.

H.-W. Goetz/J. Jarnut/W. Pohl (eds.), Regna and Gentes. Leiden 2003.

W. Goffart, Caput and Colonate. Towards a History of Late Roman Taxation. Toronto 1974.

W. Goffart, Frankish Military Duty and the Fate of Roman Taxation, in: Early Medieval Europe 16, 2008, 166–90.

W. Goffart, Rome's Fall and After. London 1989.

G. Halsall, The Ostrogothic Military, in: 12.1: Arnold/Bjornlie/Sessa, 257–97.

G. Halsall, Warfare and Society in the Barbarian West, 450–900. London 2003.

Y. Hen, Food and Drink in Merovingian Gaul, in: B. Kasten (ed.), Tätigkeitsfelder und Erfahrungshorizonte des ländlichen Menschen in der frühmittelalterlichen Grundherrschaft (bis ca. 1000). Cologne 2006, 99–110.

Y. Hen, Roman Barbarians. The Royal Court in the Early Medieval West. London 2007.

J. Jarnut, Anmerkungen zum Staat des Mittelalters. Die Kontoverse zwischen Johannes Fried und Hans-Werner Goetz, in: 11: Dilcher/Distler, 197–202.

N. Lenski, Schiavi armati e formazione del esceriti privati nell mondo tardoantico, in: G. Urso (ed.), Ordine e sovversione nell mondo greco e romano. Pisa 2009, 145–75.

J. H. W. G. Liebeschuetz, The End of the Roman Army in the Western Empire, in: J. Rich/G. Shipley (eds.), War and Society in the Roman World. London 1993, 265–76.

G. Maier, Amtsträger und Herrscher in der Romania-Gothica. Vergleichende Untersuchungen zu den Institutionen der ostgermanischen Völkerwanderungsreiche. Stuttgart 2005.

A. C. Murray, The Position of the Grafio in the Constitutional History of Merovingian Gaul, in: Speculum 61, 1986, 787–805.

A. C. Murray, From Roman to Frankish Gaul. "Centenarii" and "Centenae" in the Administration of the Merovingian Kingdom, in: Traditio 44, 1988, 59–100.

P. Paolucci (ed.), Anthimi epistolae de observatione ciborum ad Theodoricum regem Francorum concordantiae. Hildesheim 2003.

W. Pohl/V. Wieser (eds.), Der frühmittelalterliche Staat. Europäische Perspektiven. Vienna 2009.

G. Ripoll/J. Gurt (eds.), Sedes regiae (ann. 400–800). Barcelona 2000.

F. Vallet/M. Kazanski (eds.), L'armée romaine et les barbares du IIIe au VIIe siècle. Rouen 1993.

J. M. Wallace-Hadrill, Early Germanic Kingship in England and on the Continent. Oxford 1971.

D. Whittaker, Landlords and Warlords in the Later Roman Empire, in: J. Rich/G. Shipley (eds.), War and Society in the Roman World. London 1993, 277–302.

C. Wickham, Land and Power. Studies in Italian and European Social History, 400–1200. London 1994.

H. Wolfram, Intitulatio I. Lateinische Königs- und Fürstentitel bis zum Ende des 8. Jahrhunderts. Vienna 1967.

I. Wood, A Byzantine Commonwealth, 476–533, in: W. Pohl/M. Diesenberger/B. Zeller (eds.), Neue Wege der Frühmittelalterforschung. Bilanz und Perspektiven. Vienna 2018, 65–74.

J. Wood/M. Eisenberg/P. Tedesco (eds.), Approaching the Early Medieval Iberian Economy from the ground up, Special Issue, Al-Masaq, Journal of the Medieval Mediterranean 35, 2023.

M. Zerjadtke, Das Amt "Dux" in Spätantike und frühem Mittelalter. Berlin 2019.

12.2 Odoacer

M. Cesa, Il regno di Odoacre. La prima dominazione germanica in Italia, in: B. Scardigli/P. Scardigli (eds.), Germani in Italia. Roma 1994, 307–20.

A. Chastagnol, Le senat romain sous le regne d'Odoacer. Recherches sur l'épigraphie du Colisée au 5e siècle. Bonn 1966.

A. H. M. Jones, The Constitutional Position of Odoacer and Theoderic, in: JRS 52, 1962, 126–30.

A. La Rocca/F. Oppedisano, Il senato romano nell'Italia Ostrogotha. Rome 2016.

P. MacGeorge, Late Roman Warlords. Oxford 2002.

M. McCormick, Odoacer, Emperor Zeno, and the Rugian Victory Legation, in: Byzantion 47, 1977, 212–22.

12.3 Visigoths

J. Arce, Esperando a los árabes. Los visigodos en Hispania (507–711). Madrid 2011.

J. Arce, The Visigoths in Hispania. New Perspectives on their Arrival and Settlement, in: S. Panzram/P. Pachá (eds.), Visigothic Spain. The Negotiation of Power in Post-Roman Iberia. Amsterdam 2020, 59–78.

R. Barroso Cabrera/J. Morín de Pablos/I. Sánchez Ramos, Gallaecia Gothica. De la conspiración del Dux Argimundus (589-590 d. C.) a la integración en el Reino visigodo de Toledo. Toledo 2015.

L. Bourgeois (ed.), Franks et wisigoths autour de la bataille de Vouillé (507). Paris 2010.

V. Burns, The Visigothic Settlement in Aquitania. Imperial Motives, in: Historia 41, 1992, 362–73.

C. Cardelle de Hartmann (ed.), Victoris Tunnunensis Chronicon cum reliquiis ex Consularibus Caesaraugustanis et Iohannis Biclarensis Chronicon. Turnhout 2001.

S. Castellanos, The Visigothic Kingdom in Iberia. Construction and Invention. Philadelphia 2020.

R. Collins, Visigothic Spain 409–711. Oxford 2004.

W. Drews, Hermenegild's Rebellion and Conversion. Merovingian and Byzantine Connections, in: 3: Esders/Fox/Hen/Sarti, 74–86.

A. Ferreiro, The Visigoths in Gaul and Spain A. D. 418–711. A Bibliography. Leiden 1988.

A. Ferreiro, The Visigoths in Gaul and Iberia. A Supplemental Bibliography, 1984–2003. Leiden 2006.

A. Ferreiro, The Visigoths in Gaul and Iberia (Update). A Supplemental Bibliography, 2004–2006. Leiden 2008.

A. Ferreiro, The Visigoths in Gaul and Iberia (Update). A Supplemental Bibliography, 2007–2009. Leiden 2011.

A. Ferreiro, The Visigoths in Gaul and Iberia (Update). A Supplemental Bibliography, 2010–2012. Leiden 2014.

A. Ferreiro, The Visigoths in Gaul and Iberia (Update). A Supplemental Bibliography, 2013–2015. Leiden 2017.

V. Gheller, "Identità" e "arianesimo gotico". Genesi di un topos storiografico. Bologna 2017.

W. Giese, Die Goten. Stuttgart 2004.

A. Gillett, Envoys and Political Communication in the Late Antique West, 411–533. Oxford 2003, 138–43.

A. Gillett, The Accession of Euric, in: Francia 26/1, 1999, 1–40.

J. Harries, Sidonius Apollinaris and the Fall of Rome. Oxford 1994.

P. Heather, Goths and Romans 332–489. Oxford 1991.

P. Heather (ed.), The Visigoths from the Migration Period to the Seventh Century. Woodbridge 1999.

J. N. Hillgarth, Coins and Chronicles. Propaganda in Sixth-century Spain and the Byzantine Background, in: Historia 15, 1966, 483–508.

G. Kampers, Geschichte der Westgoten. Paderborn 2008.

W. E. Klingshirn, Caesarius of Arles. The Making of a Christian Community in Late Antique Gaul. Cambridge 1994.

M. Koch, Ethnische Identität im Entstehungsprozess des spanischen Westgotenreiches. Berlin 2012.

J. C. Martín, Isidori Hispalensis Chronica. Turnhout 2003.

R. Mathisen, The Settlement of the Visigoths in Aquitaine, 418 or 419?, in: Revue des Études tardo-antiques 7, 2018, 277–82.

R. Mathisen/D. Shanzer (eds.), The Battle of Vouillé, 507 CE. Where France Began. Boston/Berlin 2012.

Th. Mommsen (ed.), Monumenta Germaniae Historica, Auctores Antiquissimi XI. Munich 1981.

J. Orlandis, Historia del Reino Visigodo Español. Madrid 1988.

S. Panzram/P. Pachá (eds.), Visigothic Spain. The Negotiation of Power in Post-Roman Iberia. Amsterdam 2020.

M. Rouche/B. Dumézil (eds.), Le Bréviaire d'Alaric. Aux origins du Code civil. Paris 2009.

M. Sánchez (ed.), Vitas sanctorum patrum Emeretensium. Turnhout 1992.

R. Scharf, Der spanische Kaiser Maximus und die Ansiedlung der Westgoten in Aquitanien, in: Historia 41, 1992, 374–84.

A. Schwarcz, The Visigothic Settlement in Aquitaine. Chronology and Archaeology, in: 10: Mathisen/Shanzer, 15–25.

C. Stadermann, "Gothus". Konstruktion und Rezeption von Gotenbilden in narrativen Schriften des merowingischen Gallien. Stuttgart 2017.

K. F. Stroheker, Eurich, König der Westgoten. Stuttgart 1937.

K. F. Stroheker, Leovigild, in: K. F. Stroheker, Germanentum und Spätantike. Zürich/Stuttgart 1965, 134–91.

E. A. Thompson, The Visigoths in the Time of Ulfila. Oxford 1966.

E. A. Thompson, The Goths in Spain. Oxford 1969.

E. A. Thompson, Romans and Barbarians. The Decline of the Roman Empire. Madison 1982

Visigothic Symposia, https://visigothicsymposia.org (12.01.2023).

J. Vives, Concilios Visigóticos e Hispano-Romanos. Barcelona 1963.

H. Wolfram, Geschichte der Goten. Munich 1979, English trans. History of the Goths. Berkeley 1979.

I. N. Wood, Les wisigoths et la question arienne, in: 12.3: Bourgeois, 19–22; English version: Arians, Catholics, and Vouillé, in: 12.3: Mathisen/Shanzer, 139–49.

J. Wood, Defending Byzantine Spain. Frontiers and Diplomacy, in: Early Medieval Europe 18, 2010, 292–319.

12.4 Vandals

Association pour l'Antiquité Tardive (ed.), Antiquité Tardive, L'Afrique vandale et byzantine, 2 vols., 10–11, 2003–4.

G. Berndt, Hidden Tracks. On the Vandals' Paths to an African Kingdom, in: F. Curta (ed.), Neglected Barbarians. Turnhout 2010, 537–69.

G. Berndt, Konflikt und Anpassung. Studien zu Migration und Ethnogenese der Vandalen. Husum 2007.

G. Berndt/R. Steinacher (eds.), Das Reich der Vandalen und seine (Vor-)Geschichten. Vienna 2008.

M. Brett/E. Fentress, The Berbers. Oxford 1996.

H. Castritius, Die Vandalen. Etappen einer Spurensuche. Stuttgart 2007.

F. M. Clover, The Late Roman West and the Vandals. Aldershot 1993.

J. Conant, Staying Roman. Conquest and Identity in Africa and the Mediterranean, 439–700. Cambridge 2012.

C. Courtois/L. Leschi/C. Perrat/C. Saumagne, Tablettes Albertini. Actes privés de l'époque vandale (fin du Ve siècle), 2 vols. Paris 1952.

C. Courtois, Les Vandales et l'Afrique. Algiers 1955.

H.-J. Diesner, Das Vandalenreich. Aufstieg und Untergang. Stuttgart/Berlin/Cologne/ Mainz 1966.

E. Fentress, Romanizing the Berbers, in: P & P 190, 2006, 3–33.

J. Fraipont (ed.), Fulgence de Ruspe, Lettres ascetiques et morales. Paris 2004.

P. J. Heather, Christianity and the Vandals in the Reign of Geiseric, in: Bulletin of the Institute of Classical Studies 50, 2007, 137–146.

T. Howe, Vandalen, Barbaren und Arianer bei Victor von Vita. Frankfurt am Main 2007.

A. Isola (ed.), Anonymus, Vita S. Fulgentii episcopi. Turnhout 2016.

N. M. Kay (ed.), Epigrams from the Anthologia Latina. London 2013.

S. Lancel (ed.), Victor de Vita: Histoire de la persécution vandale en Afrique suivie de La passion des sept martyrs. Registre des provinces et des cités d'Afrique. Paris 2002.

A. H. Merrills. War. Rebellion and Epic in Byzantine North Africa. A Historical Study of Corippus' Ionannis. Cambridge 2023.

A. H. Merrills (ed.), Vandals, Romans and Berbers. New Perspectives on Late Antique North Africa. London 2004.

A. H. Merrills/R. Miles, The Vandals. Oxford 2010.

Y. Modéran, Les maures et l'Afrique romaine. IVe–VIIe siècle. Rome 2003.

J. Moorhead (trans.), Victor of Vita: History of the Vandal Persecution. Liverpool 1992.

A. Schwarcz, Religion und ethnische Identität im Vandalenreich. Überlegungen zur Religionspolitik der vandalischen Könige, in: 12.4: Berndt/Steinacher, 227–31.

K. Vössing (ed.), Victor von Vita: Kirchenkampf und Verfolgung unter den Vandalen in Africa. Historia persecutionis Africanae provinciae temporum Geiserici et Hunerici regum Wandalorum. Darmstadt 2011.

K. Vössing, Die Vandalen. Munich 2018.

H. Wessel, Das Recht der Tablettes Albertini. Berlin 2003.

R. Whelan, Being Christian in Vandal Africa. The Politics of Orthodoxy in the Post-Imperial West. Berkeley 2018.

12.5 Alans and Sueves

A. Alemany, Sources on the Alans. A Critical Compilation. Leiden 2000.

J. Arce, Bárbaros y Romanos en Hispania (400–507 A. D.). Madrid 2005.

B. Bachrach, A History of the Alans in the West from their Appearance in the Sources of Classical Antiquity through the Early Middle Ages. Minneapolis 1973.

C. W. Barlow (ed.), Martini episcopi Bracarensis opera omnia. New Haven 1950.

R. W. Burgess (ed. and trans.), The Chronicle of Hydatius and the Consularia Constantinopolitana. Oxford 1993.

P. C. Díaz Martínez, El reino suevo (411–585). Madrid 2011.

A. Gillett, Envoys and Political Communication in the Late Antique West, 411–533. Cambridge 2003, 36–83.

J. López Quiroga (ed.), In tempore Sueborum. El tiempo de los Suevos en la Gallaecia (411–585). Volumen de Estudios. Ourense 2018.

J. López Quiroga/A. M. Martínez Tejera (eds.), In tempore Sueborum. El tiempo de los Suevos en la Gallaecia (411–585). El primer reino medieval de Occidente. Ourense 2017; English trans. In tempore Sueborum. The Time of the Sueves in Gallaecia (411–585 AD). The First Medieval Kingdom of the West. Ourense 2017; Galician trans.: In tempore Sueborum. O tempo dos Suevos na Gallaecia (411–585). El primeiro reino medieval de Occidente. Ourense 2017).

E. A. Thompson, Romans and Barbarians. The Decline of the Roman Empire. Madison 1982.

E. A. Thompson, The Conversion of the Spanish Suevi to Catholicism, in: E. James (ed.), The Visigoths. New Approaches. Oxford 1980, 77–92.

J. Vives, Concilios Visigóticos e Hispano-Romanos. Barcelona 1963.

12.6 Alamans

R. Christlein, Die Alamannen. Archäologie eines lebendigen Volkes. Stuttgart 1978.

J. Drinkwater, The Alamanni and Rome 213–496. Caracalla to Clovis. Oxford 2007.

K. Fuchs/M. Kempa/R. Redies (eds.), Die Alamannen. Ausstellungskatalog. Stuttgart 1997.

D. Geuenich (ed.), Die Franken und die Alemannen bis zur "Schlacht bei Zülpich" (496/97). Berlin 1998.

H. J. Hummer, The Fluidity of Barbarian Identity. The Ethnogenesis of Alemanni and Suebi, AD 200–500, in: Early Medieval Europe 7, 1998, 1–27.

H.-P. Naumann (ed.), Alemannien und der Norden. Berlin 2004.

F. Siegmund, Alamannen und Franken. Berlin 2000.

C. Theune, Germanen und Romanen in der Alamannia. Strukturveränderungen aufgrund der archäologischen Quellen vom 3. bis zum 7. Jahrhundert. Berlin 2004.

I. Wood (ed.), Franks and Alamanni in the Merovingian Period. An Ethnographic Perspective. Woodbridge 1998.

12.7 Franks

B. S. Bachrach, The Anatomy of a Little War. A Diplomatic and Military History of the Gundovald Affair (568–586). Boulder 1994.

M. Becher, Chlodwig I. Der Aufstieg der Merowinger und das Ende der Antiken Welt. Munich 2011.

L. Bourgeois (ed.), Franks et Wisigoths autour de la bataille de Vouillé (507). Paris 2010.

B. Dumézil, La reine Brunehaut. Paris 2008.

R. Collins, Theodebert I, "Rex Magnus Francorum", in: P. Wormald (ed.), Ideal and Reality in Frankish and Anglo-Saxon Society. Oxford 1983, 7–33.

M. Coumert, La Loi salique: retour aux manuscrits. Turnhout, 2023.

K. A. Eckhardt (ed.), Pactus Legis Salicae. Hannover 1962.

B. Effros, Merovingian Mortuary Archaeology and the Making of the Early Middle Ages. Berkeley 2003.

B. Effros/I. Moreira, The Oxford Handbook of the Merovingian World. Oxford 2020.

E. Ewig, Die fränkischen Teilungen und Teilreiche (511–613), in: E. Ewig, Spätantikes und fränkisches Gallien, vol. 1. Munich 1976a, 114–71.

E. Ewig, Die fränkischen Teilreiche im 7. Jahrhundert (613–714), in: E. Ewig, Spätantikes und fränkisches Gallien, vol. 1. Munich 1976b, 172–230.

E. Ewig, Die Merowinger und das Frankenreich. Stuttgart 1988.

H. Fehr, Germanen und Romanen im Merowingerreich. Berlin 2010.

Y. Fox, Power and Religion in Merovingian Gaul. Columbanian Monasticism and the Frankish Elites. Cambridge 2014.

J. Gaudemet/B. Basdevant, Les canons des conciles mérovingiens (VIe–VIIe siècles). Paris 1989.

N. Gauthier/H. Galinié (eds.), Grégoire de Tours et l'espace gaulois. Tours 1997.

P. Geary, Before France and Germany. The Creation and Transformation of the Merovingian World. Oxford 1988.

D. Geuenich (ed.), Die Franken und die Alemannen bis zur "Schlacht bei Zülpich" (496/97). Berlin 1998.

W. Goffart, The Frankish Pretender Gundovald, 582–585. A Crisis of Merovingian Blood, in: Francia 39, 2012, 1–27.

G. Halfond, The Archaeology of the Frankish Church Councils, AD 511–768. Leiden 2009.

G. Halsall, Cemeteries and Society in Merovingian Gaul. Selected Studies in History and Archaeology, 1992–2009. Leiden 2010.

M. Hartmann, Aufbruch ins Mittelalter. Die Zeit der Merowinger. Darmstadt 2003.

E. James, The Franks. Oxford 1988.

R. Kaiser, Das römische Erbe und das Merowingerreich. Munich 1993.

E. Magnou-Nortier, Remarques sur la genèse du Pactus Legis Salicae et sur le privilège d'immunité (IVe–VIIe siècles), in: M. Rouche (ed.), Clovis. Histoire et Mémoire, vol. 1. Paris 1977, 495–538.

R. Mathisen/D. Shanzer (eds.), The Battle of Vouillé, 507 CE. Where France Began. Boston/Berlin 2012.

M. Meier/S. Patzold (eds.), Chlodwigs Welt. Organisation von Herrschaft um 500. Stuttgart 2014.

C. Mériaux, La naissance de la France. Les royaumes francs (Vᵉ–VIIᵉ siècles). Paris 2014.

K. Mitchell/I. Wood (eds.), The World of Gregory of Tours. Leiden 2002.

A. C. Murray (ed.), A Companion to Gregory of Tours. Leiden 2015.

O. Pontal, Die Synoden im Merowingerreich. Paderborn 1986.

O. Pontal, Histoire des conciles mérovingiens. Paris 1989.

D. Quast (ed.), Das Grab des fränkischen Königs Childerich in Tournai und die Anastasis Childerici von Jean-Jacques Chifflet aus dem Jahre 1655. Mainz 2015.

S. Quesnel (ed.), Venance Fortunat, Vie de saint Martin. Paris 1996.

M. Reydellet (ed.), Venance Fortunat, Poèmes, 3 vols. Paris 1994–2004.

M. Rouche (ed.), Clovis, histoire et mémoire. Actes du Congrès international d'histoire de Reims, 19–25 septembre 1996, 2 vols. Paris 1997.

S. Scholz, Die Merowinger. Stuttgart 2015.

D. Shanzer, Dating the Baptism of Clovis. The Bishop of Vienne vs the Bishop of Tours, in: Early Medieval Europe 7, 1998, 29–57.

F. Siegmund, Alamannen und Franken. Berlin 2000.

K. Ubl, Sinnstiftungen eines Rechtsbuchs. Die Lex Salica im Frankenreich. Ostfildern 2017.

M. Weidemann, Kulturgeschichte der Merowingerzeit nach den Werken Gregors von Tours. Bonn 1982.

A. Wieczorek/P. Périn/K. von Welck/W. Menghin (eds.), Die Franken. Wegbereiter Europas. 5. bis 8. Jahrhundert, 2 vols. Mainz 1996–1997.

I. Wood, Gregory of Tours and Clovis, in: Revue Belge de Philologie et d'Histoire 63, 1985, 249–72, repr. in: L. K. Little/B. H. Rosenwein (eds.), Debating Middle Ages. Blackwell 1998, 73–91.

I. Wood, Gregory of Tours. Bangor 1994.

I. Wood, The Merovingian Kingdoms, 450–751. London 1994.

I. Wood (ed.), Franks and Alamanni in the Merovingian Period. An Ethnographic Perspective. Woodbridge 1998.

E. Zöllner, Geschichte der Franken bis zum Mitte des 6. Jahrhunderts. Munich 1970.

12.8 Burgundians

P. Amory, The Meaning and Purpose of Ethnic Terminology in the Burgundian Laws, in: Early Medieval Europe 2, 1993, 1–28.

P. Amory, Names, Ethnic Identity and Community in Fifth- and Sixth-Century Burgundy, in: Viator 25, 1994, 1–30.

R. de Salis (ed.), Leges Burgundionum. Hannover 1892.

H. G. de Semainville (ed.), Les Burgondes. Apports de l'Archéologie. Dijon 1995.

M. Eisenberg, A New Name for a New State. The Construction of the Burgundian *Regio*, in: J. W. Drijvers/N. Lenski (eds.), The Fifth Century: Age of Transition. Proceedings of the 12 Biennial Shifting Frontiers in Late Antiquity Conference. Bari 2019, 157–67.

K. Escher, Genèse et évolution du deuxième royaume burgonde (443–534). Les témoins archéologiques, 2 vols. Oxford 2005.

J. Favrod (ed./trans.), La Chronique de Marius d'Avenches 455–581. Lausanne 1993.

J. Favrod, Histoire politique du royaume burgonde (443–534). Lausanne 1997.

D. G. Frye, Gundobad, the Leges Burgundionum and the Struggle for Sovereignty in Burgundy, in: CM 14, 1990, 199–212.

V. Gallé (ed.), Die Burgunder, Ethnogenese und Assimilation eines Volkes. Worms 2008.

J. Gaudemet/B. Basdevant, Les canons des conciles mérovingiens (VIe–VIIe siècles). Paris 1989.

P. Heather, Law and Society in the Burgundian Kingdom, in: A. Rio (ed.), Law, Custom and Justice in Late Antiquity and the Early Middle Ages. London 2011, 115–53.

M. Innes, Land, Freedom, and the Making of the Medieval West, in: TRHS, 6th series, 16, 2006, 39–74.

R. Kaiser, Die Burgunder. Stuttgart 2004.

E. Malaspina, Avit de Vienne, Lettres. Paris 2016.

B. Saitta, I Burgundi (413–534). Rome 2006.

D. Shanzer, Two Clocks and a Wedding. Theodoric's Diplomatic Relations with the Burgundians, in: Romanobarbarica 14, 1996, 225–58.

D. Shanzer/I. Wood, Avitus of Vienne, Letters and Selected Prose. Liverpool 2002.

A. Wagner/N. Brocard (eds.), Les royaumes de Bourgogne jusque 1032 à travers la culture et la religion. Turnhout 2018.

I. Wood, Ethnicity and the Ethnogenesis of the Burgundians, in: H. Wolfram/W. Pohl (eds.), Typen der Ethnogenese unter besonderer Berücksichtigung der Bayern. Vienna 1990, 53–69.

I. Wood, The Political Structure of the Burgundian Kingdom, in: 12.7: Meier/Patzold, 383–96.

I. Wood, The Legislation of Magistri Militum. The Laws of Gundobad and Sigismund, in: La forge du droit. Naissance des identités juridiques en Europe (IVe–XIIIe siècles), Clio@Themis, 10. March 2016, http://www.cliothemis.com, available via https://journals.openedition.org/cliothemis/1191 (05.06.2024).

I. Wood, The Making of "the Burgundian kingdom", in: Reti Medievali Rivista 22, 2, 2021, 111–40.

I. Wood, Burgundian Law-making, 451–534, in: Italian Review of Legal History 3, 2017, 1–27.

I. Wood, Roman Barbarians in the Burgundian Province, in: 11: Pohl/Gantner/Grifoni/Pollheimer-Mohaupt, 275–88.

12.9 Ostrogoths

P. Amory, People and Identity in Ostrogothic Italy, 489–554. Cambridge 1997.

J. J. Arnold, Theodoric and the Roman Imperial Restoration. Cambridge 2014.

J. J. Arnold/M. S. Bjornlie/K. Sessa (eds.), A Companion to Ostrogothic Italy. Leiden 2016.

S. J. BARNISH/F. MARAZZI (eds.), The Ostrogoths from the Migration Period to the Sixth Century. Woodbridge 2007.

M. S. BJORNLIE, Politics and Tradition between Rome, Ravenna and Constantinople. A Study of Cassiodorus and the Variae, 527–554. Cambridge 2013.

K. BLAIR-DIXON, Memory and Authority in Sixth-Century Rome. The *Liber Pontificalis* and the Collectio Avellana, in: 7: COOPER/HILLNER, 59–76.

H. BÖRM, Westrom. Von Honorius bis Justinian, 2nd. ed. Stuttgart 2013.

B. CROKE, The Chronicle of Marcellinus. A Translation and Commentary. Sydney 1995.

R. DAVIES (trans.), The Book of Pontiffs, 3 vols. Liverpool 1989–95.

F. W. DEICHMANN, Ravenna, Hauptstadt des Abendlandes, 5 vols. Wiesbaden 1969–76.

H. DEY/F. OPPEDISANO, Justinian's Legacy – l'Eredità di Giustiniano. The Last War of Roman Italy – l'Ultima Guerra dell'Italia Romana. Rome 2024.

L. DUCHESNE (ed.), Liber Pontificalis, texte, introduction et commentaire, 2 vols. Paris 1886–92.

A. GIARDINA (ed.), Le Varie di Cassiodoro. Testo, apparato critico, traduzione italiana, commentario, 6 vols. Rome 2014–20.

S. GIOANNI (ed.), ENNODE DE PAVIE, Lettres, 2 vols. Paris 2006–10.

A. GOLTZ, Barbar – König – Tyrann. Das Bild Theoderichs des Großen in der Überlieferung des 5. bis 9. Jahrhunderts. Berlin 2008.

O. GUENTHER (ed.), Epistolae Imperatorum Pontificum Aliorum Inde ab a. CCCLXVII usque DLIII datae Avellana Quae Dicitur Collectio. Vienna 1895.

P. HEATHER, Goths and Romans 332–489. Oxford 1991.

I. HUGHES, Belisarius: The Last Roman General. Yardley 2009.

S. A. H. KENNELL, Magnus Felix Ennodius. A Gentleman of the Church. Ann Arbor 2000.

I. KÖNIG, Aus der Zeit Theoderichs des Großen. Einleitung, Text, Übersetzung und Kommentar einer anonymen Quelle. Darmstadt 1997.

I. KÖNIG (ed.), Edictum Theoderici regis. Darmstadt 2018.

A. LA ROCCA/F. OPPEDISANO, Il senato romano nell'Italia Ostrogotha. Rome 2016.

S. LAFFERTY, Law and Society in the Age of Theoderic the Great. A Study of the Edictum Theoderici. Cambridge 2013.

R. LIZZI TESTA/G. MARCONI, The Collectio Avellana and its Revivals. Cambridge 2019.

M. MAAS (ed.), The Cambridge Companion to the Age of Justinian. Cambridge 2005.

D. MAUSKOPF DELIYANNIS, Ravenna in Late Antiquity. Cambridge 2010.

R. MCKITTERICK, Rome and the Invention of the Papacy. The Liber Pontificalis. Cambridge 2020.

M. MEIER, Das andere Zeitalter Justinians. Kontingenzerfahrung und Kontingenzbewältigung im 6. Jahrhundert n. Chr. Göttingen 2003.

M. MEIER, Justinian. Herrschaft, Reich und Religion. Munich 2004.

J. MOORHEAD, The Last Years of Theoderic, in: Historia 32, 1983, 106–20.

J. MOORHEAD, Theodoric in Italy. Oxford 1992.

M. REYDELLET, Théoderic et la "civilitas", in: A. CARILE (ed.), Teoderico e i Goti tra Oriente e Occidente. Congresso Internazionale (Ravenna, 28 settembre–2 ottobre 1992). Ravenna 1995.

C. ROHR, Der Theoderich-Panegyricus des Ennodius. Hannover 1995.

B. SWAIN, Goths and Gothic Identity in the Ostrogothic Kingdom, in: 12.9: ARNOLD/BJORNLIE/SESSA, 203–33.

M. Verhoeven, The Early Christian Monuments of Ravenna. Transformations and Memory. Turnhout 2011.

M. Vitiello, Momenti di Roma Ostrogota. Adventus, feste politica. Stuttgart 2005.

M. Vitiello, Il principe, il filosofo, il guerriero. Lineamenti di pensiero politico nell'Italia ostrogota. Stuttgart 2006.

M. Vitiello, Theodohad. A Platonic King at the Collapse of Ostrogothic Italy. Toronto 2014.

M. Vitiello, Amalasuintha. The Transformation of Queenship in the Post-Roman World. Philadelphia 2017.

C. Wickham, Framing the Early Middle Ages. Europe and the Mediterranean, 400–800. Oxford 2005.

H.-U. Wiemer, Theoderich der Große, König der Goten, Herrscher der Römer. Munich 2018.

12.10 Anglo-Saxons

S. Bassett (ed.), The Origins of Anglo-Saxon Kingdoms. Leicester 1989.

R. Borius, Constance de Lyon, Vie de saint Germain d'Auxerre. Paris 1965.

P. Budd/A. Millard/C. Chenery/S. Lucy/C. Roberts, Investigating Population Movement by Stable Isotope Analysis. A Report from Britain, in: Antiquity, 78, 2004, 127–41.

R. Burgess, The Gallic Chronicle of 452. A New Critical Edition with a Brief Introduction, in: 10: Mathisen/Shanzer, 52–84.

T. Charles-Edwards, Wales and the Britons 350–1064. Oxford 2013.

V. Evison, The Fifth-Century Invasions South of the Thames. London 1965.

M. Fafinski, Roman Infrastructure in Early Medieval Britain. The Adaptations of the Past in Text and Stone. Amsterdam 2021.

K. George, Gildas's De Excidio Britonum and the Early British Church. Woodbridge 2009.

D. Green/F. Siegmund (eds.), The Continental Saxons from the Migration Period to the Tenth Century. Woodbridge 2003.

G. Halsall, Worlds of Arthur. Facts and Fictions of the Dark Ages. Oxford 2013.

N. Higham, Constantius, St Germanus and Fifth-century Britain, in: Early Medieval Europe 22, 2014, 113–37.

C. Hills, The Origins of the English. London 2003.

M. Lapidge/D. Dumville (eds.), Gildas. New Approaches. Woodbridge 1984.

D. Nash-Briggs, The Language of inscriptions on Icenian coinage, in: J. A. Davies (ed.), The Iron Age in Northern East Anglia: new work in the land of the Iceni. Oxford 2011, 83–102.

J. A. W. Nicolay, The Splendour of Power. Early Medieval Kingship and the Use of Gold and Silver in the Southern North Sea Area (5th to 7th century AD). Groningen 2014.

S. Oppenheimer, The Origins of the British. London 2006.

E. A. Thompson, Saint Germanus of Auxerre and the End of Roman Britain. Woodbridge 1984.

I. N. Wood, The End of Roman Britain. Continental Evidence and Parallels, in: 12.10: Lapidge/Dumville, 1–25.

I. N. Wood, The Fall of the Western Empire and the End of Roman Britain, in: Britannia 18, 1987, 251–62.

I. N. Wood, The Roman Origins of the Northumbrian Kingdom, in: R. Balzaretti/J. Barrow/P. Skinner (eds.), Italy and Early Medieval Europe. Papers for Chris Wickham. Oxford 2018, 39–49.

D. Woods, Gildas and the Mystery Cloud of 536–7, in: Journal of Theological Studies 61, 2010, 226–34.

12.11 Lombards

C. E. G. Amorim et al., Understanding 6th-century Barbarian Social Organization Through Paleogenomics, in: Nature Communications 9, article number 3547, 2018, https://www.nature.com/articles/s41467-018-06024-4 (05.06.2024).

P. Antonopoulos, Early Peril, Lost Faith. Italy between Byzantines and Lombards in the Early Years of the Lombard Settlement, A. D. 568–608. Saarbrücken 2016.

G. Ausenda/P. Delogu/C. Wickham (eds.), The Langobards Before the Frankish Conquest. An Ethnographic Perspective. Woodbridge 2009.

J. Bemmann/M. Schmauder (eds.), Kulturwandel in Mitteleuropa: Langobarden – Awaren – Slawen. Akten der Internationalen Tagung in Bonn vom 25. bis 28. Februar 2008. Bonn 2008.

N. Christie, The Lombards. Oxford 1995.

S. Dick, Langobardi per annos decem regem non habentes, sed duces fuerunt. Formen und Entwicklung der Herrschaftsorganisation bei den Langobarden. Eine Skizze, in: 12.11: Pohl/Erhart, 335–43.

S. Fanning, Lombard Arianism Reconsidered, in: Speculum 56, 1981, 241–58.

M. Hegewisch (ed.), Die Langobarden. Das Ende der Völkerwanderung. Katalog zur Ausstellung im Rheinischen LandesMuseum Bonn, 22.8.2008–11.1.2009. Darmstadt 2008.

C. La Rocca/S. Gasparri, Forging an Early Medieval Couple. Agilulf, Theodelinda and the "Lombard Treasure" (1888–1932), in: 11: Pohl/Mehofer, 269–87.

W. Menghin, Die Langobarden. Archaeologie und Geschichte. Stuttgart 1985.

W. Pohl/P. Erhart (eds.), Die Langobarden. Herrschaft und Identität. Vienna 2005.

12.12 Avars

J. Bemmann/M. Schmauder (eds.), Kulturwandel in Mitteleuropa. Langobarden – Awaren – Slawen. Akten der Internationalen Tagung in Bonn vom 25. bis 28. Februar 2008. Bonn 2008.

F. Daim (ed.), Hunnen und Awaren. Reitervölker aus dem Osten. Eisenstadt 1996.

W. Pohl, Die Awaren. Ein Steppenvolk in Mitteleuropa 567–822. Munich 2002.

W. Pohl, The Avars. A Steppe Empire in Central Europe 567–822. Ithaca 2018.

13 The Non-theological Culture of the Sixth-century West

M. BANNIARD, Viva voce. Communication écrite et communication orale du IVe au IXe siècle en Occident. Paris 1992.

G. BARRETT/G. WOUDHUYSEN, Assembling the Austrasian Letters at Trier and Lorsch, in: Early Medieval Europe 24, 2016, 3–57.

R. BURGESS/M. KULIKOWSKI, Mosaics of Time. Chronicle Traditions from the First Century BC to the Sixth Century AD, vol. 1. Leiden 2013.

A. CAMERON (ed./trans.), Flavius Cresconius Corippus: In Laudem Iustini Minoris (In praise of Justin II). London 1976.

H. CHADWICK, Boethius, The Consolations of Music, Logic, Theology, and Philosophy. Oxford 1981.

A. S. CHRISTENSEN, Cassiodorus, Jordanes, and the History of the Goths. Studies in a Migration Myth. Copenhagen 2002.

M. DIESENBERGER/Y. HEN/M. POLLHEIMER (eds.), Sermo Doctorum. Compilers, Preachers and their Audiences in the Early Medieval West. Turnhout 2013.

J. DIGGLE/F. R. D. GOODYEAR, Iohannidos Libri VIII. Cambridge 1970.

A. FO, Il cosiddetto Epigramma Paulini attribuito a Paolino di Béziers. Testo criticamente riveduto, traduzione e studio introduttivo, in: Romanobarbarica 16, 1999, 97–168.

M. FUHRMANN/J. GRUBER (eds.), Boethius. Darmstadt 1984.

A. GALONNIER (ed.), Boèce ou la chaîne des savoirs. Louvain-la-Neuve 2003.

J. GEORGE, Poet as Politician. Venantius Fortunatus' Panegyric to King Childeric, in: JMedH 15, 1989, 5–18.

J. GEORGE, Venantius Fortunatus. A Poet in Merovingian Gaul. Oxford 1992.

M. GIBSON (ed.), Boethius. His Life, Thought and Influence. Oxford 1981.

S. GIOANNI (ed.), Ennode de Pavie, Lettres, 2 vols. Paris 2006–10.

B. GOLDLUST (ed.), Corippe. Un poète latin entre deux mondes. Lyon 2015.

R. GREEN, Latin Epics of the New Testament. Juvencus, Sedulius, Arator. Oxford 2006.

J. GRUBER, Kommentar zu Boethius, De consolatione philosophiae, 2nd ed. Berlin 2006.

N. HECQUET-NOTI (ed.), Avit de Vienne, Éloge consolatoire de la chasteté. Paris 2011.

N. HECQUET-NOTI (ed.), Avit de Vienne, Histoire spirituelle, 2 vols. Paris 1999–2005.

A. HEILMANN, Boethius' Musiktheorie und das Quadrivium. Eine Einführung in den neuplatonischen Hintergrund von "De institutione musica". Göttingen 2007.

M. HEINZELMANN, Gregor von Tours (538–594): "Zehn Bücher Geschichte". Historiographie und Gesellschaftskonzept im 6. Jahrhundert. Darmstadt 1994; English trans. Gregory of Tours, History and Society in the Sixth Century. Cambridge 2001.

Y. HEN, Culture and Religion in Merovingian Gaul, AD 481–751. Leiden 1995.

K. HERBERS/T. DESWARTES/C. SHERER (eds.), Frühmittelalterliche Briefe. Übermittlung und Überlieferung (4–11. Jahrhundert). La lettre au haut Moyen Âge. Transmission et tradition épistolaires (IVe–XIe siècles). Cologne 2017.

R. HILLIER, Arator: Historia Apostolica. Liverpool 2020.

I. KÖNIG, Aus der Zeit Theodorichs des Großen. Einleitung, Text, Übersetzung, Kommentar einer anonymen Quelle. Darmstadt 1997.

V. LAW, Grammar and Grammarians in the Early Middle Ages. London 1997.

S. MACCORMACK, Latin Prose Panegyrics. Tradition and Discontinuity in the Later Roman Empire, in: Revue d'Études Augustinienne et Patristiques 22, 1976, 29–77.

J. MARENBON (ed.), The Cambridge Companion to Boethius. Cambridge 2009.

J. MARENBON, Boethius. Oxford 2003.

R. MATHISEN, Desiderius of Cahors, Last of the Romans, in: 10: DIEFENBACH/MÜLLER, 455–69.

R. MATHISEN, Ruricius of Limoges and Friends. A Collection of Letters from Visigothic Gaul. Liverpool 1999.

C. MOUSSY/C. CAMUS, Dracontius, Œuvres, 2 vols. Paris 2002.

A. MULLEN/G. WOUDHUYSEN (eds.), Languages and Communities in the Late-Roman and Post-Imperial Western Provinces. Cambridge, 2023.

G. M. MÜLLER (ed.), Zwischen Alltagskommunikation und literarischer Identitätsbildung. Stuttgart 2018.

D. NODES, Doctrine and Exegesis in Biblical Latin Poetry. Leeds 1993.

D. NORBERG, Epistulae sancti Desiderii, Acta Universitatis Stockholmensis. Uppsala 1961.

D. NORBERG, La poésie latine rhythmique du haut Moyen Âge. Stockholm 1954.

L. OBERTELLO, Severino Boezio, 2 vols. Genoa 1974.

S. QUESNEL (ed./trans.), Venance Fortunat, Vie de saint Martin. Paris 1996.

M. REYDELLET (ed.), Venance Fortunat, Poèmes, 3 vols. Paris 1994–2004.

M. REYDELLET, La royauté dans la littérature latine de Sidoine Apollinaire à Isidore de Séville. Rome 1981.

P. RICHÉ, Éducation et culture dans l'Occident barbare (VIᵉ–VIIIᵉ siècles). Paris 1962.

M. ROBERTS, Biblical Epic and Rhetorical Paraphrase in Late Antiquity. Liverpool 1985.

M. ROBERTS (ed./trans.), Venance Fortunat, Poems. Washington DC. 2017.

C. ROHR, Der Theoderich-Panegyricus des Ennodius. Hannover 1995.

J. SCHWIND, Arator-Studien. Göttingen 1990.

D. SHANZER/I. WOOD (eds.), Avitus of Vienne, Letters and Selected Prose. Liverpool 2002.

K. SMOLAK, Zwischen Bukolik und Satire. Das sogennante Sancti Paulini Epigramma, in: International Journal of the Classical Tradition 6, 1999, 3–20.

C. SOGNO/B. STORIN/E. WATTS (eds.), Late Antique Letter Collections. A Critical Introduction and Reference Guide. Berkeley 2017.

C. SOTINEL, Arator, un poéte au service de la politique du pape Virgile, in: MEFRM, Antiquité 102, 1989, 805–20.

K. STREKER (ed.), Monumenta Germaniae Historica, Poetarum Latinorum, IV. Berlin 1923, 455–7.

A. TYRRELL, Merovingian Letters and Letter Writers. Turnhout 2019.

G. J. J. WALSTRA, Les cinq epîtres rimées dans l'appendice des formules de Sens. Leiden 1962.

I. WOOD, The Problem of Late Merovingian Culture, in: S. DUSIL/G. SCHWEDLER/R. SCHWITTER, Exzerpieren – Kompilieren – Tradieren. Transformationen des Wissens zwischen Spätantike und Frühmittelalter. Berlin 2017, 199–222.

R. Wright, Late Latin and Early Romance in Spain and Carolingian France. Liverpool 1982.

14 The Western Church in the Sixth Century

14.1 General

A. Angenendt, Das Frühmittelalter. Die abendländischen Christenheit von 400 bis 900. Stuttgart 2001.

P. Brown, The Rise of Western Christendom. Triumph and Diversity, A. D. 200–1000, 10th Anniversary Edition. London 2006.

P. Brown, Through the Eye of a Needle. Wealth, the Fall of Rome, and the Making of Christianity, 350–550 AD. Princeton 2012.

P. Brown, The Ransom of the Soul. Afterlife and Wealth in Early Western Christianity. Cambridge, Mass. 2015.

I. Fielding, Physical Ruin and Spiritual Perfection in Fifth-century Gaul. Orientius and his Contemporaries on the "Landscape of the Soul", in: Journal of Early Christian Studis 22, 2014, 569–85.

R. Klein, Der Streit um den Victoriaaltar. Die dritte Relatio des Symmachus und die Briefe 17, 18 und 57 des Mailänder Bischofs Ambrosius. Darmstadt 1972.

E. Magnani, Almsgiving. Donatio Pro Anima and Eucharistic Offering in the Early Middle Ages of Western Europe, in: M. Frenkel/Y. Lev (eds.), Charity and Giving in Monotheistic Religions. Berlin 2009, 111–21.

R. Markus, The End of Ancient Christianity. Cambridge 1990.

F. Montinaro, Les fausses donations de Constantin dans le Liber Pontificalis, in: Millennium 12, 2015, 203–30.

G. Nathan, The Rogation Ceremonies of Late Antique Gaul. Creation, Transmission and the Role of the Bishop, in: CM 21, 1998, 276–303.

I. Wood, Entrusting Western Europe to the Church, 400–750, in: TRHS 23, 2013, 37–73.

I. Wood, The Transformation of the Roman West. Leeds 2018.

I. Wood, The Christian Economy in the Early Medieval West: towards a Temple Society. Binghamton 2022.

14.2 The Structure of the Sixth-century Church

P. Allen/B. Neil, Crisis Management in Late Antiquity (410–590 CE). A Survey of the Evidence from Episcopal Letters. Brill 2013.

F. Battistella, Pelagius I. und der Primat Roms. Ein Beitrag zum Drei-Kapitel-Streit und zur Papstgeschichte des 6. Jahrhunderts. Hamburg 2017.

K. Blair-Dixon, Memory and Authority in Sixth-Century Rome. The Liber Pontificalis and the Collectio Avellana, in: 7: Cooper/Hillner, 59–76.

D. Claude, Die Bestellung der Bischöfe im merowingischen Reiche, in: ZRG KA 80, 1963, 1–75.

S. Diefenbach, "Bischofsherrschaft". Zur Transformation der politischen Kultur im spätantiken und frühmittelalterlichen Gallien, in: 10: S. Diefenbach/Müller, 91–149.

G. D. Dunn, Collectio Corbeiensis, Collectio Pithouensis, and the Earliest Collections of Papal Letters, in: 8: Neil/Allen, 175–205.

J. Durliat, Les attributions civiles des évêques mérovingien. L'exemple de Didier évêque de Cahors, in: Annales du Midi 91, 1979, 237–54.

P. Ewald/L. Hartmann, Gregorii I Papae Registrum Epistolarum. Berlin 1891–9.

P. M. Gasso/C. M. Batlle (eds.), Pelagii I Papae epistolae quae supersunt (556–61). Montserrat 1956.

J. Gaudemet/B. Basdevant, Les canons des conciles mérovingiens (VIe–VIIe siècles). Paris 1989.

R. Godding, Prêtres en Gaule mérovingienne. Brussels 2001.

G. Halfond, The Archaeology of the Frankish Church Councils, AD 511–768. Leiden 2009.

G. Halfond, Bishops and the Politics of Patronage in Merovingian Gaul. Ithaca 2019.

M. Heinzelmann, Bischofsherrschaft in Gallien. Zürich 1976.

M.-C. Isaïa, Remi de Reims, Mémoire d'un saint, histoire d'une église. Paris 2010.

B. Jussen, Über "Bischofsherrschaften" und die Prozeduren politisch-sozialer Umordnung in Gallien zwischen "Antike" und "Mittelalter", in: HZ 260, 1995, 673–718.

R. Kaiser, Bischofsherrschaft zwischen Königtum und Fürstenmacht. Studien zur bischöflichen Stadtherrschaft im westfränkisch-französischen Reich im frühen und hohen Mittelalter. Bonn 1981.

W. E. Klingshirn, Caesarius of Arles. The Making of a Christian Community in Late Antique Gaul. Cambridge 1994.

W. E. Klingshirn, Charity and Power. Caesarius of Arles and the Ransoming of Captives in Sub-Roman Gaul, in: JRS 75, 1983, 183–203.

C. Leyser, Authority and Asceticism from Augustine to Gregory the Great. Oxford 2000.

C. Leyser, Law, Memory, and Priestly Office in Rome, c. 500, in: Early Medieval Europe 27, 2019, 61–84.

R. Lizzi Testa/G. Marconi, The Collectio Avellana and its Revivals. Cambridge 2019.

R. A. Markus, Carthage – Prima Justiniana – Ravenna. Aspects of Justinian's Kirchenpolitik, in: Byzantion 49, 1979, 277–306.

R. A. Markus, Gregory the Great and His World. Cambridge 1997.

J. Martyn (trans.), The Letters of Gregory the Great, 3 vols. Toronto 2004.

R. Mathisen, Between Arles, Rome, and Toledo. Gallic Collections of Canon Law in Late Antiquity, in: 'Ilu Cuadernos, 1999, 33–46.

R. McKitterick, Rome and the Invention of the Papacy. The Liber Pontificalis. Cambridge 2020.

J. Moorhead, The Laurentian Schism. East and West in the Roman Church, in: ChurchH 47, 1978, 125–36.

H. Mordek, Kirchenrecht und Reform im Frankenreich. Die Collectio vetus Gallica – die älteste systemastische Kanonessammlung des fränkischen Gallien. Sigmaringen 1975.

C. Munier (ed.), Concilia Africae a. 345–525. Turnhout 1974.

B. Neil, De profundis. The Letters and Archives of Pelagius I of Rome (556–61), in: 8: Neil/Allen, 206–20.

D. Norberg, S. Gregorii Magni Registrum Epistolarum. Turnhout 1982.

S. Patzold, Bischöfe, soziale Herkunft und die Organisation lokaler Herrschaft um 500, in: 12.7: Meier/Patzold, 523–43.

S. Patzold, Die Bischöfe im Gallien der Transformationszeit. Eine sozial homogene Gruppe von Amsträgern?, in: S. Brather/H. U. Nuber/H. Steuer/T. Zotz (eds.), Antike im Mittelalter. Fortleben, Nachwirken, Wahrnehmung. Ostfildern 2014a, 179–93.

S. Patzold, Zur Sozialstruktur des Episkopats und zur Ausbildung bischöflicher Herrschaft in Gallien zwischen Spätantike und Frühmittelalter, in: M. Becher/S. Dick (eds.), Völker, Reiche und Namen im frühen Mittelalter. Munich 2010, 121–40.

O. Pontal, Die Synoden im Merowingerreich. Paderborn 1986.

O. Pontal, Histoire des conciles mérovingiens. Paris 1989.

R. Price, The Acts of the Council of Constantinople of 553 with Related Texts on the Three Chapters, 2 vols. Liverpool 2009.

C. Rapp, Holy Bishops in Late Antiquity. The Nature of Christian Leadership in an Age of Transition. Berkeley 2005.

J. Richards, Consul of God. The Life and Times of Gregory the Great. London 1980.

J. Richards, The Popes and the Papacy in the Early Middle Ages, 476–752. London 1979.

G. Scheibelreiter, Der Bischof in merowingischer Zeit. Vienna 1983.

K. Sessa, The Formation of Papal Authority in Late Antique Italy. Roman Bishops and the Domestic Sphere. Cambridge 2012.

C. Sotinel, Emperors and Popes in the Sixth Century. The Western View, in: 12.9: Maas, 267–91.

R. Stocking, Bishops, Councils and Consensus in the Visigothic Kingdom, 589–633. Ann Arbor 2001.

C. van Rijn/S. Patzold (eds.), Men in the Middle. Local Priests in Early Medieval Europe. Berlin 2016.

E. Wirbelauer, Zwei Päpste in Rom. Der Konflikt zwischen Laurentius und Symmachus (498–514). Munich 1993.

14.3 Doctrine

A. Angenendt, Donationes pro anima. Gift and Countergift in the Early Medieval Liturgy, in: J. Davies/M. McCormick (eds.), The Long Morning of Early Medieval Europe. London 2008, 131–54.

A. Astell, Cassiodorus's Commentary on the Psalms as an Ars rhetorica, in: Rhetorica. A Journal of the History of Rhetoric 17, 1999, 37–75.

S. Barnish/L. Cracco Rugini/L. Cuppo/R. Marchese/M. Breu, Vivarium in Context. Vicenza 2008.

F. Battistella, Pelagius I. und der Primat Roms. Ein Beitrag zum Drei-Kapitel-Streit und zur Papstgeschichte des 6. Jahrhunderts. Hamburg 2017.

G. Berndt/R. Steinacher (eds.), Arianism. Roman Heresy and Arian Creed. Farnham 2014.

F. Cardini, Cassiodoro il Grande, Roma, i barbari e il monachesimo. Milan 2009; English trans. Cassiodorus the Great. Rome, Barbarians and Monasticism. Milan 2009.

J. Cavadini (ed.), Gregory the Great. A Symposium. South Bend 1995.

H. Chadwick, Boethius, The Consolations of Music, Logic, Theology, and Philosophy. Oxford 1981.

H. Chadwick, East and West: The Making of a Rift in the Church. From Apostolic Times until the Council of Florence. Oxford 2003.

C. Chazelle/C. Cubitt, The Crisis of the Oecumene. The Three Chapters and the Failed Quest for Unity in the Sixth-Century Mediterranean. Turnhout 2007.

S. Cohen, Schism and the Polemic of Heresy. Manichaeism and the Representation of Papal Authority in the Liber Pontificalis, in: Journal of Late Antiquity 8, 2015, 195–230.

G. Declercq, Dionysius and the Introduction of the Christian Era, in: Sacris Erudiri 41, 2002, 165–246.

G. E. Demacopoulos, Gregory the Great. Ascetic, Pastor, and First Man of Rome. South Bend 2015.

P. Eich, Gregor der Große. Bischof von Rom zwischen Antike und Mittelalter. Paderborn 2016.

J. Fontaine (ed.), Grégoire le Grand. Chantilly, Centre culturel Les Fontaines, 15–19 septembre 1982: Actes. Paris 1986.

W. H. C. Frend, The Rise of the Monophysite Movement. Cambridge 1972.

T. Fuhrer, Augustinus. Darmstadt 2004.

F. Haarer, Anastasius I. Politics and Empire in the Late Roman World. Cambridge 2006.

J. Halporn/M. Vessey, Cassiodorus: Institutions of Divine and Secular Learning and On the Soul. Liverpool 2004.

U. Heil, Avitus von Vienne und die homöische Kirche der Burgunder. Berlin 2011.

R. A. Markus, Gregory the Great and His World. Cambridge 1997.

M. Meier, Anastasios I. Die Entstehung des Byzantinischen Reiches. Stuttgart 2009.

B. Neil/M. J. Dal Santo, A Companion to Gregory the Great. Leiden 2013.

J. J. O'Donnell, Cassiodorus. Berkeley 1979.

R. Price, The Acts of the Council of Constantinople of 553 with Related Texts on the Three Chapters, 2 vols. Liverpool 2009.

E. Schwartz, Publizistische Sammlungen zum acacianischen Schisma. Munich 1934.

C. Straw, Gregory the Great, Perfection in Imperfection. Berkeley 1988.

R. Whelan, Being Christian in Vandal Africa. The Politics of Orthodoxy in the Post-Imperial West. Berkeley 2018.

14.4 The Cult of the Saints

P. Brown, The Cult of the Saints. Its Rise and Function in Latin Christianity, enlarged ed. Chicago 2015.

J.-P. Caillet/S. Destephen/B. Dumézil/H. Inglebert (eds.), Des dieux civiques aux saints patrons. IVe–VIIe siècle. Paris 2016.

M. Dal Santo, Debating the Saint's Cult in the Age of Gregory the Great. Oxford 2012.

G. de Nie, Views from a Many-Windowed Tower. Studies of Imagination in the Works of Gregory of Tours. Amsterdam 1987.

G. de Nie, Gregory of Tours, Lives and Miracles. Washington D. C. 2015.

A. de Vogüé (ed.), Grégoire le Grand, Dialogues, 3 vols. Paris 1978–80.

C. Goodson, Archaeology and the Cult of Saints in the Early Middle Ages. Accessing the Sacred, in: Moyen Âge 126, 2014, 115–23.

C. Goodson, Building for Bodies. The Architecture of Saint Veneration in Early Medieval Rome, in: É. Ó Carragáin/C. L. Neuman de Vegvar (eds.), Roma Felix. Formation and Reflections of Medieval Rome. Aldershot 2007, 51–80.

G. Hartmann, Selbststigmatisierung und Charisma. Christliche Heilige der Spätantike. Heidelberg 2006.

M. Heinzelmann/J.-C. Poulin, Les vies anciennes de sainte Geneviève de Paris. Études critiques. Paris 1986.

J. Howard-Johnston/P. A. Hayward (eds.), The Cult of the Saints in Late Antiquity and the Early Middle Ages. Essays on the Contribution of Peter Brown. Oxford 1999.

B. Krusch (ed.), Gregory of Tours, Opera, vol. 2: Miracula et Opera Minora. Hannover 1885.

B. Krusch (ed.), Venantius Fortunatus, Opera Pedestria. Berlin 1885.

B. Krusch (ed.), Vita Genovefae. Hannover 1896.

B. Krusch (ed.), Vita Abbatum Acaunensium absque epitaphiis. Hannover 1920.

M. Lapidge, The Roman Martyrs. Oxford 2017.

F. Martine, Vie des Pères du Jura, SC 142. Paris 1968.

M. Maskarinec, City of Saints. Rebuilding Rome in the Early Middle Ages. Philadelphia 2018.

B. Näf, Städte und ihre Märtyrer. Der Kult des thebäischen Legion. Fribourg 2011.

S. Potthoff, The Afterlife in Early Christian Carthage. Near-Death Experience, Ancestor Cult, and the Archaeology of Paradise. London 2017.

E. Rebillard, Christians and their Many Identities in Late Antiquity, North Africa, 200–450 CE, in: E. Rebillard, Transformations of Religious Practices in Late Antiquity. Farnham 2014.

J.-F. Reynaud, Lugdunum Christianum. Lyon du IVe au VIIe s.: Topographies, nécropoles, et édifices religieux. Paris 1998.

R. Van Dam, Saints and their Miracles in Late Antique Gaul. Princeton 1993.

G. C. Wataghin, Les villes et leurs saints, dans l'Antiquité tardive et le haut Moyen Âge. Un regard archéologique sur l'Italie, in: 14.4: Caillet/Destephen/Dumézil/Inglebert, 167–83.

A. M. Yasin, Saints and Church Spaces in the Late Antique Mediterranean. Architecture, Cult and Community. Cambridge 2009.

14.5 Monasticism

H. Atsma, Les monastères urbains du Nord de la Gaule, in: Revue d'Histoire de l'Église de France 62, 1976, 163–87.

H. Atsma, Klöster und Mönchtum im Bistum Auxerre bis zum Ende des 6. Jahrhunderts, in: Francia 11, 1983, 1–96.

N. Brocard/F. Vannotti/A. Wagner (eds.), Autour de saint Maurice. Besançon-Saint-Maurice 2011.

A. Bully/S. Bully/A. Dubreucq (eds.), Colomban et son influence. Rennes 2018.

Y. Codou/M. Lauwers (eds.), Lérins, une île sainte de l'Antiquité au Moyen Âge. Turnhout 2009.

J. Courreau/A. de Vogüé (eds.), Césaire d'Arles, Œuvres monastiques, 2 vols. Paris 1988–94.

V. Desprez, La Regula Ferreoli. Texte critique, in: Revue Mabillon 60, 1982, 117–48.

A. de Vogüé/J. Neufville (eds.), Regula, La règle de saint Benoît, 6 vols. Paris 1971–2.

A. de Vogüé (ed.), La règle du maître, 3 vols., Sources Chrétiennes 105-7. Paris 1964–5.

A. de Vogüé (ed.), Les règles des saints Pères, 2 vols. Paris 1982.

A. de Vogüé, The Master and St Benedict. A Reply to Marilyn Dunn, in: EHR 107, 1992, 95–103.

H. Dey/E. Fentress (eds.), Western Monasticism ante Litteram. The Spaces of Monastic Observance in Late Antiquity and the Early Middle Ages. Turnhout 2011.

H. Dey, Das monastische Experiment. Die Rolle der Keuschheit bei der Entstehung des westlichen Klosterwesens. Münster 2005.

A. Diem/P. Rousseau, Monastic Rules, in: A. Beach/I. Cochelin (eds.), The Cambridge History of Medieval Monasticism in the Latin West, vol. 1. Cambridge 2020, 162–94.

J. Dijkstra/M. van Dijk (eds.), The Encroaching Desert. Egyptian Hagiography and the Medieval West. Leiden 2006.

M. Dunn, Mastering Benedict. Monastic Rules and their Authors in the Early Medieval West, in: EHR 105, 1990, 567–94.

M. Dunn, The Master and St Benedict. A Rejoinder, in: EHR 107, 1992, 104–11.

M. Dunn, The Emergence of Monasticism. From the Desert Fathers to the Early Middle Ages. Oxford 2000.

P. Hatlie, The Monks and Monasteries of Constantinople. Ca. 350–850. Cambridge 2007.

Y. Hirschfeld, The Judean Desert Monasteries in the Byzantine Period. New Haven 1992.

G. Jenal, Italia ascetica atque monastica. Das Asketen- und Mönchtum in Italien von den Anfängen bis zur Zeit der Langobarden (ca. 150/250–604). Stuttgart 1995.

M. Krausgruber, Die Regel des Eugippius. Die Klosterordnung des Verfassers der Vita Sancti Severini im Lichte ihrer Quellen. Text, Übersetzung, Kommentar. Innsbruck 1996.

B. Krusch (ed.), Vita Abbatum Acaunensium absque epitaphiis. Hannover 1920, 322–36.

G. Lawless, Augustine of Hippo and his Monastic Rule. Oxford 1990.

J. López Quiroga, Monasterios altomedievales hispanos. Lugares de emplazamiento y ordenación de sus espacios, in: J. A. García de Cortázar/R. Teja (eds.), Los monasterios medievales en sus emplazaientos. Lugares de memoria de lo Sagrado. Aguilar de Campo 2016, 66–99.

F. Martine, Vie des Pères du Jura, SC 142. Paris 1968.

J.-P. Migne, Patrologia Latina 68, 1844, cols. 385–408.

Monastic Manuscript Project, www.earlymedievalmonasticism.org (27.06.2024).

F. J. Moreno Martín, La arquitectura monástica hispana entre la Tardoantigüedad y la Alta Edad Media. Oxford 2011.

J. Patrich, Sabas, Leader of Palestinian Monasticism. A Comparative Study in Eastern Monasticism, Fourth to Seventh Centuries. Washington D. C. 1995.

W. Pohl/M. Diesenberger (eds.), Eugippius und Severin. Der Autor, der Text und die Heilige, Forschungen zur Geschichte des Mittelalters 2. Vienna 2001.

F. Prinz, Frühes Mönchtum im Frankenreich, 2nd. ed. Darmstadt 1988.

A. Schmidt, Zur Komposition der Mönchsregel des heiligen Aurelian von Arles, in: Studia Monastica 17, 1975, 237–56.

G. Tomás-Faci/J. C. Martín-Iglesias, Cuatro documentos inéditos del monasterio visigodo de San Martín de Asán (522–586), in: MJb 52, 2017, 261–86.

G. Tomás-Faci, The Transmission of Visigothic Documents in the Pyrenean Monastery of San Martín de Asán (6th–12th Centuries). Monastic Memory and Episcopal Disputes, in: Antiquité Tardive 25, 2017, 303–14.

L. Verheijen, La Règle de saint Augustin, 2 vols. Paris 1967.

F. Villegas/A. de Vogüé, Eugippii Regula, Corpus Scriptorum Ecclesiasticorum Latinorum. Vienna 1976.

E. Wipszycka, Monks and the Hierarchical Church in Egypt and the Levant during Late Antiquity. Warsaw 2021.

I. N. Wood, A Prelude to Columbanus. The Monastic Achievement in the Burgundian Territories, in: H. B. Clarke/M. Brennan (eds.), Columbanus and Merovingian Monasticism. Oxford 1981, 3–32.

15 Sources

15.1 General Source Collections

W. Arend (ed.), Geschichte in Quellen, vol. I: Altertum. Munich 1975.

H.-G. Beck, Byzantinisches Lesebuch. Munich 1982.

R. Blockley (ed.), The Fragmentary Classicising Historians of the Later Roman Empire, 2 vols. Liverpool 1983.

D. J. Geanakoplos (ed.), Byzantium. Church, Society and Civilization Seen Through Contemporary Eyes. Chicago/London 1984.

J. Herrmann (ed.), Griechische und lateinische Quellen zur Frühgeschichte Mitteleuropas bis zur Mitte des 1. Jahrtausends u. Z., pt. 3: Von Tacitus bis Ausonius (2. und 4. Jh. u. Z.). Berlin 1991.

V. Keil (ed. and trans.), Quellensammlung zur Religionspolitik Constantins des Großen. Darmstadt 1995.

N. Lewis/M. Reinhold (eds.), Roman Civilization. Sourcebook II: The Empire. New York 1966.

C. O. Müller/K. Müller (eds.), Fragmenta historicorum Graecorum, vol. 4. Paris 1851.

P. van Nuffelen/L. van Hoof (eds.), The Fragmentary Latin Histories of Late Antiquity (AD 300–620). Edition, Translation and Commentary. Cambridge 2020.

15.2 Sources for Church History

Acta Conciliorum Oecumenicorum, ed. E. Schwartz, J. Straub. Straßburg/Leipzig/ Berlin 1914–71.

Acta Romanorum Pontificum a. S. Clemente I (c. 90) ad Coelestinum III († 1198). Pontificia Comissio ad redigendum Codicem Iuris Canonici Orientalis, Fontes, Series III, vol. I. Vatican City 1943.

P. R. Coleman-Norton, Roman State and Christian Church. A Collection of Legal Documents to A. D. 535, 3 vols. London 1966.

C. de Clercq (ed.), Concilia Gallia, a. 511–695, CCSL 148A. Turnhout 1963.

L. Duchesne (ed.), Liber Pontificalis, 2 vols. Paris 1886–92, 2nd ed. 1955; vol. 3, ed. C. Vogel. Paris 1957; English trans. R. Davis, vol. 1: The Book of the Pontiffs; vol. 2: The Lives of the Eighth-century popes, A. D. 715–817; vol. 3: The Lives of the Ninth-century Popes. Liverpool 1989–95.

Ecclesiae Occidentalis Monumenta Juris Antiquissima, ed. C. H. Turner (with opus postumum, ed. E. Schwartz), 2 vols. Oxford 1899–1939.

K. S. Frank (ed.), Frühes Mönchtum im Abendland, vol. I: Lebensformen, vol. II: Lebensgeschichten. Zürich/Munich 1975.

J. Gaudemet/B. Basdevant (eds)., Les canons des conciles mérovingiens (V^e–VIIe siècle), Sources Chrétiennes 353–4. Paris 1989.

O. Günther (ed.), Collectio Avellana (Papal and imperial letters 367–553), CSEL 35. Prague 1895–98.

A. Heilmann/H. Kraft (eds.), Texte der Kirchenväter. Nach Themen geordnet, 5 vols. Munich 1963–66.

P. Jaffé et al. (ed.), Regesta Pontificum Romanorum. Leipzig 1885.

F. Maassen, Geschichte der Quellen und der Literatur des canonischen Rechts im Abendlande, vol. I. Graz 1870, new ed. Graz 1956.

J.-L. Maier, Le dossier du donatisme, 2 vols. Berlin 1987–89.

G. Martínez Diez (ed.), La colección canónica Hispana, 6 vols. Madrid 1966–2002.

C. Mirbt (ed.), Quellen zur Geschichte des Papsttums und des römischen Katholizismus, new ed. K. Aland, vol. 1. Tübingen 1967.

C. Munier (ed.), Concilia Galliae, a. 314–506, CCSL 148. Turnhout 1963.

C. Munier (ed.), Conciliae Africae, a. 345–525, CCSL 149. Turnhout 1974.

H. Pietras, Council of Nicaea (325). Religious and Political Context, Documents, Commentaries. Rome 2016.

R. Price/M. Gaddis (trans.), The Acts of the Council of Chalcedon, 3 vols. Liverpool 2005.

R. Price (trans.) The Acts of the Council of Constantinople. Liverpool 2009.

R. Price/T. Graumann (trans.), The Council of Ephesus of 431. Documents and Proceedings. Liverpool 2020.

E. Schwartz, Publizistische Sammlungen zum acacianischen Schisma. Munich 1934.

E. Schwartz/J. Straub (eds.), Acta Conciliorum Oecumenicorum. Straßburg/Leipzig/Berlin 1914–71.

A. Thiel (ed.), Epistolae romanorum pontificum genuinae et quae ad eos scriptae sunt a S. Hilaro usque ad Pelagium II. Braunschweig 1868.

M. Tilley (trans.), Donatist Martyr Stories. The Church in Conflict in Roman North Africa. Liverpool 1996.

J. Vives (ed.), Concilios Visigóticos e Hispano-Romanos. Barcelona 1963.

S. Wenzlowski (trans.), Die Briefe der Päpste und die an sie gerichteten Schreiben von Linus bis Pelagius II. (vom Jahre 67–590), 7 vols. Kempten 1875–80.

15.3 Sources on the Barbarians

W. J. De Boone, De Franken van hun eerste optreden tot de dood van Childerik. Amsterdam 1954

O. Fiebiger/L. Schmidt, Inschriftensammlung zur Geschichte der Ostgermanen, Denkschr. der Akad. d. Wiss. in Wien, Phil.-hist. Kl. 60, 3,1918; 70, 3, 1939; 72, 2, 1944.

P. Heather/J. Matthews, The Goths in the Fourth Century. Liverpool 1991.

P. Lakatos, Quellenbuch zur Geschichte der Gepiden. Szeged 1973.

Quellen zur Geschichte der Alamannen, ed. K. Sprigade/G. Gottlieb/W. Kuhoff (vol. 6); trans. C. Dirlmeier, 6 vols. Sigmaringen 1976–84.

15.4 Greek, Roman and Post-Roman Legal Texts

Bibliotheca Juris Antiqui, Catania 1994 (database).

Codex Euricianus, ed. A. D'Ors. Rome/Madrid 1960.

Codex Theodosianus, ed. Th. Mommsen/P. M. Mayer. Berlin 1905, new ed. 1954; English trans. The Theodosian Code, trans. C. Pharr. New York 1952; French trans. S. Crogiez-Pétrequin/P. Jaillette/J.-M. Poinsotte, Codex Theodosianus. Le Code Théodosien, V. Turnhout 2009.

Corpus iuris civilis, 3 vols., ed. P. Krüger/Th. Mommsen/R. Schoell/W. Kroll. Berlin 1877–92; English trans. S. P. Scott, The Civil Law, 17 vols. Cincinnati 1932; text and German trans. O. Behrends/R. Knütel/B. Kupisch/H. H. Seiler, vol. I: Institutionen. Heidelberg 1990; German trans.: Corpus Iuris Civilis, ed. C. E. Otto/B. Schilling/C. F. F. Sintenis, 7 vols. Leipzig 1830–33.

Edictum Theoderici regis, ed. I. König. Darmstadt 2018.

Fontes iuris Romani ante justiniani, 3 vols., ed. S. Riccobono/J. Baviera/C. Ferrini/J. Furlani/V. Arangio Ruiz. Florence 2nd ed. 1940–72 (included in vol. 2: Fragmenta Vaticana, Mosaicarum et Romanarum legum collatio, Edictum Theodorici).

Leges Burgundionum, ed. L. R. V. Salis. Hannover 1892.

Lex Romana Visigothorum, ed. G. Haenel. Berlin 1849.

Leges Visigothorum, ed. K. Zeumer. Hannover 1902.

Notitia dignitatum, ed. O. Seeck. Berlin 1876; ed. R. I. Ireland. Leipzig 1999; ed. C. Neira Faleiro, La notitia dignitatum. Nueva edición crítica y comentario histórico. Madrid 2005; online resource: https://notitiadignitatum.org.

Pactus legis Salicae, ed. K. A. Eckhardt. Hannover 1962.

15.5 Inscriptions, Papyri and Manuscripts

W. Davies et al., The Inscriptions of Early Medieval Brittany. Aberystwyth 2009.

M. A. Handley, Death, Society and Culture. Inscriptions and Epitaphs in Gaul and Spain, AD 300–750, BAR International Series 1135. Oxford 2003.

Inscriptions chrétiennes de la Gaule antérieures au VIIIe siècle, ed. E. Le Blant, 2 vols. Paris 1856–65.

Inscriptiones christianae urbis Romae, ed. J. B. de Rossi/A. Silvagni/A. Ferrua, 8 vols. Rome 1932–83.

Inscriptiones graecae christianae veteres Occidentis, ed. C. Wessel. Bari 1989.

Inscriptiones latinae christianae veteres, ed. E. Diehl, 3 vols. Berlin 1925–31.

Inscriptiones latinae selectae, ed. H. Dessau, 3 vols. Berlin 1954–55.

E. A. Lowe et al., Codices Latini Antiquiores, 14 vols. Oxford, 1934–1992; Online version: Earlier Latin Manuscripts, https://elmss.nuigalway.ie.

O. Marucchi, Christian Epigraphy, Chicago 1974.

J. F. Oates/R. S. Bagnall/W. H. Willis/K. A. Worp, Checklist of Editions of Greek Papyri and Ostraca, Chicago 1985.

Recueil des Inscriptions chrétiennes de la Gaule antérieures à la Renaissance carolingienne, ed. H.-I. Marrou et al., 3. vols. Paris 1975–85.

M. Redknap/J. M. Lewis/N. Edwards, A Corpus of Inscribed Stones and Stone Sculpture in Wales, 3 vols. Cardiff 2007-13.

Tablettes Albertini. Actes privés de l'époque Vandale (fin du Ve siècle), ed. C. Courtois/L. Leschi/C. Perrat/C. Saumagne. Paris 1952.

J.-O. Tjäder, Die nichtliterarischen lateinischen Papyri Italiens aus der Zeit 445–700, 3 vols. Lund /Stockholm 1954–82.

I. Velázquez Soriano, Las pizarras visigodas. Edición critica y estudio. Murcia 1989.

15.6 Coinage and Coin Collections

E. Arslan, Le monete di Ostrogoti, Longobardi e Vandali. Catalogo delle Civiche Raccolte Numismatiche di Milano. Milan 1978.

A. R. Bellinger (ed.), Catalogue of the Byzantine Coins in the Dumbarton Oaks Collection, vol. I: Anastasius to Maurice. 491–602. Washington D. C. 1966.

G. M. Berndt/R. Steinacher, Minting in Vandal North Africa. Coins of the Vandal Period in the Coin Cabinet of Vienna's Kunsthistorisches Museum, in: Early Medieval Europe 16 (2008), 252–98.

K. Escher, Genèse et évolution du deuxième royaume burgonde (443–534). Les témoins archéologiques, vol. 2. Oxford 2005, 603–35.

P. Grierson, Byzantine Coinage. Washington D. C. 1999.

P. Grierson/M. Blackburn, Medieval European Coinage, vol. 1: The Early Middle Ages. With a Catalogue of the Coins of the Fitzwilliam Museum Cambridge. Cambridge 1986.

P. Grierson/M. Mays (eds.), Catalogue of Roman Coins in the Dumbarton Oaks Collection and in the Whittemore Collection. Washington D. C. 1992.

P. Guest, The Late Roman Gold and Silver Coins from the Hoxne Treasure. London 2005.

W. Hahn (ed.), Moneta Imperii Byzantini, pt. 1: Von Anastasius I. bis Justinianus I. (491–565). Vienna 1973.

W. Hahn, Die Ostprägung des römischen Reiches im 5. Jh. (408–491). Vienna 1989.

P. V. Hill/J. P. C. Kent/R. A. G. Carson (eds.), Late Roman Bronze Coinage A. D. 324–498. London 1965.

C. Morrisson (ed.), Catalogue des monnaies byzantines de la Bibliothèque Nationale, vol. I: D'Anastase à Justinian II (491–711). Paris 1970.

R. Pliego, La moneda visigoda, 2 vols. Seville 2009.

A. S. Robertson, An Inventory of Romano-British Coin Hoards. London 2000.

A. S. Robertson (ed.). Roman Imperial Coins in the Hunter Coin Cabinet, vol. V: Diocletian (Reform) to Zeno. Oxford 1982.

C. H. V. Sutherland/R. A. G. Carson et al. (eds.), The Roman Imperial Coinage, vols. VI–IX (Diocletian–Theodosius I). London 1967–81.

D. R. Walker, The Metrology of the Roman Silver Coinage, 3 vols. Oxford 1976–78.

W. W. Wroth, Catalogue of the Coins of the Vandals, Ostrogoths and Lombards, and the Empires of Thessalonica, Nicaea, and Trebizond in the British Museum. London 1911.

15.7 Individual Authors

Agathias
Historian and poet from Myrina, c. 532–c. 580. His histories cover the years from 552–559.

Text and trans.:

Histories, ed. R. Keydell. Berlin 1967; Engl. trans. J. Frendo. Berlin 1975; French ed. and trans. P. Maraval. Paris 2007.

Lit:

A. Cameron, Agathias. Oxford 1970.

Ambrose
Ca. 339–397, Bishop of Milan (since 374) and Church Father; his numerous theological works are available in PL, CSEL, CCSL, and SC.

Text and trans.:

Letters, ed. O. Faller/M. Zelzer, CSEL 82, 1–3, 1968–90; also PL 16; major speeches in CSEL 73, ed. O. Faller. English trans. J. H. W. G. Liebeschuetz, Ambrose of Milan, Political Letters and Speeches. Liverpool 2005. German trans. of theological works and the speech on the death of Theodosius J. E. Niederhuber, BKV 17, 21 and 32; R. Klein, Der Streit um den Victoriaaltar. Die dritte Relatio des Symmachus und die Briefe 17, 18 und 57 des Mailänder Bischofs Ambrosius. Darmstadt 1972.

Lit.:

E. Dassmann, Ambrosius von Mailand. Leben und Werk. Stuttgart 2004.

F. H. Dudden, The Life and Times of St Ambrose, 2 vols. Oxford 1935.

N. McLynn, Ambrose of Milan: Church and Court in a Christian Capital. Berkeley 1994.

J. Moorhead, Ambrose. Church and Society in the Late Roman World. London 1999.

K.-P. Schneider, Christliches Liebesgebot und weltliche Ordnungen. Historische Untersuchungen zu Ambrosius von Mailand, Diss. Cologne 1975.

Ammianus Marcellinus

Roman historian, born in Antioch, died c. 395. Author of Res gestae, which covered the period form Nerva to 378, but only survives for the years 353–78.

Text and trans.:

Res gestae, ed. and trans. W. Seyfarth, 4 vols. Berlin 1968–71; ed. and English trans. J. C. Rolfe, 3 vols. Cambridge Mass. 1950–56; ed. and French trans. E. Galletier/ G. Sabbah et al., 6 vols. Paris 1968–99.

Comm.:

J. den Boelt/D. den Hengst/H. C. Teitler, Philological and Historical Commentary on Ammianus Marcellinus XXI. Groningen 1991.

J. den Boelt/J. W. Drijvers/D. den Hengst/H. C. Teitler (eds.), Ammianus after Julian. The Reign of Valentinian and Valens in Books 26–31 of the Res Gestae. Leiden 2007.

P. de Jonge, Philological and Historical Commentary on Ammianus Marcellinus, 18 vols. Groningen/Leiden 1935–2018.

J. Szidat, Historischer Kommentar zu Ammianus Marcellinus Buch XX–XXI, 2 vols. Wiesbaden 1977–81.

Lit.

T. D. Barnes, Ammianus Marcellinus and the Representation of Historical Reality. Ithaca 1998.

R. C. Blockley, Ammianus Marcellinus. Brussels 1975.

G. A. Crump, Ammianus Marcellinus as a Military Historian. Wiesbaden 1975.

G. de Bonfils, Ammiano e l'imperatore. Bari 1986.

A. Demandt, Zeitkritik und Geschichtsbild im Werk Ammians, Diss. Marburg. Bonn 1965.

J. W. Drijvers/D. Hunt (eds.), The Late Roman World and its Historian. Interpreting Ammianus Marcellinus. London 1999.

F. Jenkins, Ammianus Marcellinus. An Annotated Bibliography, 1474 to the Present. Leiden 2017.

G. Kelly, Ammianus Marcellinus. The Allusive Historian. Cambridge 2008.

J. Matthews, The Roman Empire of Ammianus. London 1987.

V. Neri, Ammiano e il cristianesimo. Bologna 1985.

R. L. Pike, Apex omnium. Religion in the Res Gestae of Ammianus. Berkeley 1987.

K. Rosen, Ammianus Marcellinus. Darmstadt 1982.

R. Syme, Ammianus and the Historia Augusta. Oxford 1968.

G. Sabbah, La méthode d'Ammien Marcellin. Paris 1978.

R. Seager, Ammianus Marcellinus. Seven Studies in His Language and Thought, Columbia 1986.

R. Syme, Emperors and Biography. Studies in the Historia Augusta. Oxford 1971.

E. A. Thompson, The Historical Work of Ammianus Marcellinus. Cambridge 1947; new ed. Groningen 1969.

M. G. M. van der Poel, Online bibliography at Bibliographia Latina Selecta, http://an-cientworldonline.blogspot.com/2012/10/bibliographia-latina-selecta.html.

Anonymus de rebus bellicis

Anonymous author of a memorandum on finance and war, writing in the Western Empire in the late 4th century (or 5th century according to Brandt).

Text and trans.:

E. A. Thompson, A Roman Reformer and Inventor. Oxford 1952; R. Ireland, De rebus bellicis. The Text. Oxford 1979; Italian trans. A. Giardina, Le cose della guerra. Florence 1989; Spanish trans. Á. Sánchez-Ostiz, Anónimo sobre asuntos militares. Pamplona 2004.

Lit:

H. Brandt, Zeitkritik in der Spätantike. Munich 1988.

Anonymus Valesianus

Two texts, the first on Constantine and the second on Italy under Theodoric.

Text and trans.:

Ed. and English trans. J. C. Rolfe, in: Ammianus Marcellinus, vol. 3. Cambridge Mass. 1939, available online in the Greek and Roman Materials of the Perseus Digital Library, http://www.perseus.tufts.edu/hopper/collections (27.06.2024); German trans. of part 2 O. Veh, in: Prokop, Gotenkriege. Munich 1966, pp. 1213–1237.

Text and comm.:

I. König, Origo Constantini: Anonymus Valesianus, pt. 1. Trier 1987; I. König, Aus der Zeit Theoderichs des Großen. Darmstadt 1997.

Anthimus

Diplomat, physician, and author of culinary treatise, active in Ostrogothic Italy.

Text and trans.:

Anthimi, De observatione ciborum ad Theodoricum regem Francorum epistula. Leipzig 1928; ed. P. Paolucci. Hildesheim 2003; English trans. M. Grant. London 1996.

Lit:
Y. Hen, Food and Drink in Merovingian Gaul, in: B. Kasten, Tätigkeitsfelder und Erfahrungshorizonte des ländlichen Menschen in der frühmittelalterlichen Grundherrschaft. Cologne 2006, 99–110.

Anthologia Latina
Collection of poetry compiled, at least in part, in Vandal Africa.
Text and trans.:
Anthologia Latina mit den Vergil-Centonen, ed. W. Fels. Stuttgart 2014; English trans. N. M. Kay, Epigrams from the Anthologia Latina. London 2006.

Arator
Sixth-century Italian poet, active in Milan and Ravenna; later, suvolsacon of the Church of Rome under pope Vigilius; author of an epic poem on the Acts of the Apostles.
Text and trans.:
De actibus Apostolorum, ed. A. P. McKinlay, CSEL 72. Vienna 1951; English trans. R. Hillier, Arator, Historia Apostolica. Liverpool 2020.
Lit:
R. Green, Latin epics of the New Testament, Juvencus, Sedulius, Arator. Oxford 2006.
J. Schwind, Arator-Studien. Göttingen 1990.
C. Sotinel, Arator, un poète au service de la politique du pape Vigile, in: MEFRA 102 (1989), 805–20.

Athanasius
295–373, from 328 Bishop of Alexandria, although frequently in exile. A leading eastern Church Father. In addition to his theological writings, the Vita Antonii.
Text:
Urkunden zur Geschichte des arianischen Streites, in: Athanasius, Werke, vol. III, ed. H.-G. Opitz/W. Schneemelcher. Berlin/Leipzig 1934.
Vita Antonii, ed. A. Gottfried, trans. H. Przybyla, Leipzig 1986; G. M. J. Bartelink, Athanase d'Alexandrie, Vie d'Antoine, SC 400. Paris 1994; also H. Hertel, BKV 31; Latin text, P. Bertrand, L. Gandt, Vitae Antonii Versiones latinae, CCSL 170. Turnhout 2018.
Deux apologies, ed. J. Scymusiak: SC 56, 2nd ed.1987.
History of the Arians, trans. R. Flower, Imperial Invectives against Constantius II. Liverpool 2016.
Lit:
C. Kannengiesser (ed.), Politique et Théologie chez Athanase d'Alexandrie. Paris 1974.
E. Schwartz, Gesammelte Schriften, vol. III: Zur Geschichte des Athanasius, Berlin 1959.

Augustine
354–430. From 395 bishop of Hippo in Africa and a leading Christian writer in Antiquity.
Text and trans.:

Epistulae, ed. A. Goldbacher, CSEL 34, 1895; 44, 1904; 57, 1911; 58, 1923; Epistulae, ed.
    J. Divjak: CSEL 88, 1981 (newly discovered letters); new ed. 1987.
De civitate dei, ed. B. Dombart, A. Kalb, 2 vols. Stuttgart 1981; German trans. W.
    Thimme, 2 vols. Zürich/Munich 1977–78; English trans. R. W. Dyson, Augustine,
    The City of God against the Pagans. Cambridge 1998.
Confessiones, ed. M. Skutella. Leipzig 1934; Latin and German trans., W. Thimme.
    Zurich/Stuttgart 1950; Latin text and comm. J. J. O'Donnell, Augustine, Confes-
    sions, 3 vols. Oxford 1992; Latin and English trans. C. Hammond. Cambridge
    Mass., 2014–16; English trans. H. Chadwick. Oxford 2008.
Regulae, ed. L. Verheijen, La Règle de saint Augustin, 2 vols. Paris 1967.
Lit.
P. Brown, Augustine of Hippo. London 1967.
E. Dassmann, Augustinus. Heiliger und Kirchenlehrer. Stuttgart et al. 1993.
V. H. Drecoll, Augustin-Handbuch. Tübingen 2007.
T. Fuhrer, Augustinus. Darmstadt 2004.
W. Geerlings, Augustinus – Leben und Werk. Eine bibliographische Einführung.
    Paderborn 2002.
E. Kenyon, Augustine and the Dialogue. Cambridge 2018.
R. Lane Fox, Augustine. Conversions and Confessions. London 2015; German trans.
    Augustinus. Bekenntnisse und Bekehrungen im Leben eines antiken Men-
    schen. Stuttgart 2017.
G. Lawless, Augustine of Hippo and his Monastic Rule. Oxford 1990.
C. Lepelley (ed.), Les lettres de Saint Augustin découvertes par J. Divjak. Paris 1983.
F. G. Maier, Augustin und das antike Rom. Stuttgart 1955.
R. A. Markus, Saeculum. History and Society in the Theology of St. Augustine. Cam-
    bridge 1970.
H.-I. Marrou, Saint Augustin et la fin de la culture antique. Paris 1938, 1958.
H.-I. Marrou, Le dogme de la résurrection des corps et la théologie des valeurs hu-
    maines selon l'enseignement de saint Augustin, in: Revue des Etudes Augus-
    tiniennes 12, 1966, 111–136.
H.-I. Marrou, Saint Augustin, Orose et l'augustinisme historique, in: La storiografia
    altomedievale I. Settimane di studio 17, Spoleto 1970, 59–87.
G. O'Daly, Augustine's City of God. A Reader's Guide. Oxford 1999.
J. J. O'Donnell, Augustine: Saint and Sinner. A new biography. London 2005.
K. Rosen, Augustinus. Genie und Heiliger. Wiesbaden 2015.
E. Stump/N. Kretzmann (eds.), The Cambridge Companion to Augustine. Cambridge
    2001.
J. van Oort, Jerusalem und Babylon. Leiden et al. 1993.
J. Wetzel (ed.), Augustine's City of God. A Critical Guide. Cambridge 2012.

Aurelian of Arles

Bishop of Arles, author of a monastic rule.
Text and trans.:
ed. PL 68.

Lit:

A. Schmidt, Zur Komposition der Mönchsregel des heiligen Aurelian von Arles, in: Studia Monastica 17, 1975, 17–54.

Aurelius Victor

Governor of Pannonia Secunda under Julian and praefectus urbi *under Theodosius. Author of Historiae abbreviatae (Caesares, covering the period up to 360) with an Epitome de Caesaribus (from Augustus to Theodosius) also attributed to him.*

Text, trans., comm.:

Ed. and French trans. P. Dufraigne, Aurelius Victor, Livre des Césars. Paris 1975; ed. and German trans. C. Scardino, M. A. Nickbakht, Aurelius Victor, Historia Abbreviatae. Paderborn 2021; English trans. H. W. Bird, Aurelius Victor, De Caesaribus. Liverpool 1994.

Lit.:

H. W. Bird, Sextus Aurelius Victor. A Historiographical Study. Liverpool 1984.

W. den Boer, Some Minor Roman Historians. Leiden 1972.

V. Neri, Le fonti della Vita de Caesaribus nell' Epitome de Caesaribus, in: RSA 17–18, 1987–88, 249–280.

D. Rohrbacher, The Historians of Late Antiquity. London 2002.

J. Schlumberger, Die Epitome de Caesaribus. Munich 1974.

J. A. Stover/G. Woudhuysen, The Lost History of Sextus Aurelius Victor. Edinburgh 2023.

Ausonius

Gallic rhetor and poet, c. 310–393/4. Tutor of the emperor Gratian, 378 praefectus Galliarum, 379 consul. Author of a praise poem on the Moselle, a gratiarum actio for his consulship, and the Parentalia, important for the history of his family.

Text and trans.

R. Green. Oxford 1991; B. Combeaud. Paris 2010; H. G. Evelyn-White, 2 vols. Cambridge Mass. 1919–21.

Lit.:

A. Coşkun, Die gens Ausoniana an der Macht. Untersuchungen zu Decimius Magnus Ausonius und seiner Familie. Oxford 2002.

R. Etienne, Ausone ou les ambitions d'un notable aquitain. Bordeaux 1986.

B. Gibson, Gratitude to Gratian. Ausonius' Thanksgiving for his Consulship, in: 4.1: Burgersdijk/Ross, 270–88.

H. Sivan, Ausonius of Bordeaux. Genesis of a Gallic Aristocracy. London/New York 1993.

Avitus of Vienne

Ca. 460–518, from c. 494 bishop of Vienne. Author of an important, but fragmentary, collection of letters which constitute the major source for the Middle Rhône valley at the start of the sixth century. Also the author of epic poems versifying the Old Testament Books of Genesis and Exodus, and on the chastity of his sister.

Text and trans.

De consolatoria de castitatis laude, ed. and French trans. N. Hᴇǫᴜᴇᴛ-Nᴏᴛɪ, SC 546. Paris 2011.

De Spiritalis Gestis, ed. and French trans. N. Hᴇǫᴜᴇᴛ-Nᴏᴛɪ, 2 vols., SC 444, 492. Paris 1999–2005; Bks. 1–III, ed. D. Nᴏᴅᴇs, Toronto 1985; Engl. trans. G. W. Sʜᴇᴀ, Tempe 1997.

Alcimi Ecdicii Aviti Viennensis episcopi Opera quae supersunt, MGH AA VI, 2, 1883, ed. R. Pᴇɪᴘᴇʀ; ed. U. Cʜᴇᴠᴀʟɪᴇʀ, Lyon 1890; Lettres, ed. and French trans., E. Mᴀʟᴀsᴘɪɴᴀ/M. Rᴇʏᴅᴇʟʟᴇᴛ. Paris 2016; English trans. and comm. D. Sʜᴀɴᴢᴇʀ/I. N. Wᴏᴏᴅ, Avitus of Vienne, Letters and Selected Prose. Liverpool 2002.

Lit.:

U. Hᴇɪʟ, Avitus von Vienne und die homöische Kirche der Burgunder. Berlin 2011.

I. N. Wᴏᴏᴅ, Letters and Letter-collections from Antiquity to the Early Middle Ages, in: M. A. Mᴇʏᴇʀ (ed.), The Culture of Christendom. London 1993, 29–43.

Basil (the Great) of Caesarea

Ca. 330–379, from 370 bishop of Caesarea in Cappadocia. Regarded as the Father of Eastern Cenobitism.

Text:

Greater Asketikon, in: PG 31, 889–1306.

Lesser Asketikon (surviving only in the Latin translation of Rufinus), in: PL 103, 483–554.

Text and trans.:

Letters, ed. R. J. Dᴇғᴇʀʀᴀʀɪ, 4 vols. Cambridge Mass. 1926–34.

Benedict of Nursia

Ca. 480–547. From a noble family; founded a monastery at Subiaco, then 529 at Monte Cassino. After the Carolingian period his Rule became the model for Western monasticism.

Text and trans.:

Regula Benedicti, ed. A. ᴅᴇ Vᴏɢüᴇ; J. Nᴇᴜғᴠɪʟʟᴇ, La règle de saint Benoît, 6 vols., SC 181–6. Paris 1971–2; ed. B. Sᴛᴇɪᴅʟᴇ. Beuron 1980.

Lit.:

U.-K. Jᴀᴄᴏʙs, Die Regula Benedicti als Rechtsbuch. Cologne 1987.

Boethius

Born c. 477, executed 524. Senator, Consul 510, magister officiorum 522. Philosopher.

Text and trans.:

L. Bɪʟᴇʀ (ed.), Anicii Manlii Severini Boethii Philosophiae Consolatio. CCSL 94. Turnhout 1957; C. Mᴏʀᴇsᴄʜɪɴɪ (ed.), De consolatione philosophiae, opuscula theologica. Leipzig 2005.

Lit.:

H. Cʜᴀᴅᴡɪᴄᴋ, The Consolations of Music, Theology, and Philosophy. Oxford 1981.

M. Fᴜʜʀᴍᴀɴɴ/J. Gʀᴜʙᴇʀ, (eds.), Boethius. Darmstadt 1984.

A. Gᴀʟᴏɴɴɪᴇʀ (ed.), Boèce ou la chaîne des savoirs, Louvain-la-Neuve 2003.

M. Gibson (ed.), Boethius. His Life, Thought and Influence. Oxford 1981.

J. Gruber, Kommentar zu Boethius, De consolatione philosophiae, 2nd ed. Berlin 2006.

A. Heilmann, Boethius' Musiktheorie und das Quadrivium. Eine Einführung in den neuplatonischen Hintergrund von "De institutione musica". Göttingen 2007.

J. Marenbon, Boethius. Oxford 2003.

J. Marenbon (ed.), The Cambridge Companion to Boethius. Cambridge 2009.

L. Obertello, Severino Boezio, 2 vols. Genoa 1974.

Bordeaux pilgrim

Fourth-century pilgrim account of a visit to the Holy Land.

Text:

Ed. P. Geyer/O. Cuntz, Itinerarium Burdigalense, CCSL 175 (Itineraria et alia geographica). Turnhout 1965.

Lit:

E. D. Hunt, Holy Land Pilgrimage in the Later Roman Empire AD 312–460. Oxford 1982.

Caesarius of Arles

Born c. 470 in Chalon-sur-Saône, monk at Lérins, Bishop of Arles, 502–42, monastic legislator and theologian.

Text and trans.:

Sermones, ed. G. Morin, CCSL 103-4. Turnhout 1953.

Regulae: J. Courreau/A. de Vogüé (eds.), Césaire d'Arles, Œuvres monastiques, 2 vols., SC 345, 398. Paris, 1988–94.

Eng. trans. W. Klingshirn, Caesarius of Arles, Life, Testament, Letters. Liverpool 1994.

Lit:

W. Klingshirn, Caesarius of Arles. The Making of a Christian Community in Late Antique Gaul. Cambridge 1994.

Cassian, John

d. 430/35. Lived as a monk in Egypt, in 404 moved to the West and founded a male and a female monastic community in Marseille. His writings played a major role in the transmission of the traditions of eastern monasticism to the West.

Text and trans.:

Conlationes patrum, ed. M. Petschenig, CSEL 13, 1886; French trans. E. Pichery, Jean Cassien, Conférences, 3 vols. SC 42 bis, 54, 64. Paris 1966–68.

De institutis coenobiorum et de octo principalium vitiorum remediis, ed. M. Petschenig, CSEL 17, 1888; French trans. J. C. Guy, Institutions cénobitiques, SC 109, 1965.

Lit.:

R. Goodrich, Contextualizing Cassian. Aristocracts, Asceticism, and Reformation in Fifth-century Gaul. Oxford 2007.

O. Chadwick, John Cassian. A Study in Primitive Monasticism. London 2nd ed. 1968.

Cassiodorus

Ca. 485–ca. 580. Senator, 514 consul, 523–527 magister officiorum, 533–537 praefectus praetorio. The collection of his Variae epistolae contains his official writings from 507–537 and is a major source for Ostrogothic Italy. From the later stages of his life there are significant religious writings, the Institutiones and the Commentary on Psalms.

Text:

Variae epistolae, ed. Th. Mommsen, MGH AA XII, 1894; ed. Ä. J. Fridh/J. W. Halporn, CCL 96, 1973; ed. G. Cecconi/A. Giardina et al., 6 vols. Rome 2017–21. Selected letters trans. S. J. B. Barnish, Cassiodorus Variae. Liverpool 1992.

Institutiones divinarum et saecularium litterarum, ed. R. A. B. Mynors. Oxford 1937; English trans. J. W. Halporn/M. Vessey, Cassiodorus, Institutions of Divine and Secular Learning. On the Soul. Liverpool 2004.

De anima, ed. J. W. Halporn, CCSL 96. Turnhout 1973; English trans. J. W. Halporn/M. Vessey, Cassiodorus, Institutions of Divine and Secular Learning. On the Soul. Liverpool 2004.

Expositio Psalmorum, ed. M. Adrien, CCSL 97-8. Turnhout 1958.

Lit.:

A. Astell, Cassiodorus's Commentary on the Psalms as an Ars rhetorica, in: Rhetorica. A Journal of the History of Rhetoric 17 (1999), 37–75.

M. S. Bjornlie, Politics and Tradition between Rome, Ravenna and Constantinople. A Study of Cassiodorus and the Variae, 527–554. Cambridge 2013

F. Cardini, Cassiodoro il Grande. Roma, i barbari e il monachesimo. Milan 2009; English trans. Cassiodorus the Great. Rome, barbarians and monasticism. Milan 2009.

Å. J. Fridh, Contributions à la critique et à l'interprétation des Variae de Cassiodore. Stockholm 1968.

A. Giardina, Cassiodoro politico. Rome 2006.

G. Heydemann, Cassiodors Psalmenkommentar. Exegese, Politik und did christliche Neuordnung der römischen Welt. Stuttgart 2024.

S. Krautschick, Cassiodor und die Politik seiner Zeit. Bonn 1983.

R. MacPherson, Rome in Involution. Cassiodorus' Variae in their Literary and Historical Setting. Poznan 1989.

M. Mazza, La Historia tripartita di Flavio Magno Aurelio Cassiodore senatore. Metodi e scopo, in: S. Leanza (ed.), Flavio Magno Aurelio Cassiodoro. Atti della settimana di Studi. Catanzaro 1984, 210–44.

J. J. O'Donnell, Cassiodorus. Berkeley 1979.

G. Vidén, The Roman Chancery Tradition. Studies in the Language of Codex Theodosianus and Cassiodorus' Variae. Gothenburg 1984.

Chromatius of Aquileia

Bishop of Aquileia, d. c. 406/7.

Text and trans.:

Chromace d'Aquilée, Sermons, ed. J. Lemarié, 2 vols., SC 154, 164. Paris 1969–71.

Lit.:

P. F. Beatrice/A. Peršič (eds.), Chromatius of Aquileian and his Age. Proceedings of the International Conference held in Aquileia, 22–24 May 2008. Turnhout 2011.

R. Lizzi Testa, Vescovi e strutture nella città tardoantica. L'Italia annonaria nel IV–V secolo d. C. Como 1989.

R. McEachnie, A History of Heresy Past. The Sermons of Chromatius of Aquileia, 388–407, in: ChurchH 83, 2014, 273–96.

R. McEachnie, Chromatius of Aquileia and the Making of a Christian City. London 2020.

Chronica Minora

Latin Chronicles, see also Prosper Tiro, Hydatius und Marcellinus Comes

Text:

Ed. Th. Mommsen, MGH AA IX, 1892; XI, 1894; XIII, 1898.

Chronicle of 452: ed. R. W. Burgess, The Chronicle of 452. A New Critical Edition with a Brief Introduction, in: 10: Mathisen/Shanzer, 52–84; J. M. Kötter/C. Scardino (eds.), Gallische Chroniken. Paderborn 2017.

Chronicle of 511: ed. R. W. Burgess, The Chronicle of 511. A New Critical Edition with a Brief Introduction, in: 10: Mathisen/Shanzer, 85–100; J. M. Kötter/C. Scardino, (eds.), Gallische Chroniken. Paderborn 2017.

Chronicle of Saragossa/Zaragoza: C. Cardelle de Hartmann (ed.), Victoris Tunnunensis Chronicon cum reliquiis ex Consularibus Caesaraugustanis et Iohannis Biclarensis Chronicon, CCSL CLXXIII A. Turnhout 2001.

The Chronograph of 354, ed. J. Divjak, W. Wischmeyer, Das Kalenderhandbuch von 354, der Chronograph des Filocalus, 2 vols. Vienna 2014.

Consularia Constantinopolitana, ed. with English trans. R. W. Burgess, The Chronicle of Hydatius and the Consularia Constantinopolitana. Oxford 1993; ed. and trans. M. Becker/B. Bleckmann/M. A. Nickbakht/J. Gross, Consularia Constantinopolitana und verwandte Quellen. Paderborn 2016.

Ravenna Annals, ed. B. Bischoff/W. R. W. Koehler, Eine illustrierte Ausgabe der spätantiken Ravennater Annalen, in: W. R. W. Koehler (ed.), Studies in Memory of A. Kingsley Porter. Cambridge Mass. 1939, 125–38.

Lit.:

R. W. Burgess, The Chronograph of 354. Its Manuscripts, Contents and History, in: Journal of Late Antiquity 5, 2012, 345–96.

R. W. Burgess, The New Edition of the Chronograph of 354. A Detailed Critique, in: Zeitschrift für antikes Christentum 21, 2017, 383–415.

S. Muhlberger, The Fifth-century Chroniclers. Prosper, Hydatius and the Galllic Chronicle of 452. Leeds 1990.

M. R. Salzman, On Roman Time. The Codex Calendar of 354 and the Rhythms of Urban Life in Late Antiquity. Berkeley 1990.

I. N. Wood, Chains of Chronicles. The Example of London, British Library ms. Add. 16974, in: R. Corradini/M. Diesenberger/M. Niederkorn (eds.), Zwischen Niederschrift und Wiederschrift. Frühmittelalterliche Hagiographie und Historiographie im Spannungsfeld von Kompendienüberlieferung und Editionstechnik. Vienna 2010, 67–77.

Chronicon Paschale
Greek World Chronicle, up to 628.
Text and trans.:
Ed. L. Dindorf, 1832; English trans. M. Whitby/M. Whitby. Liverpool 1989.

Claudian
Poet, born in Alexandria c. 370, by 395 active in Rome as a writer of panegyrics (e. g. for
Stilicho) and invectives (e. g. against Rufinus und Eutropius); d. c. 404.
Text and trans.:
Ed. T. Birt, MGH AA X, 1892; J. B. Hall, Leipzig 1985; ed. and English trans. M. Plat-
nauer, 2 vols. Cambridge Mass. 1922; ed. and French trans. J.-L. Charlet, Clau-
dien, Œuvres, 2 vols. Paris 1991–2000; German trans. P. Weiss/C. Wiener,
Claudius Claudianus, vol. 1: Politische Gedichte. Berlin 2020.
Panegyricus de consulatu Manlii Theodori, ed. W. Simon. Berlin 1975.
Panegyricus dictus Olybrio et Probino consulibus, ed. W. Taegert. Munich 1988.
Lit.:
A. Cameron, Claudian. Poetry and Propaganda at the Court of Honorius. Oxford 1970.
S. Döpp, Zeitgeschichte in Dichtungen Claudians. Wiesbaden 1980.
H. L. Levy, Claudian's In Rufinum. An Exegetical Commentary. Cleveland 1971.
P. L. Schmidt, Politik und Dichtung in der Panegyrik Claudians. Konstanz 1976.

Claudianus Mamertus
Theologian and priest of Vienne; author of the De Statu animae.
Text and trans.:
Ed. A. Engelbrecht, CSEL 11. Vienna 1885.
Lit.:
E. L. Fortin, Christianisme et culture philosophique au Ve siècle. La querelle de l'âme
humaine en Occident. Paris 1959.

Constantius of Lyon
Hagiographer, and friend of Sidonius Apollinaris.
Text and trans.:
Ed. W. Levison, MGH, SRM VII. Hannover 1920; ed. and French trans. R. Borius, Con-
stance de Lyon, Vie de saint Germain d'Auxerre, SC 112. Paris 1965; English
trans. F. R. Hoare, The Western Fathers. London 1965.
Lit.:
N. Higham, Constantius, St Germanus and Fifth-century Britain, in: Early Medieval Eu-
rope 22, 2014, 113–37.
E. A. Thompson, Saint Germanus of Auxerre and the End of Roman Britain. Wood-
bridge 1984.
I. N. Wood, The End of Roman Britain. Continental Evidence and Parallels, in: 12.10:
Lapidge/Dumville, 1–25.

Corippus

Byzantine poet, active in the reigns of Justinian I and Justin II.

Text and trans.:

J. DIGGLE/F. R. D. GOODYEAR (eds.), Iohannidos Libri VIII. Cambridge 1970.

A. CAMERON (ed.), Flavius Cresconius Corippus, In laudem Iustini Augusti minoris. London 1976.

English trans. G. W. SHEA, The Iohannis or the De Bellis libycis of Flavius Cresconius Corippus. Lewiston 1998.

Lit.:

T. GÄRTNER, Untersuchungen zur Gestaltung und zum historischen Stoff der "Iohannis" Coripps. Berlin 2008.

B. GOLDLUST (ed.), Corippe. Un poète latin entre deux mondes, Lyon 2015.

A. H. MERRILLS, War, Rebellion and Epic in Byzantine North Africa. A Historical Study of Corippus' Iohannis. Cambridge 2024.

C. SCHINDLER, Per carmina laudes. Untersuchungen zur spätantiken Verspanegyrik von Claudian bis Coripp. Berlin 2009.

Cyprian of Toulon

Born c. 476, Bishop of Toulon 516–46; leading author of the Vita Caesarii and author of theological letter to Maximus of Geneva.

Text and trans.:

Ed. M.-J. DELAGE/M. HEIJMANS, Vie de Césaire d'Arles, SC 536. Paris, 2010; English trans. W. KLINGSHIRN, Caesarius of Arles, Life, Testament, Letters. Liverpool 1994.

Ep. to Maximus, ed. W. GUNDLACH, E. DÜMMLER, MGH Ep. I, 1982.

Lit.:

R. W. MATHISEN, Between Arles. Rome, and Toledo. Gallic Collections of Canon Law in Late Antiquity, in: Cuadernos 'Ilu 2, 1999, 33–46.

Damasus

Born c. 305, bishop of Rome 366–84.

Text and English trans.:

D. TROUT, Damasus of Rome. The Epigraphic Poetry: Introduction, Texts, Translations and Commentary. Oxford 2015.

Lit.:

A. LIPPOLD, Ursinus and Damasus, in: Historia 14, 1965, 105–28.

N. MCLYNN, Damasus of Rome. A Fourth-century Pope in Context, in: T. FUHRER (ed.). Rome und Mailand in der Spätantike. Repräsentationen städtischer Räume in Literatur, Architektur und Kunst. Berlin 2012, 305–26.

U. REUTTER, Damasus, Bischof von Rom (366–384). Leben und Werk. Tübingen 2009.

Dracontius

Poet active in Vandal Africa, c. 455–ca. 505; author of religious, political and occasional verse.

Text and trans.:

Ed. C. MOUSSEY/C. CAMUS/J. BOUQUET/E. WOLFF, Dracontius, Œuvres, 4 vols. Paris 2002.

Lit.:

L. Castagna (ed.), Studi Draconziani (1912–1996). Naples 1997.

K. Pohl (ed.), Dichtung zwischen Römern und Vandalen. Tradition, Transformation und Innovation in den Werken des Dracontius. Mit einer Gesamtbibliographie zu Dracontius. Stuttgart 2019.

R. Simons, Dracontius und der Mythos. Christliche Weltsicht und pagane Kultur in der ausgehenden Spätantike. Munich 2005.

Egeria

Fourth-century author of an account of a pilgrimage to the Holy Land.

Text and trans.:

Itinerarium Egeriae, ed. A. Franceschini, R. Weber, CCSL 175 (Itineraria et alia geographica). Turnhout 1965; ed. with French trans. P. Maraval, Égérie, Journal de Voyage, SC 296. Paris 1982: German trans. H. Donner, Pilgerfahrt ins Heilige Land. Die ältesten Berichte christlicher Palästinapilger (4.–7. Jahrhundert). Stuttgart 1979, rev. and expand. ed. 2002; English trans. J. Wilkinson, Egeria's Travels, Warminster 1999.

Lit.:

E. D. Hunt, Holy Land Pilgrimage in the Later Roman Empire AD 312–460. Oxford 1982.

Ennodius

Bishop of Pavia 514–521; previously deacon of Milan. Author of Letters, a Vita Epiphanii and a Panegyric on Theodoric.

Text and trans.:

Ed. F. Vogel, MGH AA VII, 1885); ed. with French trans. S. Gioanni, Ennode de Pavie, Lettres. Paris 2006–10; ed. with German trans. C. Rohr, Der Theoderich-Panegyricus des Ennodius. Hannover, 1995; English trans. G. M. Cook, The Life of Saint Epiphanius by Ennodius. Washington D. C. 1942.

Lit.:

S. Gioanni, La contribution épistolaire d'Ennode de Pavie à la primauté pontificale sous le règne des papes Symmaque et Hormisdas, MEFRM 113, 2001, 245–68.

S. A. H. Kennell, Magnus Felix Ennodius, a Gentleman of the Church. Ann Arbor 2000.

B.-J. Schröder, Bildung und Briefe im 6 Jahrhundert. Studien zum Mailänder Diakon Magnus Felix Ennodius. Berlin 2007.

Epistolae Arelatenses genuinae

Letters relating to the church of Arles in the fifth and sixth centuries. The origins of the collection seem to be sixth-century, but the earliest manuscript which gathers most of the letters dates to the ninth century.

Text.:

Ed. W. Gundlach, MGH Epp III. Berlin 1892.

Lit.:

S. Gioanni, Césaire d'Arles et la collection des Epistolae Arelatenses genuinae. La construction documentaire d'un lien juridique entre l'Église de Rome et la métropole d'Arles au VIe siècle, in B. Dumézil/L. Vissière (eds.), L'épistolaire politique. France et monde francophone V^e–XVe siècles. Paris 2014, 183–97.

I. N. Wood, Why Collect Letters?, in: 8: Müller, 45–61.

Epistolae Austrasicae

Collection of Gallo-Roman and Merovingian letters, dating from the late fifth to the late sixth century. The full collection may have been put together as late as the early ninth century.

Text:

Ed. W. Gundlach, MGH Epp III, 1892; ed. E. Malaspina, Il Liber epistolarum della cancelleria austrasica (sec. V–VI). Rome 2001.

Lit.:

G. Barrett/G. Woudhuysen, Assembling the Austrasian Letters at Trier and Lorsch, in: Early Medieval Europe 24, 2016, 3–57.

B. Dumézil/T. Lienhard, Les lettres austrasiennes. Dire, cacher, transmettre les informations diplomatiques au haut Moyen Âge, in: Les relations diplomatiques au Moyen Âge. Formes des enjeux. Paris 2011, 69–80.

A. V. Tyrell, Merovingian Letters and Letter Writers. Turnhout 2019.

Eucherius of Lyon

Born c. 380, monk of Lérins, elected bishop of Lyon c. 434, d. c. 449. Author of treatises on the ascetic life and of an account of the martyrdom of the Theban legion.

Text and trans.:

Opera ed. C. Wotke, CSEL 31. Vienna 1894, also in PL 50.

S. Pricoco, Eucherii De Laude eremi. Catania 1965.

Passio Acaunensium martyrum, ed. B. Krusch, MGH SRM III, 1896; ed. B. Näf, Duo Passiones Acaunensium martyrum, available at https://passiones.textandbytes.com.

Lit.:

C. J. Kelly, The Myth of the Desert in Western Monasticism. Eucherius of Lyon's In Praise of the Desert, in: Cistercian Studies Quarterly 46, 2011, 129–41.

Eugippius

Abbot of Castellum Lucullanum near Naples, the burial site of Severinus of Noricum; d. after 533. His Vita Severini is the major source for the history of Noricum in the second half of the fifth century. Also, the author of a florilegium of works by Augustine, and, less certainly, of a monastic rule.

Text and trans.:

Eugippius, Excerpta ex operibus Augustini, ed. P. Knöll, CSEL IX, 1 1885.

Eugippius, Vita Sancti Severini, ed. P. Knöll, CSEL IX, 2, 1886; Vita Severini, ed. R. Noll, 2nd ed. Berlin 1963 (with commentary).

Eugippe, Commemoratorium vita sancti Severini, ed. and French trans. P. Régerat, SC 374. Paris 1991.

Eugippius, Regula, ed. A. de Vogüé/F. Villegas, CSEL 87, 1976; text, German trans. and comm. M. Krausgruber, Die Regel des Eugippius. Die Klosterordnung des Verfassers der Vita Sancti Severini im Lichte ihrer Quellen. Text, Übersetzung, Kommentar. Innsbruck 1996.

Lit.:

A. K. Gometz, Eugippius of Lucullanum. A Biography. Ph. D. thesis Leeds 2008.

W. Pohl/M. Diesenberger, (eds.), Eugippius und Severin. Der Autor, der Text und der Heilige. Vienna 2002.

C. Stancliffe, Review of P. Régerat, Eugippe: Vie de saint Séverin, in: Journal of Theological Studies 4, 1994, 351–3.

G. Wirth, Anmerkungen zur Vita des Severin von Noricum, in: Quaderni Catanesi di Studi Classici e Medievali 1, 1979, 219–266

Eunapius of Sardis

Philosopher and Rhetor, c. 345–c. 420. Author of a now-fragmentary work of history covering the period from 270 to 404.

Text and trans.:

A. Baldini, Ricerche sulla "Storia" di Eunapio. Bologna 1984.

Lit.:

R. C. Blockley, The Fragmentary Classicising Historians of the Later Roman Empire. Liverpool 1983.

A. Breebart, Eunapius of Sardes and the Writing of History, in: Mnemosyne 32, 1979, 360–75.

Eusebius of Caesarea

Bishop of Caesarea (Palastine) from c. 314, d. 339/40. Ecclesiastical historian, was involved in the Arian controversy, wrote apologetic and dogmatic works, as well as a Chronicle (which does not survive in its original Greek, but can be reconstructed from early translations), the earliest Ecclesiastical History, and a eulogy of the emperor Constantine (Vita Constantini). For the Latin version of the Chronicle, see under Jerome.

Text and trans.:

Historia ecclesiastica, ed. E. Schwartz, 3. vols.: GCS 9. Berlin 1903–09; German trans. Ph. Haeuser: BKV II 1, 1932; English trans. K. Lake/J. E. L. Oulton/H. J. Lawlor, 2 vols. London 1926–42.

Vita Constantini, ed. F. Winkelmann, GCS, unnumbered. 2nd ed. Berlin 1975; German trans. J. M. Pfättich, BKV 9, 1913; English trans. and comm. A. Cameron/S. G. Hall, Eusebius, Life of Constantine. Oxford 1999.

Lit.:

R. W. Burgress, The Dates and Editions of Eusebius' Chronici canones and Historia Ecclesiastica, in: The Journal of Theological Studies 48,1997, 471–504.

R. W. Burgress, M. Kulikowski, Mosaics of Time, the Latin Chronicle Traditions from the First Century BC to the Sixth Century AD. Turnhout 2013.

R. Farina, L'impero e l'imperatore cristiano in Eusebio di Cesarea. La prima teologia politica del cristianesimo. Zürich 1966.

P. Franchi de'Cavalieri, Constantiniana. Studi e Testi 171, Vatican City 1953.

K. M. Girardet, Das christliche Priestertum Konstantins d. Gr. Ein Aspekt der Herrscheridee des Eusebius von Caesarea, in: Chiron 10, 1980, 569–592.

M. Gödecke, Geschichte als Mythos. Eusebs "Kirchengeschichte". Frankfurt am Main 1987.

A. Johnson/J. Scott (eds.), Eusebius of Caesarea. Tradition and Innovations. London 2013.

R. Laqueur, Eusebius als Historiker seiner Zeit. Berlin 1929.

J.-M. Sansterre, Eusèbe de Césarée et la naissance de la théorie césaropapiste, in: Byzantion 42, 1972, 131–195, 532–593.

D. Timpe, Was ist Kirchengeschichte? Zum Gattungscharakter der Historia Ecclesiastica des Eusebius, in: Xenia 22, 1989, 171–204.

D. S. Wallace-Hadrill, Eusebius of Caesarea. London 1960.

F. Winkelmann, Zur Geschichte des Authentizitätsproblems der Vita Constantini, in: Klio 40, 1962, 187–243.

F. Winkelmann, Die Textbezeugung der Vita Constantini des Eusebius von Caesarea: TU 84, 1962.

Eusebius Gallicanus

Homily collection from the early sixth century. Once attributed to Faustus of Riez, it contains some of his sermons.

Text.:

F. Glorie (ed.), Eusebius Gallicanus, Sermones, CCSL 101, 101A, 101B. Turnhout 1970–1.

Lit.:

L. K. Bailey, Christianity's Quiet Success. The Eusebius Gallicanus Sermon Collection and the Power of the Church in Late Antique Gaul. South Bend 2010.

Eutropius

Historian, active in the mid fourth century, composed a compendium of Roman history from the beginnings to Jovian (364).

Text and trans.:

Breviarium ab urbe condita, ed. C. Santini. Stuttgart 1979; ed. and trans. B. Bleckmann/J. Gross, Eutropius, Breviarium ab urbe condita. Paderborn 2018; English trans. H. W. Bird. Liverpool 1993.

Lit.:

D. H. Rohrbach, The Historians of Late Antiquity. London 2002.

Faustus of Riez

Born c. 410. monk at Lérins, bishop of Riez, c. 457–90, and theologian.

Text and trans.:

Ed. A. Engelbrecht, CCEL 21. Vienna 1891; epistolae, ed. B. Krusch, MGH, AA VIII, 1987; ed. R. Demeulenaere, Foebadius, Victricius, Leporius, Vincentius Lerinensis, Eva-

grius, Ruricius, CCSL 64. Turnhout 1985; also see under Eusebius Gallicanus.
Letters in English trans. R. W. Mathisen, Ruricius of Limoges and Friends. A Collection of Letters from Visigothic Gaul. Liverpool.

Lit.:

E. L. Fortin, Christianisme et culture philosophique au Ve siècle. La querelle de l'âme humaine en Occident. Paris 1959.

T. A. Smith, De Gratia. Faustus of Riez's Treatise on Grace and its Place in the History of Thought. South Bend 1990.

Ferrandus, Fulgentius

African theologian, d. 546/7, involved in the Tricapitoline debate. Once regarded as the author of the Life of Fulgentius of Ruspe who he accompanied into exile.

Text.:

PL 67.

Ferreolus of Uzès

Born c. 520; bishop of Uzès, 553–81; author of a monastic rule.

Text:

Ed. V. Desprez, La Regula Ferreoli. Texte critique, in: Revue Mabillon 60, 1982, 117–48.

Fulgentius Bishop of Ruspe

Born 462 or 477, appointed Bishop of Ruspe, d. 527 or 533. Anti-theologian active in the Vandal kingdom.

Text and trans.:

Ed. and French trans. J. Fraipont, Fulgence de Ruspe, Lettres ascetiques et morales, SC 487. Paris 2004.

Anon., Vita Fulgentii, ed. A. Isola, CCSL 91F. Turnhout 2016.

Lit.:

Y. Modéran, La chronologie de la Vie de Fulgence de Ruspe et ses incidences sur l'histoire de l'Afrique vandale, in: MEFRM 105, 1993, 135–88.

Gelasius I

Born in Africa, bishop of Rome 492–6.

Text and trans.:

Letters, in: A. Thiel, Epistolae romanorum pontificum genuinae et quae ad eos scriptae sunt a S. Hilaro usque ad Pelagium II, Braunschweig 1868.

Lit.:

B. Neil/P. Allen, The Letters of Gelasius I (492–496). Pastor and Micro-Manager of the Church of Rome. Turnhout 2014.

W. Ullmann, Gelasius I (492–496). Das Papsttum an der Wende der Spätantike zum Mittelalter. Stuttgart 1981.

Gennadius of Marseille
Author, d. c. 496, author of continuation of Jerome's De Viris Illustribus.
Text and trans.:
C. A. Bernoulli, Hieronymus und Gennadius De Viris Illustribus, Freiburg im Breisgau
    1895.
E. Sottocorno, Genadio de Marsella, Sobre los Hombres Ilustres. Madrid 2021.

Gildas
British theologian active in Britain and Brittany in the early sixth century.
Text and trans.:
De Excidio Britonum, ed. K. GEORGE, Gildas's De Exfidio Britonum and the early
    British Church. Woodbridge 2009; ed. M. Winterbottom, The Ruin of Britain and
    other documents. Chichester 1978.
Lit.:
L. Larpi, Prologomena to a new edition of Gildas Sapiens "De Excidio Britanniae".
    Florence 2012.

Gregory I
Born c. 540, bishop of Rome 590–604. Theologian, letter-writer. There has been debate
    about the authorship of the Dialogues. His theological works are collected in CSEL
    and CCSL.
Text and trans.:
Register, ed. D. Norberg, CCSL CLX-CLXA. Turnhout 1982; ed. P. Ewald, L. Hartmann,
    MGH, Epp. I–II. Berlin 1891–2; English trans. J. R. C. Martin, The Letters of Gre-
    gory the Great, 3 vols. Turnhout 2004.
Dialogorum Libri Quattuor, ed. A. de Vogüé, 3 vols. SC 251, 260, 265. Paris 1978–80.
Cura pastoralis, ed. with French trans., B. Judic, Grégoire le Grand, Régle pastorale, 2
    vols., SC 381–2. Paris 1992.
Lit.:
M. Dal Santo, Debating the Saint's Cult in the Age of Gregory the Great. Oxford
    2012.
R. A. Markus, Gregory the Great and his World. Cambridge 1997.
J. Richards, Consul of God. The Life and Times of Gregory the Great. London 1980.

Gregory of Nazianzus
Leading Greek theologian, bishop of Nazianzus 372–9, and of Constantinople 379–81.
    The author of letters and speeches, especially against Julian.
Text and trans.:
PG 35-6.
Discours 4–5: Contre Julien, ed. J. Bernardi: SC 309, 1983.
Lit.:
A. Kurmann, Oratio 4 gegen Julian. Ein Kommentar, Basel 1988.
J. A. McGuckin, St Gregory of Nazianzus. An Intellectual Biography. Crestwood 2001.

Gregory of Tours

538–94. From a senatorial family, bishop of Tours from 573. Wrote a work of history and several hagiographical works.

Text and trans.:

Decem Libri Historiarum, ed. B. Krusch/W. Levison, MGH, SRM I, 1; ed. and German trans. R. Buchner, 2 vols.: I 5th ed. Darmstadt 1977, II 6th ed. 1974; English trans. L. Thorpe, Gregory of Tours, History of the Franks, Harmondsworth 1974; partial English trans. A. C. Murray, Gregory of Tours, The Merovingians.

Opera hagiographica, ed. B. Krusch, MGH, SRM, I, 2, 1885; ed. and English trans. G. de Nie, Gregory of Tours, Lives and Miracles. Cambridge Mass. 2015; ed. and French trans. L. Pietri, Grégoire de Tours, La Vie des Pères. Paris 2016; English trans. E. James, Gregory of Tours, Life of the Fathers. Liverpool 1985; R. Van Dam, Gregory of Tours, Glory of the Confessors. Liverpool 1988; B. Krusch, Gregory of Tours, Glory of the Martyrs. Liverpool 1988; B. Krusch, Saints and their Miracles in Late Antique Gaul. Princeton 1993.

Lit.:

G. de Nie, Views from a Many-windowed Tower. Studies in the Imagination in the Works of Gregory of Tours. Amsterdam 1987.

N. Gauthier/H. Galinié (eds.), Grégoire de Tours et l'espace gaulois, Tours 1997.

W. Goffart, The Narrators of Barbarian History (A. D. 550–800). Jordanes, Gregory of Tours, Bede and Paul the Deacon. Princeton 1988.

M. Heinzelmann, Gregor von Tours (538–594), "Zehn Bücher Geschichte". Historiographie und Gesellschaftskonzept im 6. Jahrhundert. Darmstadt 1994; English trans. Gregory of Tours, History and Society in the Sixth Century. Cambridge 2001.

A. E. Jones, Death and Afterlife in the Pages of Gregory of Tours, Amsterdam 2020.

K. Mitchell/I. N. Wood (eds.), The World of Gregory of Tours. Leiden 2002.

A. C. Murray (ed.), A Companion to Gregory of Tours. Leiden 2016.

H. Reimitz, History, Frankish Identity, and the Framing of Western Ethnicity, 350–850. Cambridge 2015.

M. Weidemann, Kulturgeschichte der Merowingerzeit nach den Werken Gregors von Tours, 2 vols. Mainz 1982.

Hilary of Arles

Born c. 403, monk of Lérins, succeeds Honoratus as bishop of Arles, 429, d. 449. Author of the Life of Honoratus.

Text and trans.:

Vita Honorati, ed. and French trans. M.-D. Valentin, Hilaire d'Arles, Vie de saint Honorat, SC 235. Paris 1977; with German trans. F. Jung, Hilarius von Arles, Leben des hl. Honoratus. Eine Textstudie zu Mönchtum und Bischofswesen im spätantiken Gallien mit lateinisch-deutschem Text des "Sermo" sowie zweier Predigten über den hl. Honoratus von Faustus von Riez und Caesarius von Arles. Fohren/Linden 2013.

Lit.:

L. Håkanson, Some Critical Notes on the "Vitae Honorati et Hilarii", in: Vigiliae Christianae 31, 1977, 55–9.

Hilary of Poitiers

Born c. 310, elected bishop of Poitiers c. 350, d. 367. Leading Western anti-Arian apologist, exiled by Constantius II c. 357-61.

Text and trans.:

Ed. A. Zingerle, CSEL 22. Vienna 1891, ed. A. Feder, CSEL 65. Vienna 1916.

Against Constantius, English trans. R. Flower, Imperial Invectives against Constantius. Liverpool 2016; L. R. Wickham (trans.), Hilary of Poitiers. Conflicts of Conscience and Law in the Fourth-century Church. Liverpool 1997.

Lit.:

C. Beckwith, Hilary of Poitiers on the Trinity. From De Fide to De Trinitate. New York 2009.

J. Doignon, Hilaire de Poitiers avant l'exil. Recherches sur la naissance, l'enseignement et l'épreuve d'une foi épiscopale en Gaule au milieu du IVe siècle. Paris 1971.

Historia Augusta

Collection of imperial biographies covering the years 117-285, perhaps written c. 395.

Text and trans.:

Scriptores Historiae Augustae, ed. E. Hohl, 2 vols., Leipzig 1965; ed. and English trans. D. Magie. Cambridge Mass. 1921-2; ed. and French trans. F. Paschoud (ed.), Histoire Auguste, 5 vols. Paris, 2002-11; German trans E. Hohl, 2 vols. Zürich 1976-85.

Lit.:

T. D. Barnes, The Sources of the Historia Augusta. Brussels 1978.

Beiträge zur Historia-Augusta-Forschung: Antiquitas Reihe 4. Bonn 1963 ff.

G. Bonamente/F. Paschoud (eds.), Historiae Augustae. Colloquium Genevense, Bari 1994, 1999.

G. Bonamente/K. Rosen (eds.), Historiae Augustae. Colloquium Bonnense V. Bari 1997.

A. Chastagnol, Constantinople et ombres chinoises dans l'Histoire Auguste, in: 15.7: Bonamente/Rosen, 85-96.

A. Lippold, Die Historia Augusta. Eine Sammlung römischer Kaiserviten aus der Zeit Konstantins. Stuttgart 1998.

M. Meckler, The Beginning of the "Historia Augusta", in: HZ 45, 1996, 364-75.

A. Momigliano, An Unsolved Problem of Historical Forgery. The Scriptores Historiae Augustae (1954), in: A. Momigliano, Secondo contributo alia storia degli studi classici. Rome 1960, 105-43.

B. Pottier, L'Histoire Auguste, le consul Aurelianus et la réception de la Notitia Dignitatum en Occident, in: Antiquité Tardive 14, 2006, 225-34.

J. Stover, M. Kestemont, The Authorship of the "Historia Augusta". Two New Computational Studies, in: Bulletin of the Institute of Classical Studies 59, 2016, 140-57.

J. Straub, Heidnische Geschichtsapologetik in der christlichen Spätantike. Bonn 1963.

R. Syme, Ammianus and the Historia Augusta. Oxford 1968.

R. Syme, Emperors and Biography. Studies in the Historia Augusta. Oxford 1971.

Honoratus of Marseille

Bishop of Marseille, c. 483–94. Author of the Life of Hilary of Arles, c. 480.
Text and trans.:
Honoratus, Vita Hilarii, ed. with French trans. S. Cavallin/P.-A. Jacob, Honorat de Marseille, La Vie d'Hilaire d'Arles, SC 404. Paris 1995.
Lit.:
L. Håkanson, Some Critical Notes on the "Vitae Honorati et Hilarii", in: Vigiliae Christianae 31, 1977, 55–9.

Hydatius

Ca. 400–ca. 469, bishop of Aqua Flaviae, author of a chronicle covering the years 379–468.
Text and trans.:
Chronicon, ed. MGH AA XI, 1894; ed. with English trans. R. W. Burgess, The Chronicle of Hydatius and the Consularia Constantinopolitana,. Oxford 1993; ed. J.-M. Kötter/C. Scardino, Chronik des Hydatius. Fortführung der Spanischen Epitome. Paderborn 2019.
Lit.:
J. Arce, El catastrofismo de Hydacio y los camellos de la Gallaecia, in: A. Velásquez/E. Cerrillo/P. Mateos, Los ultimos romanos en Lusitania. Mérida 1995, 219–29.
H. Börm, Hydatius von Aquae Flaviae und die Einheit des römischen Reiches im fünften Jahrhundert, in: B. Bleckmann/T. Stickler (eds.), Griechische Profanhistoriker des fünften nachchristlichen Jahrhunderts. Stuttgart 2014, 195–214.
S. Muhlberger, The Fifth-century Chroniclers. Prosper, Hydatius and the Gallic Chronicle of 452. Leeds 1990.

Jerome

Father of the Church, c. 345–419/420. Born in Stridon, travelled throughout the Empire, moved to Rome in 382, where he worked for pope Damasus. In 384 he returned to the Holy Land. In addition to translating the Bible into Latin, he wrote numerous works of Biblical commentary (edited in PL, CSEL, CCSL, and SC) and letters, as well as works of hagiography (the Lives of Hilarion, of Malchus, and Paul the first Hermit). He also translated and continued Eusebius' Chronicle.
Text:
Chronicle, ed. R. Helm, GCS 24, 34, Leipzig 1913–26; French trans. B. Jeanjean/B. Lançon, Saint Jérôme Chronique, Rennes 2004.
De Viris Illustribus, ed. A. Ceresa-Gastaldo, Florence 1988.
Letters, ed. I. Hilberg: CSEL 54–56, 1910–18.
Lit.:
A. Cain/J. Lössl (eds.), Jerome of Stridon. His Life, Writings and Legacy, Farnham 2009.
E. A. Clerk, Jerome, Chrysostom and Friends. New York 1979.
Y.-M. Duval (ed.), Jérôme entre l'Occident et l'Orient. Paris 1988.
J. N. D. Kelly, Jerome. His Life, Writings and Controversies. London 1975.

S. Rebenich, Hieronymus und sein Kreis. Prosopografische und sozialgeschichtliche
Untersuchung. Stuttgart 1992.

S. Rebenich, Jerome. London 2002.

John of Biclaro
Born c. 540, d. post 621. Bishop of Girona, author of a chronicle.
Text and trans.:
C. Cardelle de Hartmann, ed., Victoris Tunnunensis Chronicon cum reliquiis ex Con-
sularibus Caesaraugustanis et Iohannis Biclarensis Chronicon, CCSL CLXXIII A.
Turnhout 2001; English trans. K. B. Wolf, Conquerors and Chroniclers of Early
Medieval Spain. Liverpool 1990.

John Chrysostom
Greek Father of the Church, 344/354–407. Priest in Antioch; 397 Bishop of Constantinople,
exiled 404, d. 407. Author of letters, homilies, tractates.
Text and trans:
Tractates in: SC 13, 28, 50, 79, 117, 125, 138, 188, 272, 277, 300, 304.
Letters (selection) in: SC 13 und 103.
BKV 23, 25–27.
Chrysostom's Homilies Against the Jews, English trans. C. M. Maxwell, PhD. Diss.
Univ. of Chicago, University Microfilms. Ann Arbor 1967.
Lit.:
J. Stenger, Johannes Chrysostomos und die Christianisierung der Polis. "Damit die
Städte Städte warden". Tübingen 2019.
C. Tiersch, Johannes Chrysostomos in Konstantinopel, 398–404. Weltsicht und
Wirken eines Bischofs in der Hauptstadt des Oströmischen Reiches. Tübingen
2002.

Jordanes
Gothic historian, d. after 551. Author of Roman and Gothic histories.
Text:
De origine actibusque Getarum ("Getica"), De summa temporum vel origine
actibusque gentis Romanorum ("Romana"), ed. Th. Mommsen, MGH AA V 1,
1882; F. Giunta, Jordanis de origine actibus Getarum. Rome 1991; text and
French trans. O. Devillers, Jordanès, Histoire des Goths. Paris 2008; English
trans. P. Van Nuffelen/L. Van Hoof, Jordanes Romana and Getica. Liverpool 2020;
German trans., L. Möller, Jordanes, Die Gotengeschichte. Wiesbaden 2012.
Lit.:
A. S. Christensen, Cassiodorus, Jordanes and the History of the Goths. Studies in a Mi-
gration Myth. Copenhagen 2002.
W. Ensslin, Des Symmachus Historia Romana als Quelle für Jordanes. Munich 1948.
W. Goffart, The Narrators of Barbarian History. Jordanes, Gregory of Tours, Bede,
and Paul the Deacon. Princeton 1988.

R. Kasperski, Propaganda im Dienste Theoderichs des Großen. Die dynastische Tradition der Amaler in der "Historia Gothorum" Cassiodors, in: FMSt 52, 2018, 13–42.

R. Kasperski, Jordanes versus Procopius of Caesarea. Considerations Concerning a Certain Historiographic Debate on How to Solve "the Problem of the Goths", in: Viator 49, 2018, 1–23.

B. Luiselli, Sul de summa temporum di Jordanes, in: Romanobarbarica 1, 1976, 84–108.

L. Várady, Jordanes-Studien. Jordanes und das Chronicon des Marcellinus Comes – Die Selbständigkeit des Jordanes, in: Chiron 6, 1976, 441–487.

Julian

Emperor 361-3.

Text and trans.:

Ed. and English trans. W. C. Wright, 3 vols. Cambridge Mass. 1913–23; ed. and French trans. J. Bidez, 2 vols. Paris 1932–60; Letters, Greek with German trans, ed. B. K. Weiss. Munich 1973.

Lit.:

P. Athanassiadi, Julian and Hellenism. An Intellectual Biography. London 1981.

N. Baker-Brian/S. Tougher (eds.), Emperor and Authors. The Writings of Julian the Apostate. Swansea 2012.

G. W. Bowersock, Julian the Apostate. London 1978.

J. Fontaine/C. Prato/A. Marcone, Alia madre degli dei e altri discorsi. Milan 1987.

B. Gentili (ed.), Giuliano Imperatore. Urbino 1986.

K. Rosen, Julian. Kaiser, Gott und Christenhasser. Stuttgart 2006.

R. Smith, Julian's Gods. Religion and Philosophy in the Thought and Action of Julian the Apostate. London 1995.

H. C. Teitler, The Last Pagan Emperor. Julian the Apostate and the War against Christianity. Oxford 2017.

Juvencus

Spanish poet, active c. 330.

Text and trans.:

Evangelium libri, ed. J. Hümer, CSEL 24. Vienna 1891; English trans. S. McGill, Juvencus. Four Books of the Gospels – Evangeliorum libri quattuor. London 2016. Oxford 1984; German trans. A. Hartl, BKV 36, 1919.

Lactantius

Rhetorician in Nicomedia under Diocletian, c. 317 tutor of Crispus, son of Constantine. His major work is a history of the Great persecution.

Text and trans.:

De mortibus persecutorum, ed. with French trans. and comm. J. Moreau, 2 vols. SC 39, 1954/55; ed. with English trans. and comm. J. L. Creed. Oxford 1984; German trans. A. Hartl, BKV 36, 1919.

Lit.:
T. D. Barnes, Lactantius and Constantine, in: JRS 63, 1973, 29–46.
A. S. Christensen, Lactantius the Historian. Copenhagen 1980.
J. Fontaine/M. Perrin (eds.), Lactance et son temps. Paris 1978.

Laterculus regum Vandalorum
Text:
M. Becker/J.-M. Kötter (eds.), Prosper Tiro, Chronik. Laterculus regum Vandalorum et Alanorum. Paderborn 2016.

Leo I
Born c. 400, bishop of Rome 440–61. Played an important role in negotiations leading to the Council of Chalcedon. His works are collected in PL 54–6.
Text and trans.:
Letters in: A. Thiel, Epistolae romanorum pontificum genuinae et quae ad eos scriptae sunt a S. Hilaro usque ad Pelagium II. Braunschweig 1868.
Sermons, ed. J. Leclercq/R. Dolle, SC 22, 49, 74, 200. Paris 1949–73.
Lit.:
B. Neil, Leo the Great. London 2009.
B. Neil, Leo Magnus, in: A. Dupont (ed.), Preaching in the Patristic Era. Sermons, preachers, Audiences in the Latin West. Leiden 2018, 327–46.
K. Uhalde, Pope Leo on Power and Failure, in: The Catholic History Review 95, 2009, 671–88.

Libanius
Antiochene Rhetor, 314–393.
Text:
Ed. R. Foerster, 12 vols. Hildesheim 1903–23; Selected Orations, ed. and English trans. A. F. Norman, 2 vols. Cambridge Mass. 1969–71; text and German trans. G. Fatouros/T. Krischer, Auswahl. Munich 1980; English trans. A. F. Norman, Antioch as a Dentre of Hellenic Culture as Observed by Libanius. Liverpool 2000; English trans. R. Cribiore, Between City and School. Selected Orations of Libanius. Liverpool 2015; English trans. S. Bradbury, Selected Letters of Libanius from the Age of Constantius and Julian. Liverpool 2004; German trans. Autobiographische Schriften, P. Wolf. Zurich/Stuttgart 1967.
Lit.:
A. J. Festugière, Antioche paienne et chrétienne. Paris 1959.
J. H. W. Liebeschuetz, Antioch. City and Imperial Administration in the Later Roman Empire. Oxford 1972.
P. Petit, Libane et la vie municipale à Antioche. Paris 1955.

Liberatus of Carthage
Archdeacon of the Church of Carthage, theologian; active pre 566.
Text and trans.:

Libératus de Carthage, Abrégé de l'histoire des Nestoriens et des Eutychiens, ed. P. Bladeaux, SC 607. Paris 2019.

Lucifer of Cagliari
Bishop of Cagliari, d. ca 380, anti-Arian theologian whose own religious position was attacked by Jerome.
Text and trans.:
Ed. G. F. Diercks, CCSL VIII. Turnhout 1978; English trans. R. Flower, Imperial Invectives against Constantius II. Liverpool 2016.

Luxorius
Poet in Vandal Africa whose epigrams are preserved in the Anthologia Latina.
Text, trans., and comm.:
Ed. H. Happ, Luxurius. Text, Untersuchung, Kommentar. Stuttgart 1986; English trans. M. Rosenblum, Luxurius, a Latin Poet among the Vandals. Together with a Text of the Poems and an English trans., New York 1961.
Lit.:
M. Giovini, Studi su Lussorio. Genoa 2004.

Lydus, John
490–post 552. Active in imperial service and in scholarship. The most important of his works for Late Antique historians is the De Magistratibus.
Text and trans.:
J. le Lydien (ed.), Des magistratures de l'état romain, ed. and French trans. M. Dubuisson/J. Schamp. Paris 2006; ed. and English trans. T. F. Carney, On the Magistrates of the Roman Constitution. Sydney 1965.
Lit.:
J. Caimi, Burocrazia e diritto nel De magistratibus di Giovanni Lido. Milan 1984.
C. Kelly, Ruling the Later Roman Empire. Cambridge Mass. 2004.
M. Maas, John Lydus and the Roman Past. London 1992.

Macrobius
Latin author active in the early fifth century.
Text:
Opera, ed. J. Willis, 2 vols. Stuttgart 1970; ed. and English trans. R. A. Kaster, Macrobius, The Saturnalia, 3 vols. Cambridge Mass. 2011; English trans. W. H. Stahl, Macrobius, Commentary on the Dream of Scipio. New York 1952.
Lit.:
A. Cameron, The Date and Identity of Macrobius, in: JRS 56, 1966, 25–38.
S. Döpp, Zur Datierung von Macrobius' "Saturnalia", in: Hermes 106, 1978, 612–32.
J. Flamant, Macrobe et le néo-platonisme latin à la fin du IVe siècle. Leiden 1977.

Malalas, John

Author of a World Chronicle from the time of Justinian.
Text:
Ed. J. Thurn, Corpus Fontium Historiae Byzantinae. Berlin 2000; English trans. E. Jeffreys/R. Scott et al., Melbourne 1986; English trans. M. Spinka/G. Downey, Chronicle of John Malalas. Books VIII–XVIII. Chicago 1940.
Lit.:
E. Jeffreys/B. Croke/R. Scott, (eds.), Studies in John Malalas. Sydney 1990.

Malchus

Byzantine chronicler of the late fifth century who continued the work of Priscus, covering the years from 473–80. Fragments of his work are preserved in later texts.
Text and trans.:
Ed. with Latin trans., K. W. L. Müller, Fragmenta historicorum Graecorum; ed. with English trans. R. C. Blockley, The Fragmentary Classicising Historians of the Later Roman Empire. Eunapius, Olympiodorus, Priscus and Malchus, 2 vols. Liverpool 1981.
Lit.:
B. Baldwin, Malchus of Philadelphia, in: Dumbarton Oaks Papers 31, 1977, 89–107.
M. Errington, Malchos von Philadelphia, Kaiser Zenon und die zwei Theoderiche, in: Museum Helveticum 40, 1983, 82–110.

Marcellinus Comes

Byzantine chronicler at the court of Constantinople, d. c. 534.
Text and trans.:
Chronicon, ed. Th. Mommsen, MGH AA XI, 1894; English trans. and comm. B. Croke, The Chronicle of Marcellinus. A Translation and Commentary. Sydney 1995.
Lit.:
B. Croke, Count Marcellinus and his Chronicle. Oxford 2001.

Marius of Avenches

532–96, bishop of Avenches from 574.
Text and trans:
Chronicon, ed. Th. Mommsen, MGH AA XI, 1894; J. Favrod, La chronique de Marius d'Avenches (455–581), Lausanne 1991.
Lit.:
J. Favrod, Les sources et la chronologie de Marius d'Avenches, in: Francia 17, 1990, 1–22.

Martianus Capella

Probably active in Carthage in the late fifth century. Author of the encyclopedic De nuptiis Philologiae et Mercurii, which was the foundational text for the medieval categorisation of the Seven Liberal arts.

Text and trans.:

Ed. J. A. Wıllıs, De nuptiis Philologiae et Mercurii, Leipzig 1983; ed. and French trans. Martianus Capella, Le noces de Philologie et de Mercure, ed. J.-F. Chevalıer/B. Ferré/M. Ferré/J.-Y. Guıllaumın. Paris 2003; English trans. W. H. Stahl/R. W. John-son, 2 vols. New York 1971–77.

Lit.:

L. Crıstante, Martiani Capellae De nuptiis Philologiae et Mercurii Liber IX. Padua 1987.

L. Lenaz, Martiani Capellae De nuptiis Philologiae et Mercurii liber secundus. Padua 1975.

D. R. Shanzer, A Philosophical and Literary Commentary on Martianus Capella's De Nuptiis Philologiae et Mercurii Book 1. Berkeley 1986.

K. Vössıng, Augustinus und Martianus Capella. Ein Diskurs im spätantiken Kartago?, in: T. Fuhrer (ed.), Die christlich-philosophischen Diskurse der Spätantike. Stuttgart 2006.

Martin of Braga

Born in Pannonia, travelled to the Holy Land, then to Gallaecia, becoming Bishop of Braga c. 550, d. 580. Monastic founder and author of works of moral theology.

Text and trans.:

Ed. C. W. Barlow. New Haven 1950; ed. with French trans. Martin de Braga, Œuvres morales et pastorales, ed. C. W. Barlow/G. Sabbah, SC 594. Paris 2018.

Lit.:

A. Ferreıro, The Westward Journey of St Martin of Braga, in: Studia monastica 22, 1980, 243–51.

A. Ferreıro, The Missionary Labours of St Martin of Braga in 6th-century Galicia, in: Studia monastica 23, 1981, 11–26.

Maximus of Turin

Born c. 380, bishop of Turin, d. between 408 and 423.

Text.:

Ed. A. Mutzenbecher, CCSL 23. Turnhout 1962.

Lit.:

R. Lızzı Tesıa, Vescovi e strutture nella città tardoantica. L'Italia annonaria nel IV–V secolo d. C., Como 1989.

Merobaudes

Fifth-century Latin rhetorician and poet; author of a panegyric on Aetius, of which fragments survive, and also of religious verse.

Text:

Ed. I. Becher, Corpus Scriptorum Historiae Byzantinae. Bonn 183; ed. T. Bırt, in Clau-dian, MGH, AA X, 1892; ed. F. M. Clover, Flavius Merobaudes. A Translation and Historical Commentary, in: Transactions of the American Philosophical Society 61, 1971, 1–78.

Olympiodorus

Greek historian of the first half of the 5th century, author of a now-fragmentary work of history, covering the years 407–425.

Text and trans.

Ed. with Latin trans. K. W. L. Müller, Fragmenta historicorum Graecorum; ed. with English trans. R. C. Blockley, The Fragmentary Classicising Historians of the Later Roman Empire. Eunapius, Olympiodorus, Priscus and Malchus, 2 vols. Liverpool 1981.

Lit.:

A. Baldini, Ricerche di tarda storiografia (da Olimpiodoro di Tebe). Bologna 2004.

A. Gillett, The Date and the Circumstances of Olympiodorus of Thebes, Traditio 48, 1993, 1–29.

J. F. Matthews, Olympiodorus and the History of the West (A. D. 407–425), in: JRS 60, 1970, 79–97.

F. Paschoud, Eunape, Olympiodore, Zosime. Bari 2006.

D. Rohrbacher, The Historians of Late Antiquity. London 2002.

Optatus of Milevis

Fourth-century bishop of Milevis, noted for his anti-Donatist writings.

Text and trans.:

Ed. J. Labrousse, Optate contre les Donatistes, 2 vols. SC 412–3. Paris 1995–6; English trans. M. Edwards, Optatus against the Donatists. Liverpool 1997.

Orientius of Auch

Bishop of Auch and author of a verse Commonitorium.

Text and trans.:

Ed. R. Ellis, in Poetae Minores, CSEL 16. Vienna 1888; English trans. M. D. Tobin, Orientii Commonitorium. A Commentary with an Introduction and Translation. Washington D. C. 1945.

Lit.:

I. Fielding, Physical Ruin and Spiritual Perfection in Fifth-century Gaul. Orientius and his Contemporaries on the "Landscape of the Soul", in: Journal of Early Christian Studies 22, 2014, 569–85.

Orosius

Spanish priest, although perhaps born in Brittany, who studied with Augustine before moving to the Holy Land, where he was involved in the Synods of Jerusalem and Diospolis. Author of the Historiarum adversus paganos.

Text and trans.:

Ed. J. Zangemeister: CSEL 5, 1882; ed. with Italian trans. A. Lippold/G. Chiarini, 1976; ed. with German trans. A. Lippold/C. Andresen, 2 vols. Zurich/Munich 1985–86; ed. with French trans., M.-P. Arnaud-Lindet. Paris 1990–1. English trans. A. T. Fear. Liverpool 2010.

Lit.:

C. Corsini, Introduzione alle Storie di Orosio, Turin 1968.

B. Lacroix, Orose et ses idées, Montreal 1965.

F. Fabbrini, Paolo Orosio uno storico. Rome 1979.

H.-W. Goetz, Die Geschichtstheologie des Orosius. Darmstadt 1980.

D. Koch-Peters, Ansichten des Orosius zur Geschichte seiner Zeit. Frankfurt am Main et al. 1984.

E. T. Mommsen, Orosius and Augustine, in: E. T. Mommsen/E. Rice (ed.) Medieval and Renaissance Studies. New York 1966, 299–324.

D. Ó Corráin, Orosius, Ireland and Christianity, in: Peritia 26, 2017, 113–34.

P. Van Nuffelen, Orosius and the Rhetoric of History. Oxford 2012.

Pachomius

d. 346. Founded c. 320 the monastery of Tabennisi (Thebais), instituting the tradition of coenobitic monasticis. His monastic rule only survives in Jerome's Latin translation.

Text and trans.:

Œuvres de S. Pachome et de ses disciples. Corpus scriptorum christianorum orientalium 159–160. Louvain 1956.

The Life of Pachomius, trans. A. N. Athanassakis, 1975; A. Veilleux (trans.), Pachomian Koinonia, 3 vols.: The Life of Saint Pachomius; Pachomian Chronicles and Rules; Instructions, Letters and Other Writings). Kalamazoo 1980–2.

Lit.:

P. Rousseau, Pachomius. The Making of a Community in Fourth-century Egypt. Berkeley 2nd ed. 1999.

E. Wipszycka, The Second Gift of the Nile. Monks and Monasteries in Late Antique Egypt. Warsaw 2018.

Palladius

Fourth/fifth-century author of agricultural works.

Text and trans.:

Opus agriculturae de veterinaria medicina, de insitione, ed. R. H. Rodgers. Stuttgart 1975; Traité d'agriculture, ed. R. Martin, vol. I. Paris 1976.

Lit.:

E. Frézouls, La vie rurale au Bas-Empire d'apres l'œuvre de Palladius, in: Ktema, 1980, 193–210.

Palladius of Galatia

Early fifth-century author of the Lausiac History, an account of the monks of Egypt, written for Lausus, chamberlain at the court of Theodosius II.

Text and trans.:

Palladius, Historia Lausiaca, die frühen Heiligen der Wüste, ed. and trans. J. Laager, Zurich 1987; Palladio, La storia lausiaca, ed. and trans. G. J. M. Bartelink. Milan 1974; English trans. R. T. Meyer. London 1965; French trans. N. Molinier. Bellefontaine 1999.

Panegyrici Latini

Late fourth-century Collection of 12 panegyrics addressed to various emperors.

Text and trans.:

Panégyriques latins, 3 vols., ed. L. Galletier. Paris 1949–55; ed. R. A. B. Mynors. Oxford 1964; C. E. V. Nixon/B. S. Rogers, In Praise of Later Roman Emperors. Berkeley 1994; B. Müller-Rettig, Panegyrici Latini. Lobreden auf römische Kaiser. Lateinisch und deutsch, 2 vols. Darmstadt, 2008–12; H. Gutzwiller, Die Neujahrsrede des Konsuls Claudius Mamertinus vor dem Kaiser Julian. Text, Übers. und Komm., Basel 1942; A. Guida, Un anonimo panegirico per l'imperatore Giuliano. Florence 1990; B. Müller-Rettig, Der Panegyricus des Jahres 310 auf Konstantin den Großen. Übers. und histor.-philol. Komm. Stuttgart 1990; English trans. C. E. V. Nixon, Pacatus. Panegyric to the Emperor Theodosius. Liverpool 1987.

Lit.:

S. MacCormack, Latin prose Panegyrics. Tradition and Discontinuity in the Later Roman Empire, in: Revue d'Études Augustinienne et Patristiques 22, 1976, 29–77.

W. Portmann, Geschichte in der spätantiken Panegyrik. Frankfurt am Main 1988.

B. S. Rodgers, Divine Insinuation in the Panegyrici Latini, in: Historia 35, 1986, 69–104.

Patrick

British missionary active in Ireland.

Text:

Libri Epistolarum sancti Patricii episcopi, ed. L. Bieler, 2 vols. Dublin 1952; The Book of Letters of Saint Patrick the Bishop, ed. D. R. Howlett. Blackrock 1994; Saint Patrick. His Writings and Muirrchu's Life, ed. and English trans. A.B. E. Hood, Chichester 1978.

Paulinus?

Disputed author of the Carmen ad Uxorem.

Text:

Sanctii Pontii Meropii Paulini carmina, ed. G. Hartel, CSEL 30. Leipzig 1894.

Lit.:

R. Chiappiniello, The Carmen ad Uxorem and the Genre of the Epithalamium, in: W. Otten/K. Pollmann (eds.) Poetry and Exegesis in Premodern Latin Christianity. Leiden 2007, 115–38.

Paulinus of Beziers?

Text and Italian trans.:

A. Fo, Il cosiddetto Epigramma Paulini attribuito a Paolino di Béziers. Testo criticamente riveduto, traduzione e studio introduttivo, in: Romanobarbarica 16, 1999, 97–168.

Lit.:

K. Smolak, Zwischen Bukolik und Satire. Das sogenannte "Sancti Paulini Epigramma", in: International Journal of the Classical Tradition 6, 1999, 3–20.

Paulinus of Milan

Deacon of Milan, notary of bishop Ambrose, whose Life he wrote in 422 at the request of Augustine.

Text and trans.:

M. Pellegrino (ed.), Paolino di Milano, Vita di S. Ambrogio. Rome, 1961; English trans. F. H. Hoare, The Western Fathers. London, 1954.

Lit.:

E. Lamirande, Paulin de Milan et la "Vita Ambrosii". Aspects de la religion sous le Bas-Empire. Paris 1983.

Paulinus of Nola

Bishop of Nola, theologian.

Text and trans.:

Ed. G. de Hartel, CSEL 29. Vienna 1894; G. Santaniello, Paolino di Nola, Le Lettere, 2 vols. Naples 1992; Ausonius et Paulin de Nole, Correspondence, ed. and French trans. D. Amherdt, Bern 2004; English trans. P. G. Walsh, The Letters of Paulinus of Nola, Westminster Md. 1975.

Paulinus Nolanus, Carmina, ed. F. Dolceck, CCSL 21. Turnhout 2012; A. Ruggiero (ed.) Paolino di Nola, I Carmini, Naples 1996; English trans. P. G. Walsh, The Poems of Paulinus of Nola, 2 vols. Westminster Md. 1966–7.

Lit.:

C. Conybeare, Paulinus Noster. Self and Symbols in the Letters of Paulinus of Nola. Oxford 2000.

P. Fabre, Saint Paulin de Nole et l'amitié chrétienne. Paris 1949.

S. Mratschek, Der Briefwechsel des Paulinus von Nola. Göttingen 2002.

D. Trout, Paulinus of Nola. Life, Letters and Poems. Berkeley 1999.

Paulinus of Pella

Senatorial aristocrat, descended from Ausonius, born 377 in Pella in Macedonia, d. in Gaul after 461. After a career in which he was associated with the Visigoths in Provence, he fell on hard times which he described in his poem, the Eucharisticos.

Text and trans.:

Ed. C. M. Lucarini. Munich 2006; ed. with English trans. in H. G. Evelyn White, Ausonius, vol. 2. Cambridge Mass. 1921; ed. and French trans. C. Moussy, Paulin de Pella, Poéme d'action de grâces et Prière, SC 209. Paris 1974.

Lit.:

N. McLynn, Paulinus the Impenitent. A Study of the Eucharisticos, in: Journal of Early Christian Studies 3, 1995, 461–86.

Paulinus of Périgueux

Active c. 470, author of a poetic Life of St Martin.

Text and trans.:

Ed. M. Petschenig, CSEL 16. Milan 1888; Books I–III, ed. with French trans. S. Labarre, SC 581. Paris 2016.

Lit.:

S. Labarre, Le manteau partagé. Deux métaphoses poétiques de la Vie de saint Martin chez Paulin de Périgueux (Vᵉ s) et Venance Fortunat (VIᵉ s). Paris 1998.

Pelagius I

Bishop of Rome, 556–61.
Text:
Pelagii Papae epistolae quae supersunt (556–61), ed. P. M. Gasso/C. M. Batlle. Montserrat 1956.
Lit.:
F. Battistella, Pelagius I. und der Primat Roms. Ein Beitrag zum Drei-Kapitel-Streit und zur Papstgeschichte des 6. Jahrhunderts. Hamburg 2017.
B. Neil, "De Profundis". The Letters and Archives of Pelagius I of Rome (556–561), in: 8: Neil/Allen, 206–20.

Pelagius

Born c. 354, d. 418, British theologian active in Rome whose ideas on grace were attacked by Augustine and Jerome.
Text and trans.:
B. R. Rees, Pelagius, Life and Letters. Woodbridge 1998.
Lit.:
A. Bonner, The Myth of Pelagianism. Oxford 2018.
B. R. Rees, Pelagius, a Reluctant Heretic. Woodbridge 1988.

Peter the Patrician

Imperial administrator at the court of Justinian I, fragments of whose history survive.
Text and trans.:
Fragmenta historicorum Graecorum, vol. 4, ed. C. O. Müller/K. Müller. Paris 1851; English trans. T. M. Banchich, The Lost History of Peter the Patrician. London 2015.

Philostorgius

Born 368, d. c. 439; active in Constantinople. Church historian who wrote a history of the Arian controversy from an non-orthodox viewpoint.
Text and trans:
Ed. B. Bleckmann, M. Stein, Philostorgius Kirchengeschichte, 2 vols. Paderborn 2015; ed. J. Bidez/F. Winkelmann, Philostorgius, Kirchengeschichte, Mit dem Leben des Lucian von Antioch und den Fragmenten eines arianischen Historiographen. Berlin 1981; English trans. P. R. Amidon, Philostorgius, Church History, Atlanta 2007.

Polemius Silvius

Friend of Hilary of Arles.
Text and German trans:
B. Bleckmann/J.-M. Kötter/M. A. Nickbakht/I.-Y. Song/M. Stein (eds.), Origo gentis Romanorum, Polemius Silvius, Narratio de imperatoribus. Paderborn 2017.

Pomerius

Julianus Pomerius, probably born in Africa, but fled to Gaul and settled in Arles, where he taught Caesarius in the early sixth century.

Text and trans.:

De vita contemplativa, PL 59; English trans. M. J. Suelzer, The Contemplative Life. Washington D. C. 1947; French trans. R. Jobard/L. Gagliadi, La vie contemplative. Paris 1995.

Porcarius of Lérins

Fifth-century moral theologian.

Text and trans.:

Ed. A. Wilmart, Porcarius Monita, in: Revue Bénédictine 26, 1909, 475–80; M. Delcogliano, Porcarius of Lérins and his Counsels. A Monastic Study, Part 1, in: American Benedictine Review 53, 2002, 400–25; A. Wilmart, Porcarius of Lérins and his Counsels. A Monastic Study, Part 2, in: American Benedictine Review 54, 2003, 30–58.

Possidius of Calama

Bishop of Calama in North Africa from c. 397; expelled from his see in c. 437, d. soon after in Apulia. Friend and biographer of Augustine.

Text and trans.:

Possidius, Vita Augustini, ed. with German trans. W. Geerlings. Paderborn 2011; English trans. H. T. Weiskotten, Merchantville 2008.

Lit.:

E. Zocca, L'impatto della Vita Augustini (e di Agostino) sulla produzione letteraria di età vandalica. temi martiriali e agiografici, in: RQA 15, 2020, 1–17.

Priscillian of Avila

Spanish ascetic and charismatic leader; condemned as a heretic by Spanish and Gallic bishops and executed on the orders of Magnus Maximus, c. 385.

Text and English trans.:

M. Conti, Priscillian of Avila. Complete Works. Oxford 2009.

Lit.:

H. Chadwick, Priscillian of Avila. Oxford 1976.

A. Olivares Guillem, Prisciliano a través del tiempo. Historia de los estudios sobre el priscilianismo. Madrid 2004.

Priscus

Fifth-century Greek historian and diplomat. His work, which is only preserved in fragments, is important for the history of the Huns.

Text and trans.:

Ed. L. Dindorf, Historici Graeci minores, vol. 1, Leipzig 1870; ed. C. Pia, Priscus Panita, Excerpta et fragmenta. Berlin 2008; ed. with English trans. R. C. Blockley, The Fragmentary Classicising Historians of the Later Roman Empire. Eunapius, Olympiodorus, Priscus and Malchus, 2 vols. Liverpool 1981; ed. with Italian

trans. F. Bornman, Prisci Panitae Fragmenta. Florence 1979; English trans. C. D.
Gordon, The Age of Attila. Ann Arbor 1966.
Lit.:
D. Rohrbacher, The Historians of Late Antiquity. London 2002.

Procopius Caesariensis

Mid-sixth-century Byzantine historian; author of the Wars, the Buildings, and the Anecdota (a satire on Justinian and Theodora).
Text and trans.:
Ed. J. Haury/G. Wirth, 3 vols., Leipzig 1962–4; ed. O. Veh, 5 vols. Munich 1961–77; ed.
with English trans. H. B. Dewing, 7 vols. Cambridge Mass. 1914–40; ed. with
French trans. D. Roques, La Guerre contre les Vandals. Paris 1990; ed. with
French trans. P. Maraval, Histoire secrète. Paris 1990; ed. with French trans. D.
Roques, Constructions de Justinien I. Alexandria 2011; ed with French trans. D.
Roques/J. Auberger, Histoire des Goths. Paris 2015.
Lit.:
A. Cameron, Procopius and the Sixth Century. London 1985.
B. Rubin, Prokopios von Kaisareia, in: RE 23, 1957, 252–599.

Prosper Tiro

Born c. 390 in Aquitaine, active in Rome in the 430s and 440s. Augustinian theologian and author of a chronicle. Probable author of the poem De Providentia Dei.
Text.:
Ed. PL 51; Chronicle, ed. Th. Mommsen, MGH AA IX, 1892; M. Becker/J.-M. Kötter, Kleine
und fragmentarische Historiker. Paderborn 2016.
De Providentia Dei, ed. and English trans. M. Marcovich. Leiden 1989.
For the Ad Uxorem see Pauilinus? above.
Lit.:
S. Muhlberger, The Fifth-century Chroniclers. Prosper, Hydatius and the Galllic Chronicle of 452. Leeds 1990.

Prudentius

Spanish Christian poet and imperial official (348–post 405). Wrote about the cult of the martyrs and about the Altar of Victory controversy between Ambrose and Symmachus.
Text and trans.:
Carmina, ed. M. P. Cunningham, CCSL 126. Turnhout 1966; ed. with English trans. H. T.
Thomson, 2 vols. Cambridge Mass. 1949–53; ed. with French trans. M. Lavarenne,
4 vols. Paris 1955–63.
H. Tränkle (ed.), Prudentius Contra Symmachum. Gegen Symmachus. Turnhout
2008.
M. Frisch, Psychomachia. Einleitung, Text und Kommentar. Berlin 2020.
Lit.:
T. D. Barnes, The Historical Setting of Prudentius' Contra Symmachum, in: American
Journal of Philology 17, 1976, 373–86.

V. Buchheit, Christliche Romideologie im Laurentius-Hymnus des Prudentius, in: Poly-chronion. Festschr. f. F. Dölger. Heidelberg 1966, 121–144.

R. Herzog, Die allegorische Dichtkunst des Prudentius. Munich 1966.

M. A. Malamud, A Poetics of Transformation. Prudentius and Classical Mythology. Ithaca/London 1989.

A.-M. Palmer, Prudentius on the Martyrs. Oxford 1989.

M. Roberts, Poetry and the Cult of the Martyrs. Ann Arbor 1993.

Querolus sive Aulularia
Unique Latin comedy of the fifth century.
Text and trans.:
Ed. R. Peiper, Leipzig 1885; ed. G. Ranstrand. Gothenburg 1951; ed. C. Jacquemard-Le Saos. Paris 1994.
Lit.:
J. Küppers, Die spätantike Prosakomödie "Querolus sive Aulularia" und das Problem ihrer Vorlagen, in: Philologus 133, 1989, 82–103.

D. Lassandro, E. Romano, Rassegna bibliografica degli Studi sul Querolus, in: Bollet-tino di Studi Latini 21, 1991, 26–51.

Regula Magistri
Monastic rule of unknown authorship, arguably a source for Benedict.
Text, trans., comm.:
Ed. A. de Vogüé SC 105–107, 1964–65.
Lit.:
M. Dunn, Mastering Benedict. Monastic Rules and their Authors in the Early Me-dieval West, in: EHR 105, 1990, 567–94.

M. Dunn, The Master and St Benedict. A rejoinder [to A. de Vogüé], in: HER 107, 1992, 104–11.

A. de Vogüé, The Master and St Benedict. A Reply to Marilyn Dunn, EHR 107, 1992, 95–103.

Regulae
Rules from the circle of Lérins.
Text and trans.:
Text and French trans.: A. de Vogüé, Les règles des saints pères. Introduction, texte, traduction, 2 vols., SC 297–8. Paris 1982; ed. and German trans. M. Puzicha, Mönchsregel von Lérins. Regel der Vier Väter – Zweite Regel der Väter – Macarius-Regel – Regula Orientalis – Dritte Regel der Väter. Sankt Ottilien 2010.

Rufinus of Aquileia
Monk and theologian, born c. 345. Met Jerome c. 370; moved to Rome c. 400. Translator of Greek texts, including works by Origen and Eusebius, into Latin.

Text and trans.:
Ed. in PL 21; E. Schulz-Flügel (ed.), Tyrannius Rufinus. Historia Monachorum sive De
  Vita Sanctorum Patrum. Berlin 1990.
Lit.:
M. Humphries, Rufinus' Eusebius. Translation, Continuation, and Edition in the Latin
  Ecclesiastical History, in: Journal of Early Christian Studies 16, 2008, 143–64.

Ruricius of Limoges
*Gallo-Roman aristocrat, born c. 440, elected bishop of Limoges, c. 485, d. c. 510. Author of
  a collection of letters which also included the letters of his correspondents.*
Text and trans.:
Ed. C. Luetjohann, MGH AA VIII. Berlin 1887; English trans. R. W. Mathisen, Ruricius of
  Limoges and Friends. Liverpool 1999.
Lit.:
R. W. Mathisen, The Letters of Ruricius of Limoges and the Passage from Roman to
  Frankish Gaul, in: 10: R. W. Mathisen/Shanzer, 101–15.

Rutilius Namatianus
*Member of the Gallic senatorial aristocracy, poet, wrote an account of his return from
  Rome to Gaul in 417.*
Text and trans.:
De reditu suo sive Iter Gallicum, ed and trans. E. Doblhofer, 2 vols. Heidelberg 1972–
  77.
Lit.:
H. Fuchs, Zur Verherrlichung Roms und der Römer in dem Gedicht des Rutilius Na-
  matianus, in: Basler Z 42, 1943, 37–58.
S. Ratti, Le De reditu suo de Rutilius Namatianus. Élégie ou voyage vers l'au-delà?,
  in: Antiquité Tardive 24, 2016, 185–92.

Salvian of Marseille
*Ca. 400–ca. 480, priest in Marseille. Wrote the De gubernatione dei in 8 books, and the
  Ad Ecclesiam (ad avaritiam), theological works that include important social com-
  mentary on fifth-century Gaul.*
Text and trans.:
Œuvres, ed. G. Lagarrigue, SC 176, 220, 1971–75; German trans. A. Mayer, BKV 11, 1935.
Lit.:
J. Badewien, Geschichtstheologie und Sozialkritik im Werk Salvians von Marseille. Göt-
  tingen 1980.
J. M. Blasquez Martinez, La Sociedad del Bajo Imperio en la obra de Salviano de
  Marsella. Madrid 1990.
S. Elm, New Romans. Salvian of Marseilles On the Governance of God, in: Journal of
  Early Christian Studies 25, 2017, 1–28.

Sedulius
Fifth-century rhetorician and poet, active in Italy.
Text:
Carmen Paschale, Opus Paschale, ed. J. Hümer, CSEL 10. Vienna 1885; rev. ed. V. Panagi. Vienna 2007.
Lit.:
R. Green, Latin Epics of the New Testament. Juvencus, Sedulius, Arator. Oxford 2006.

Severus of Menorca
Early fifth-century bishop of Menorca, author of a letter on the conversion of the Jews of Menorca. The letter has, however, been seen by some as a seventh-century fabrication.
Text and trans.:
S. Bradbury (ed.), Severus of Menorca, Letter on the Conversion of the Jews. Oxford 1996.

Sidonius Apollinaris
432–479. Gallo-Roman aristocrat, born in Lyon, City Prefect of Rome, 467/8, elected bishop of Clermont c. 470. Author of poems (especially panegyrics) and letters that are important for the understanding of the culture and politics of Gaul in the later fifth century.
Text and trans.:
Poems and Letters, ed. W. Anderson, 2 vols. Cambridge Mass. 1963–65.
Poèmes, ed. A. Loyen. Paris 1960.
Lettres, ed. A. Loyen, 2 vols. Paris 1970.
German trans. H. Köhler. Stuttgart 2014.
Lit.:
H. Harich-Schwarzbauer/J. Hindergarten (eds.), Leisure and the Muses in Sidonius Apollinaris, Journal of Late Antiquity 12, Special Issue, 2020.
J. Harries, Sidonius and the Fall of Rome. Oxford 1994.
G. Kelly/J. van Waarden, The Edinburgh Companion to Sidonius Apollinaris. Edinburgh 2020.
A. Loyen, Recherches historiques sur les panégyriques de Sidoine Apollinaire. Paris 1942.
F. Oppedisano, In lode di Antemio. L'ultimo panegirico di Roma imperiale. Rome 2020.
Sidonius Appollinarius Research Companion, https://sidonapol.org

Socrates
Church historian, c. 380–440, author of a continuation of the Ecclesiastical History of Eusebius up to 439.
Text and French trans.:
G. C. Hansen/P. Périchon/P. Maraval, 4 vols. SC 477, 493, 505, 506. Paris 2004–7.

Lit.:

H. Leppin, Von Constantin dem Großen zu Theodosius II. Das christliche Kaisertum bei den Kirchenhistorikern Socrates, Sozomenus und Theodoret. Göttingen 1996.

T. Urbainczyk, Socrates of Constantinople. Ann Arbor 1997.

Sozomenos

Born c. 400 near Gaza, became a lawyer in Constantinople; wrote a Church history dependent on that of Socrates, covering the period from 324–425.

Text and trans.:

Ed. J. Bidez/G. C. Hansen, GCS 50,1960; ed. and French trans. A. J. Festugière/B. Grillet/ G. Sabbah/L. Angleviel de la Beaumelle, 4 vols., SC 306, 418, 495, 516. Paris 1983.

Lit.:

H. Leppin, Von Constantin dem Großen zu Theodosius II. Das christliche Kaisertum bei den Kirchenhistorikern Socrates, Sozomenus und Theodoret. Göttingen 1996.

Sulpicius Severus

d. 420. rhetor, then ascetic. Author of a World Chronicle and the Life of Martin of Tours.

Text and trans.:

Ed. C. Halm, CSEL 1, 1866; English trans. R. J. Goodrich, Sulpicius Severus, The Complete Works. Introduction, Translation and Notes. New York 2015.

Vie de S. Martin, ed. with French trans. J. Fontaine, 3 vols. SC 133–135, 1967–69; German trans. P. Bihlmeyer: BKV 20, 1914.

Gallus, ed. with French trans. J. Fontaine, SC 510. Paris 2006.

Chroniques, ed. with French trans. G. de Senneville-Grave, SC 441. Paris 1999.

Lit.:

C. Stancliffe, Saint Martin and his Hagiographer. History and Miracle in Sulpicius Severus. Oxford 1983.

Symmachus

Roman Senator (ca. 345–402), 384 praefectus urbi, senatorial advocate in the Altar of Victory controversy. Author of speeches and letters which provide important information on the period.

Text and trans:

Ed. O. Seeck, MGH AA VI/1, 1883.

Lettres, ed. with French trans. J. P. Callu, 4 vols. Paris 1972–.

Relationes, ed. with English trans. and comm. R. H. Barrow, 1973; ed. with Italian trans. and comm. D. Vera, Pisa 1981.

Reden, ed. with German trans. and comm. A. Pabst. Darmstadt 1989.

R. Klein, Der Streit um den Victoriaaltar. Die dritte Relatio des Symmachus und die Briefe 17, 18 und 57 des Mailänder Bischofs Ambrosius. Darmstadt 1972.

Lit.:

Commentaries on Books IV and VI of the Letters, by A. Marcone, Pisa 1983/1987, on Book IX by S. Roda, Pisa 1981, on Book V by P. R. Tiberga, Pisa 1992.

J. F. Matthews, The Letters of Symmachus, in: J. W. Binns (ed.), Latin Literature of the
Fourth Century. London 1974, 58–99.

F. Paschoud (ed.), Colloque Genevois sur Symmaque. Paris 1986.

M. R. Salzman, Reflections on Symmachus' Idea of Tradition, in: Historia 38, 1989,
348–364.

Themistius

*Greek rhetor and senator, praefectus urbi of Constantinople 383/384. His speeches con-
tain important information on politics.*

Text:

Orationes, ed. G. Downey, A. F. Norman, 3 vols. Stuttgart 1965–74; ed. and English
trans. S. Swain, Themistius, Julian and Greek Political Theory under Rome.
Texts, Translations and Studies of Four Key Works. Cambridge 2014; German
trans. H. Leppin, Themistius, Staatsreden. Stuttgart 1998; English trans. P.
Heather/D. Moncur, Politics, Philosophy and Empire in the Fourth Century. Selected Orations of Themistius. Liverpool 2001.

Lit.:

R. M. Errington, Themistius and his Emperors, in: Chiron 30, 2000, 861–904.

A. Garzya, In Themistii orationes index auctus, Naples 1989.

P. J. Heather, Themistius. A Political Philosopher, in: M. Whitby (ed.), The Propaganda
of Power. The Role of Panegyric in Late Antiquity. Leiden 1998, 125–50.

J. Vanderspoel, Themistius and the Imperial Court. Ann Arbor 1995.

Theodoret

*Ca. 393–ca. 466, bishop of Cyrrhus from 423. Anti-Monophysite Theologian whose views
were subsequently condemned, and Church historian, who wrote an Ecclesiastical
history and a monastic history (Philotheos historia).*

Text and trans.:

Kirchengeschichte, ed. L. Parmentier/F. Scheidweiler, GCS 44, 1954; German trans. A.
Seider, BKV 51, 1926; ed. J. Bouffartigue/P. Canivet/A. Martin/L. Pietri/F. Thelamon, 2
vols. SC 501, 530. Paris 2006/2009.

Histoire Philothée, ed. P. Canivet/A. Leroy-Molinghen, 2 vols. SC 234, 257, 1977–79; German trans. K. Gutberlet: BKV 50, 1926.

Lit.:

H. Leppin, Von Constantin dem Großen zu Theodosius II. Das christliche Kaisertum
bei den Kirchenhistorikern Socrates, Sozomenus und Theodoret. Göttingen
1996.

Valerian of Cimiez

Bishop of Cimiez, present at councils between 439 and 451.

Text.:

Ed. PL 52.

Lit.:

L. K. Bailey, Preaching in Fifth-century Gaul. Valerian of Cimiez and the Eusebius Gallicanus Collection, in: A. Dupont/S. Boodts/G. Partoens/J. Leemans (eds.), Preaching

in the Patristic Era. Sermons, Preachers and Audiences in the Latin West. Leiden 2018, 253–73.

Venatius Fortunatus

Italian poet and hagiographer, born c. 530, active in Gaul, elected bishop of Poitiers, c. 600, d. pre 609.

Text and trans.:

Ed. F. Leo, Venantius Fortunatus, Opera Poetica. Berlin, 1881; ed. and French trans. M. Reydellet, Venance Fortunat, Poèmes, 3 vols. Paris, 1994–2004; ed. and French trans. S. Quesnel, Venance Fortunat, Vie de saint Martin. Paris 1996; ed. and English trans. M. Roberts, Venantius Fortunatus, Poems. Washington D. C. 2017.

Ed. B. Krusch, Venantius Fortunatus, Opera Pedestria. Berlin, 1885.

English trans. J. George, Venantius Fortunatus, Personal and Political Poems. Liverpool 1995.

Lit.:

J. George, Poet as Politician. Venantius Fortunatus' Panegyric to King Childeric, in: JMedH 15, 1989, 5–18.

J. George, Venantius Fortunatus. A poet in Merovingian Gaul. Oxford 1992.

M. Roberts, The Humblest Sparrow. The Poetry of Venantius Fortunatus. Ann Arbor 2009.

Verus of Orange

Bishop of Orange, between 475 and 517, author of a Life of his predecessor, Eutropius (d. 475).

Text:

Vita Eutropii, ed. P. Varin, in: Bulletin du Comité Historique des monuments écrits de l'histoire de France, 1, 1849, 53–64.

Vegetius

Military theorist.

Text and trans.:

Epitoma rei militaris, ed. and English trans. L. F. Stelten, New York 1990; ed. and German trans. F. L. Müller, Publius Flavius Vegetius Renatus, Epitoma rei militaris – Abriß des Militärwesens. Stuttgart 1997; English trans. N. P. Milner, Vegetius, Epitome of Military Science, rev. ed. Liverpool 2011.

Lit.:

T. D. Barnes, The Date of Vegetius, in Phoenix 33, 1979, 254–7.

W. Goffart, The Date and Purpose of Vegetius' De re militari, in: W. Goffart, Rome's Fall and After. London 1989, 45–80.

Victor of Tunnuna

Bishop of Tunnuna in North Africa, d. c. 570, keen upholder of the Three Chapters, author of a chronicle.

Text.:

Victoris Tunnunensis Chronicon cum reliquiis ex Consularibus Caesaraugustanis et Iohannis Biclarensis Chronicon, ed. C. Cardelle de Hartmann, CCSL 173 A. Turnhout 2001.

Victor of Vita

African bishop, in 488/89 wrote a history of the persecution of the Catholics under the Vandal kings Geiseric and Huneric.

Text and trans.:

Historia persecutionis Africanae provinciae, ed. C. Halm, MGH AA III/l, 1879; ed. and French trans. S. Lancel, Victor de Vita. Histoire de la persécution vandale en Afrique suivie de La passion des sept martyrs. Registre des provinces et des cités d'Afrique; ed. and German trans. K. Vössing, Victor von Vita. Kirchenkampf und Verfolgung unter den Vandalen in Africa. Historia persecutionis Africanae provinciae temporum Geiserici et Hunerici regum Wandalorum. Darmstadt 2011; English trans. J. Moorhead. Liverpool 1992.

Lit.:

C. Courtois, Victor de Vita et son œuvre. Étude critique. Algiers 1954.

Victricius of Rouen

Born c. 330, bishop of Rouen, c. 390–ca. 407. Author of a letter on the cult of relics.

Text and trans.:

De laude sanctorum, ed. R. Demeulenaere, Foebadius, Victricius, Leporius, Vincentius Lerinensis, Evagrius, Ruricius, CCSL 64; English trans. G. Clark, Victricius of Rouen, Praising the Saints (introduction and annotated translation), in: Journal of Early Christian Studies 7, 1999, 365–99.

Lit.:

G. Clark, Translating relics. Victricius of Rouen and Fourth-century Debate, in: Early Medieval Europe 10, 2001, 161–76.

Vitae sanctorum

Anonymous hagiographical works. Many of the most important are edited by B. Krusch and W. Levison, MGH SRM III, VII, 1896, 1920. A few have been the subject of individual editions.

Text and trans.:

Vita Genovefae, ed. and French trans. M.-C. Isaïa, Vie de sainte Geneviève, SC 610. Paris 2020.

Vita Patrum Iurensium, ed. and French trans. F. Martine, Vie des Pères du Jura, SC 142. Paris, 1968; English trans. T. Vivian/K. Vivian/J. B. Russell, The Lives of the Jura Fathers, Kalamazoo 1999.

Vitas sanctorum patrum Emeretensium, ed. M. Sánchez, CSEL 116. Turnhout, 1992; English trans. A. T. Fear, Lives of the Visigothic Fathers. Liverpool 1997.

Lit.:

M. Goullet/M. Heinzelmann/C. Veyrard-Cosme (eds.), L'hagiographie mérovingienne à travers ses réécritures. Ostfildern 2010.

M. Heinzelmann/J.-C. Poulin, Les vies anciennes de sainte Geneviève de Paris, Études critiques. Paris 1986.

M. Lapidge, The Roman Martyrs. Introduction, Translations and Commentary. Oxford 2018.

G. Philippart (ed.), Hagiographies. Turnhout, 1994–.

Zonaras

Byzantine monk, active in the mid-12th century. Author of a World Chronicle containing material from earlier authors and reaching to 1118.

Text:

Epitome Historion, ed. L. Dindorf, 6 vols. Leipzig 1868–75.

Zosimus

Pagan historian, writing in Constantinople c. 500, who saw the Christian emperors as responsible for the collapse of Rome.

Texts, trans. and comm.:

Histoire nouvelle, ed. and French trans., F. Paschoud, 5 vols. Paris 1971–89; English trans. R. T. Ridley. Sydney 1982; German trans. O. Veh/St. Rebenich. Stuttgart 1990.

Lit.:

W. Goffart, Zosimus, the first Historian of Rome's Fall, in: W. Goffart Rome's Fall and After. London 1989, 81–110.

F. Paschoud, Cinq études sur Zosime. Paris 1975.

R. T. Ridley, Zosimus the Historian, in: ByzZ 65, 1972, 277–302.

1 Alpes Cottiae
2 Liguria
3 Venetia et Histria
4 Aemilia
5 Flaminia et Picenum
6 Tuscia et Umbria
7 Picenum suburbicarium
8 Valeria

9 Samnium
10 Campania
11 Apulia et Calabria
12 Lucania et Brutti
13 Sicilia
14 Praevalitana
15 Dardania
16 Haemimontus

--- Borders at death of emperor Justinian (565 A.D.)

▨ Eastern Roman Empire

Map 1: The Byzantine Empire and the Successor States c.565.

https://doi.org/10.1515/9783110352658-004

Slavic peoples

Volga

Dnieper

Donez

Don

Dniester

Antes

Avars

Tisza

Avars

Bug

Bulgars

Sclavines

Danube

Alans

Avars

Abasgians

Caucasus

Caspian Sea

Oids

Chersonesus

Scythia

Black Sea

Sebastopolis

Lazica

Iberia

Albania

Dacia

Moesia II

Odessus

Sinop

Trapezunt

Tzani

Ssus

Thracia

Hadrianopolis

Paphla-gonia

Heleno-pontus

I

Rhodope

16 Constantinople

Europe

Bithynia

Honorias

II

Armenia

NEWPERSIA
EMPIRE OF THE
SASSANIDS

Donia

Thessalonika

Hellespontus

Ancyra

Galatia

I

II

III

Mesop.

Nisibis

Ecbatana

Essalia

Lydia

I

II

Cappadocia

Edessa

Osroene

II

Euphratensis

Ath

Athens

Ephesos

Phrygia

Pisidia

Iconium

Lycaonia

I

Cilicia

Syria

Hala

Caria

Pamphylia

Isauria

Antiochia

II

Lycia

Cyprus

Tripolis

Palmyra

Babylon

Creta

Berytus

Damascus

Phoenice

Mediterranean Sea

II

Palaestina I

Arabia

Lakhmid Arabs
(under Sasanian sovereignty)

Jerusalem

Rene

Ya

Ip.

Libya Inf.

Alexandria

Augustamnica

Aegyptus

Palaestina III

Ghassanid Arabs
(under Byzantine sovereignty)

Nile

Arcadia

Thebais

Red Sea

Theben

0 100 200 300 km

Mediterranean Sea

Euphrates

Tigris

Map 2: The Roman Empire c.380.

Moesia
superior
Dacia
Ripensis *Danube*
Scythia
THRACIA
Moesia inferior
Haemimontus
Dardania
valitana
9
Thracia
Rhodope
Europe
Macedonia
MOESIAE
Hellespontus
Thessalia
Lydia
Asia
Caria
Achaia
Creta
Mare Internum

Pontus Euxinus

C a u c a s u s

Diospontus
(Heleno-
pontus)
Pontus
Polemoniacus
Paphlagonia
Bithynia
PONTICA
Galatia
Cappadocia
Armenia
minor
Mesopotamia *Tigris*
10
11
Pisidia
Isauria
Pamphylia
et Lycia
Cilicia
12
Osrhoene
Coelesyria
Euphrates
Cyprus
Augusta
Libanensis
Phoenice
Palaestina
Arabia

Aegyptus
Iovia
Arabia
Nova
ORIENS
Libya
inferior
Aegyptus
Herculia
Libya superior
Nile
Sinus Arabicus
Thebais

0 100 200 300 km

Map 3: The Byzantine Empire and the Successor States c.510.

Volga

Slavs

Avars

Dnieper

Gepids

Caspian
Sea

Danube

C a u c a s u s

Black Sea

Constantinople

Tigris

Thessalonika

Aegean

Aleppo

Athens

Cyprus

Damascus

Crete

Euphrates

Mediterranean Sea

Jerusalem

Alexandria

Nile

Red Sea

0 100 200 300 km

Index of Authors

https://doi.org/10.1515/9783110352658-005

Index of People

https://doi.org/10.1515/9783110352658-006

Index of Places

https://doi.org/10.1515/9783110352658-007

Subject Index

https://doi.org/10.1515/9783110352658-008

Oldenbourg Grundriss der Geschichte

Herausgegeben von Hans Beck, Karl-Joachim Hölkeskamp, Achim Landwehr, Benedikt Stuchtey und Steffen Patzold

Band 1a
Wolfgang Schuller
Griechische Geschichte
6., akt. Aufl. 2008. 275 S., 4 Karten
ISBN 978-3-486-58715-9

Band 1b
Hans-Joachim Gehrke
Geschichte des Hellenismus
4. durchges. Aufl. 2008. 328 S.
ISBN 978-3-486-58785-2

Band 2
Jochen Bleicken
Geschichte der Römischen Republik
6. Aufl. 2004. 342 S.
ISBN 978-3-486-49666-6

Band 3
Werner Dahlheim
Geschichte der Römischen Kaiserzeit
3., überarb. und erw. Aufl. 2003. 452 S.,
3 Karten
ISBN 978-3-486-49673-4

Band 4
Jochen Martin
Spätantike und Völkerwanderung
4. Aufl. 2001. 336 S.
ISBN 978-3-486-49684-0

Band 5
Reinhard Schneider
Das Frankenreich
4., überarb. und erw. Aufl. 2001. 224 S.,
2 Karten
ISBN 978-3-486-49694-9

Band 6
Johannes Fried
Die Formierung Europas 840–1046
3., überarb. Aufl. 2008. 359 S.
ISBN 978-3-486-49703-8

Band 7
Hermann Jakobs
Kirchenreform und Hochmittelalter
1046–1215
4. Aufl. 1999. 380 S.
ISBN 978-3-486-49714-4

Band 8
Ulf Dirlmeier/Gerhard Fouquet/Bernd
Fuhrmann
Europa im Spätmittelalter 1215–1378
2. Aufl. 2009. 390 S.
ISBN 978-3-486-58796-8

Band 9
Erich Meuthen
Das 15. Jahrhundert
4. Aufl., überarb. v. Claudia Märtl 2006.
343 S.
ISBN 978-3-486-49734-2

Band 10
Heinrich Lutz
Reformation und Gegenreformation
5. Aufl., durchges. und erg. v. Alfred
Kohler 2002. 283 S.
ISBN 978-3-486-48585-2

https://doi.org/10.1515/9783110352658-009

Band 11
Heinz Duchhardt / Matthias Schnettger
Barock und Aufklärung
5., überarb. u. akt. Aufl. des Bandes
„Das Zeitalter des Absolutismus" 2015.
302 S.
ISBN 978-3-486-76730-8

Band 12
Elisabeth Fehrenbach
Vom Ancien Régime zum Wiener
Kongreß
5. Aufl. 2008. 323 S., 1 Karte
ISBN 978-3-486-58587-2

Band 13
Dieter Langewiesche
Europa zwischen Restauration und Re-
volution 1815–1849
5. Aufl. 2007. 261 S., 4 Karten.
ISBN 978-3-486-49734-2

Band 14
Lothar Gall
Europa auf dem Weg in die Moderne
1850–1890
5. Aufl. 2009. 332 S., 4 Karten
ISBN 978-3-486-58718-0

Band 15
Gregor Schöllgen/Friedrich Kießling
Das Zeitalter des Imperialismus
5., überarb. u. erw. Aufl. 2009. 326 S.
ISBN 978-3-486-58868-2

Band 16
Eberhard Kolb/Dirk Schumann
Die Weimarer Republik
8., aktualis. u. erw. Aufl. 2012. 349 S.,
1 Karte
ISBN 978-3-486-71267-4

Band 17
Klaus Hildebrand
Das Dritte Reich
7., durchges. Aufl. 2009. 474 S., 1 Karte
ISBN 978-3-486-59200-9

Band 18
Jost Dülffer
Europa im Ost-West-Konflikt 1945–1991
2004. 304 S., 2 Karten
ISBN 978-3-486-49105-0

Band 19
Rudolf Morsey
Die Bundesrepublik Deutschland
Entstehung und Entwicklung bis 1969
5., durchges. Aufl. 2007. 343 S.
ISBN 978-3-486-58319-9

Band 19a
Andreas Rödder
Die Bundesrepublik Deutschland 1969–
1990
2003. 330 S., 2 Karten
ISBN 978-3-486-56697-0

Band 20
Hermann Weber
Die DDR 1945–1990
5., aktual. Aufl. 2011. 384 S.
ISBN 978-3-486-70440-2

Band 21
Horst Möller
Europa zwischen den Weltkriegen
1998. 278 S.
ISBN 978-3-486-52321-8

Band 22
Peter Schreiner
Byzanz
4., aktual. Aufl. 2011. 340 S., 2 Karten
ISBN 978-3-486-70271-2

Band 23
Hanns J. Prem
Geschichte Altamerikas
2., völlig überarb. Aufl. 2008. 386 S.,
5 Karten
ISBN 978-3-486-53032-2

Band 24
Tilman Nagel
Die islamische Welt bis 1500
1998. 312 S.
ISBN 978-3-486-53011-7

Band 25
Hans J. Nissen
Geschichte Alt-Vorderasiens
2., überarb. u. erw. Aufl. 2012. 309 S.,
4 Karten
ISBN 978-3-486-59223-8

Band 26
Helwig Schmidt-Glintzer
Geschichte Chinas bis zur mongoli-
schen Eroberung 250 v. Chr.–1279
n. Chr.
1999. 235 S., 7 Karten
ISBN 978-3-486-56402-0

Band 27
Leonhard Harding
Geschichte Afrikas im 19. und 20. Jahrhundert
2., durchges. Aufl. 2006. 272 S.,
4 Karten
ISBN 978-3-486-57746-4

Band 28
Willi Paul Adams
Die USA vor 1900
2. Aufl. 2009. 294 S.
ISBN 978-3-486-58940-5

Band 29
Willi Paul Adams
Die USA im 20. Jahrhundert
2. Aufl., aktual. u. erg. v. Manfred Berg
2008. 302 S.
ISBN 978-3-486-56466-0

Band 30
Klaus Kreiser
Der Osmanische Staat 1300–1922
2., aktual. Aufl. 2008. 262 S., 4 Karten
ISBN 978-3-486-58588-9

Band 31
Manfred Hildermeier
Die Sowjetunion 1917–1991
3. überarb. und akt. Aufl. 2016. XXX S.
ISBN 978-3-486-71848-5

Band 32
Peter Wende
Großbritannien 1500–2000
2001. 234 S., 1 Karte
ISBN 978-3-486-56180-7

Band 33
Christoph Schmidt
Russische Geschichte 1547–1917
2. Aufl. 2009. 261 S., 1 Karte
ISBN 978-3-486-58721-0

Band 34
Hermann Kulke
Indische Geschichte bis 1750
2005. 275 S., 12 Karten
ISBN 978-3-486-55741-1

Band 35
Sabine Dabringhaus
Geschichte Chinas 1279–1949
3. akt. und überarb. Aufl. 2015. 324 S.
ISBN 978-3-486-78112-0

Band 36
Gerhard Krebs
Das moderne Japan 1868–1952
2009. 249 S.
ISBN 978-3-486-55894-4

Band 37
Manfred Clauss
Geschichte des alten Israel
2009. 259 S., 6 Karten
ISBN 978-3-486-55927-9

Band 38
Joachim von Puttkamer
Ostmitteleuropa im 19. und 20. Jahrhundert
2010. 353 S., 4 Karten
ISBN 978-3-486-58169-0

Band 39
Alfred Kohler
Von der Reformation zum Westfälischen Frieden
2011. 253 S.
ISBN 978-3-486-59803-2

Band 40
Jürgen Lütt
Das moderne Indien 1498 bis 2004
2012. 272 S., 3 Karten
ISBN 978-3-486-58161-4

Band 41
Andreas Fahrmeir
Europa zwischen Restauration, Reform und Revolution 1815–1850
2012. 228 S.
ISBN 978-3-486-70939-1

Band 42
Manfred Berg
Geschichte der USA
2013. 233 S.
ISBN 978-3-486-70482-2

Band 43
Ian Wood
Europe in Late Antiquity
2025. 408 S., 3 Karten
ISBN 978-3-11-035264-1

Band 44
Klaus Mühlhahn
Die Volksrepublik China
2017. 324 S.
ISBN 978-3-11-035530-7

Band 45
Jörg Echternkamp
Das Dritte Reich. Diktatur, Volksgemeinschaft,
Krieg
2018. 344 S., 2 Karten
ISBN 978-3-486-75569-5

Band 46
Christoph Ulf/Erich Kistler
Die Entstehung Griechenlands
2019. 328 S., 26 Abb.
ISBN 978-3-486-52991-3

Band 47
Steven Vanderputten
Medieval Monasticisms
2020. 304 S.
ISBN 978-3-11-054377-3

Band 48
Christine Hatzky/Barbara Potthast
Lateinamerika 1800–1930
2021, 370 S., 2 Karten
ISBN 978-3-11-034999-3

Band 49
Christine Hatzky/Barbara Potthast
Lateinamerika seit 1930
2021, 416 S., 1 Karte
ISBN 978-3-11-073522-2

Band 50/1
Raimund Schulz/Uwe Walter
Griechische Geschichte ca. 800–322
v. Chr.
Band 1: Darstellung
2022. 278 S., 7 Karten
ISBN 978-3-486-58831-6

Band 50/2
Raimund Schulz/Uwe Walter
Griechische Geschichte ca. 800–322
v. Chr.
Band 2: Forschung und Literatur
2022. 378 S.
ISBN 978-3-11-076245-7

Band 51
Peter-Franz Mittag
Geschichte des Hellenismus
2023. 348 S., 2 Karten
ISBN 978-3-11-064859-1

Band 52
Jörg Requate
Europa an der Schwelle zur Hochmo-
derne (1870-1890)
2023. 350 S., 3 Karten
ISBN 978-3-11-035937-4

Band 53
Friedrich Kießling
Europa im Zeitalter des Imperialismus
1890–1918
2023. 385 S.
ISBN 978-3-486-76385-0

Band 54
Matthias Schnettger
Das 17. Jahrhundert
2024. 348 S., 3 Karten
ISBN 978-3-11-073767-7

Band 55
Stefan Jordan
Geschichtsschreibung. Geschichte und
Theorie
2024. 256 S., 13 Abbildungen
ISBN 978-3-11-061078-9